Computer-Assisted
Reporting

A Comprehensive Primer

Fred Vallance-Jones
and David McKie

with Aron Pilhofer and Jaimi Dowdell

D1249364

OXFORD
UNIVERSITY PRESS

OXFORD
UNIVERSITY PRESS

70 Wynford Drive, Don Mills, Ontario M3C 1J9
www.oupcanada.com

Oxford University Press is a department of the University of Oxford.
It furthers the University's objective of excellence in research, scholarship,
and education by publishing worldwide in

Oxford   New York

Auckland   Cape Town   Dar es Salaam   Hong Kong   Karachi
Kuala Lumpur   Madrid   Melbourne   Mexico City   Nairobi
New Delhi   Shanghai   Taipei   Toronto

With offices in

Argentina   Austria   Brazil   Chile   Czech Republic   France   Greece
Guatemala   Hungary   Italy   Japan   Poland   Portugal   Singapore
South Korea   Switzerland   Thailand   Turkey   Ukraine   Vietnam

Oxford is a trade mark of Oxford University Press
in the UK and in certain other countries

Published in Canada by Oxford University Press

Library and Archives Canada Cataloguing in Publication

Vallance-Jones, Fred
Computer-assisted reporting : a Canadian primer / Fred Vallance-Jones,
David McKie.

Includes index.
ISBN 978-0-19-542457-7

1. Journalism—Data processing.   2. Journalism—Computer network
resources.   3. Reporters and reporting—Computer network resources.
I. McKie, David C. (David Carlos), 1959–   II. Title.

PN4784.E53V35 2008   070.4'30285   C2008-903807-X

Cover image: Stock Photography/Camilo Jimenez

This book is printed on permanent acid-free paper.
Printed and bound in Canada.

1 2 3 4 — 12 11 10 09

Contents

Acknowledgements

We would like to thank the following people and organizations who helped make this book possible:

ESRI Canada, which provided its ArcView software for the chapter on mapping.

The City of Hamilton, Ontario, which made available its map files. Special thanks to Al Little, Hamilton's manager of GIS services.

Statistics Canada, which provided both map boundary files and census data. A special thank you to Roy Jones, director of the client services division, and to Lily Eisenberg of census communications.

The *Hamilton Spectator*, which gave permission to reproduce copyright material.

The reviewers of the manuscript, including the CBC's Phil Harbord, and Jennifer LaFleur of the *Dallas Morning News*.

Aron Pilhofer of the *New York Times*, who provided not only inspiration, but wrote the section on web scraping. Jaimi Dowdell of the *St. Louis Post-Dispatch* wrote the section on social network analysis, an emerging field in computer-assisted reporting.

Our thanks also goes out to Brant Houston, Jim Rankin, Glen MacGregor, Dana Robbins, Steve Doig, Karen Kleiss, Tamsin McMahon, Phil Harbord, Kevin Donovan, and David Akin, Debbie Wolfe, Natalie Johnson, Rob Washburn and Carla Heggie, all of whom took the time to share their stories and insights with us.

Our editors at Oxford University Press, Roberta Osborne, Dina Theleritis, and Laurna Tallman, who kept us on track throughout this project; and Cliff Newman, who brought the idea to Oxford in the first place.

Finally, we would like to thank everyone in the CAR community across North America for all of the help and inspiration over the years.

———

I would like to thank my wife Louise, who has always been there to support and encourage my work, and our four girls, Laura, Anna, Kathleen, and Caroline.

I also want to thank David McKie, who, by accepting my invitation to co-author this project, stengthened it immeasurably with his talents, enthusiasm, and ideas.

—Fred Vallance-Jones

I would like to thank those journalists whose intelligence, patience, and creativity have inspired me to continue to strive higher. It is difficult to single out individuals because computer-assisted reporting is the result of like-minded journalists coming together in a spirit of collegiality to produce stories that make a difference. In the United States the National Institute for Computer-Assisted Reporting has been instrumental in providing a forum in which journalists—even those from competing media outlets—share their ideas and expertise. In this country, the Canadian Association of Journalists provides an indispensable training ground that brings computer-assisted reporting to a new generation of journalists. Fred Vallance-Jones has been a key and inspirational figure for me, and I am indebted to him for inviting me to help write this book. And, finally, none of this would be possible without the continued support of my family, especially my wife Deirdre, for her patience with the long hours frequently necessary to do this kind of work.

—David McKie

Chapter 1

Introduction to Computer-Assisted Reporting

Fred Vallance-Jones and David McKie

Computer-assisted reporting (CAR) has expanded in the last decade from the exclusive practice of a few pioneering specialists to an essential part of the journalist's craft. By learning some powerful new skills, ordinary reporters can break important stories and make mundane copy crackle.

Editors are taking notice and some of the reporters who first pioneered these techniques are themselves moving into management. CAR is a niche skill no longer. Job notices now demand CAR skills. Reporters need to learn CAR to keep up with their rapidly changing profession.

What exactly is computer-assisted reporting? At heart, it simply is reporting. Reporters use the raw data-crunching power of computers to manipulate information in order to uncover trends, patterns, and facts that otherwise would remain hidden on some government hard drive. The same news judgement, story-finding skills, and writing abilities needed for any journalism story also are required for successful CAR. We could drop the 'CA' part of the term and treat computers as we do pens and telephones—just tools of the trade. But the term was devised at a time when CAR was new and has stuck. So we'll stick with it, too.

As with any newly evolving skill, CAR at first was passed on informally. Later, the US-based National Institute for Computer Assisted Reporting began to offer 'boot camps': week-long intensive training sessions. Then along came the first books, particularly Brant Houston's seminal *Computer-Assisted Reporting, A Practical Guide*, now in its third edition.[1] *Computer-Assisted Reporting: A Comprehensive Primer* will add to the growing library, providing the most comprehensive, detailed guide yet. This book is intended primarily for journalists, journalism students, and researchers interested in using new skills to uncover information. Since the techniques are universal, we hope this book will be a valuable resource for English-language journalists worldwide.

A Short History of CAR

The techniques that eventually became CAR were practiced first in the United States. Although a 'birthday' for these methods is difficult to pin down, many point to the 1952 presidential election when CBS used the Remington Rand UNIVAC (an enormous computer that filled a room) to predict the outcome of the race between Republican candidate Dwight Eisenhower and his Democratic opponent Adlai Stevenson. The application of UNIVAC was by no means investigative journalism—that would not come for another 15 years—but it marked an important change in data analysis.

In one of the most authoritative books about computer-assisted reporting, Margaret H. DeFleur relates one of the first examples of investigative CAR when Philip Meyer, then a reporter with the Detroit Free Press, used a computer in 1967 to analyze survey data from blacks who lived in an area that was torn apart by race riots. He was able to successfully challenge popular theories about the causes of the riots, namely that the black people caught up in the problem were poorly educated, situated at the bottom of the socio-economic ladder, and had no opportunities for advancement or expression. Meyer's analysis demonstrated that people who attended college were just as likely to have participated in the riots as individuals who dropped out of high school. His story won a Pulitzer Prize.[2] Meyer's success as a pioneer led others to emulate him.

The arrival of desktop computing in the 1980s heralded the real explosion of CAR, as ever-more-powerful computers and software became available at modest cost. The days when one had to use a large mainframe computer, as Meyer had done, were gone. CAR started to move into the mainstream.

These days, many journalists have at least heard of CAR. It is an active part of news-gathering in growing numbers of newsrooms around the world. In the US, even some small, regional papers and broadcast outlets have CAR specialists.

In Canada, a handful of individuals learned about the development of CAR in the United States and endeavoured to learn as much as they could about a type of reporting that would evolve into a cutting edge technological skill. Among these early advocates was Bill Doskoch, then a reporter with the *Leader Post* in Regina. He produced what likely was Canada's first guide to CAR, a photocopied introduction to spreadsheets.[3]

Another pioneer was Rob Washburn, then of the *Cobourg Star*, now with Loyalist College in Belleville, Ontario. He organized the country's first CAR workshop at Loyalist in 1994. 'A reporter from the *Buffalo Evening News* traveled in an ice storm to deliver the main session. The meeting was held at Loyalist because the college had Internet connectivity. There were not very many ISPs at the time.'[4]

Washburn helped to organize a larger event the same year at Carleton University, and was a founder of the CAR caucus of the Canadian Association of Journalists, which worked for several years to make Canadian reporters and editors aware of this new branch of journalism.

> I used to work all week at the *Cobourg Star* and then travel on weekends to deliver seminars. I slept on many floors and couches because I did it for free. Groups would pay my airfare and feed me. But I met amazing people.[5]

After attending a week-long seminar at the Poynter Institute in Florida in 1995, Washburn started to help the Canadian Association of Journalists expand its training efforts.

> When I returned from Poynter, I offered my services to the CAJ. I organized practical workshops at conventions that year, something we continue to do until this day. Steve Ross, from the Columbia University School of Journalism, did it for the first few years, since most of us didn't have the expertise. One of the proudest moments was when Fred Vallance-Jones and Robert Cribb (of the *Toronto Star*) started doing the sessions and we stopped having to rely on our American colleagues.'[6]

The mid-1990s was a period that would prove critically important to the development of CAR in Canada. It was also a time of great ambition for the small band pursuing CAR. Reporters started building or going after major government data sets.

In 1995, CBC Manitoba battled to get a copy of the database containing details of projects funded by the federal-provincial Infrastructure Works program. As has been typical in such struggles, it took months to get the data, so the first stories proving political patronage in Manitoba's version of the program were based on a database built from paper records.[7] Later, when the database was released, CBC followed up with a second series of stories showing, among other things, that 'infrastructure' could mean something as small as a lawn mower.[8]

Canada's CAR pioneers had the distinct advantage of being able to learn from the prior experience in the US. Some other early efforts included Adrian Humphreys's work at the *Hamilton Spectator* chronicling murder,[9] Paul Schneidereit's series based on the census in Nova Scotia, published in the *Halifax Chronicle Herald*,[10] and Kevin Donovan's work at the *Toronto Star* showing how the NDP government was spending millions on subsidized housing without any controls.[11]

> When I first started doing this, I remember people in the newsroom being quite hostile to it, and they would say 'this is all you do is sit at the computer and ker-ching, ker-ching,' Donovan recalls. 'And I used to get really upset at that. But I think that they don't realize that it's not a substitute for reporting, it's just allowing you to do better reporting.[12]

Donovan is now in charge of investigations at the *Toronto Star*. In 1999, the Canadian Association of Journalists moved to recognize the best CAR story of the year as part of its annual awards. Since then, the CAR Award (Computer-Assisted Reporting Award) has become one of the most competitive.

CAR is also gradually making its way into daily reporting in Canada and online resources are appearing, such as www.carincanada.ca. 'Slowly, more journalists are realizing this is a good tool for bringing precision to daily reporting. And, it helps spot trends and makes analyzing numbers simpler,' Washburn said. 'With a growing number of journalism schools offering some form of CAR, it is also becoming part of the newsroom culture. They are arriving with the skills and they use them. Editors are still wary, but I think it is economic more than philosophical.'[13]

Dana Robbins, now publisher of the *Hamilton Spectator*, oversaw many of the CAR efforts at the paper where he was editor-in-chief from 2000 to late 2006. 'I probably shouldn't admit this, but I didn't immediately see how it would be applied in a daily news environment,' he said. 'I had this vague notion that CAR was a tool that financial auditors might use, not journalists.'[14] But after a series of groundbreaking stories at the paper, his views changed.

> I'm a convert. It would be difficult for me to overstate how much value I believe CAR can bring a news organization.
>
> At its most basic level, it allows us to tell stories that we simply would not have been able to tell. It is not within the capacity of even the largest news organization to manually analyze millions of documents. CAR gives us that capability.
>
> At a more strategic level—and this is the piece that most engaged me as an editor—it allows news organizations to create content that clearly differentiates themselves from the competition. In an age in which news is increasingly a homogenous commodity, this is ever more important.[15]

Brant Houston, who for many years was executive director of IRE/NICAR and is now Knight Chair in Investigative and Enterprise Reporting at the University of Illinois at Urbana-Champaign, has similar thoughts. 'I think it's the salvation of what we consider to be the mainstream journalism. I think investigative reporting in all its formats and data analysis is what's going to separate journalists from casual forms of journalism by citizens, periodic journalism, and spot news journalism,' he said. 'I mean people with a cell phone can now beat us to the punch on news. So our ability to gather information, to filter it, and make sense of it in a credible and non-partisan fashion is what's going to separate us, and to do that you're going to need these tools.'[16]

The Tools

The tools of CAR range from the relatively familiar to the highly specialized.

Perhaps the most basic and commonly used tool is the Internet, which hardly needs much introduction. But journalists don't always know how to get everything they can from the Internet. A few tips and tricks can turn the ordinary into the extraordinary.

Among specific software tools, probably the most popular is the spreadsheet. There are many such programs available, including Microsoft Excel, Corel Quattro Pro, Lotus 123, OpenOffice and NeoOffice (which are free), and Google's online free spreadsheet. Spreadsheets are best for doing math and are exceptionally convenient for doing calculations on long columns of numbers, as well as for-sorting information into a more revealing order. They also perform simple data analysis. Spreadsheets are extremely easy to use and are the tool employed most often in daily reporting.

The next most popular software tool is the database manager. These programs pick up where spreadsheets leave off in the sense that database programs can deal with very large and complicated data sets with many data tables and are much more powerful in terms of their analytical capabilities. Common desktop products include Microsoft Access, Corel Paradox, and Filemaker Pro. Powerful server database systems are capable of handling enormous amounts of data. These include Microsoft SQL Server, and MySQL, a free open-source database system. Databases allow for sophisticated analysis of large sets of data, and have been behind many of Canada's most successful CAR stories.

Mapping programs, or geographic information systems, plot geographic data on maps. Some regard mapping to be the 'killer application' in CAR, because it turns rows and columns of data into something the reader, viewer, or web surfer can see. Common mapping programs include ArcView, MapInfo, and Maptitude.

Beyond these big three, a number of other CAR tools are used by journalists. Many of these are utility programs that massage data to the point where it can be analyzed in one of the other programs. And then there are the truly niche tools, such as the PERL programming language, which can be used to extract data from searchable, online databases.

We will cover all of these tools, and more, in this book. But always, the focus will be on what you can achieve as a journalist.

An Ongoing Example

A good example of how CAR has started not only to reshape journalism, but to foster positive social change is the country's system of public health inspections of restaurants in their respective municipalities.

In Canada at least three major investigations have been done into food safety by reporters who obtained databases of restaurant inspections done by public health staff in their communities. Food safety is a topic that had been pursued in the United States with great success, so it is hardly surprising that journalists in Canada followed suit. Of course, before CAR came along, journalists were doing stories on food inspections, but they were anecdotal because there was no way to look at the overall picture. There were stories about dirty restaurants, but no independent reporting as to how many restaurants were dirty. Reporters followed inspectors, who inevitably found problems, but the reporters had no way to know how the inspection system was working as a whole.

Access to databases changed all of that.

The first story broke in 2000, when the *Toronto Star* analyzed inspection data to show not only disgusting conditions in many restaurant kitchens, but that municipal inspectors were doing little to crack down on the restaurant owners. The *Star* series sparked an inspection blitz. It also persuaded health officials to bring plans off the drawing board for a system of public disclosure of inspection results. Many of Canada's largest city restaurants have to display in their front windows a colour-coded announcement of the level of certification granted by the Department of Health.[17]

The Toronto Health Department initially resisted giving the data to the *Star*, but eventually relented. Sylvanus Thompson, a manager with the department, says the newspaper's access to the data allowed it to tell a story that otherwise it could not have done. 'I think it is important for journalists to have access to the actual data. Without that access you cannot really put that true story out there.'[18]

The *Star* series was followed soon after by a similar effort in the *Hamilton Spectator* that reached many of the same conclusions, prompting a wholesale reshaping of the food inspection system there, including hiring more inspectors, and instituting better internal controls to ensure inspectors visit premises on a required schedule. Since the series was run, the city also has promised to disclose the results of inspections to the public. Compliance with provincial inspection requirements by the city Health Department has increased from 10 per cent to higher than 90 per cent.[19]

Most recently, the *Edmonton Journal* tackled the subject of restaurant food safety in the fall of 2006, starting off with this compelling lead:

> 99 violations in four years
> 72 breaches likely to make patrons sick
> 13 hand-washing infractions
> 9 citations for leaving food out
> 6 cases of vermin
> This restaurant is still open[20]

The conclusions of the investigation were familiar. Dirty restaurants, missed inspections, and almost no enforcement. For *Edmonton Journal* reporter Karen Kleiss, the story proved to be a spectacular introduction to CAR. She said:

> The public reaction was astounding. We had hundreds of phone calls, letters, and e-mails, and filled two pages with extraordinarily thoughtful reader response after the series ran. We put the database online and made it searchable, so readers could look at the records of their favourite restaurants. We had more than half a million hits in the week after the series ran, and tens of thousands in the month that followed, making it the most successful online venture in the history of edmontonjournal.com. All the other media followed the story, and several other news outlets, including the *Journal's* sister paper, the *Calgary Herald*, conducted similar investigations.[21]

Kleiss says that without the database, the story would have been impossible.

> There was almost no publicly available information on the program: no internal or external reports, no advocacy groups compiling information, no leaks, and no previous reporting. The database told us everything, from the dirtiest restaurants to the most common violations. It was like a well-placed source telling us exactly where to look for the story.[22]

A day after the series completed its run, the Auditor General of Alberta released a report that echoed the *Journal*'s findings. As a result, health authorities across the province implemented a disclosure program to make restaurant inspection information readily available to the public.

These public health inspections are only one among the growing list of successful forays by Canadian journalists into CAR. Others include:

- The monumental 'Race and Crime' series that ran in the *Toronto Star* in 2002. It revealed disturbing patterns in the way blacks were being treated by the police and the justice system[23] The series led to a renewed effort to stamp out racism in the police force. It won numerous awards, including the Michener Award, Canada's most prestigious journalism award.
- The *Hamilton Spectator*'s 2004 investigation of Ontario's Drive Clean emissions testing program. The series revealed rampant fraud in the program, and showed that most newer cars passed the test. After the series, the Ontario government moved to crack down on fraud and exempted newer cars from testing. The series won a National Newspaper Award.[24]
- The CBC's two series on dangerous reactions to prescription drugs in 2004 and 2005. After a five-year fight to obtain data on adverse drug reactions from Health Canada, the CBC reporters showed that both the young and the elderly were prescribed drugs not approved for use in those age groups, sometimes with tragic results. The series won several awards, including the Canadian Association of Journalists CAR award, mentioned above, and the Overall Award for two successive years.[25]
- A joint effort by the *Hamilton Spectator*, the *Toronto Star*, and the *Record* of Waterloo Region that revealed disturbing cracks in Canada's air safety system. The series won two Ontario Newspaper Awards, the CAJ's CAR award and Overall Award, and received a citation of merit in the Michener Award competition.

The Structure of this Book

Many books on the market teach you how to use computer programs. With the notable exceptions of Houston's work and the introduction to CAR in *Digging Deeper: A Canadian Reporter's Research Guide*, most are written with business or personal uses in mind. This book addresses the specialized needs of journalists and other researchers whose purpose is to mine data for meaning and truth.

Our approach is user-friendly. We take you step-by-step through each of the key techniques, with ample illustrations. And while we use Canadian examples, the methods are equally applicable in other countries.

Our focus is journalistic uses of data. We don't burden you with unnecessary technical information and we do not document features of computer programs that journalists rarely use.

We do not ask you to work with fictional 'demonstration' data. Instead, throughout the chapters on spreadsheets, databases, mapping programs, and specialized applications we focus on real-life examples. You can download actual data sets obtained from government agencies at <www.oup.com/ca/he/companion/reporting>.

Each chapter begins with a short summary of what it covers. In addition, many of the chapters conclude with a section called 'Five Stories You Can Use.' Each of these provides five ideas for CAR stories you can do, so you can get started right away.

Throughout the text, you will find a generous number of screenshots to guide you through the intricacies of the computer programs we demonstrate. Tech Tips point out quirks and tricks you need to know to do your job better.

TECH TIP ⚠

Throughout the text we have used the 2007 versions of Microsoft Excel and Access. While these versions have a somewhat different user interface from the earlier versions, most of the program functions in the latest versions are available in older versions. We have included 'older version' tip boxes to help you locate the commands in the old user interfaces. Go to <www.oupcanada.com/CAR.html> for tip sheets that summarize and locate features in both the 2007 and earlier versions.

Our goal is not to turn you into software experts—although you definitely will gain much expertise as you go—but instead to show you the tools you need to add to your reporting arsenal, so you will have a competitive edge in journalism. As Robbins of the *Spectator* has observed:

> If you are a journalist, and you're looking for a clear, unequivocal way to distinguish yourself from the pack, CAR will do that. In the longer term, I think CAR will eventually become an assumed skill, and that reporters without this capacity will find themselves at an increasing disadvantage.[26]

Internet Research Strategies

David McKie

What We'll Cover:

- How to create an effective and efficient research strategy
- How to find specific types of records
- How to use site operators
- How to find people using discussion groups and social networking sites
- How to use tools such as alerts and Google desktop

Introduction

When investigative documentary-maker Julian Sher set out for Iraq to shoot the footage for *The Battle for Baghdad*, he had already done much of his legwork—even before setting foot inside the besieged country. His hour-long documentary chronicled the continued violence in Iraq's capital through the eyes of a doctor who had abandoned all hope of a bright future and gone into hiding to stay alive amid the sectarian violence. In Sher's account of the doctor's situation, he writes:

> A secular Shia professional who chafed under the repression of Saddam Hussein's regime, he was overcome with joy when American troops entered Baghdad four years ago this Sunday. 'I was screaming, rejoicing in happiness', he told me during a recent trip to Baghdad. 'The tyranny has ended.'[1]

But the tyranny has continued, not only for the once-idealistic doctor, but for many of his fellow Iraqis who also dreamed of a brighter future in a post-Saddam era. Getting the story of hopelessness and despair was a challenge, in large part because moving around Iraq was dangerous for its citizens—and for journalists. It is for this reason that Sher had to rely on his ability to search efficiently on the Internet, a skill that he has spent the past several years honing as a former producer with CBC Television's *The Fifth Estate*, a trainer on Internet search techniques, and webmaster of journalismnet.com.

A large focus of *The Battle for Baghdad* was human rights abuses by the Iraqi government. 'We knew that the United Nations had carried out investigations', he recalls. 'But by using the advanced search techniques to find the pdf (portable document format) reports, and key words of certain prison sites . . . we were able to bullet down (i.e., drill or dig deeper for information using key-word searches). And just before I met the chief human rights investigator, he was surprised at how much I knew about his investigations because I could find them on-line and read the extract that I needed. There was a UN human rights site for Iraq.'[2]

Sher was able to 'bullet down'—to use the research techniques we'll discuss in this chapter to be very surgical in his pursuit—for the essential information for his documentary using a feature of search engines that many journalists and journalism students, surprisingly, still ignore: the advanced search. Whether it be Google, or search engines for the sites of newspapers, it's important to use the advanced function to help tell better stories.

But even before Sher turned to the web, he developed a research strategy that allowed him to locate online sites, find documents, and identify safe places to send his cameras. This advance work offline increased Sher's productivity on-line. By the time he was ready to turn to the Internet, he was armed with all the information he needed. He later produced a documentary in conjunction with the *New York Times*.

Whether you're producing award-winning documentaries, writing books or feature articles, or covering city hall for a local radio or television station, the approach you take to using the Internet should borrow from that of Sher and of other able researchers: Develop a strategy to ensure you find the best information possible. Study tools such as search engines and discussion groups to discover ways they can help. The payoff? You'll stay on top of your beat, avoid being handed boring assignments, and break stories.

It is also important to develop a strategy for a second key reason: staying out of trouble. The Internet is so vast and chaotic that it's easy to be duped. People aren't always who they say they are. Information can't always be trusted. Websites and blogs become tools for propaganda and spin.

'Just because it's on the Internet in 25 places, doesn't mean that it's true, even if those sites are different', warns Mary McGuire, associate professor at Carleton University's School of Journalism in Ottawa and co-author of *The Internet Handbook for Writers, Researchers and Journalists*. 'There are too many examples of mistakes that live forever on line.'[3] Having a reliable checklist of verification tools will also help avoid these minefields that can turn the Internet into a dangerous place.

Though we will be examining specific search engines such as Google, websites, and types of documents such as pdfs, the goal of this chapter is not to provide a definitive catalogue of web resources. The Internet is too fluid for that. Rather, the task at hand is to provide strategies that will allow you to find what you're looking for, whether on deadline or for a long-term project.

When Julian Sher began formally writing about the Internet for the Canadian Association of Journalists' *Media* magazine back in the winter of 1995, cyberspace was a new and mysterious entity. In his inaugural column, Sher tried to calm journalists' phobia about this emerging public sphere, a 'hosepipe' as some users have now taken to calling it. After telling journalists, in essence, to check their phobias at the door, he advised readers to 'get on the learning curve fast. Because the Internet will become as central to journalism as the phone.'[4] We hope this chapter will make that journey a little easier.

The Need to Think Offline before You Begin Hunting

One Strategy and an Example

Being strategic is simple. It means taking time offline to think about what you want to search on line. Who are you researching? What does she do for a living? Is she involved in any volunteer activities or charities? How can I find someone with a fresh perspective? What city department or government ministry is ultimately accountable? The answers to some, or all, of these questions could provide useful terms to plug into search engines, or hints about websites to visit using some of the domain searches we'll discuss later in the chapter.

Internet research pioneer, Nora Paul, has six steps to what she calls 'sensible searching on the World Wide Web'. Her advice? Know the difference between search tools; think of the task, and then the topic; understand the searching aids on the site you're perusing; use your logic; evaluate your sources; (and) know when to stop.[5]

Offline Thinking for Online Success

The claim that you should do your initial thinking offline is a view that underscores the philosophy of experts such as Nora Paul and Julian Sher.

> First and foremost, I make a list of what do I want to find? Who do I want to find? Where am I likely to find it? It's not hard to find the official government report on cigarette smuggling. But if you're trying to find activists, if you're trying to find supporters of Al-Qaeda or Internet child predators, you have to think like them. Where are they going to be? What words are they likely to use?
>
> I'm amazed how journalists . . . put in a certain key word and then say 'I can't find anything about it.' Well, maybe it's because you're only using a word that only journalists would use.[6]

It's important to understand that this philosophy of 'think before you get too deeply into searching' is a strategy that transcends all kinds of investigations, from Sher's longer-term research to breaking news. A case in point is the bridge accident in Laval, Quebec, that killed five people on 30 September 2007. It was noon on a Saturday. Tonnes of concrete from a collapsed highway overpass rained down on two cars, crushing them and killing the five people inside, including a pregnant woman. Ironically, about 45 minutes before the tragedy an inspector had visited the structure to examine pieces of concrete that fell from the overpass. Jules Bonin would later testify before an inquiry into the accident, 'I didn't think the overpass would fall. I didn't think it was an emergency.'[7]

In the newspaper account shortly after the accident, the Laval mayor, Gilles Vaillancourt, claimed that 'It is a viaduct that had never, until now, shown any signs of weakness. It wasn't on the list of viaducts and bridges that needed to be repaired or replaced.' Vaillancourt also told reporters that the viaduct had passed an inspection the previous year.[8]

A few important details to be gleaned from that article and subsequent television stories came in handy. First of all, the accident happened in Laval. Since the mayor was quoted, perhaps city councillors or bureaucrats had expressed concerns about the bridge. It was also clear from media reports that Quebec's Ministry of Transport was responsible for the overpass and that the bridge had been inspected, meaning that bridges must undergo regular inspections. So already there were places to begin searching: the websites of the City of Laval and the Quebec Ministry of Transport, to name two. The key research terms (we'll delve more deeply into terms later in this chapter) were 'inspection' and 'bridges'.

Now, who is watching the inspectors who gave this bridge and others a clean bill of health? Well, every year, journalists dutifully write and broadcast stories about the reports of auditors general. However, only the most sensational problems in government spending and programs receive attention. Had the auditor in Quebec ever expressed concerns about bridge safety? Entering the terms 'bridge' and 'inspection' into the search engine of the auditor general's website uncovered gold. It turns out the auditor sounded the alarm back in 2002.[9]

Fig. 2.1

As you can see, the search terms produce two results, with the first one showing the most promise. Clicking on that link will take you to the report. In most web browsers, the key combination 'Ctrl + F' will give you a search box, in which you can also plug in the term 'inspection'. Given that this isn't a very long document, you can read it all. It becomes clear from this passage halfway into the document that the auditor general was concerned.

> As there are deficiencies in the planning strategies related to repair and major rehabilitation works, there is a risk that the amount of the budget recommendation will be underestimated.[10]

So, there's a follow-up story to be done in Quebec. What about other provinces? Searches in other provinces turned up similar results, which became the focus of a story by CBC Radio's national reporter, Derek Stoffel. His piece pointed out that audits in provinces such as Quebec, Ontario, and Newfoundland and Labrador uncovered serious deficiencies in the bridge inspection programs.[11] 'Fishing trips' are not a great idea because they are akin to randomly sticking your line into the water rather than first researching the best sites that have the most fish. Or, like trawling, you go after everything and end up throwing most of it back overboard—wasteful of both time and resources. Although, as Julian Sher points out, it doesn't hurt to run across pleasant surprises every now and then.[12]

That's why it's important to think through what you're doing, as in the example of the overpass in Laval. Before indiscriminately plugging terms into search engines, give the topic some preliminary thought and analysis to determine what those terms should be. Where are the best fishing spots? And what time of day is best to show up? This kind of research can be conducted offline, and then going online. 'The Internet is too much of a hosepipe to be your first stop. Go there after you've read some stories and have a better idea of what you're looking for', warned Bloomberg News's Erik Schatzker at a joint conference of the Canadian Association of Journalists and Investigative Reporters and Editors.[13]

He advises that if you are trying to build a profile of a company, try to read past profiles and focus on articles of 1,500 words or longer because they tend to contain richer detail than run-of-the-mill news reports. Determine whether the company is public or private. If it's the former, then you'll be able to find a lot of information online. Begin by visiting the company's website to see what it says about itself in news releases and then compare that self-assessment with the financial information that the company must disclose in financial statements to the securities commission in Canada or the United States.[14] Then, once you've done this kind of research and have an idea of the categories and keywords you might want to use in searches, you can begin with the real research.

In the preliminary, planning stages of your research, you might also ask yourself who has tackled this topic before. Though we would like to think that our ideas are original, chances are someone else in another market in Canada or the United States has already done the story. Restaurant inspection is a prominent example of this kind of piggybacking effect. After a number of exposés in US newspapers on dirty restaurants, based on obtaining electronic inspection records, the *Toronto Star*'s Robert Cribb was the first to Canadianize the story, in 2000.[15] Reporters in other cities, most recently Edmonton, followed with similar stories. So, before phoning the mayor to ask about the state of restaurants in your city, poke around to see if there are any articles in which reporters in other markets explained how they got the story. There could be valuable clues in that explanation.

In addition to searching for similar stories written by other journalists, it's also a good idea to seek out academics or researchers with advocacy groups who have conducted studies on your topic. They may have already compiled the data, which formed the basis of an obscure article in an academic journal or report buried deep inside a web page that few people have seen.

Assess the Tools

If you know all the tools and how to use them and if you use a disciplined approach to finding the information, you will have more luck than someone who does not. Think of it as a probability experiment. You can find what you're looking for (if it actually exists on the web) 95 per cent of the time if you have good search habits, and 20 per cent of the time if you are sloppy.[16] So what are some of these tools?

1. Knowing already where the information will be stored.
2. Guessing correctly where the information is stored.
3. Key word search engines.[17]

If you already know and/or can guess correctly, then, obviously, you should proceed with your search, which is what we did in the example of the collapsed bridge. It's difficult to know where the information is stored if you lack an understanding of the websites that are vital to your beat. If part of your beat covers infrastructure such as roads and bridges, then it's important to understand the part the federal, provincial, and municipal governments play in the maintenance of those structures.

A lot of the money flows from the federal government, but the province is responsible for the network of highways and the bridges that cross over them. Cities are responsible for municipal roads and bridges. Next, ask who talks about bridges. Politicians, businessmen, bureaucrats, and citizens' groups all are potential characters for your eventual story. Find out where they live online (websites, blogs, social networking sites, discussion groups, listservs) and what concerns they may be expressing. Treat the websites and other online resources as you would any other source of information. Get to know them.

The Need to Evaluate

Evaluating is important once you've located a website or page. Fortunately, finding tips on ways to evaluate is easy. There are many online resources, such as the University of British Columbia (UBC) library, that run through a checklist of questions you should be asking when visiting a web page or site. The questions are many, but the UBC site covers useful common ground.

- *Source or author:* Is there a credentialed author responsible for the page's content, and if so, is she part of a group?
- *Accuracy:* Can the information be verified through footnotes, bibliographies, or other sources deemed to be credible?
- *Currency:* How frequently is the site updated? If there are links to other web pages, are they current?
- *Objectivity:* Is there any information on the page, such as advertising or views from another organization, that would compromise the page's objectivity?
- *Coverage:* Is the page incomplete or still under construction?
- *Purpose:* What's the primary purpose of the site or page? Is that purpose clearly stated? What is the emphasis of the presentation: technical, scholarly, clinical, popular, or elementary?[18]

These questions should be kept in mind when creating a hierarchy of websites. Stephen C. Miller, assistant to the technology editor at *The New York Times* uses the acronym MIDIS (Miller Internet Data Integrity Scale) as a guide to help determine if the information gathered from the Net can be trusted. He has a hierarchy that goes as follows:

Websites that contain government data: federal, state/provincial or municipal: 'While you may personally question the data, you are safe in quoting it.'

Websites that contain university studies: They tend to be published by professors who are recognized experts in their fields and whose work is reviewed by peers. 'Quoting from these studies is also a safe bet with attribution.' Miller also notes that an increasing number of students are doctoral candidates publishing their ongoing work on the Net, much of which is also peer-reviewed. A 'surprising' number of post-graduate students are publishing their masters theses. 'While the validity of the data might be in question, it usually contains links or references to the supporting data. You might not want to quote directly from the study, but it will give you lots of leads if you check the bibliography.' The National Library of Canada also maintains an online repository of graduate theses.

Websites maintained by special interest groups: They publish a lot of data. They may have a political agenda but that doesn't mean their statistics are unreliable. It's also safe to use the data since it is attributable: 'a study by Amnesty International claims that . . .'

Websites that fall into the 'other' category: This includes information published on someone's homepage. Validity of data can be a 'coin toss' but the saving grace is that there is usually a way to contact the page's owner. 'Often the value of this information is to find sources. The person owning the homepage may, in fact, be an expert in his field and can safely be used as a source. Check them out, and if they turn out okay, you've now got a source who is not one of the 'usual suspects. We're all looking for new sources of good information and good quotes.'[19]

Getting Deep Inside the Web

Part of the importance of evaluating websites and pages is assessing how deeply the information is buried. Certain documents, particularly if they have been recently uploaded, run the risk of escaping the reach of keyword search engines such as Google, which use robots to automatically index sites. Google uses criteria such as how many other sites link to a site, so a search tends to produce popular sites.

Chances are few people even bothered to read the bridge safety audits in provinces such as Quebec and Ontario or link to them. This lack of popularity means that they will be buried deeper within the web. As journalists, we're constantly on the lookout for the obscure report that few people are talking about, or the little-noticed audit that can shed light on government spending.

These nuggets are invaluable for reporters looking to advance or break stories. Taking an inventory of a site's contents is one way to ferret out these documents. But what if you don't know they exist or only have a hunch?

Search Engines

Now that we have assessed the websites on our beat, we're ready to begin searching, a process that has been dubbed more an art than science because there is no exact formula. If you used the correct search terms and combination of terms, you're likely to find success most of the time; that is, if the information is online. But before you can harness the power of the particular search engine, it's important to have a general understanding of searching.

'We have reached this conclusion as a result of our experience with Internet users', writes Jim Carroll in the *1997 Canadian Internet Handbook*. 'We are always amazed when we watch people use the Internet—we ask them if they have used the help screens on a search system, only to be told no and then they complain when they cannot find anything ! Good gosh! What do you expect? Learn to swim before you dive in. It is generally the thing to do.'[20]

For city hall reporters, for instance, the city's website should be mined for important nuggets buried in the minutes of committee meetings, long-forgotten reports, and audits. But before using the site, it's a good idea to read the Search Tips page.

On the City of Ottawa's 's Help section, you are encouraged to 'type in your question as you would have asked it when speaking to another person, and you will receive better results than a typical Keyword or Boolean query would return. Being able to use natural language also means that your questions can be quite elaborate, thus leading to more accurate, concise results'.[21] So, for instance, if you were looking for information about the level of chlorine and other chemicals in the drinking water, you're instructed to phrase the query as a natural question such as 'What are the levels of chlorine and other chemicals in our drinking water? Or simply the phrase: chlorine in water?[22]

Three terms mentioned in the paragraph are important to understand. Natural language, as the Search Tips page explains, uses plain language as search terms. Keyword search is just what the word implies: The search engine will return documents that contain the words or phrases that you've specified. So, for instance, if you were looking for all documents related to 'chlorine' on the city of Ottawa website, then you would type the word and take your chances. It wouldn't be the most efficient search, but you would get many results.

Finally, there was a reference to a 'Boolean' query which more than any other searches can be the key to finding what you want. It is for that reason that we will spend some time learning how to conduct searches using Boolean logic.

Boolean Logic

The syntax for many search terms comes in the form of Boolean Logic and when using the Internet you must learn to 'think Boolean', which is a form of math that involves ways of examining the relationships between different bits of information. Many search engines on the web, like the one belonging to the city of Ottawa, allow you to use Boolean logic to specify the relationships that exist between the words on a web page.[23]

Boolean logic allows you to both enlarge and narrow your search using key operators: 'AND'; 'OR'; and 'NOT'.

'AND' allows you to use more than one search term. For instance, if you're researching the food made by Monsanto, you would want to use the term 'food AND Monsanto' to find the sites that may be of interest. The operator returns web pages and websites that contain both words. 'AND' is the operator you'd use if you knew for sure that Monsanto is in the food business. If not, you might want to increase your research by using the operator 'OR', which asks the search engine to return sites that contain the words 'Monsanto OR food'.

During the course of your research, as the CBC did during its profile of the company,[24] you may discover that during its earlier life as a chemical company it made the deadly pesticide Agent Orange. As far as Monsanto is concerned, that's ancient history. The company now bills itself as a 'life sciences' firm that produces genetically modified foods.

If you were doing a story about these foods and wanted to know how Monsanto was involved, the fact that it once produced Agent Orange may be of little interest. Therefore, you'd want to eliminate references to Agent Orange. This is where the operator 'NOT' comes into play. The search would look like this: 'Monsanto OR food NOT pesticides'. You are telling the search engine to return results with the terms 'Monsanto' and 'food' but NOT 'pesticides.' However, we're using the 'AND' operator because we know for sure that Monsanto is in the food business.

Boolean Logic also allows you to search by strings of characters, which is accomplished by putting the phrase between quotation marks. So, upon further research, if we determined that Monsanto was involved in the making of genetically modified foods, then we would want to include that text string in our search like this: 'Monsanto AND "genetically modified foods"'.

Because this logic is so useful when conducting research, it's essential to find out if the search engine you're using—especially if it's on a government or company website—supports this logic. The answer probably will be 'yes'. The answer will be contained in the 'Help' section.

As we have seen, narrowing the number of sites is of vital importance. It's a good idea to try to whittle down the number of sites to about 50 or less before you begin perusing, and in order to do this, you need to go one step further, and combine Boolean operators.[25] For instance, if we continue with the Monsanto example, we could conduct a search that would only give us references to the company's genetically modified foods and eliminate any references to Agent Orange with the following search: 'monsanto AND "genetically modified foods" NOT "agent orange"'. The first part of the query produced

141,000 hits. When we specified that we didn't want references to 'Agent Orange', the number of results was reduced to 552.

Search engines usually are not case sensitive. So there's no need for upper-case letters, though it's probably a good idea to get into the habit of using caps just to make sure. (Here, the operators are in upper case for clarity and emphasis.) You will also notice that we used quotation marks to ensure that the search engine, in this case Google, searched the phrase as one term 'Agent Orange', rather than as two separate words. In many search engines, such as Google, the 'AND' operator is implicit, meaning that if you type: 'Monsanto "genetically modified food"', the search engine treats it as if you were using 'AND'. This is why you need to know how your search engine handles Boolean Logic. For instance, many search engines use the '+' and '−' signs in place of 'AND' and 'NOT'. (For a resumé of advanced searching tips, see Table 1.)

While understanding Boolean logic is vital for successful searches, sometimes it's necessary to go even further by using a feature called 'the wild card'. The asterisk (*) is a special symbol that stands for one or more characters. It allows searches for words with similar spellings.

If we take the example of 'teenage suicide', many terms could come into play. We can probably use the wild card 'teen*' to capture the terms 'teen' and 'teenage' in the search phrase 'teen* suicide'. The asterisk not only produced titles such as 'teen suicide', but similar-sounding titles such as 'teen-aged suicide' and 'teenaged suicide'.

Combining Boolean searches in combination with the wild card might also be in order if we want to capture even more results. Given that the term 'adolescent' is used interchangeably with 'teen,' we might broaden our search with the operator 'OR'. The new search might look something like this:

"teen*suicide" OR "adolescent suicide"

The result? More than double the number of hits. Then, if we were interested in narrowing the search by limiting it to teens who committed suicide while on an 'anti-depressant', we would use the operator 'AND'. The combinations are almost endless.

Site Operators

These are powerful operators contained in the 'advanced search' features of the more popular search engines such as Google, Yahoo, and MSN. Search engines for major websites also support the operators, which is why you must read the background information. Site operators allow journalists to maximize their searches by limiting them to specific web pages or types of files. Why would you want to limit a search to a particular web page when that page already has a search engine? The answer is simple. Many search engines, especially for organizations that may not have a lot of money, lack advanced searching capabilities. But by telling Google that you want to search that site, you are enabled to use all of its advanced features to locate specific information. Let's use Health Canada as an example.

Most government departments tend to release documents such as audits and studies in pdf format because they're easy to save, download, and print. So, before searching Health Canada's site, we might want to find out how the department stores its information. If the answer is 'pdf', then we can conduct exact searches. But there's a problem. While Health Canada's search engine does contain advanced features that allow for a variety of key-word searches, it does not allow users to specify the type of document. You can specify that you want a publication; you can't specify the exact file format, such as a .xls (spreadsheet), .pdf (portable document format), or .ppt (PowerPoint). This is why you'd want to use Google's advanced capabilities. To do this, visit Google's Advanced

Search page, and go to the 'File Format' section. Clicking on the arrow in the box to the right produces a menu of choices. The file type we want is pdf.

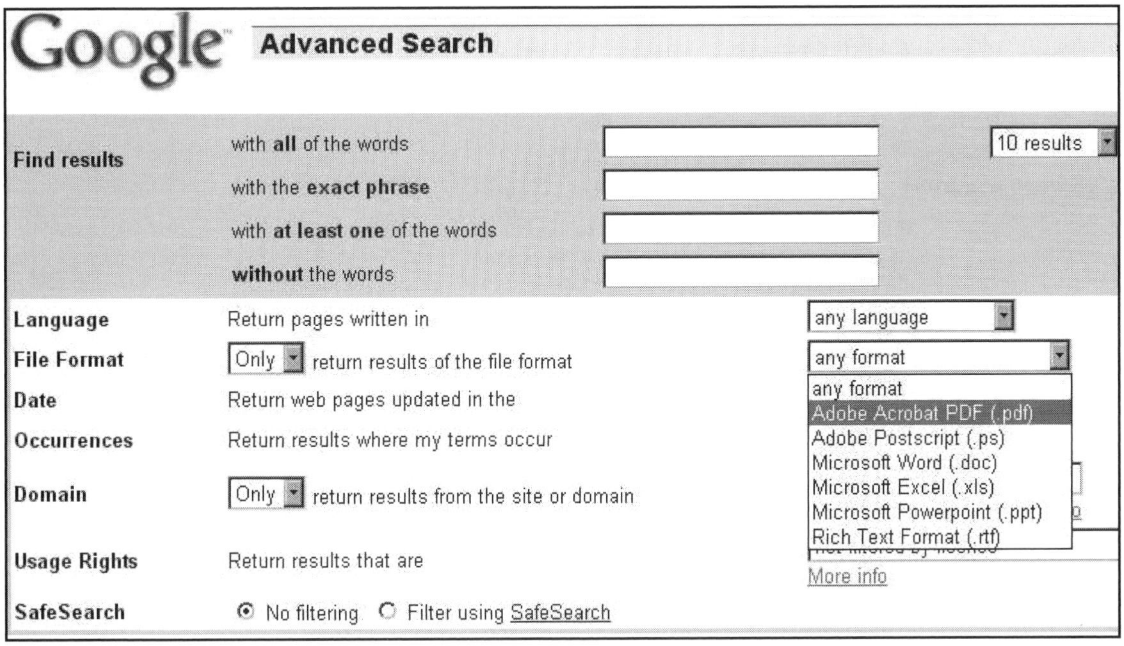

Fig. 2.2

As you can see, Google provides a drop-down menu of format choices. This list is not exhaustive in that it doesn't include all the file types. For instance, you can search for database files which go by the extension mdb. However, you won't find that extension in Google's drop-down menu. For instance, Google also searches file formats such as Post-Script, Corel, WordPerfect, Lotus 1-2-3, mdb (databases), and others. In this case, we're interested in the pdf file, which our advanced function allows us to specify. Once we've done that, let's copy (Ctrl + c) the domain from Health Canada's web address (hc-sc. gc.ca) and paste (Ctrl + v) it into Google's 'Domain' section.

To this point, we have used the 'File Format' option to specify the type of document, and then asked Google to look for that type of file on Health Canada's homepage. Now we need only indicate the subject. On any given month, the department publishes warnings about dangerous drugs. On 30 March 2007, it alerted Canadians that Novartis, the company that makes Zelnorm, the drug to treat 'irritable bowel syndrome', had agreed to withdraw the product from the market. So let's enter the drug's name into the 'this exact wording or phrase' section in the advanced search.

We have to document what we need. The 'Search' box contains the operators Google used to conduct the search:

site:hc-sc.gc filetype:pdf zelnorm

If you knew the operators by heart, using the Google Advanced Search option would have been unnecessary. You could have just typed the operators. Table 1 contains the most commonly used operators. Many search engines use these operators in their Advanced Search options. However, the options are not always clearly spelled out. While there is a common set of operators, a few engines have their own variations. Table 2.1 is an amalgamated list. The 'Site' operators are followed by a colon (:), which is then followed by a word, URL, or domain name, etc. There should be no spaces on either side of the colon.[26]

Table 2.1
Operators

What is it?	What it does	Example
General query operator		
' '	quotation marks to find exact phrases	'to be or not to be'
Boolean operators		
OR	Most search engines are not case sensitive, still the operator should be capitalized just to make sure. It allows you to capture either of the items identified. The OR expands the search by including either of the words or phrases.	'to be or not to be' OR Shakespeare
+	This is the absolute AND. In Google, and many other search engines, this is the default operator. The '+' sign narrows your search by returning both words or phrases that are specified.	'to be or not to be' + Shakespeare
−	The minus sign, which can also be the word NOT, is the opposite of 'and' in that it tells the search engine to exclude a term. For example, we may be interested in the life sciences company Monsanto and its present-day genetically modified foods, but not in any of the products such as Agent Orange that it made during its days as a chemical company. In this case, we would have to specify that we don't want the term 'agent orange'.	Monsanto −'agent orange'
~	This operator is called a tilde (pronounced til-dee), and is used to capture terms that resemble the one you have specified. For instance, in the aftermath of the 2006 ferry accident off the coast of British Columbia, you may be conducting some research. If you're interested in ferry accidents, you might also want to include words such as 'boats' and 'crashes'. With the tilde you can broaden the search to include similar tragedies, thus allowing you to draw possible parallels to past events. Google replicates this with its 'stemming' technology that allows you to search for similar words to the ones you've specified.[27]	~ferry~accident
Wildcard	The wildcard feature allows you to specify that your search should cover several similar phrases.[28]	
*	The asterisk is a wild card that substitutes for a word. Let's say that for some reason you forgot the middle name of former Canadian Prime Minister, Pierre Elliot Trudeau. You could use the wild card to locate the word Elliot.	'Pierre * Trudeau'
Site operators	These are powerful operators that most engines have but that are not always well-known. While there is a common set of operators, a few engines have their own variations. Here is an amalgamated list. All of them consist of a predefined keyword and a colon (:) character, which are then followed by a word or URL or domain name, etc. There should be no spaces on either side of the colon.[29]	
Site:	This advanced operator is a query word that has a special meaning in search engines such as Google and AltaVisa and allows searches within a specific site. For instance, if you wanted to limit your search to the website of the Canadian Association of Journalists, you would preface the phrase with the word 'site' followed immediately with a colon (:). Once you're on the site, you can use the regular search terms, and other operators to continue your research. This option is also available	Site: www.caj.ca

Table 2.1 (continued)

What is it?	What it does	Example
	in the 'domain' section of the advanced option in Google and AltaVista. Simply put the Canadian Association of Journalists domain (www.caj.ca) into the box next to 'domain.' Note, there are no spaces between the 'Site' and the URL.	
Link:	The 'link' advanced operator allows you to find all the sites that link to a particular page. This is handy if you're researching a controversial group and you want to find out if there are any legitimate sites from governments or institutions that link to it. For example, do well-known and respected charity groups link to the website of a group that espouses hate? The connection may be unintentional, but one worth investigating nonetheless. Or Industry Canada may be linked to an obscure and controversial company that makes dubious products. This is a handy operator because you never know what connections may be worth investigating. This option, too, is available in the advanced search function for Google. Note, that you can not combine a Link search with a regular keyword search.	Link:www.world vision.ca
Cache:	This operator allows you to find web pages that are hidden in Google's cache. This is handy for finding controversial sites that may have been taken down in a hurry, but still exist in the form it took the last time it was indexed by Google. As with the other advanced operator, the word 'Cache' is followed by a colon and then the website's domain, and then the word or term that you might want to find on the website. Google will highlight the word or phrase that matches your query. This operator is not accessible through the Advanced Search page.	Cache: www. journalismnet.com
Related:	Engines determine topic similarity of web pages on different sites. This operator, when used with an URL, will return pages from other sites that are similar.	related:www.lii.org[30]
allinanchor:, inanchor:	Use allinanchor: to specify one or more words that must all be in anchor text. Use inanchor to specify one word in anchor text and one or more words in the rest of the document body.	allinanchor:www. librarian[31]
allintitle: , intitle:	Use allintitle: to specify one or more words that must all be in the title of a web page. Use intitle: to check for a single word in the title, and one or more words in the document body.	allintitle:www. librarians[32]
allinurl:, inurl:	Use allinurl: to specify one or more words to be checked in the URL of a web page. Use inurl: to check one word in the URL and one or more words in the document body.	allinurl:librarians[33]
define:	Returns definitions of a specific word, from various sources.	define:librarian[34]
filetype:	Use with a media file type (e.g., PDF) to limit searches to that type of record.	Filetype:pdf
info:	Provides engine-specific info about a particular URL or its parent site.	info:become alibrarian.org[35]

Search Engines

Catalogue Search Engines

If you lack a specific idea about a topic, then perhaps it's wise to use a catalog search engine. A 'catalog' engine is also called a 'dictionary search engine' or a 'hierarchical' index. The websites in the index are rated and put together by actual humans, who work 'behind the scenes' for some of the most popular catalogue search engines such as Yahoo and Looksmart. The fact that the rating is done by experts means a lot of thought has been put into the choices. This is different from the robots used by the keyword search engines such as Google, where the 'index' of websites and pages is compiled automatically by robots that use a variety of criteria to rank sites, but not necessarily the site's actual merit. So you may receive fewer hits compared to keyword search engines such as Google, but the results will be more relevant. This is why catalogue engines are good places to begin investigations.[36]

Meta Search Engines

A 'meta' search engine is one that obtains results from two or more other search engines, instead of its own efforts. This is another efficient way to maximize your results. Clusty (clusty.com) is one example of a search engine that uses the results of several other engines in what it calls a 'metasearch approach that helps raise the best results to the top, and push search engine spam to the bottom.[37] But the engine's most useful function appears after the results are posted. To stick with our Health Canada example, let's say that you're interested in drug recalls, but are unsure of what drug to focus on. Use the term 'drug recall' in the search engine, and you'll obtain a number of categories that could offer further clues.

Clusty.com's menu on the left side contains the results that are 'clustered' into categories, which could provide clues for future stories. For instance, plugging in terms about recalled prescription drugs produces references to medical devices. So not only do you have drug recalls, but also recalls of medical devices, and sites of lawyers who may become good sources for information about a particular recalled drug, which may be the subject of a class action suit.

Keyword Search Engines

Unlike catalogue search engines, these monsters use the brute force of technology to pick the best websites. Some of the most popular keyword engines, such as Google, use an automated technology called web worms or web bots that hunt the web for new pages. The worm sends all the information back to the master index. So, when you're using a keyword search engine such as Google, you are actually perusing its index, not the web.

While catalogue search engines are 'selective' in that they add only the most relevant sites, the keyword search selects everything; that is, the sites that are visited most frequently, including obscure and useless ones.

To understand the difference between catalogue and keyword search engines, think of a book's table of contents and its index. The 'index' would be the keyword search engine that allows you to zero in on a specific term or word. By contrast, the table of contents allows you to view the chapters. 'A catalogue search engine is like the table of contents of a book. It lists the chapters and when using the contents, readers will figure out which chapter is most likely to have the information they are looking for. A keyword search engine is like the index at the back of a book where you find the search term you're interested in and it tells you what page to go to.'[38]

Keyword searches are best used when looking for individual pages within websites. For instance, if you already know that the drug Zelnorm has been the subject of a recall, then it makes sense to go directly to Health Canada's website with the help of Google. Then, Google's 'advanced features' allows you to find the pdf document about the recall that the department posted on the site.

Going Deep into the 'Invisible' Web

Of course, search engines miss a lot of information available in cyberspace. About half of the content on the web is located in hard-to-find locations. Here, we're talking about material that exists in formats such as <ppt> (PowerPoint presentations), <xls> (spreadsheets), <doc> (Word documents), and many others.

Many experts have labelled the place where this hard-to-find material resides as the 'invisible' web. While the term 'invisible' has gained a lot of currency, it may also be misleading. It's not that the information is invisible. It can be found quickly using many of the techniques we've discussed thus far. Many search engines have advanced features that allow you to limit your searches according to the type of file—as we saw in the Health Canada example—and the date the file was produced.

Apart from obscure file formats, valuable information also exists in places such as minutes of committee meetings. Health Canada, and the US Food and Drug Administration, for instance, have a number of advisory committees that meet to discuss drug and food safety. Health Canada provides summaries of those meetings on its website.[39] While Health Canada lacks the FDA's transparency—FDA's committee meetings are open to the public, and the minutes are verbatim accounts—the summaries of the meetings do provide valuable clues. For instance, the committee that reviews drug safety began raising concerns about the anti-inflammatory drug, Vioxx, before Merck 'voluntarily' pulled it from the Canadian and US market in 2004. The committee on medical device safety heard a disturbing presentation about hospitals reusing devices that are supposed to be used only once. This warning came before the major outbreak in hospital infections across the country.

A similar research methodology came in handy for follow-up stories in the aftermath of the problems BC's Greater Vancouver region experienced with its drinking water. On 16 November 2006, torrential rains caused landslides into the region's three reservoirs that are sources for drinking water. The mud turned the tap water cloudy and brown. City officials ordered hospitals, daycares, and schools to boil or use bottled water. Residents were forced to do the same. Speaking to a room full of reporters after the city had ordered one of the province's largest tap-water advisories, the city's medical health officer, Patricia Daly, addressed the news conference with a rather technical explanation of what had happened and emphasized her warning to residents.

> I think they should be concerned with the level of turbidity. Having said that, it's their choice. But if they ask my opinion, they shouldn't be drinking water from the taps with turbidity levels this high.[40]

Once the story broke and the boil-water advisory was in place, it was time to think of a follow-up. That's because whenever disaster strikes, such as a bridge collapsing or drinking water becoming contaminated, chances are somebody had already sounded the alarm previously. The quest is to find out who expressed concerns and why those concerns were ignored. Such research is essential to making public officials more accountable. You need to ask, for instance, 'Did the medical health officer know of any previous problems with the city's water quality when she addressed reporters at the news conference?'

Before attempting to zero in on specific documents, it is necessary to conduct the kind of legwork we've stressed in this chapter. Essential in that exercise is trying to think like the experts responsible for water safety. What terms would they use? 'Turbidity' is the technical term for what happens when the water is filled with mud that turns it brown. So that word became important in the keyword search. Also important were the names of the three reservoirs that would be plugged in along with the term 'turbidity'. Next, it was necessary to identify potential players who would have crucial information about water quality. Top on the agenda was finding out if anyone in the city had ever expressed concerns about water quality. So it made sense to use our search terms on the city's website. Since the city's site lacks a search engine with advanced capabilities, it was necessary to use the 'site' operator to convert Google into the search engine for the city's website. Entering the term 'turbidity' produced 135 hits (compared to the 22 hits produced by the city's search engine). The key document happened to be the first one on the list.

The chapter in this city document was crucial because it discussed the problem of turbidity in detail. Waiting about halfway down the page was a nugget: there were concerns already about the city's drinking water and, as a matter of fact, the quality of Vancouver's water quality was below the national standards set by Health Canada.

You can see why using Google's domain and filetype search is an important tool for mining the web for nuggets. 'If you know how to use Google domain search capabilities', explains Sher, 'you can plough through the city hall and get the specific bylaw that even the mayor doesn't know exists. You can get council records. If you know how to do an address search for a whole street, you make sure that you can find everybody who lives on a certain block with sewage problems, or find neighbours of a controversial person. It's standard stuff, and even people who are local can broaden their horizons. You're doing a story on prostitutes who are getting killed. Well, if you know how to use the web, you can find out how other cities are reacting and dealing with it. Medical stories. You're dealing with a hospital, and how it's handling a particular epidemic, you have to know how other ones are dealing with it.'[41]

The same technique can be used to find databases that exist in programs such as Access, Microsoft's popular database manager, which we discuss in Chapters 5 and 6. Database files support the extension 'mdb'. As mentioned previously in this chapter, .mdb is not one of the file formats that Google officially recognizes. (For a full list of extensions, see Table 2.)

However, there is a way to search for databases using the advanced Google domain searches. To specify that you're looking for a database, simply type the extension '.mdb' after the operator 'filetype' (filetype:mdb). Now that you've identified the file, you can use the 'site' operator to locate websites that might contain databases. The complete syntax[42] is:

filetype:mdb 'site:.gov'

Another method that can be used to mine for databases is to use Google's Advanced Search 'with the exact phrase' field and enter terms such as 'downloadable database', 'record layout', 'searchable database', or 'search database'. These are some the common terms that government agencies employ when instructing users to download databases. Even if the databases aren't immediately available, you've just discovered that they *are* available for the asking.

Table 2.2
Extensions for Domain Names

Extension	What it means
.com	commercial site
.org	non-profit site
.gov	governmental site
.mil	US military site
.edu	educational site
.net	Internet service provider
.nato	NATO site
.int	International site

Countries

.ba	Bosnia-Herzegovina
.us	United States
.de	Germany
.nl	Netherlands
.fr	France
.ca	Canada

The domain name is usually something easy to remember, and the extension indicates the type of website. Table 2.2 provides a partial list.

Finding People and Their Backgrounds for Your Stories

Wes Williams of the *New York Times* talks about the order he generally goes through when conducting a background search. One of the first places he goes is the Internet to find 'web Droppings', i.e., traces the person has left in cyberspace. You can find droppings by at first just entering the person's name into a general search engine such as Google. On the plus side, this is a quick, easy, and free technique. On the negative side, you can end up with too many hits for reasons we've already explored.

Next, Williams visits public records, which he categorizes as the 'best and most accurate'. He's talking about records such as court documents.

Next in line are newspaper databases followed by professional, and other directories; and private people-finding databases. About private databases, he says: 'These types of things are the ultimate tools for quick and thorough research. It's like putting your search on steroids or bringing in the big guns. The catch: they're very expensive and can waste your time when you come up with a hundred John Doe listings and don't even have a middle initial. Use them wisely, and sparingly. These are great for locating hard-to-find people, locating relatives, crisscrossing addresses, and turning up non-local leads and assets. If I'm in a hurry, and it's worth the cost, this may be my first step instead of my last.'[43]

Williams suggests that you begin with as much information as possible and ask lots of questions that could lead to different venues for research. 'Who are you searching for and why? Even if you're starting with just a name, it helps to know why you're looking for this person and what the story is about. This will give you other ideas of where to look for information. Is your subject a lawyer? Check the legal directory online. Does his bio say where he went to school? Check the school's alumni web page for profiles. Every nugget of info you have will help, but look especially for approximate age, geography, and occupation.'[44] You may not follow the exact order as Wes Williams. But it is important to ask some of the same questions about the person you're researching. Answers to those questions will determine the kinds of online resources you use. The right strategy will take you to the appropriate resources. There are too many of them to cover in this chapter. Instead, we'll focus on a few of the most popular ones and explain how some journalists have used them.

Newsgroups

'The Internet proved invaluable in finding children who had lived on the Clinton Air Force base in 1959, but then had scattered across the country, married, and sometimes changed names. Chat groups and reunion pages on the web for Canadian "military brats" were a useful resource; *The Fifth Estate* contacted these sites appealing for help, information, and even home videos.'[45] That was Julian Sher's account of how he managed to find people for his award-wining documentary on Steven Truscott. *Steven Truscott: His Word Against History*, told a grim story that chronicled the pursuit to clear a name and attain redemption.

At the tender age of 14, Truscott was sentenced to hang for the 1959 murder of Lynne Harper, who lived on the Clinton airbase. His sentence eventually was commuted to life. After serving 10 years in prison, he was set free and lived for years under an assumed name. In the documentary, Truscott broke a 40-year silence that sparked calls for a new inquiry into the case.

A news or discussion group became a vital tool. In essence, they are public meeting places in cyberspace where like-minded people gather to chat about a range of topics. The main players, such as Google, Yahoo, and MSN, host these groups that, generally speaking, anyone can join. The path to membership is painless. Just follow the easy instructions. To monitor the discussion, bookmark the group the way you would any other site and visit it periodically. The discussion is continuous, so you'll want to check it daily if your deadline is pressing and you need information.

The fact that virtually anyone can join means that these groups become easy ways for journalists to monitor discussions around a certain topic, then post questions looking for people to interview. The downside of newsgroups is that the discussion tends to go off on tangents and become dominated by people who like to hear themselves talk. People don't always use their real names, but do provide contact information. Still, as Julian Sher found out, they are excellent places to find sources—in this case people who lived on the Air Force base in Clinton, Ontario, at the time of the murder Steven Truscott allegedly committed.

One of the largest challenges in investigating a 40-year-old story was finding witnesses. Working on the story full time with a second producer, Sher tracked down 24 witnesses, three former jurors, and 50 people from the area, and a dozen military and police officials.[46] Some of the important interviewees proved to be people who were on the same military base at the time of the teenager's murder, and he found them through a newsgroup called <can.military.brats>. Asks Sher,

> How are you going to find kids who had witnessed a murder . . .
> or who were there in 1959, forty years later when they were all par-
> ents and the women had changed their names, and they've scattered
> across the country and across the world? We used the military brat

newsgroups. And through them we contacted people, and we even got some video from one of them that showed the base at the time [and] that we used in the documentary. We eventually found can.military.brats. It's only for people who had grown up on a military base. So think of journalists who never knew about newsgroups or who never knew how to find newsgroups.[47]

Be very careful when posting questions to newsgroups. You want to give people just enough information about the nature of your research, not the story itself. That's because it's easy to spy on newsgroups using the Advanced Search in Google. So you don't want another reporter stealing your idea.[48]

Listservs

All Wilma Johannesma wanted was a pill to make her feel less anxious, and for a while, Ativan, did the trick. The drug calmed her nerves. Life was easier. She could deal with the broken marriage and other rough spots in her life. But when Johannesma wanted to stop taking Ativan, which is in a family of drugs called benzodiazepines, she couldn't. Johannesma had turned into an 'accidental addict'. Her story became the centrepiece of the CBC's series on the use of prescriptions among the elderly called *Prescribed to Death*.[49]

Her story provided the perfect anecdote for exploring the tendency of doctors to give the elderly too many pills. Originally, Johannesma was supposed to be on the drug for only a few months. Her doctor prescribed the medication for four years, and with each passing year, her addiction grew stronger and stronger. Thanks to the wonders of the Internet, finding Johannesma was fairly easy. All it took was posting a question on Biojest, a listserv comprised of advocates concerned about the state of the health care system in Canada, and the United States.

Unlike discussion groups that are easily accessible and freewheeling, the discussion on listservs is more controlled, and closed to outsiders. A listserv is a discussion group comprised of people who provide their e-mail addresses. The e-mail exchanges are sent to all members of the group, though members have the option of responding to people 'offline' to discuss confidential matters. Just as a discussion group exists for virtually every topic, so is there a listserv that covers an equally vast terrain.

However, the discussion on listservs tends to be more on topic, and serious-minded, given that the listservs are usually comprised of professionals, everyone from health care advocates, to lawyers to journalists. The really useful listservs exchange information for professional reasons. Either you have to be invited to join, or you can subscribe by simply typing the words 'subscribe' in the body of your first e-mail. Once your membership has been confirmed, you will begin receiving regular e-mail from the group. Some groups are more active then others. Biojest, for instance, is a busy place, with several e-mails a day.

The rules for asking for information are the same as in discussion groups. Identify yourself, your news organization, and explain what you're looking for. In the case of drugs and seniors, the CBC made it clear that its investigative team was searching for a man or woman over the age of 65 who was addicted to a benzodiazepine. Victoria-based health care advocate Janet Curry responded quickly, and provided Johannesma's phone number.

Whatever your beat, there are listservs that could be of use. For instance, if you're a local reporter, there are all kinds of people concerned about traffic, garbage, bicycle paths, etc. who can become excellent contacts. Many of them use listservs to vent, exchange information, and keep up to date with latest developments, because members also tend to post articles they think might be of interest to the broader group. Members also use them as a place to learn about upcoming events, or a post mortem on important events. If you feel that the listserv has outlived its usefulness, just send an e-mail message with the phrase 'unsubscribe'. It's a good idea to subscribe to several listservs at once, and monitor them closely.

Given that they are good sources, you should find ways to become a member, either by subscribing to ones that deal with journalism, or asking people to sign up for others that deal with specialized topics such as law and medicine.[50]

Blogs

'Blog' is shorthand for 'weblog', which is an online diary that can be kept by anyone. The diary can be full of personal details of little relevance to many people. The diary can also be replete with useful background information or the names of people who could become sources for future stories. There are two basic ways blogs can be used: either as passive tools that dispense information; or as active tools that blog owners can use to solicit information.

First, the passive tool. Just like a website, listserv, or discussion group, a blog is a place on the Internet that contains information the owner finds relevant. The blog also links to other blogs or websites. These weblogs cover a variety of topics. To get a sense of which ones may interest you, try search engines such as Technorati[51] that will allow you to search for blogs by subject. For instance, many columnists now have blogs that allow them to get into much more detail than they could ever dream of printing. This value-added information can range from personal opinion to views of experts in a particular topic.

However, a word of caution. The popularity of blogs has made them less trustworthy. Says Carleton University journalism professor, Mary McGuire:

> Blogs that did provide information and political points of view were interesting in the beginning, But they are increasingly hard to depend on as reliable because people have learned to use those tools for spin. You've got lots of evidence that campaign operatives are using them without being honest about who they are to spread rumours, and then once the rumours are on the Internet, and get enough attention, then the mainstream media pays attention. And it's a way of planting rumours.[52]

This is why journalists must use blogs with the same caution exercised with the other online tools we've been discussing in this chapter.

The second way journalists can use blogs is as an active tool. A growing number of journalists are maintaining blogs that serve as more than vanity projects. Because an increasing number of people are visiting blogs and sticking around to read the content, these visitors constitute a ready supply of possible sources.

The Canwest's News Service's national affairs correspondent David Akin, who maintains a blog,[53] estimates that he receives about 35,000 visitors a month. He recalls a time when, after reading the website of the *Atlanta Journal-Constitution*, he came across an idea to do a story on pre-teen magazines, and the questionable content they were peddling to girls aged 10 to 12. Akin thought the idea would travel well south of the border. But there was only one problem: how would he find a pre-teen and a parent who would agree to be the subject of his story? 'So at my blog, I put out the call, and asked some people to respond to me. Sure enough, I got quite a few responses, and through that was able to find some sources that were perfectly suitable, had something interesting to say, and away we went and did the story. So there's a case where the Internet was where

I found the inspiration for the story, then my blog became a helpful tool in finding a source.'[54]

The key concept in Akin's explanation is the word 'tool.' Like many of these web resources, once you figure out the strengths and weaknesses, then you can use them to the maximum benefit. Akin continues, 'I think blogs are wonderful, but I'm not on the blog hype. I take a little bit more of a pragmatic approach, saying blogs have not changed journalism . . . .[i]t was the Internet that did it. Blogging is just simply an interactive website. We know the perils and pitfalls of using web sources for journalists. So, as always, take caution and use the telephone at the end of the day.'[55]

Social Network Sites such as 'Facebook'

'My students live on "FaceBook"', says Carleton University's Mary McGuire. 'When they do profiles on any of their sources, they go check them out on "Facebook" and "MySpace". And when you check someone out on "Facebook" or "Myspace", if they've been indiscrete enough to post everything, you can find out what colour they like, their favourite movies, music, . . .their past sexual history. People post their life stories on their "Facebook" pages, and if they've left them open in any way, then other people can find them, and use them.'[56]

'Facebook' and other so-called social networking sites have become so popular that some recruiters on college and university campuses have been using them to spy on potential employees. Such a campaign became the subject of a major exposé in the *New York Times*.

> Many companies that recruit on college campuses have been using search engines like Google and Yahoo to conduct background checks on seniors looking for their first job. But now, college career counsellors and other experts say, some recruiters are looking up applicants on social networking sites like Facebook, MySpace, Xanga and Friendster, where college students often post risqué or teasing photographs and provocative comments about drinking, recreational drug use and sexual exploits in what some mistakenly believe is relative privacy.[57]

Navigating a social network site is trickier than using newsgroups, listservs or blogs. Anyone can set up a page on the network site, but then you have to be invited into a group to participate in a discussion. Says McGuire:

> You can look people up by name and up will come their picture, if they have a Facebook page. If their page is open, depending on how they've set their permissions, you might be able to link on to it. And from there, you can check out their friend's list, and from those lists, you can you can find others.'[58]

This is why the employers have to use the services of young people who already have accounts. That being said, social networks are emerging tools that journalists would be foolish to ignore. They can also be used to find people for profiles. Says Julian Sher,

> I've investigated them because they're prime ways that predators use to find victims. If you were trying to find everyone from fans of a certain rock group to those that are using a certain kind of drug or are troubled by a social phenomenon, it's a natural. It's the modern version

of those newsgroups that we used to use. They are harder to navigate, but they're not impossible, and search tools will be developed more and more.[59]

Effective searching is impossible without setting up an account. And it is for this reason the learning curve for social networking sites is a little steeper than it is for listservs or discussion groups. Although people in various age groups now have 'Facebook' pages, it is predominantly young journalists like former Carleton student Natalie Johnson who have become experts in using "Facebook". Johnson used a column in the Canadian Association of Journalists' *Media* magazine to explain how she uses the tool to find background information and people.

> Unlike in newsgroups, where the journalist is often forced to make a general post regarding his or her call for sources, with Facebook he or she can pinpoint the specific individual believed to be the most relevant or helpful and send that source a personal, for-their-eyes-only message. I was able to find a student who had written to the *Ottawa Citizen*, complaining about a story that had referred to Carleton University as "Last Chance U."[60]

After setting up their accounts, Johnson advises users to use the 'groups' section to search for individuals who can be sources or characters for stories. Groups are important because an increasing number of people are creating groups to talk about a range of topics including the sexual assault that they endured and some of the ways they, as a group, can help each other deal with the devastation. But there are limits to these kinds of searches that are important to take into account.

> Where you as a reporter will find sources are in groups that are considered open; these are the only groups in which you can see the wall, discussion board, and posted items. You can, of course, request permission to become a member of a closed group, but you're taking a gamble, especially if you're facing a deadline; the group's description might not reveal enough about it to actually let you know whether helpful sources lurk within it. Secret groups won't be of any help to you because they won't appear in search results.[61]

As is the case with listservs and discussion groups, Johnson cautions journalists to be up-front about their own identities, and be aware that sending a message will also reveal some of the personal details (such as interests, age, beats) that may appear in their profiles.

'WHOIS'

The message went out at 5:25 p.m. on 25 November 2006, the same day the new Harper government announced over a billion dollars in cuts to federal programs the party had long criticized while sitting as Canada's Official Opposition to the governing Liberals of Jean Chrétien and Paul Martin. Many groups were quick to respond, including the Institute for Canadian Values. It fired off a news release 'applauding today's announcement by the federal government that it will be terminating the Court Challenges Program and cutting funding to the Status of Women.' The contact person on the news release was Joseph Ben-Ami, the group's executive director. 'Let groups funded through Ministries like Status of Women do what the rest of us do,' said Ben-Ami. 'Let them raise funds among the people who they claim to speak for, and those who support their efforts.'[62] Who was the Institute for Canadian Values?

Type the group's name into a search engine and a website turns up that looks pretty standard. There were contact numbers, and many of the articles posted on other pages were from columnists considered to be right-wing. But who is behind the page? Well, that's where a 'WHOIS' search comes into play.

Every website has to be registered, and basic details are stored in so-called 'whois' databases. Of course, someone could simply be acting as a front for a group—but at least you have a real name and usually a phone number or address.

'Geek Tools' is one of the easiest tools to use, but there are many others such as 'BetterWhoIs'. For Canadian sites—that is, sites registered with a '.ca' domain—you are best to use the Canadian Internet Registration Authority at www.cira.ca.[63] The search box is at the top left. Simply put in any address—but be sure *not* to put in the 'www' at the front. Out pops an easy-to-read results page. The Institute for Canadian Values is registered to Charles McVety. Charles McVety is a member of a controversial Christian movement. He had run-ins with the Conservative Party before the federal election in 2006. Charles McVety's name is nowhere to be found on the news release, nor is it featured prominently on the website. So, if you were doing a story on the Institute, a 'WHOIS' search would provide valuable background information on the people behind the group and that may become an important part of your follow-up story on cuts to the Court Challenges Program.

Similar searches can be conducted on websites in other countries with tools such as the 'Whois' database at www.allwhois.com. They monitor all the domains, although the results can sometimes be difficult to decipher.

Public Records

The emergence of the Internet has been a boon for journalists with a 'document state of mind', i.e., the mindset that forces you to follow paper trails that inevitably lead to breaking stories—such as the sponsorship scandal that sank Paul Martin's Liberal government in 2006, or the revelations that led to the 2006 resignation of RCMP commissioner Giuliano Zaccardelli. He was forced to step down in the aftermath of the inquiry that led to the exoneration of Maher Arar, the Canadian who was assumed to be a terrorist and who the United States deported to Syria, where he endured a year of torture.

While the Internet hasn't triggered a revolution of government transparency in Canada and the United States, there has been a steady increase in the kinds of information that are now becoming publicly available, including audits, financial disclosure, salaries, and business dealings. Once you've done the legwork to determine what documents may contain valuable information about your subject, search for them online using the techniques we've discussed in this chapter.

Levels of disclosure vary; you might have better luck in some provinces than in others. For instance, Quebec publishes many of its court documents online, whereas in other provinces you have to take a trip down to the courthouse. BC Online allows reporters to gain access to records such as land titles, property assessments, and corporate information. If you need information in a hurry, the cost associated with the search may be worth it, considering the cab fare for a return trip to the court house and the extra time travel takes.

So when 'back-grounding' an individual, it's best to use your document state of mind to think in terms of where public records can be found online. Phone directories such as Canada 411 are obvious for phone number searches, though they can be a hit-and-miss proposition. Here are some strategic questions to keep in mind when sleuthing for background information.

Where does the person work? If the person works for a company or government department, then it is fairly easy to access the employer's home page and staff directory. For instance, federal government employees can be found in a directory called the 'Government Electronic Directory Services'.[64] GEDS's advanced search engine allows queries by surname, given name, phone number, and job title. It's also a good way to find out who else works in the person's office. If, for instance, you were doing a story on Serge Nadeau, the Director General of analysis in the tax policy branch at the Finance Department, and his breach-of-trust charges in the income trust scandal that rocked former Liberal finance minister, Ralph Goodale, in December 2006, the GEDS directory would come in handy.[65] You'd be able to identify people in his branch who may want to speak on or off the record about Nadeau.

Is the person a member of a professional association, and if so, has she ever been disciplined? Professionals such as lawyers and doctors have provincial regulatory bodies that also discipline their members. For instance, the colleges of physicians and surgeons post their disciplinary decisions online. In BC, details about disciplinary actions date back to 1998. The decisions are only summaries, but provide enough details to help move your investigation forward; and in Ontario, the cases heard by the College's discipline committee date back to 1993, where you can have access to the summary or detailed account. Be forewarned, though, Ontario's level of disclosure is rare. The college was forced into being more open after the *Toronto Star* ran a series in 2001 called 'Medical Secrets', which we discuss in greater detail in Chapter 6.[66]

The level of disclosure surrounding municipally licensed businesses or trades people is much better. Formal charges under municipal bylaws are a matter of public record, along with the resulting court decisions. If you're investigating taxi drivers, driving school owners, owners of adult entertainment parlours, or owners of automobile body repair shops, and so on, then there is much that can be found online.

Has the person ever worked as a lobbyist, or donated money to a political party? Whenever we do stories that measure influence in federal, provincial, or municipal politics, it's always helpful to know about the political involvement of the person you're investigating. If she donates to a federal party, the date the donation was made, the amount, and the candidate who received the money is recorded on Elections Canada's database.[67] Similarly, in provinces such as Quebec, Ontario, and British Columbia you can also track the same information.[68]

Has the person ever appeared before a government committee? Much of the grunt work that escapes the attention of journalists is conducted in committees. They could be committees comprised of city politicians who meet regularly to discuss such seemingly mundane topics such as street and bridge safety. Or it could be an advisory committee comprised of government bureaucrats and representatives from the pharmaceutical industry that meet regularly to discuss issues such as drug safety and regulations. Or it could be provincial or federal politicians who sit on various committees that study proposed legislation, and grill bureaucrats and cabinet ministers. Though most of these meetings are public, they seldom make news, in large part because they may not be tracking the hot issues of the day.[69] Fortunately, the minutes of these committee meetings are dutifully recorded in Hansard, the official transcript of the proceedings of Parliament.

Hansard transcripts are easy to find. Simply visit the government's home page, and type the term 'Hansard' into the search engine. Once you're at the appropriate page, you'll have an option of using an Advanced Search feature to conduct keyword searches. You'll also be able to narrow your searches by date, subject, name, and Boolean operators such as 'AND' and 'OR'.

Let's take the example of Serge Nadeau; the bureaucrat in the federal finance department was charged with breach of trust in the income trust scandal. There were a series of profiles that featured comments from shocked former colleagues. But a simple Hansard search would have unearthed his testimony on 30 May 2006, before the Standing Committee on Finance where he was grilled on the goods and services tax. From his detailed answers, it was clear that he was an authority who knew his files.[70] Though the testimony didn't reveal anything related to his charges, it would have helped to paint a more complete portrait of a man considered by many to be a straight-shooter and workaholic whose expertise was unquestioned and who was an ambassador for the department.

Is the person a volunteer in the community? Does she coach soccer, belong to the local Kiwanis club? Is she on a parent-teacher advisory committee? It's no secret that people spend much of their time volunteering, whether in their community or on the board of a local arts group. Many of these groups post information about their events online.

Does the person work for a public company? Unlike private companies, public companies must reveal a lot of information about themselves: how much money they make. If they're being sued. The salaries of their top executives. When the salary of a top executive is revealed, it's not necessarily because the reporter had inside knowledge. Rather, it's because that information is disclosed in what's called a proxy circular, a document that is circulated before the company's annual meeting. In the circular, you'll find concerns of investors that may have received little or no public attention, the salaries of the top executives, and a listing of the board of directors. You can locate these documents by visiting a website called 'SEDAR', an acronym for the System for Electronic Document Analysis and Retrieval.[71] As its name suggests, 'SEDAR' is a database that contains many—although not all—of the documents that public companies are required to file to regulators such as the Ontario Securities Commission. Similar information for companies filing documents with the US Securities and Exchange Commission can be found in 'EDGAR', a similar system on its website.

Organizing Your Information

Once you've conducted all your searches and have the information you need, how do you organize it and ensure that the information keeps coming? Good journalists are also masters of organization, meaning that they catalogue the information in a way that makes it easy to find. Though the methods may vary, there are some basic tools that are worth a brief mention.

Google Desktop

You may have your own indexing system for your articles and transcripts, but it may not be foolproof. There's nothing more frustrating than being unable to find a key document when you need to check quickly a fact for a story. This is where the Google Desktop feature comes into play. It is exactly what the name suggests, a search engine that sits on your desktop and allows you to use keyword searches to find that important document on your hard drive that has eluded your grasp. The instructions for setting up the desktop are fairly straightforward. 'I can track every e-mail I've written,' says Julian Sher, who also uses it to find legal documents he may need when vetting his work with lawyers. 'I survive on Google desktop all the time.'[72]

Setting Up Alerts (Google News, websites, RSS feeds, FreeEdgar Watch List, Alerts)

An alert does what the name suggests: it alerts you to breaking stories that may have escaped your attention. It's a useful tool for journalists to obtain a range of material on the Internet. These alerts have become so popular that many news organizations are now offering them. However, that offer increasingly is coming with a price tag. This may not be a problem for journalists working for established news organizations. However, for journalism students, freelancers, and staffers working at smaller media outlets, the price tag may be too steep. The good news is that the lack of ability to subscribe to certain alert services or pay for searches such as Lexis/Nexis need not be an obstacle. Search engines such as Google offer these services free. Just go to the Google News section, scroll down to the alert section on the left-hand side, and you're in business.

The advantage of an alert system is that it puts in your mailbox only news that addresses the subject areas that you've specified. Many websites also offer their own alert services, which e-mail messages every time the page is updated. This is particularly handy for beat reporters who may be monitoring a set number of websites for breaking news.

Back in 2005, Real Simple Syndication feeds were being touted as one of the newest and most useful trends on the Internet. Now many media outlets are using the RSS feeds to push their headlines into cyberspace. To find out if the organization you're monitoring offers the service, look for a distinctive small, orange box with the letters XML. 'RSS is essentially a list of headlines encoded in such a way that it can be used by another program or website. XML is the coding language—just like HTML is the language used to write web pages—that allows any media organization, or anybody else for that matter, to push or deliver a stream of news and information to anyone who wants it. Think of it as your own private wire service—only you get to choose the sources and topics.'[73]

You can read the news feed with either downloaded software or on a web page. All the programs are basically the same. An icon sits on your desktop taskbar; click on it, a box opens up. On the left is the list of news feeds they have already programmed in. You can delete some and add others. Some of the programs can be configured to run inside your e-mail service, such as Outlook.[74]

Creating Word Documents

We've all done it: thrown away all those news releases that we think will never come in handy, until the day when we need some information about an individual or company that's attracting attention. For instance, when the CBC's Investigative Unit was conducting research into workplace safety, it received news releases through an alert system that provided details about penalties such as fines and charges that the Ontario government had levelled against companies in breach of the province's workplace safety laws. Instead of throwing them away, members of the unit created a document in Microsoft Word, then copied and pasted the contents of each news release into the document. Within a year, the document became a searchable database for companies and individuals who had run afoul of the law.

The same technique can also be used with news releases that exist on government or company websites, or any other kinds of information, such as minutes of committee meetings.

Creating Blogs and Web Sites

We know what you're thinking: "Have you lost your mind? Me? Create a blog or website? These are legitimate questions. But the idea of creating a blog or a website isn't as far-fetched as it seems. The mechanics of setting them up are fairly straightforward these days. Several online services, including Google's Blogger, allow you to set up a blog with almost no specialized knowledge.

And many Internet service providers allow extra space for setting up personal websites. This may be a good option for freelancers. If you want more space than providers are able to set aside, you may have to buy space from another commercial provider. Journalists who work for medium and large media outlets may be able to grab some space from their employer, though it might be smarter to have an independent provider in order to maintain some independence from an employer who might feel compelled to control some of your content.

As we learned earlier in this chapter, blogs can be used for finding people for your stories. But it can also be a place to store your working notes. This is exactly how the Canwest's David Akin uses his blog. When he was doing calculations with the federal government's spending estimates, he crunched some numbers and figured out which cultural programs would be the best off over the course of the next few years. There was no news hook. No outstanding revelations. So, no reason to do a story. Instead, he wrote up his analysis and placed it on his blog for everyone to see.[75]

The downside is that someone may steal the idea, but they would have to do the similar legwork and conduct interviews to flesh out the story—an unlikely event. Instead, Akin is now able to use his working notes on cultural spending for future stories. He also does the same on a host of other issues. Even when he's on the road, covering a political event, he'll use his Blackberry to upload notes to his blog. The same thing can be done with websites.

'Wikis'

The details of the lobbying scandal were breathtaking. Washington lobbyist Jack Abramoff's lobbying fees to Indian tribes exceeded 45-million dollars. Even other well-heeled lobbyists were left slack-jawed. Three reporters from the *Washington Post* dug into the extent of Abramoff's influence on Capitol Hill. The stories exposed congressional corruption, proposed ways to reform the system, and won the 2006 Pulitzer Prize for investigative reporting.

'This was an octopus story', recalls Derek Willis, the former database editor at *Washingtonpost.com,* who is now at the *New York Times*. 'And every time we would write a story, other leads would come up, and eventually, the reporters got tired of passing notes around, and holding meetings to figure out what people were working on. The investigative reporter on it, Jim Grimaldi, came to me, and asked "Can you help?" and the first thing I thought of was a Wiki.'[76]

Whether you're part of a large investigative unit, working a regular beat, or helping out on a breaking story, Wikis can make the job of updating and sharing information a lot easier, more efficient.

'Wiki' software allows you to set up a website with the added bonus of allowing users to upload and edit content on the fly. The Wiki usually functions within a news organization such as the *Washington Post* or the *St. Paul Pioneer Press* as an intra-Net site. The web pages the software creates are simple and devoid of photos or graphics. Think of the pages as Word documents that can be accessed through a web browser. All of the software products have search capabilities. This means that you can use the kind of keyword searches we've discussed in this chapter to find information. You can also hyperlink to documents in a variety of formats, including pdfs and spreadsheets.

The Wiki, and the database that stores all the text, sits on a separate computer, anything possessing a hard drive of 60 gigabytes and up should be adequate. Access to the site can be controlled through the use of passwords—reporters need not worry about unwelcome visitors. Wikis also log every change and identify the authors of those changes. You can also rollback or reverse any additions that may have been inaccurate.

In the Abromoff investigation, the team used the Wiki to upload notes about the lobbyist, and other key players in the story. Willis says that the reporters were able to use the Wiki as a reference, ensuring that everyone was working with the same information.

'All three reporters were really using it pretty heavily to the point where it became part of their natural behaviour. They would e-mail me and ask, 'Hey, is that is that on the Wiki, or can you get that on the Wiki?' That was probably a textbook example.'[77]

You can visit websites such as www.wikimatrix.org/, which offer lots of tips, and if that's not good enough, then post a question on the listservs of the IRE (Investigative Reporters and Editors) or NICAR (the National Institute for Computer Assisted Reporting), and chances are experienced users such as Willis and Webster can offer some assistance.[78]

'When people come to see how it can be used, how it can make you more efficient, more productive, and avoid you losing stuff, then I think it's a natural thing,' says Willis.[79]

Bringing It All Together

The challenge with writing anything concerning the Internet is that it changes so quickly. Many books that were written in the 90s when the Internet came into its own are now hopelessly out-of-date. This is why we chose to focus on research techniques and strategies, rather than on specific websites, and what they have to offer. Effective research techniques and sound knowledge of search engines will produce better results.

Internet research is the first phase of CAR that we perform everyday. Yet, like the telephone or any other tool, we must not take it for granted. The challenge will be maintaining our knowledge of the well-known search-engines and websites, while keeping track of innovations and adapting them to our use.

Now that you're more comfortable with the Internet, let's turn our attention to some of the more sophisticated ways we can harness information, not only from the Internet, but data that government departments would prefer we ignore. It's time to learn about spreadsheets.

Introduction to Spreadsheets

David McKie

Chapter 3

What We'll Cover

- Fundamentals of spreadsheets and Microsoft Excel.
- Formatting your data.
- Importing and exporting data.
- Simple sorting and filtering.

Introduction

It was the first time anyone had ever conducted an audit of the city of Ottawa's payroll system, and the results were disturbing. The city's general auditor, Alain Lalonde, concluded that there were too many employees working overtime. In 2004, he found that the city paid out $13.7 million more than it budgeted. The figure was the same for the subsequent year.

He came to the conclusion after looking at 39 claims by employees chosen randomly that 'Overall, we found management were not using the corporate financial system's full functionality to plan, monitor, and manage overtime,' he concluded in his report.[1]

While the findings of the auditor led the local coverage, the seeds of that story were buried in a so-called 'sunshine' list that the province of Ontario posts online every year. The list contains the salaries of public sector workers such as municipal employees, health care workers, or nurses who earn more than 100-thousand dollars a year. Most municipal workers such as firemen or nurses don't earn salaries that high. If they do make the list, it's for one reason: they've been working overtime. Instead of conducting a random audit of employees, an astute journalist with knowledge of the sunshine list, could have downloaded data from municipalities across the province, filtered the information, reached a similar conclusion, and broken a good story.

The same method of downloading the salary data and performing simple calculations could have been used to obtain information about Tom Parkinson, the former president of Hydro One, Ontario's transmission utility. Parkinson raised more than a few eyebrows when it was revealed that he was the province's highest paid public servant, pulling in an annual $1.6-million paycheque. The fuss about his salary occurred at a time when a panel appointed by the provincial government was investigating the executive salaries of Ontario's electricity agencies.

'I think Ontarians understand the complexity of a multibillion-dollar system and I think they wanted us to take action first on executive compensation, and then subsequently on the issue of efficiency within the system', Ontario Energy Minister Dwight Duncan was quoted as saying at the time.[2]

Parkinson's high salary may have been a surprise to many, but not to journalists and students who make it a regular practice of downloading the salary data into Excel and looking for stories. Anyone familiar with the information would know that Parkinson's salary skyrocketed during the course of a few years, just as the salaries of other top executives in many government departments and Crown corporations did. There was no need to wait until the controversy exploded to begin asking questions about executive compensation within the Ontario public service. The data had always been there for the taking.

Such is the advantage of using a spreadsheet to analyze data sitting on government websites at the federal, provincial, and municipal levels. To do this initial work, there is no math involved, no complicated calculations or deep knowledge of everything that a spreadsheet has to offer. To get started, all you need is to be able to cut and paste information or save and export files. With these few steps, you can routinely stay ahead of the pack by adding context to your stories and breaking new ground.

Because of its ease and versatility, the spreadsheet is the basic tool for journalists who have graduated to the next level of computer-assisted reporting. Journalists can use these programs to accomplish a range of tasks from the relatively easy ones such as sorting and filtering, to intermediate tasks such as doing mathematical calculations to advanced statistical analysis.

'The spreadsheet is the basic building block of computer-assisted journalism,' writes Rich Gordon in his tipsheet for the Missouri-based Investigative Reporters and Editors regional conference. 'You can start with database software if you like, but you will be readier to use it if you master a spreadsheet first.'[3]

Although there are many products on the market, Microsoft Excel is the most popular. Much of the appeal of Excel is due to the fact that it's so versatile. Excel's forte, of course, is performing numerical calculations, but Excel is also very useful for non-numerical applications such as creating charts, organizing lists, accessing other data, creating graphics and diagrams, and automating complex tasks. For this reason we'll be using Excel as our model, and more specifically, Excel 2007. Excel 2007 is bigger and, some would argue, better than earlier versions. It contains larger worksheets: 1,048,576 rows and 16,384 columns.[4]

The goal of this chapter is to get you up and running in Excel. We'll begin with a general discussion of a spreadsheet, and how this computer-assisted reporting tool is being adapted by journalists. From there, we'll learn how to enter data into Excel, download data from websites, analyze the data using simple methods such as sorting. Then, before moving on to the slightly more advanced chapter on Excel, we'll end with a discussion about ideas that you can adopt after learning these techniques. Throughout, we will refer to a number of stories, particularly two series on workplace safety done by CBC Radio's investigative unit, and Glen Macgregor's investigation of gun ownership, published in the *Ottawa Citizen*. You can download some of this data from <www.oupcanada.com/CAR.html>. More downloadable datasets are available at <www.carincanada.ca>.

What Is a Spreadsheet?

The following illustration shows you a blank spreadsheet.

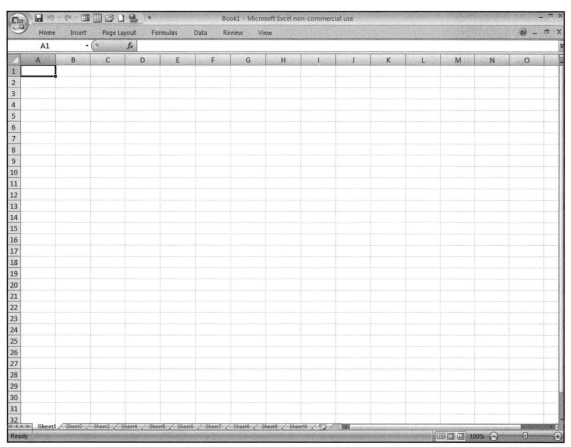

Fig. 3.1

Spreadsheets see the world as grids, with numbered rows along the left side, and columns labelled with letters across the top or bottom. The places where the columns and rows intersect are called cells. A1—the rectangle on the top left corner of the table that is highlighted—is an intersection of column A and row 1. When you want to refer to a cell, you do so by using the cell reference—A1.

Every worksheet consists of rows, which, in Excel 2007, are numbered 1 through 1,048,576, and columns, which are labeled A through XFD. Once you work through the alphabet and reach column Z, then the next column becomes AA, followed by AB, AC, and AD. Column AZ is then followed by BA, BB. The pattern continues with the next round after ZZ being AAA, AAB, and AAC. You won't necessarily be dealing with data-sets that large, but it helps to understand the pattern Excel uses to keep labelling cells.

You can navigate through the cells either by using the arrows on your keyboard to go in any direction; pressing the Enter key to move down, and Tab to move from left to right; or by pointing your mouse on the cell you desire and clicking. You can also use the scroll bars on the right side and the bottom of the screen, and the wheel on your mouse to scroll vertically. If you press the 'Ctrl' key while manipulating the wheel, you'll be able to zoom in, making the worksheet larger and easier to see. You can also use the zoom control on the right side of the status bar.

Office 2007 has a new interface that sets it apart from the earlier versions, which use traditional menus and toolbars. Ribbons, something of a combination of both menus

> ⚠ **TECH TIP**
>
> We know some readers have earlier versions of Excel. The features are sometimes in different places on the screen in older versions, and we'll point them out when that's the case.

and toolbars, are arranged into groups of similar commands and accessed by clicking on tabs.

You can also access features using the keyboard, just as in earlier versions of Excel. If you press the Alt key the accompanying keyboard letters will appear directly below each tab. Hold the Control key down and click the appropriate letter to use the command. To give yourself more space to see about five more rows, just double-click on one of the tabs and the ribbon will be hidden from view.

There is also a quick-access toolbar. By default it contains three tools: save, undo, and redo. You can add other tools that you frequently use by right-clicking on the downward arrow for an additional set of commands such as e-mail or spelling. For even more commands, click on the 'More Commands' option, which allows you to upload more options to the window on the right-hand side. You can click the 'Add' button to put more options on your 'Quick Access Toolbar'.

Excel can undo up to 100 steps going backward. But a word of warning, anything accomplished using the big, round 'Office' button—such as saving or deleting a file—can't be undone.

> ⚠ **TECH TIP**
>
> In older versions of Excel, icons for basic functions such as opening and saving files, cutting, copying, pasting, undoing, redoing, and printing are located on the standard toolbar. If it is not visible, click 'Toolbars', then 'Standard' under the 'View' menu.

You can also find many of these features by right-clicking a cell. The mini-tool bar allows you to see a pull-down menu that contains many of the frequently-used tools from the home tab.

How Can the Spreadsheet Be Adapted by Journalists?

Excel's biggest claim to fame is performing numerical calculations, which come in handy for journalists doing stories on such subjects as government budgets.

Usually, budgets are handed out to journalists as paper documents. Government officials perform the calculations, the most significant of which can end up as headlines: 'Mayor takes credit for freezing property taxes'; 'Police service gets a three per cent increase.' What those headlines fail to reveal is whether the mayor cut services in order to freeze taxes or whether money was taken from another program area to give the police an increase. Or more generally, has the city achieved its tax freeze, and given more money to the police by increasing user fees for services such as water and paramedic services? If this is this the case, then the real story is the fact that the city, while boasting about its budget-making prowess, actually is taking more money—not less—out of the pockets of its some of its residents.

These realities may not be evident to the journalists pouring through the stacks of budget paper documents with an eye on the upcoming deadline. But what if the budget came in a spreadsheet, with all the spending summaries arranged in easily identifiable rows and columns? And what if you were able to obtain the budgets for the past several years, allowing you to track increases over a significant duration of time? Well, this is not just a hypothetical question. It is possible. That would give you new power to make sense of the information.

The following illustration shows the summary expenses for the city of Ottawa's budget for the years 2005 and 2006 in the department of Community & Protective Services. The rows represent specific services residents receive from such providers as paramedics and bylaw officers. The 'Net Exp' in column B represents the amount of money the city earmarked to be spent on the program. The 'Revenue' in column C represents the money the service was able to generate in the form of a user fee. The 'Net' in column C is the actual amount that was spent on the service once the revenue was subtracted from the money earmarked at the beginning of the city's fiscal year. The revenue figure is in brackets because Excel reads it as a negative number that is subtracted from the Net expenditure.

If we look at 'Parks & Recreation' highlighted below, the city earmarked $119,169.00. But because it generated about $94,000 in revenue, the cost to the city was only a little over $25,000. If we calculate the percentage increase of the user fee (we'll learn more about calculations in Chapter 4) from 2005 to 2006, it works out to 12 per cent, as you can see in column L, row 42. In keeping with the headlines we have identified, the city may have been able to keep tax increases to a minimum (as it did that year), but it achieved the results on the backs of people forced to pay more in user fees.

		2005 Budget				2006 Budget					
	A	B	C	D	E	F	G	H	I	J	K	L
1	2006 Operating Budget Corporate Summary											
2												
3		**2005 Budget**					**2006 Budget**					
4												
5		*Net Exp	Revenue	Net	FTE's		*Net Exp	Revenue	Net	FTE's	Gross	
33	Committee of Adjustment	896	(896)	-	10.00		922	(922)	-	10.00	26	
34												
35	Community & Protective Services											
36	- Deputy City Manager	2,317	-	2,317	23.00		2,565	-	2,565	22.00	248	
37	- Paramedic Service	43,792	(17,635)	26,157	420.00		49,880	(18,284)	31,596	439.00	6,088	
38	- By-law Services	12,114	(17,386)	(5,272)	146.40		13,308	(17,684)	(4,376)	146.40	1,194	
39	- Emergency Measures Unit	1,742	(97)	1,645	5.33		1,763	(97)	1,666	5.33	21	
40	- Fire Services	99,059	(509)	98,550	988.76		104,365	(544)	103,821	990.00	5,306	
41	- Housing	117,686	(50,132)	67,554	68.40		116,396	(45,422)	70,974	65.40	(1,290)	
42	- Parks & Recreation	119,169	(93,950)	25,219	916.60		131,084	(105,036)	26,048	936.30	11,915	12%
43	- Public Health	36,899	(24,284)	12,615	438.00		39,430	(28,672)	10,758	448.00	2,531	
44	- Employment & Financial Assistance	257,587	(153,044)	104,543	604.00		262,761	(155,159)	107,602	602.00	5,174	
45	- Cultural Services & Community Funding	30,723	(2,673)	28,050	87.70		32,925	(3,015)	29,910	104.70	2,202	
46	- Long Term Care	39,800	(33,867)	5,933	567.20		41,469	(35,676)	5,793	559.35	1,669	
47	Total	760,888	(393,577)	367,311	4,265.39		795,946	(409,589)	386,357	4,318.48	35,058	

Fig. 3.2

Entering Data into the Spreadsheet

You can enter numerical values and text just by clicking on the cell and typing. The number or character will be displayed not only in the cell but also in the formula bar just below the ribbon. To move to the next cell in the row, you can hit the tab key or the arrow. To move down, hit the 'Enter' key or the 'Downward Arrow' key.

Cells in Excel 2007 can handle lots of text—32,000 characters, to be exact. If there is a lot of text in the cell, you may not be able to see all of it in the formula bar. To give yourself a more complete view, click at the bottom of the formula bar and drag it down to increase the height.

If you enter text that exceeds the cell's width, one of two things can happen. First, if the next cell is blank, Excel allows the text to spill into that adjacent cell, seeming to overwrite it. If the adjacent cell contains information, Excel will display as much text within the confined space as possible, meaning that the only way to read it is to refer to the formula bar. You can always improve your view by making the font smaller, but a better option is to 'wrap' the text within the cell. To do this go to the 'Home' ribbon and click on the 'wrap text' icon in the upper right of the 'Alignment' area of the ribbon. Choose 'Format Cells'. This will bring up the 'Format Cells' dialogue box. Under the 'Alignment' tab, check the 'wrap text' option.

You can perform a similar function by placing your cursor on cell C5 and right-clicking. The same box will appear. Once you have selected the 'Wrap Text' option, you can manually adjust the size of the cell, by placing the cursor on the border between rows 5 and 6. Upon doing so, the cursor will turn into a cross, at which time you go back to the spreadsheet and adjust the size of the cell—either by double-clicking or by dragging the cross while holding down the mouse with your index finger—until all the text appears as one block in the cell. You can see the result here.

DATE of issue (mm/dd/yr)	Number	Order	Number of Orders	Section(s) Quoted
		Inspection Reports for Weyerhaeuser (location 30) from 2000 to 2006 (includes most pertinent orders)		
3/7/2000	2000110210047	**Order 1:**A worker who works on machinery or equipment requiring lockout failed to take responsibility for locking out **Order 2:** A worker failed to take responsibility for maintaining immediate control of the key(s) to personal locks. **Order 3:** (preventative order) A worker must be notified at the start of his or her next shift if the worker's personal lock(s) have been removed since the worker's previous shift.	3	OHS 10.7(a), OHS 10.7(c), OHS 10.8(3)
3/8/2000	2000030370044	dures are to be based on the hazard assessment. Specif	5	OHS 9.10, 9.5
5/3/2000	2000110210121	astal Planer operator, sharpening cutting head). This is a follow up to inspection 2000110210047 Order#3. Every wo		
9/6/2000	2000030370132	or developing written procedures (as required by Section 9.10)	6	OHS 9.10, OHS 9.5

Fig. 3.3

If you want to edit the contents of the cell with all that text, or any other material, there are two simple ways among many: double-clicking the mouse places the cursor inside the field, which then allows you to edit just as you would in a Word document. The insertion point becomes a vertical bar that can be moved about using the arrow keys. Use the 'Ctrl' and 'Home' keys at the same time to move the insertion point to

⚠ TECH TIP

When a range of cells is selected, pressing the 'Enter' key automatically moves the cursor to the next cell in the range. If you want to enter the same data into a number of cells, you don't have to keep retyping the same information. Type the entry into the cell at the beginning of the range. Next, copy the cell by using the keystrokes Ctrl+C. Now, place your mouse pointer in the centre of the cell, hold the left mouse button down, and drag in any direction until you have highlighted the desired range. Finally, copy the entry with the keystrokes Ctrl+V. The entry will be copied to all the cells.

the beginning of the text in the cell, and the 'Ctrl' and 'End' keys to move the insertion point to the end of the text; or you can click on the formula bar which also contains the contents.

⚠ TECH TIP

If you want a column of consecutive numbers, type the first number, e.g., '1', into a cell. The cell now is active. Move the mouse pointer to the bottom right corner of the cell until it becomes a small cross. Drag through to the end of your range of consecutive numbers. Before you let go of the left mouse button simultaneously right-click on your mouse, which will make a small icon appear. Click on the icon and select the 'Fill Series' option on the menu that appears. Sequential numbers will fill in automatically.

Excel's AutoComplete function facilitates your data entry, which comes in handy if you want to enter the same data into a number of cells. This is how AutoComplete works. Say you type in the word 'Government' into cell A1. Excel stores the word in memory. Once you begin typing the first few letters of the same word in cell A2, Excel draws upon its memory bank to complete the word. If you want to keep the same word, all you have to do is press Enter to move to A3. Not only does the AutoComplete feature reduce the typing, but it reduces mistakes. If, in subsequent cells, your word is a slight variation on 'Government,' you can just ignore Excel's AutoComplete and keep typing.

Just remember that the AutoComplete works only within a range of cells that are attached. If, for instance, you leave A3 blank, and then want to continue typing in A4, the memory bank is wiped clean, meaning the AutoComplete function only identifies the contents below that A4 cell. If you don't like this feature, just go to the Excel 'Options' dialogue box by clicking on the 'Office' button and deactivate it by clicking the check box entitled 'Enable AutoComplete for cell values'.

⚠ TECH TIP

In addition to features such as AutoComplete, there are other ways to speed up your data entry. You can use the AutoCorrect feature to create shortcuts to commonly used words that may be too long to be typed repeatedly. For instance, if you didn't want to type the rather long name of the Canadian Broadcasting Corporation, you can use the feature to create an AutoCorrect entry for the abbreviation CBC. This means every time you type CBC, the feature replaces that abbreviation with the full word. Excel has many built-in Auto-Correct terms to deal with common misspellings, but you can add your own by going to the 'Options' dialogue box, clicking on the 'Proofing' tab, and then the 'AutoCorrect' 'Options' tab, as you can see in the image below. Once you've got this far, make sure that you're in the AutoCorrect section where about three-quarters down you'll see features that allow you to 'replace' your abbreviation (CBC) 'With' the actual phrase: Canadian Broadcasting Corporation. Once you've finished typing everything in, click on 'Okay'. Now your abbreviation will become one of the AutoCorrect terms.

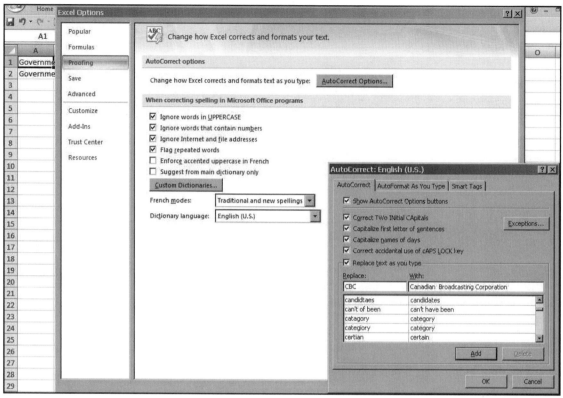

Fig. 3.4

To customize some of your options, such as the number of decimal places you want, and the capability of editing inside the cells, follow the same procedure. Once you get to the Excel 'Options' box, click on the options tab on the bottom, left-hand side. If you're stuck, go to the spreadsheet's 'Help' function, and type in the word 'Option'.

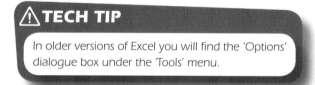

⚠ TECH TIP

In older versions of Excel you will find the 'Options' dialogue box under the 'Tools' menu.

Formatting Numbers

There is no need to format text because Excel recognizes it as such. But numbers are a different story. Numbers can be currency, percentages, dates or times. Once the information is entered, you have to tell Excel how you want that number to be expressed or formatted. Formatting doesn't affect the value of the number, just the appearance. To format your cell, go to the 'Home' tab on the ribbon, go to the 'Cell' box on the far right side, click on the arrow next to 'Format', and proceed to the last option in the drop-down menu: 'Format Cells'.

Make sure you're in the 'Number' tab, which gives you a series of options located in the left side of the box. Say you want to express '0.125' in A2 as a percentage. You would choose the 'Percentage' option from the list, and then exercise the option to give it decimal places, in this case, two. Click 'OK', and the cell will be reformatted to express the per cent as 12.50%.

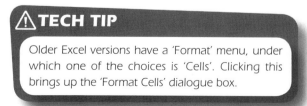

⚠ TECH TIP

Older Excel versions have a 'Format' menu, under which one of the choices is 'Cells'. Clicking this brings up the 'Format Cells' dialogue box.

Of course, you can use a shortcut to accomplish the same task. You could have simply clicked on A1, and chosen the 'Format Cells' option from the shortcut menu, then followed the same process. There are many number format categories, which you can see in Table 3.1.

Table 3.1
Number-Format Categories

General The default format: it displays numbers as integers, as decimals, or in scientific notation if the value is too wide to fit in the cell.

Number Enables you to specify the number of decimal places, whether to use a comma to separate thousands, and how to display negative numbers (with a minus sign, in red, in parentheses, or in red, and in parentheses.)

Currency Enables you to specify the number of decimal places, whether to use a currency symbol, and how to display negative numbers (with a minus sign, in red, in parentheses, or in red and parentheses). This format always uses a comma to separate thousands.

Accounting Differs from the Currency format in that the currency symbols always line up vertically.

Date Enables you to choose from several different date formats.

Time Enables you to choose from several different time formats.

Percentage Enables you to choose from the number of decimal places, and always displays a percent sign.

Fraction Enables you to choose from among nine fraction formats.

Scientific Displays numbers in exponential notation (with an E): 2.00E+05=200,000;2.05E+05=205,000. You can choose the number of decimal places to display to the left of E.

Text When applied to a value, causes Excel to treat the value as text (even if it looks like a number). This feature is useful for such items as part numbers.

Special When adapted for the English (Canada) in the 'Location' menu, this category contains two additional number formats: Phone Number, and Social Insurance Number.

Custom Enables you to define custom number formats that aren't included in any other category.[5]

Putting Data from Websites into Spreadsheets

While it's crucial to learn how to enter data into a spreadsheet, there are many instances when all you have to do is import the data from a website. Data is available in many downloadable formats. We'll concentrate here on two common formats: text and html files.

Importing Text Files

For this exercise, we'll use Health Canada's Drug Product Database. It contains all the drugs that have received approvals, and those that have been pulled off the market. For anyone covering the health beat, this would be a valuable resource, especially if a drug has been recalled. You can quickly use the database to find such information as the manufacturer, the company's address, and the drug's claimed therapeutic value when it was on the market.

Let's go to the website that contains the files <www.hc-sc.gc.ca/dhp-mps/prodpharma/databasdon/dpd_bdpp_data_extract_e.html>. There is a link to this site on the companion website to this book.

From the full screen view, you can see a table with three columns: the name of the table that captures all the information for the purposes of categorization, the name of the actual file, and when it was last updated. Let's take 'drug.txt,' the second category down from the top. Right-click on the txt link and you'll get a menu of options. Choose the 'Save Target As' option, which will produce the following result.

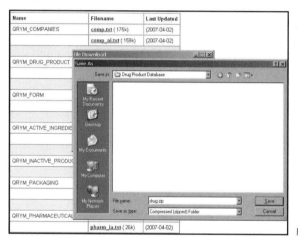

Fig. 3.5

You'll notice two important points: We have created a special folder for the text file, making it easy to find. The file is in a zip archive called 'drug.zip' If you open the zip file in a zip utility, such as WinZip, you can extract the text file to your hard drive. Then you can import the text file into Excel. But before we do, let's see what it looks like in a word processor.

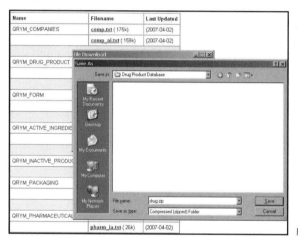

Fig. 3.6

This is what is called a 'delimited text file'. As the name implies, a delimited text file uses delimiters, in this case commas, to replace the column separators in data tables. Each row is ended with a carriage return. These files are popular for transferring data from one computer to another because they cut the file down to its essentials, making for a much-reduced- size file.

You'll notice that in this file, all of the data entries are surrounded by quotation marks. This is done to ensure that any commas contained within the data entries themselves are not misinterpreted by Excel as column separators, putting the data out of alignment.

Now that you are familiar with the text file, close it and open a worksheet in Excel. Be sure to activate A1, the first cell in the worksheet, by clicking on it with the mouse. Go to the 'Data' menu on the ribbon, and on the far left you'll notice three options for obtaining external data: 'From Access', 'From the Web', and 'From Text'. We want to choose 'From Text'. That opens this dialogue box in which you can navigate to and choose the text file.

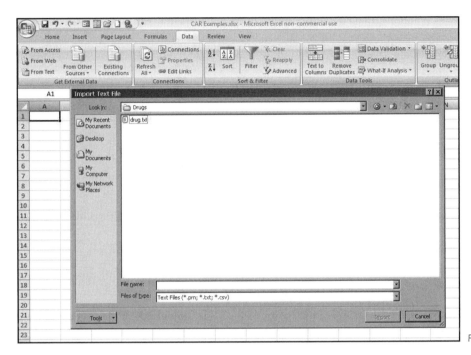

Fig. 3.7

Click 'Import' to go to the next step and see this screen:

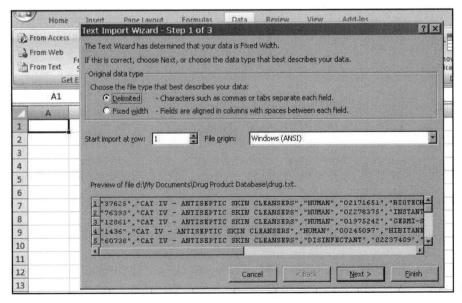

Fig. 3.8

We are ready to import in three easy steps, as you can see from the Text Import Wizard. Step one: make sure you check the circle beside the 'Delimited', option. Remember, you're importing a text file, which is delimited by commas. Hit the 'Next' tab.

In the next image we have chosen the 'Comma' as the delimiter. To the right, you'll notice that the 'Text Qualifier' is a quotation mark we saw in the 'Text' file. Select the 'Next' button.

⚠ **TECH TIP**

In older versions, click on 'Get External Data' then, under the 'Data' menu, 'Import Text File'.

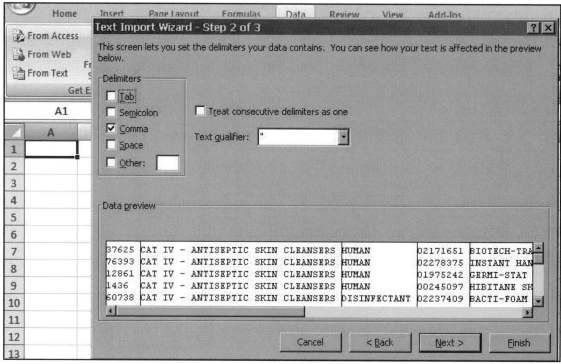

Fig. 3.9

We're almost there. As you can see in the next image the Import Wizard makes 'General' the default for data type. This option works fine for most entries. Sometimes you will want to set a field explicitly as a date or text field. In this example we set the 'date' field as a date type in month-day-year order, and the fourth field from the left as text. It's important to use the 'Text' format for fields with numbers with a leading 'zero', as is the case in the fourth field to the right. If you forget to do this, and leave the field as 'General', those zeros will disappear, rendering sorting on that field inaccurate. Press the 'Finish' key.

Excel now wants to know where you intend to place the data? Since A1 is already activated '=$A$1', go ahead and hit 'OK'.

You have successfully imported the drug file into Excel in a few easy steps, and you'll notice that the leading zeros have been preserved in column D. Whenever working with

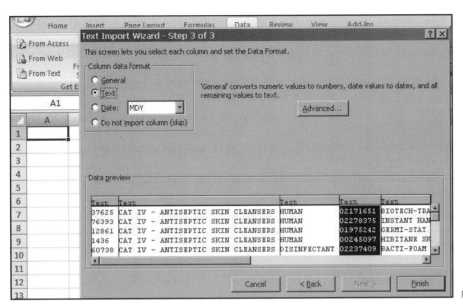

Fig. 3.10

data in any table, the first thing you should do is use the horizontal and vertical scroll bars to navigate your way around the file to see what you have. For instance, are any of the cells blank? Are there inconsistencies in spelling?

Upon scrolling, you'll notice that none of the columns has a heading, which is problematic because the information in the columns is meaningless if we don't know what it is. Many downloadable files will contain the headings in the first row, but Health Canada keeps them in a separate place. Most data sets must have some kind of document that gives the user crucial information such as the column headings and their meanings; explanations for certain codes and numbers. It is these explanations, along with your own familiarity with the data that are keys to finding newsworthy information and to avoiding errors.

Back at Health Canada's website, you'll notice a link in the middle of the page entitled 'ReadMe'. Click on the link. As you can see in the first few paragraphs, the ReadMe file tells you all about the database, including the tables it contains, and the field names. The part we want is a little farther down the page under the heading 'DATA STRUCTURE FOR MARKETED PRODUCTS'.

Let's scroll down to the table that is of interest to us, 'QRYM_DRUG_PRODUCT'.

```
ENTITY:    QRYM_DRUG_PRODUCT;
Name                                    Null?      Type
------------------------------------ -------- ----
DRUG_CODE                              NOT NULL  NUMBER(8)
PRODUCT_CATEGORIZATION                           VARCHAR2(80)
CLASS                                            VARCHAR2(40)
DRUG_IDENTIFICATION_NUMBER                       VARCHAR2(8)
BRAND_NAME                                       VARCHAR2(200)
GP_FLAG                                          VARCHAR2(1)
ACCESSION_NUMBER                                 VARCHAR2(5)
NUMBER_OF_AIS                                    VARCHAR2(10)
LAST_UPDATE_DATE                                 DATE
AI_GROUP_NO                                      VARCHAR2(10)
```

Fig. 3.11

Under the heading 'Name', you'll see the field names that are linked by an underscore. While Excel (and Access for that matter) will accept spaces in field names, many database applications will not. So Health Canada defaults to using underscores to link words in field names.

Now, let's go back to our spreadsheet, and insert a row into which we can plug in these headings. To insert a row, place your cursor on cell A1, go to the 'Cells' tab in the 'Home' section of the ribbon. Click on 'Insert Sheet Rows' and you'll see the result.

You'll notice that the whole worksheet drops in order to accommodate the new row, which is where you'll copy and paste your headings. Now, let's go back to the 'ReadMe' file and copy (by clicking and dragging to highlight the term, (Ctrl + c) each of the column headings, pasting them (Ctrl + v) into the appropriate columns in the spreadsheet. You should be familiar with typing or pasting text or numbers into cells. Begin by activating cell A1 with your cursor, copying the first column heading, DRUG_CODE, and pasting it. Next is B1, and the heading PRODUCT_CATEGORIZATION. Repeat the process for the remaining columns.

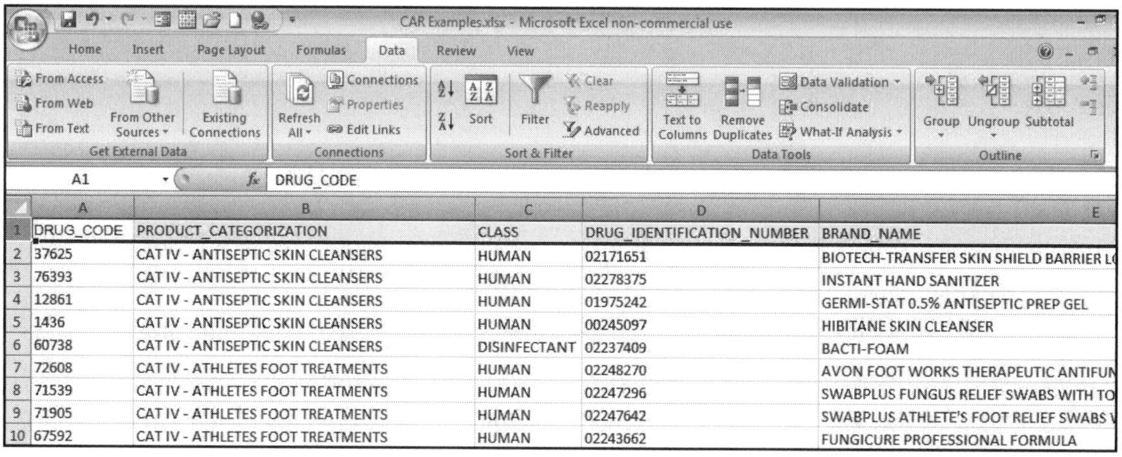

> **⚠ TECH TIP**
>
> In older versions, click on 'Rows' under the 'Insert' menu.

Fig. 3.12

All the headings are in place. To make sure, click on each cell and the heading will appear in the status bar, as you can see in Figure 3.12. We'll be able to see all the columns on the spreadsheet by readjusting the size of the columns. To do so, place your cursor at the top of the column between A and B. The cursor will turn into a cross, at which point you can do one of two things: double click with your index finger and Excel will automatically adjust the size of the cell; or you can hold your index finger on the mouse and drag the column to the desire spot, and then let go. Once you've readjusted the columns, you're set.

We now know what's in each column. Double-check the titles by referring back to the website. Not every cell is filled in. Sometimes information is missing that Health Canada may fill in later. Or there may be simply no information available at all. Still, we have a table that will, at the very least, add more heft to our reporting about prescription drugs. For instance, every time a drug company pulls one of its products from the market, you'll be able to consult this table for such details as the length of time the product has been on the market, when it was first approved, and the reason it was approved.

A little later in this chapter, we'll run through some of the most common methods journalists use to analyze the material they gather and store in spreadsheets. But before we get to that, let's run through another import.

Sometimes, comma-delimited files are given the file extension .csv, which stands for comma-separated values. To make things even more confusing, agencies sometimes use this extension when the delimiter isn't a comma at all!

Let's examine the tables that track contributions citizens make to provincial political parties in Quebec. Let's go to the website with the tables, which you can see in these images.[6]

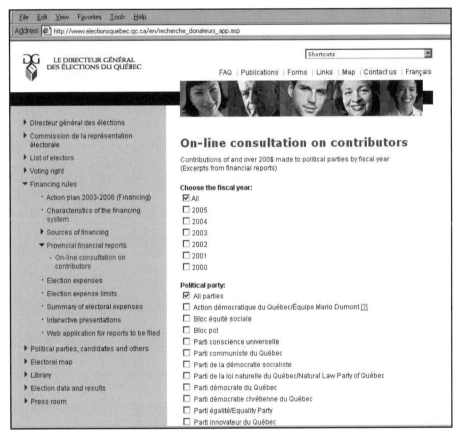

Fig. 3.13

Each category on the website represents a column of information, in this case, the table of donors will have five columns of information:

1. Fiscal year
2. Political party
3. Surname of contributor
4. Given name of contributor
5. Contributions

We can get to the database by clicking on the 'Search' button at the bottom of the page of the website, taking us to a table. Look for the 'CSV' link at the bottom left side.

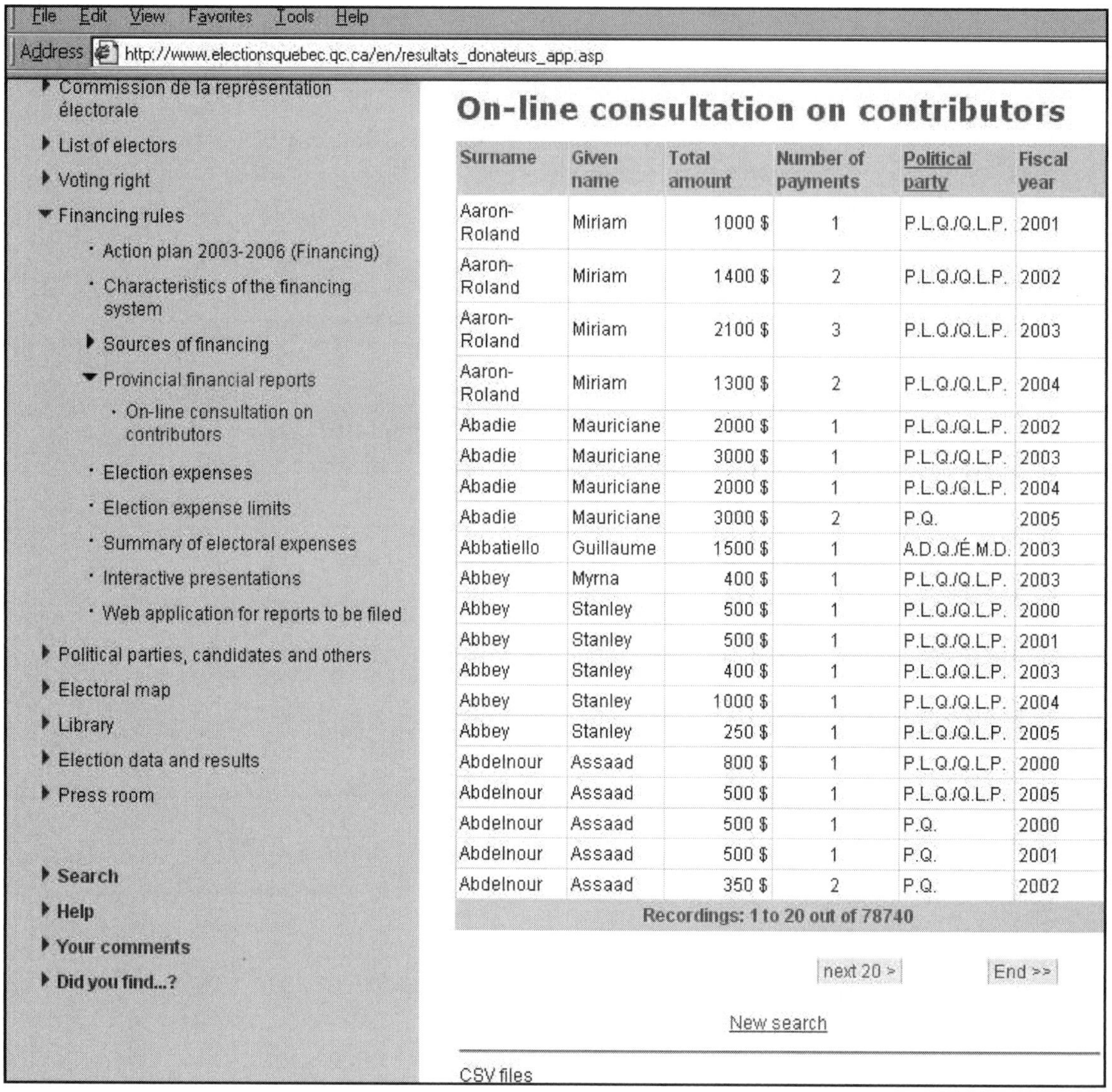

| File Edit View Favorites Tools Help |
| Address http://www.electionsquebec.qc.ca/en/resultats_donateurs_app.asp |

▶ Commission de la représentation électorale

▶ List of electors

▶ Voting right

▼ Financing rules
  • Action plan 2003-2006 (Financing)
  • Characteristics of the financing system
  ▶ Sources of financing
  ▼ Provincial financial reports
    • On-line consultation on contributors
  • Election expenses
  • Election expense limits
  • Summary of electoral expenses
  • Interactive presentations
  • Web application for reports to be filed

▶ Political parties, candidates and others

▶ Electoral map

▶ Library

▶ Election data and results

▶ Press room

▶ Search

▶ Help

▶ Your comments

▶ Did you find...?

On-line consultation on contributors

Surname	Given name	Total amount	Number of payments	Political party	Fiscal year
Aaron-Roland	Miriam	1000 $	1	P.L.Q./Q.L.P.	2001
Aaron-Roland	Miriam	1400 $	2	P.L.Q./Q.L.P.	2002
Aaron-Roland	Miriam	2100 $	3	P.L.Q./Q.L.P.	2003
Aaron-Roland	Miriam	1300 $	2	P.L.Q./Q.L.P.	2004
Abadie	Mauriciane	2000 $	1	P.L.Q./Q.L.P.	2002
Abadie	Mauriciane	3000 $	1	P.L.Q./Q.L.P.	2003
Abadie	Mauriciane	2000 $	1	P.L.Q./Q.L.P.	2004
Abadie	Mauriciane	3000 $	2	P.Q.	2005
Abbatiello	Guillaume	1500 $	1	A.D.Q./É.M.D.	2003
Abbey	Myrna	400 $	1	P.L.Q./Q.L.P.	2003
Abbey	Stanley	500 $	1	P.L.Q./Q.L.P.	2000
Abbey	Stanley	500 $	1	P.L.Q./Q.L.P.	2001
Abbey	Stanley	400 $	1	P.L.Q./Q.L.P.	2003
Abbey	Stanley	1000 $	1	P.L.Q./Q.L.P.	2004
Abbey	Stanley	250 $	1	P.L.Q./Q.L.P.	2005
Abdelnour	Assaad	800 $	1	P.L.Q./Q.L.P.	2000
Abdelnour	Assaad	500 $	1	P.L.Q./Q.L.P.	2005
Abdelnour	Assaad	500 $	1	P.Q.	2000
Abdelnour	Assaad	500 $	1	P.Q.	2001
Abdelnour	Assaad	350 $	2	P.Q.	2002

Recordings: 1 to 20 out of 78740

[next 20 >]   [End >>]

New search

CSV files

Fig. 3.14

Click the 'CSV' link and then the 'Save' tab. The files are in a zipped folder. Save it, then copy and extract the csv files from the zip folder into 'Donations', or whatever folder you have designated. Now, you're ready to import the files into Excel.

Make sure you have activated A1, the first cell in the worksheet. Go to the 'Data' section on the Ribbon and select 'From Text' in the 'Get External Data' tab.

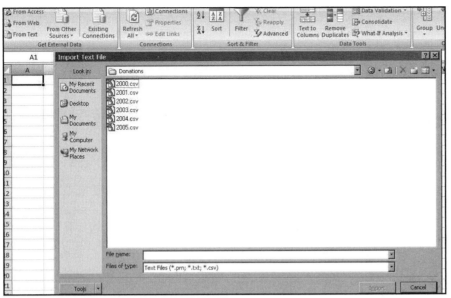

Fig. 3.15

Choose the 2000.csv, the first file in the menu. Press the 'Import' button and, as was the case with the text file in the Health Canada example, the import wizard will walk you through the steps. Select the 'Delimited' file type and hit 'Next'.

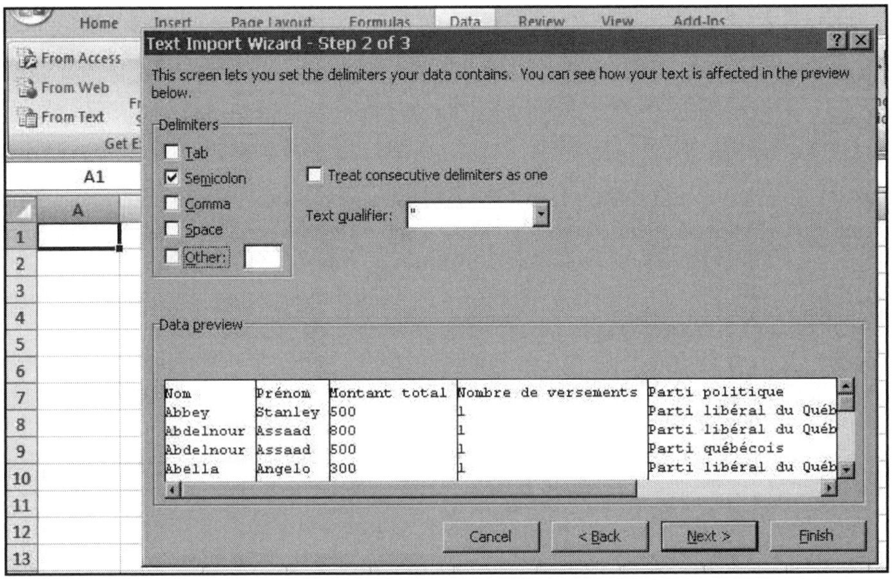

Fig. 3.16

Since the delimiter in this csv file is a semi-colon you must select the 'Semicolon' option. Selecting the semicolon will separate the material into the appropriate columns. So the view that you see in the 'Data Preview' window is what you'll see in Excel. Leave the text qualifier as is, and proceed to the next step.

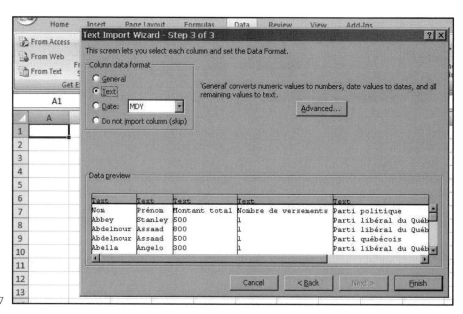

Fig. 3.17

You'll notice that this table contains the column headers, unlike the Health Canada example. We're almost there. Just make sure to format the columns as 'Text'. Click 'Finish'.

	A	B	C	D	E	F
1	Nom	Prénom	Montant total	Nombre de versements	Parti politique	Année financière
2	Abbey	Stanley	500	1	Parti libéral du Québec/Quebec Liberal Party	2000
3	Abdelnour	Assaad	800	1	Parti libéral du Québec/Quebec Liberal Party	2000
4	Abdelnour	Assaad	500	1	Parti québécois	2000
5	Abella	Angelo	300	1	Parti libéral du Québec/Quebec Liberal Party	2000
6	Aberman	Jill	1000	1	Parti libéral du Québec/Quebec Liberal Party	2000
7	Aberman	Jordan	3000	2	Parti libéral du Québec/Quebec Liberal Party	2000
8	Abikhzer	Charles	1450	4	Parti québécois	2000
9	Abitbol	Gérard	500	1	Parti libéral du Québec/Quebec Liberal Party	2000
10	Abitbol	Gilda	3000	1	Parti libéral du Québec/Quebec Liberal Party	2000

Fig. 3.18

Voila! The table is ready. Now let's find out how to import an HTML file. For this example, we'll use Ontario's salary disclosure tables.

Importing HTML Files

 **TECH TIP**

Note that right-clicking on the table and using the 'Export to Microsoft Excel' option in the shortcut menu only works in Explorer and not in other browsers, such as Firefox.

There are three ways to import tables in HTML format. (1) copy and paste the table into a worksheet; (2) left-click inside the table, right-click, and then choose the 'Export to Microsoft Excel' option; or, (3) as in the case of text files, have Excel import the entire file. We'll begin with the latter.

Importing Tables

The website shown in the next illustration is run by the Ontario Ministry of Finance. The link is on the companion site to this book. It lists public employees in Ontario who make $100,000 or more in a calendar year. The salary disclosures, which date back to 1997, are updated every year. Below the 'Select Years' drop-down menu, you'll notice the different employers. The first one in the group, 'Ministries', represents all the provincial ministries such as Agriculture, and Health and Long Term Care. To get a better look, let's click on the 'Ministries' link. This is the table for 2006 salaries and benefits of employees of government ministries.

Fig. 3.19

In the illustration above, you can see the bilingual title and a pdf icon on the right side. You can download the pdf. But it takes a bit more effort to work with pdfs. So we won't worry about that file format for the time being. (See Chapter 10 for a discussion on using data in pdf files). Notice that the information is in tabular form, perfect for importing into a spreadsheet. You could simply copy this table and paste it into Excel, so long as you are working in the Internet Explorer browser. That option works best with smaller tables, as we'll see a little later in this section. What we want to do is import the entire table into Excel. So, let's open a worksheet, activate cell A1, go to the 'Data' portion on your ribbon, and choose the 'From Web' option in the 'Get External Data' section. Click on the 'From Web' option. Now, go back to the web page that contains the table for import, and copy the URL. Paste it into the address bar, which will give you the page with the table we want to import. You have now instructed Excel to go to the web page, find the table, and import it into the worksheet. Select the 'Import' tab. Hit the 'OK' tab. What you see in the illustration is unwanted material that we'll delete. But to make sure the table has been imported, scroll down to row 78, the place where the table begins.

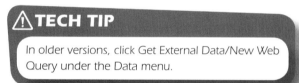

Fig. 3.20

The imported table probably has unwanted material at the top that should be removed. Let's get rid of everything above row 54. To do so, you have to scroll to the top of the table to begin the process of deleting all the fields from one to 54. Clicking on number one will highlight the entire first row. You can either highlight the rest of the cells by holding down the left mouse button and dragging down to row 72, or by holding down the Shift key and pressing on the down arrow. Either method is fine. Now we have highlighted the first 77 rows.

> **⚠ TECH TIP**
>
> In older versions, click Get External Data/New Web Query under the Data menu.

Go to the 'Home' section in the ribbon; go to the 'Cells' section; and select the 'Delete' option. Or, you can right-click and use the same option from the short-cut menu.

You also want to delete the sheet rows from 54 to number one. So make sure that entire block is highlighted and again select the 'Delete' option. These deletions go a long way to cleaning up your table.

We're almost there. Let's repeat the same clean-up process for the bottom of the table. Scroll down, highlight the extraneous information, and delete it.

> **⚠ TECH TIP**
>
> You can also avoid the cleaning by using a feature in Excel's import wizard that allows you to select only the table and exclude everything else.

Scroll back to the top; you have a clean table. To get a better view of all the fields, adjust the size of the fields. Now we're ready to work with the information in the spreadsheet with some exercises we'll learn a little later in this chapter.

Excel has a shortcut that avoids importing unwanted rows. You import the salary table from the web in the same manner described earlier in this chapter, but before pressing

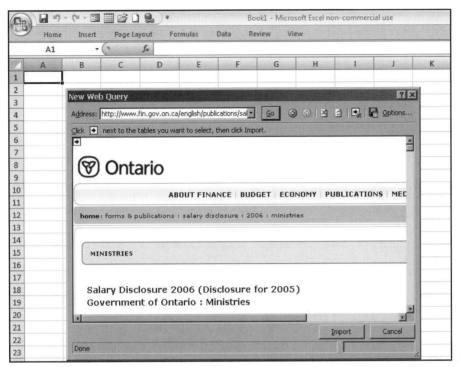

Fig. 3.21

the 'Import' button, you'll notice an instruction just below the address bar that tells you to 'click the (arrow) next to the tables you want to select, then click import.' Use the vertical scroll bar on the right side to find the table. At the top left, you'll see an arrow pointing to the right. Clicking on it will highlight only the table.

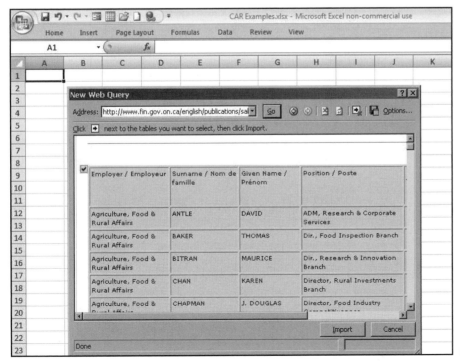

Fig. 3.22

Once this task has been carried out, select the 'Import' button and proceed from there. While this is a handy shortcut that allows you to avoid cleaning, doing it the long way forces you to become familiar with the data and learn how to do the kind of cleaning that will be necessary with many datasets imported from the web.

Exporting Tables from Excel

As discussed previously, you can also export tables on the web directly into Excel by placing your cursor anywhere in the table in Microsoft Internet Explorer, right-clicking on your mouse and using the 'Export to Microsoft Excel' option. A word of caution, though. This technique works well if all you have to import is one table. If you have many tables to import into one worksheet, or if you have many worksheets, then this right-click shortcut doesn't work. That's because each time you use the shortcut, the table is exported into a *new* Excel file. Still, it's handy if you're on deadline and want to dump a table into Excel for some quick analysis. You'll still have to do the same kind of clean-up as we performed when importing the salary disclosure table. Note that this method does *not* work in other browsers, such as Firefox or Netscape.

Pasting Information

You can also copy and paste information from web-based tables into Excel. In many instances it's easier to use this method, either because the table is too small to warrant pulling in the entire web page, or because doing so is impossible.

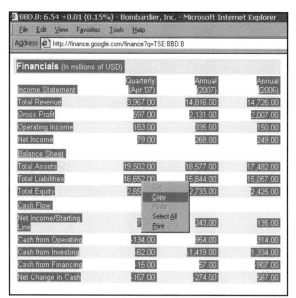

Fig. 3.23

The files may also be posted in HTML format, which means selecting and copying material is as easy as for any Word document. Once selected, it can be pasted into Excel. You'll notice that all of the text and numbers have "wrapped" to fit the size of the cells. This feature can take up a lot of space, especially if you have a fairly large table. To remove this feature, right-click anywhere in the table, and select the 'Format Cells' option. Now go to the 'Format' tab at the top of the dialogue box and deselect the 'Wrap text' option situated right under the 'Text Control' section.

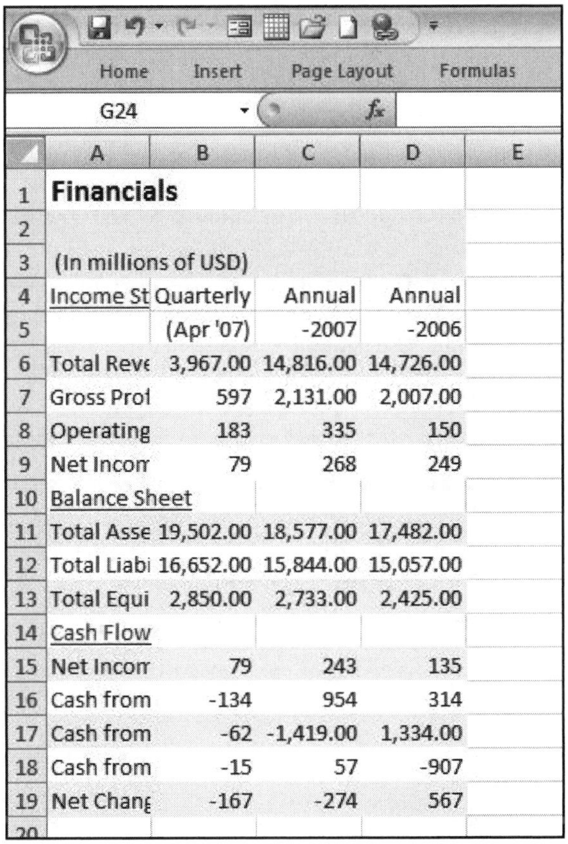

	A	B	C	D	E
1	Financials				
2					
3	(In millions of USD)				
4	Income St	Quarterly	Annual	Annual	
5		(Apr '07)	-2007	-2006	
6	Total Reve	3,967.00	14,816.00	14,726.00	
7	Gross Prol	597	2,131.00	2,007.00	
8	Operating	183	335	150	
9	Net Incor	79	268	249	
10	Balance Sheet				
11	Total Asse	19,502.00	18,577.00	17,482.00	
12	Total Liabi	16,652.00	15,844.00	15,057.00	
13	Total Equi	2,850.00	2,733.00	2,425.00	
14	Cash Flow				
15	Net Incor	79	243	135	
16	Cash from	-134	954	314	
17	Cash from	-62	-1,419.00	1,334.00	
18	Cash from	-15	57	-907	
19	Net Chang	-167	-274	567	
20					

Fig. 3.24

The result is a table that takes up less room. After adjusting the size of the columns, you'll be able to see all the financial data.

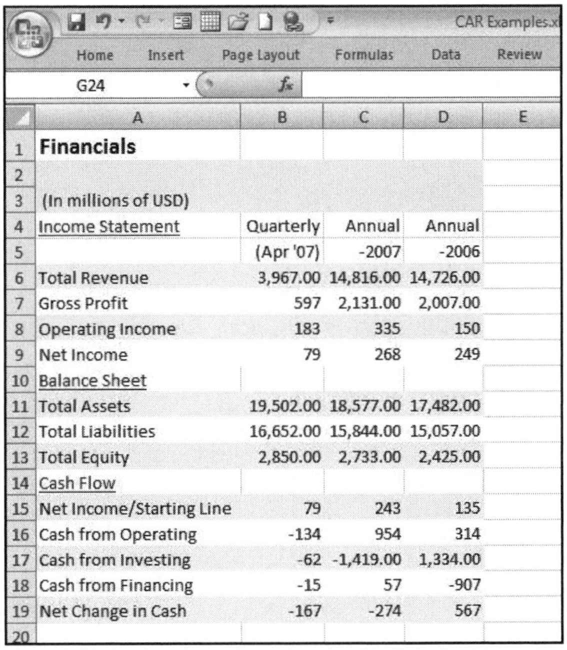

	A	B	C	D	E
1	Financials				
2					
3	(In millions of USD)				
4	Income Statement	Quarterly	Annual	Annual	
5		(Apr '07)	-2007	-2006	
6	Total Revenue	3,967.00	14,816.00	14,726.00	
7	Gross Profit	597	2,131.00	2,007.00	
8	Operating Income	183	335	150	
9	Net Income	79	268	249	
10	Balance Sheet				
11	Total Assets	19,502.00	18,577.00	17,482.00	
12	Total Liabilities	16,652.00	15,844.00	15,057.00	
13	Total Equity	2,850.00	2,733.00	2,425.00	
14	Cash Flow				
15	Net Income/Starting Line	79	243	135	
16	Cash from Operating	-134	954	314	
17	Cash from Investing	-62	-1,419.00	1,334.00	
18	Cash from Financing	-15	57	-907	
19	Net Change in Cash	-167	-274	567	
20					

Fig. 3.25

Some Simple Methods for Analyzing Data

Sorting

Now that we have data in a spreadsheet; have done the necessary cleaning; have checked to see that all the numbers, names, and titles are in place; and have obtained a clear understanding of what all our data means we are on our way to finding stories. And, for the time being, we don't have to worry about math, just simple tasks such as sorting, and filtering.

Let's begin using the salary disclosure information we discussed previously. We'll focus on the Hydro One example that caused such as fuss when the seven-figure pay cheque for its former top executive, Tom Parkinson, was revealed. Let's first download the figures for 2006 in Excel for Hydro One and Ontario Power Generation, and clean up the table.[7] Again, there is a link to the data on the companion website to this book.

	A	B	C	D
	Employer / Employeur	Surname / Nom de famille	Given Name / Prénom	Position / Poste
1	Employer / Employeur	Surname / Nom de famille	Given Name / Prénom	Position / Poste
2	Hydro One	ABBOTT	BRAD	Regional Maintainer I - Lines
3	Hydro One	ABBOTT	MARK	Customer & Business Services Manager
4	Hydro One	ADAM	MIKE	Regional Maintainer I - Lines
5	Hydro One	ADAMS	DAN	Regional Maintainer I - Lines
6	Hydro One	ADAMS	DAVID	Senior Manager - Outsourcing
7	Hydro One	ADAMS	GREG	Regional Maintainer - Lines Union Trades Supervisor 3
8	Hydro One	AGARWAL	ARVIND	Cad Operator Electrical & Telecom
9	Hydro One	AGNELLO	PETE	Customer Operations Manager
10	Hydro One	AGOSTINO	JOSEPH	Assistant General Counsel

Fig. 3.26

Given that readers, viewers, and listeners usually are more interested in people who make the most money, pay the highest taxes, or give the largest amounts to politicians, we'll have to sort column E in descending order. That way, those who made the most will appear at the top.

In order to sort column E, we'll first need to highlight the entire table. Place your cursor in the grey box at the top left corner of the table with the white arrow, and click the mouse. Go to the 'Data' section on the 'Home' ribbon, and choose 'Sort & Filter.' Choose 'Custom Sort'. Click on the downward arrow to the right of the 'Sort by' option. Choose 'Salary Paid'.

⚠ TECH TIP

In older versions, click on 'Sort' under the 'Data' menu.

You'll notice that you've been given options in the 'Order' section on the right side of the dialogue box. We want 'Largest to Smallest' (which is called 'Descending Order' in previous versions of the program). So, click on the arrow to the right, and from the pull-down menu, choose 'Largest to Smallest'.

Make sure that you click the box beside the 'My data has headers' option on the top right side of the dialogue box. Activating that option ensures that the column titles stay in place and don't get sorted with the rest of the information. Now, select the 'OK' key.

You should recognize the name of Tom Parkinson. Also interesting is the number of other executives earning high salaries: two others over $1-million, and several others pulling in more than $500,000.

CAR Examples.xlsx - Microsoft Excel non-commercial use

Home Insert Page Layout Formulas Data Review View

E2 | fx 1560900.85

	A	B	C	D	E
1	Employer	Surname	Given Name	Position	Salary Paid
2	Hydro One	PARKINSON	TOM	President/Chief Executive Officer	$1,560,900.85
3	Ontario Power Generation	HANKINSON	JAMES F	President & Chief Executive Officer	$1,480,804.01
4	Ontario Power Generation	CHARLEBOIS	PIERRE R	Executive Vice President & Chief Operating Officer	$1,015,540.32
5	Ontario Power Generation	DICERNI	RICHARD	Executive Vice President, Corporate Secretary	$923,499.96
6	Ontario Power Generation	ROBINSON	WILLIAM	Senior Vice President, Nuclear Programs & Training	$901,634.48
7	Ontario Power Generation	SMITH	GREGORY	Senior Vice President, Nuclear Generation Development & Services	$897,316.96
8	Ontario Power Generation	TWOMEY	JAMES	Executive Vice President, Fossil	$776,029.44
9	Ontario Power Generation	MURPHY	JOHN D	Executive Vice President, Hydro	$733,116.24
10	Ontario Power Generation	MITCHELL	THOMAS	Chief Nuclear Officer	$707,647.84
11	Ontario Power Generation	BURPEE	JAMES R	Executive Vice President, Corporate Development	$609,972.56
12	Ontario Power Generation	HANBIDGE	DONN W	Senior Vice President & Chief Financial Officer	$581,603.35
13	Ontario Power Generation	COLEBY	JOHN	Senior Vice President, Pickering A	$555,559.92
14	Ontario Power Generation	BOLAND	BRUCE	Senior Vice President, Corporate Affairs	$505,603.28
15	Ontario Power Generation	LONG	FREDERICK	Vice President, Financial Planning Corporate Finance	$496,738.52
16	Hydro One	SUMMERS	BETH	Chief Financial Officer	$474,166.14
17	Hydro One	D'ARCEY	MYLES	Senior Vice President, Customer Operations	$471,016.50
18	Hydro One	GOLDIE	TOM	Senior Vice President, Corporate Services	$467,990.40
19	Hydro One	FORMUSA	LAURA	General Counsel And Secretary	$462,272.60
20	Ontario Power Generation	PECKHAM	MICHAEL	Deputy Site Vice President	$396,420.71
21	Hydro One	OGRAM	GEOFF	Vice President, Asset Management	$383,792.39
22	Ontario Power Generation	NASH	KENNETH	Senior Vice President, Nuclear Waste	$380,448.78
23	Hydro One	MCQUEEN	NAIRN	Vice President, Engineering & Construction Services	$378,269.98
24	Ontario Power Generation	MCNEIL	PATRICK	Senior Vice President, Plant Life Extension Projects	$378,173.65
25	Ontario Power Generation	ALLEN	MICHAEL	Director, Work Management	$358,147.98
26	Ontario Power Generation	REED	JEROME	Director, Work Management	$357,438.03
27	Ontario Power Generation	REINER	DIETMAR E	Chief Information Officer	$352,931.00

Fig. 3.27

Just from sorting the information we can now add more context to the Tom Parkinson story by pointing out that there are also other highly paid executives at Hydro One and Ontario Power Generation.

Filtering

Scrolling down column E (Figure 3.27), you'll notice that quite a few officials earn more than $300,000 a year, which is a high salary for a public-sector worker. Filtering allows us to select only those employees who earned more than that amount. To begin the process, click on any cell below the header row. Next, select the 'Filter' option in the 'Editing' area of the ribbon.

Excel now adds downwards arrows at the top of each column, allowing for the option of filtering on any one of the columns. We're still interested in salaries, so let's click on the arrow in the 'Salary Paid' column.

The drop-down menu provides all the salaries in the range. This allows you to isolate or filter for specific salaries. Instead, we want to choose everyone earning more than $300,000. For that, we'll need the advanced features in the 'Number Filters' option. Excel gives us the options we want to use. We're interested only in people making more than $300,000, so choose 'Greater Than'.

TECH TIP ⚠

In older versions, click 'Filter/Autofilter' under the 'Data' menu.

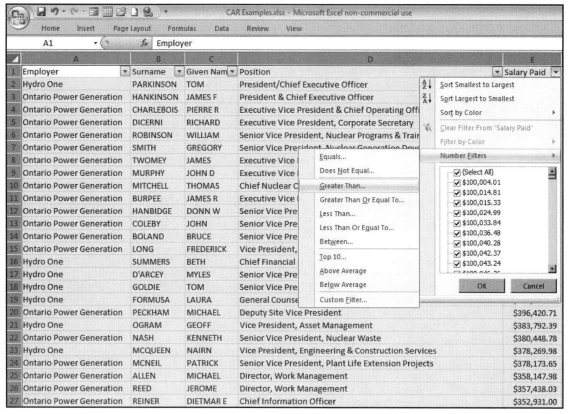

Fig. 3.28

You can do one of two things: choose a number from a drop-down menu you'll obtain by clicking on the downward arrow to the far right of the box, or type the figure into the blank space to the right of the 'Is greater than' option, and select 'OK'.

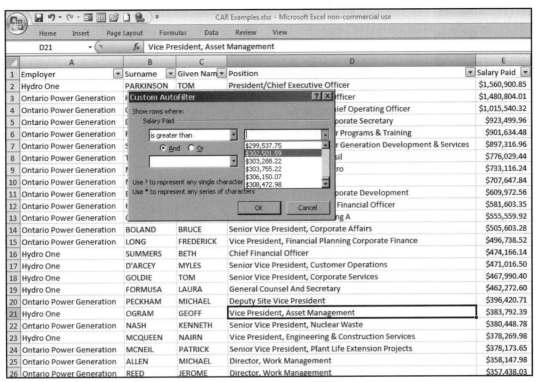

Fig. 3.29

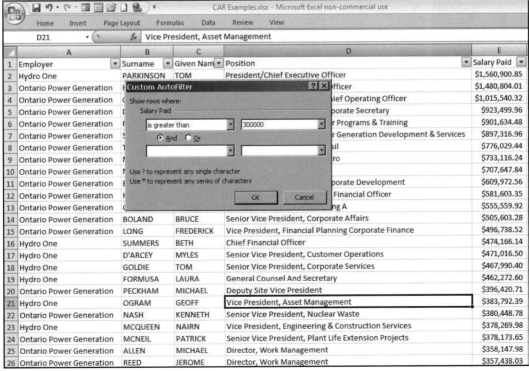

Fig. 3.30

Scrolling down to the bottom of the filtered table, you can see 70 employees who earn more than $300,000.

	A	B	C	D	E	F
1	Employer	Surname	Given Nam	Position	Salary Paid	Taxable Benefits / Avantages impos
2	Hydro One	PARKINSON	TOM	President/Chief Executive Officer	$1,560,900.85	$37,1
3	Ontario Power Generation	HANKINSON	JAMES F	President & Chief Executive Officer	$1,480,804.01	$7,5
4	Ontario Power Generation	CHARLEBOIS	PIERRE R	Executive Vice President & Chief Operating Officer	$1,015,540.32	$5,4
5	Ontario Power Generation	DICERNI	RICHARD	Executive Vice President, Corporate Secretary	$923,499.96	$3,1
6	Ontario Power Generation	ROBINSON	WILLIAM	Senior Vice President, Nuclear Programs & Training	$901,634.48	$3,6
7	Ontario Power Generation	SMITH	GREGORY	Senior Vice President, Nuclear Generation Development & Services	$897,316.96	$2,7
8	Ontario Power Generation	TWOMEY	JAMES	Executive Vice President, Fossil	$776,029.44	$4,3
9	Ontario Power Generation	MURPHY	JOHN D	Executive Vice President, Hydro	$733,116.24	$3,5
10	Ontario Power Generation	MITCHELL	THOMAS	Chief Nuclear Officer	$707,647.84	$2,4
11	Ontario Power Generation	BURPEE	JAMES R	Executive Vice President, Corporate Development	$609,972.56	$5,1
12	Ontario Power Generation	HANBIDGE	DONN W	Senior Vice President & Chief Financial Officer	$581,603.35	$2,8
13	Ontario Power Generation	COLEBY	JOHN	Senior Vice President, Pickering A	$555,559.92	$1,9
14	Ontario Power Generation	BOLAND	BRUCE	Senior Vice President, Corporate Affairs	$505,603.28	$2,5
15	Ontario Power Generation	LONG	FREDERICK	Vice President, Financial Planning Corporate Finance	$496,738.52	$1,7
16	Hydro One	SUMMERS	BETH	Chief Financial Officer	$474,166.14	$2,5
17	Hydro One	D'ARCEY	MYLES	Senior Vice President, Customer Operations	$471,016.50	$2,5
18	Hydro One	GOLDIE	TOM	Senior Vice President, Corporate Services	$467,990.40	$2,5
19	Hydro One	FORMUSA	LAURA	General Counsel And Secretary	$462,272.60	$8
20	Ontario Power Generation	PECKHAM	MICHAEL	Deputy Site Vice President	$396,420.71	$1,7
21	Hydro One	OGRAM	GEOFF	Vice President, Asset Management	$383,792.39	$2,3
22	Ontario Power Generation	NASH	KENNETH	Senior Vice President, Nuclear Waste	$380,448.78	$1,4
23	Hydro One	MCQUEEN	NAIRN	Vice President, Engineering & Construction Services	$378,269.98	$1,4
24	Ontario Power Generation	MCNEIL	PATRICK	Senior Vice President, Plant Life Extension Projects	$378,173.65	$2,5
25	Ontario Power Generation	ALLEN	MICHAEL	Director, Work Management	$358,147.98	$1,3
26	Ontario Power Generation	REED	JEROME	Director, Work Management	$357,438.03	$1,2
27	Ontario Power Generation	REINER	DIETMAR E	Chief Information Officer	$352,931.00	$6
28	Ontario Power Generation	BOGUSKI	ROBERT	Vice President, Nuclear Supply Chain	$346,334.42	$1,5
29	Hydro One	SMITH	WAYNE	Vice President, Grid Operations	$337,248.25	$2,1
30	Ontario Power Generation	ROBBINS	WAYNE	Senior Vice President, Darlington	$334,768.27	$1,4
31	Hydro One	KELLESTINE	RICK	Vice President, Culture	$333,366.04	$1,9
32	Hydro One	STROME	STEVE	Vice President Labour Relations	$316,622.67	$1,6
33	Ontario Power Generation	JAGER	G. A	Director, Operations & Maintenance	$315,934.66	$1,5
34	Ontario Power Generation	ELSAYED	EMAD E	Vice President, Hydroelectric Development	$314,129.26	$18,1
35	Ontario Power Generation	DUNCAN	BRIAN	Director, Operations & Maintenance	$312,173.09	$1,5

Fig. 3.31

If this is a table you want to keep for further analysis, copy and paste it into a new worksheet. If not, you can get rid of the filter by returning to the 'Filter' option on the ribbon and clicking on the icon.

To copy the table, make sure that the entire table is highlighted, right-click, and hit 'Copy.' Now you have to insert a new worksheet in one of three ways: Go to the 'Insert' area on the 'Home' ribbon, and select 'Insert Sheet'.

Second, you can press the Shift and F11 keys at the same time; or, third, you can click on the tab at the bottom of the spreadsheet that contains the envelope-shaped icon with what looks like a star on the top left corner. Choosing the second option that appears will give you a blank worksheet into which you can paste the new table.

We're almost there. But first, we have to get rid of the hash marks (###). Excel uses these marks to tell you when the cell is too narrow to display a value or number. As it turns out, all the columns should be wider. Simply readjust the widths of the columns by clicking on the boundary between the headers, waiting for the cursor to turn into a cross, and then dragging the column to the desired width. Or, you can do so automatically by double-clicking on the cursor after it has turned into a cross. Then, we should name the worksheet, by right-clicking on the 'Sheet' tab at the bottom of the worksheet and choosing the 'Rename' option.

Now you have a table that contains only those civil servants who made more than $300,000 in 2006. Using the same method, you can build tables containing the salaries of specific groups of employees. For instance, you may be interested only in the salaries of the very top executives such as the President and Vice Presidents.

Using Colours

Excel 2007 has a feature not available in earlier versions, sorting by colour. That is, you can select a certain colour for certain rows of information and then sort accordingly. This comes in handy if you want to group certain kinds of information. Let's take, as an example, the 'Community & Protective Services' expenditures in the city of Ottawa's 2005 and 2006 budgets.

Although there is a range of services, we may be interested in just a few of them, such as those that deal with emergency response: in this case, Paramedic, Emergency Measures Unit, and Fire Services. First of all, we can select the rows simultaneously by holding down the Control key while clicking on the row numbers: 8, 10, and 11.

	A	B	C	D	E	F	G	H	I	J
1					2006 Operating Budget Corporate Summary					
2										
3			2005 Budget					2006 Budget		
4										
5		*Net Exp	Revenue	Net	FTE's		*Net Exp	Revenue	Net	FTE's
6	Community & Protective Services									
7	- Deputy City Manager	2,317	-	2,317	23.00		2,565	-	2,565	22.00
8	- Paramedic Service	43,792	(17,635)	26,157	420.00		49,880	(18,284)	31,596	439.00
9	- By-law Services	12,114	(17,386)	(5,272)	146.40		13,308	(17,684)	(4,376)	146.40
10	- Emergency Measures Unit	1,742	(97)	1,645	5.33		1,763	(97)	1,666	5.33
11	- Fire Services	99,059	(509)	98,550	988.76		104,365	(544)	103,821	990.00
12	- Housing	117,686	(50,132)	67,554	68.40		116,396	(45,422)	70,974	65.40
13	- Parks & Recreation	119,169	(93,950)	25,219	916.60		131,084	(105,036)	26,048	936.30
14	- Public Health	36,899	(24,284)	12,615	438.00		39,430	(28,672)	10,758	448.00
15	- Employment & Financial Assistance	257,587	(153,044)	104,543	604.00		262,761	(155,159)	107,602	602.00
16	- Cultural Services & Community Funding	30,723	(2,673)	28,050	87.70		32,925	(3,015)	29,910	104.70
17	- Long Term Care	39,800	(33,867)	5,933	567.20		41,469	(35,676)	5,793	559.35
18	Total	760,888	(393,577)	367,311	4,265.39		795,946	(409,589)	386,357	4,318.48

Fig. 3.32

On the 'Home' ribbon, go to the 'Font' area, the second from the left. You'll notice an icon at the bottom right side of that section with what looks like a paint bucket tilted to the right. Click on the icon for a list of colour options. Let's choose a colour. We'll try yellow, the fourth option from the left. The rows shown on your monitor will now be coloured yellow. To isolate these rows, click on field A6, right-click on your mouse, and choose the option in the 'Filter' section that allows you to choose by colour. Select 'Filter by Selected Cell's Color'. Excel has given the filter on the 'Community & Protective Services' column an option that will allow you to isolate the colours.

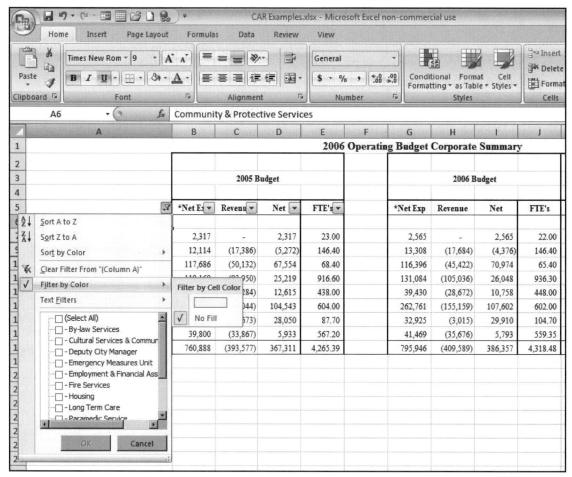

Fig. 3.33

Notice that the filter has already identified the colour of the cells you've chosen to highlight. Click on the 'Filter by Color'.

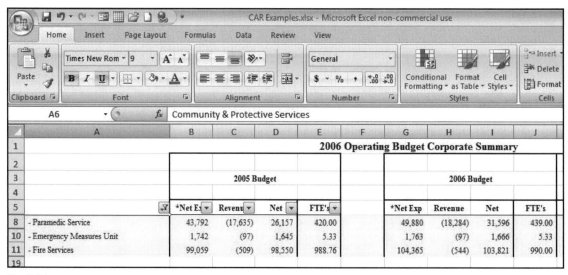

Fig. 3.34

You can now copy and paste this table into another worksheet. To do this, hold down the Control key on cell A3, press the right-arrow key until you get to J3, then press the downward arrow key to J11.

Splitting Cells

In addition to the techniques we have reviewed so far, you also can get ideas from simply putting certain rows and columns together to compare numbers. To do this, you can 'split' the view of the worksheet that contains the table. To see how this works, let's take a look at a table from Elections Canada that tracks campaign donations.

TECH TIP ⚠

You do have the option of left-clicking on the mouse and dragging the cursor across the rows in the table you want to copy, but this can be dangerous in that you risk making mistakes. That's because Excel allows you to copy the contents from one cell to the next using key strokes. Once you've highlighted the table, copy and paste into another worksheet, and continue your work.

	A	B	C	D	E
	Name of contributor	Name of candidate	Political party	Electoral district	Date re
1	Name of contributor	Name of candidate	Political party	Electoral district	Date re
2	0438959 BC Ltd dba Speedpro Signs (Jay Bella)	Profili, Bill	Liberal Party of Canada	British Columbia Southern Interior	23
3	0699072 BC Ltd. (Chris Dalton)	Mulroney, David	Liberal Party of Canada	Victoria	16
4	0710056 BC Ltd. (Dale Hewitt)	Strahl, Chuck	Conservative Party of Canada	Chilliwack--Fraser Canyon	27-
5	115164 HOLDINGS	Day, Stockwell	Conservative Party of Canada	Okanagan--Coquihalla	20
6	1371327 Ontario Limited -O/A Famous Magazine	Robinson, Svend	New Democratic Party	Vancouver Centre	23
7	1398030 Ontario Inc. DBA IMG Imports (Maninder Singh)	Dosanjh, Ujjal	Liberal Party of Canada	Vancouver South	30-
8	1578341 Ontario Inc. (Baklar Dosanjh)	Dosanjh, Ujjal	Liberal Party of Canada	Vancouver South	30-
9	1636658 Ontario Inc. (Edward Chou)	Scott, Brian	Liberal Party of Canada	Nanaimo--Cowichan	12
10	264076 B.C. Limited (D. Telep)	Kamp, Randy	Conservative Party of Canada	Pitt Meadows--Maple Ridge--Mission	29-

Fig. 3.35

There are actually more columns on this worksheet, but Excel will let you see only so many of them at a time. What if we wanted to see a certain number of columns, and hide the rest? Well, we would do exactly that—hide the columns we don't want. In this example, we want to line two columns side by side: the name of the candidate and donations. Having these two columns next to each other will make it easier to compare candidates' donations. To hide the unwanted columns, hold down the Shift key and click all the column headers between C and J. Then right-click on the mouse to get to the shortcut menu. Choose the 'Hide' option. Now we can see the donations that each candidate received, and make visual comparisons. If we are interested in a certain candidate, we can now apply the filter.

To get rid of the 'Hide', hold down the 'Shift' key and select the two cells on each side of the cell range that is hidden, in this case C and J. Once they're selected, right-click on the mouse to obtain the shortcut menu, and then select the 'Unhide' option. But in this case, we want to continue with our hunt for stories, so we'll stay with the 'Hide' option. Now, if you are interested in the donations to the Conservative Party only of MP Chuck Strahl, you can isolate his donations by applying the 'Filter' and the 'Custom' option.

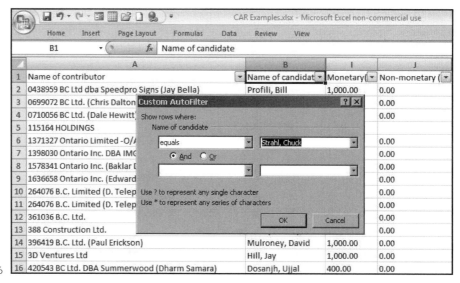

Fig. 3.36

Select 'OK. You've successfully narrowed your choices. If this is the table you want, then copy it and paste it into another worksheet. Once you've finished, return to the federal elections worksheet and return to the original table by getting rid of the hide and filter functions.

Freezing

Scrolling down a worksheet is fine for double checking that all the information is in place. But analyzing the information is difficult because as you scroll down, the column titles disappear. It's much easier to 'freeze' the titles or have them stay in place when scrolling up and down the worksheet. When you freeze, you are dividing the view into two horizontal panes with the upper portion containing the titles staying in place. To exercise this option, select Row 1, go to the 'View' section of the ribbon and then to the 'Window' tab on the far right. Choose the 'Freeze Panes' option.

⚠ TECH TIP

In older versions, click on 'Split' under the 'Window' menu.

You'll end up with the view dividing into two horizontal panes. The thick black line at the bottom of Row 1 indicates that it is frozen. Now you're free to scroll up and down the worksheet with the titles held in place. (To get rid of the freezing option, return to the 'View' section on the ribbon, and choose 'Unfreeze Panes'.)

If you want to put the columns with the name of the candidate and the donation amount beside each other, you can go through the same process as above. Using the freezing and hiding options, you made the worksheet easier to analyze for stories. You can also copy a slice of the table that may be of interest onto another worksheet.

Using Excel to Build Chronologies

So far we have focused on using Excel to analyze data. But Excel can come in handy for organizing data that hits closer to home: your own notes. Frequently, when you're working on a longer- or medium-term story, one of the big challenges is organizing your material in a way that makes it easy to find specific bits of information or to spot trends.

Using chronologies is one of the most effective ways of organizing your material, and while word processing programs such as Word can be used to accomplish this task, it becomes much easier in Excel.

This technique helped Halifax-based CBC reporter Bob Murphy when he was investigating a ferry accident in Nova Scotia. Captain Donald LeBlanc was killed while clearing snow on the Englishtown ferry ramp. Murphy discovered problems with the investigation into the death, and concerns of LeBlanc's family. In order to help with the investigation and story-telling, Murphy built a chronology in Excel.

Murphy' chronology consists of two columns, one with the date, and the other containing the significant details. The small red triangle at the top right corner of cell B9 indicates that there is a note 'hidden' beneath the icon. You can right-click on the mouse and select the 'Insert Comment' option from the shortcut menu.

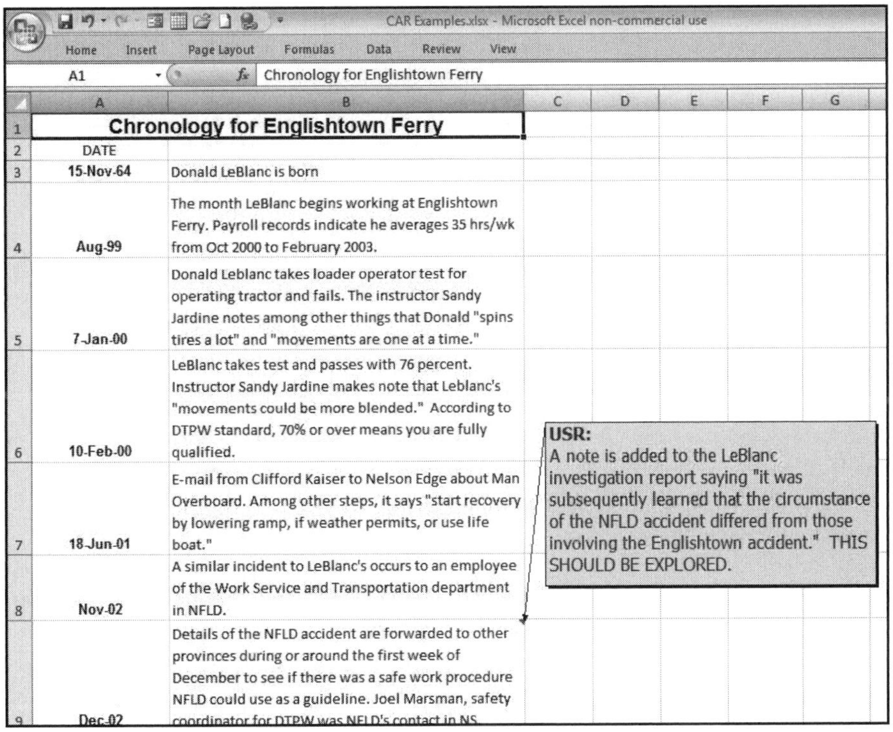

Fig. 3.37

The 'insert comment' option allows you to type notes in a box, which you can make disappear behind a small, red, triangular icon wedged in the top right-hand corner of the cell, or you can choose the 'Show/Hide Comments' option from the short-cut menu to make the comments appear. This comes in handy if you're sending your chronology to a colleague who can just open up the spreadsheet and have everything in front of her.

This is a good option to use when your chronology, like Murphy's, only has a few columns. He says it took hours to build this chronology. 'Because first of all, I had to eyeball the individual documents, decide what would be important, and then put it in the spreadsheet. But the hours spent are well worth it, not only because it helps identify key points that you might otherwise miss, but it also becomes a useful reference as you continue your research. So you can quickly refresh your memory of the story without having to review all of the documents.'

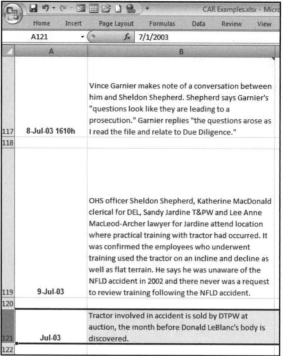

Fig. 3.38

In Murphy's case, he was able to show that Nova Scotia's ministry of Labour disposed of the tractor before its own investigators were able to examine the evidence. He was never able to determine the ministry's motivation for its actions.[8]

Murphy says the Jul-03 entry may seem insignificant to some, but no one, including the family and the retired police officer investigating the case, realized the government had sold the tractor before Donald LeBlanc's body was recovered. 'That only became apparent after I entered the information into a chronology. According to the family, it was further proof the government was not trying very hard to get to the bottom of Donald's death. 'It just becomes an interesting point because it shows some of the problems with the investigation.'

It is also possible to build chronologies with many more fields with details such as phone numbers, e-mail address, hyperlinks to websites, and documents on your hard drive.

Bringing It All Together

This chapter provides you with the skills you need to get going in Excel. But there is so much more to the program, including its forte, doing math. We explore these features in Chapter 4.

Five Stories You Can Do

1. Go the website for the Canada Foundation for Innovation. Use sorting and filtering to see who got the largest grants and to find the largest grants to your local university.

2. Using an Excel worksheet, download, paste, or type in political donations for your city or province. See who gave the most. Then, look through news archives to find references to contracts or favours they received.

3. If you work in Ontario, paste the latest year's public sector salary disclosure information into an Excel sheet. Add a new column for 'sector' and fill it in with the sector names. Now, sort the whole sheet, and see who was paid the most across all sectors.

4. Many publicly traded companies like to convince governments that they need tax breaks, grants, or special privileges. In exchange, the companies promise to spend more money on research and development. Use Excel to figure out if those companies are keeping their word. Copy and paste the financial statements two to three years before and after they made that promise, and compare the money the company spends on R&D to what it spends on activities such as marketing. If the marketing expenses dwarf what the company spends on R&D, then you might want to ask why.

5. All federal departments and agencies must disclose online who gets contracts to do work for the government. Go to the central federal government site for disclosure of information about contracts awarded by government departments at <www.tbs-sct.gc.ca/pd-dp/gr-rg/index_e.asp>. Copy and paste the lists for some agencies active in your area, then sort and filter to see which firms in your area got the most work from government. You could also compare those names to the donors from idea 2 above.

Chapter 4

Taking Spreadsheets to the Next Level
David McKie

What We'll Cover:

- Doing simple math in a spreadsheet.
- Percentage and percentage change calculations.
- Using functions.
- String manipulation functions
- Creating charts and graphs.

Introduction

Breaking stories is what the *Ottawa Citizen*'s Glen McGregor had in mind when he became curious about gun ownership in Canada. After negotiating for and obtaining the massive gun registry database, he also used Excel to conduct much of the analysis for his series 'Rapid Fire'.[1]

He told his readers about the areas of the country that had the highest per capita gun ownership. He also explained why an increasing number of guns were being stolen and, perhaps more disturbingly, that an increasing number of people were buying the Beretta CX4 Storm, the gun used by Kimveer Gill during his murderous shooting rampage at Montreal's Dawson College on 13 September 2006. Excel helped McGregor to beef up his analysis for a series that provoked an important discussion about guns and how they are used.

> It showed that gun theft was rising, and that Ontario had an overwhelmingly higher rate of recovery—probably because it has a special firearms taskforce dedicated to getting illegal or stolen guns off the street.[2]

For his part, Canwest's national affairs correspondent, David Akin, also manages to work Excel into his journalism in many ways.[3] Given that delving into spending habits is one of the best ways to investigate governments at all levels, he routinely goes through the spending estimates for federal government departments, compiling the numbers for successive years to see which departments will end up receiving more or less money.[4] Though government spending draws lots of attention from journalists covering federal, provincial, and municipal administrations, the numbers buried in the spending estimates can help journalists find out how the government department in question actually is spending money.

In this chapter, we'll delve into some examples to discover how you can use the power of Excel to help tell better stories.

Formulas

Spreadsheets derive much of their power from formulas. 'If it weren't for formulas, writes John Walkenbach, author of Excel 2007 Bible, 'a spreadsheet would simply be a glorified word-processing document that has great support for tabular information.'[5]

The advantage of formulas is that they can be copied repeatedly to perform the same calculation over and over again on long rows or columns or figures. Once they are in place, if the underlying figures change, the formulas will automatically recalculate the results.

Any calculation performed in Excel has to begin with an 'equals' sign: =. You can write the formula either in the cell where you want the result to appear or, with that cell selected, directly in the formula bar. The formula bar displays the formula in a cell or, if there is no formula, the actual contents of the cell.

What follows '=' can be either a simple mathematical formula—addition, subtraction, division, or multiplication, or some combination of these—or a more complicated mathematical operation, using one of Excel's built-in functions, or a statement that manipulates a string of text.

The Key Math

No matter how dismissive we may be of our math skills, everyone can do the basics such as addition. Let's take this simple example.

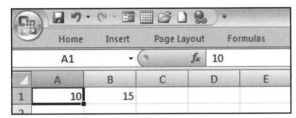

Fig. 4.1

The numbers '10' and '15' are in cells A1 and B1, respectively. The simplest formula for addition just adds cell references: A1 + B1. You'll notice that we are not entering the values themselves, that is, 10 and 15. We simply enter the cell references. If the values in the cells change later, the formulas will still work but on the new numbers. We're going to perform our calculation in cell C1, so we type the 'equals' sign there: =.

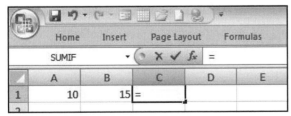

Fig. 4.2

Now hit 'Enter'.

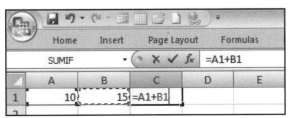

Fig. 4.3

The formula '=A1+B1' produces the answer 25 in cell C1. If you want to see the formula again, double-click on the cell and it will reappear, and can be edited. The formula also appears in the Formula bar above and to the right of cell C1.

Now, the ability to add up two cells is nice; but so far, we haven't done anything we couldn't do with a calculator. The real power of Excel comes into play when there are many pairs or groups of values to be added up. There is no need to retype the same formula into the cells below C1. Excel has stored the formula, and can now apply it automatically to the rest of the cells where we would like to see the results of adding data from columns A and B. The formula can be copied in a number of ways. The easiest way is to use what Microsoft calls the 'fill handle'. Place the cursor on the thick black square at the bottom right side of cell C1, wait until the cursor turns into a small cross, hold the left mouse button, and drag down to C9. The formula will now be copied downwards and the answers will appear.

⚠ TECH TIP

The only caution with double-clicking on the small box at the bottom right side of the cell to automatically copy the formula is that it will stop as soon as it encounters a blank cell to the left. If you're going to use this method, be sure that you first manually scroll down the worksheet to ensure that the formula has been copied all the way to the bottom. If necessary, use the first method to complete the fill.

You can also place the cursor on the square, wait until it turns into the small cross, and then double-click the left mouse button. Again, the formula will be copied instantly.

This works just as well with much larger tables. Let's apply this method to the Ontario salary disclosure table for the highest paid executives at Hydro One and Ontario Power Generation that we used in the previous chapter.

Columns E and F contain the 'Salary Paid' and 'Taxable Benefits', the two numbers we want to add to obtain total remuneration paid. In column G, we'll begin a new category with the title 'Salary Total' and put the formula '=E2+F2' into cell G2. Now, using either of the two methods we just learned, copy the formula down to the end of the table.

	A	B	C	E	F	G
1	Employer	Surname	Given Name	Salary Paid	Taxable Benefits / Avantages imposables	Salary Total
2	Hydro One	PARKINSON	TOM	$1,560,900.85	$37,104.11	$1,598,004.96
3	Ontario Power Generation	HANKINSON	JAMES F	$1,480,804.01	$7,318.90	$1,488,122.91
4	Ontario Power Generation	CHARLEBOIS	PIERRE R	$1,015,540.32	$5,427.60	$1,020,967.92
5	Ontario Power Generation	DICERNI	RICHARD	$923,499.96	$3,168.00	$926,667.96
6	Ontario Power Generation	ROBINSON	WILLIAM	$901,634.48	$3,652.80	$905,287.28
7	Ontario Power Generation	SMITH	GREGORY	$897,316.96	$2,714.59	$900,031.55
8	Ontario Power Generation	TWOMEY	JAMES	$776,029.44	$4,312.80	$780,342.24
9	Ontario Power Generation	MURPHY	JOHN D	$733,116.24	$3,542.40	$736,658.64
10	Ontario Power Generation	MITCHELL	THOMAS	$707,647.84	$2,444.46	$710,092.30

Fig. 4.4

If we were following up the story about the salaries being earned by the top executives at Hydro One and Ontario Power Generation, we would be able to add some context by not only sorting the salaries from top to bottom—as we did in the previous chapter—but by adding the taxable benefits to the salary paid to get a more complete picture of their compensation.

Later in this chapter, we'll show you how to use the SUM function, and the 'autosum' button to simplify addition of long rows or columns of numbers.

Subtracting

In this table from the City of Ottawa's budget, columns B and C contain FTEs for the Community & Protective Services department. An FTE is a 'full time equivalent', so the total FTEs is the number of equivalent full-time positions achieved by adding up all the part-, and full-time jobs. One equivalent could be comprised of two people working half-time.

The number of FTEs is an indicator employers use to determine the size of their work force. In this case, we will subtract B5 from C5 using the subtraction operator: '-'. Let's put the formula in column D and label it 'Difference in FTEs': '=C5-B5'.

| | Home | Insert | Page Layout | Formulas | Data | Review | View | |

| SUMIF | ▾ | ✗ ✓ f_x | =B5-C5 |

	A	B	C	D
1	**2006 Operating Budget Corporate Summary**			
2		**2006**	**2005**	
3		FTE's	FTE's	Difference in FTEs
4	**Community & Protective Services**			
5	- Deputy City Manager	22.00	23.00	=B5-C5
6	- Paramedic Service	439.00	420.00	
7	- By-law Services	146.40	146.40	
8	- Emergency Measures Unit	5.33	5.33	
9	- Fire Services	990.00	988.76	
10	- Housing	65.40	68.40	
11	- Parks & Recreation	936.30	916.60	
12	- Public Health	448.00	438.00	
13	- Employment & Financial Assistance	602.00	604.00	
14	- Cultural Services & Community Funding	104.70	87.70	
15	- Long Term Care	559.35	567.20	

Fig. 4.5

Hit enter and copy the formula.

One way Excel indicates a negative number is by putting it in brackets. The Deputy City Manager, Housing, Employment & Financial Assistance, and Long Term Care all were areas that received cuts. But as you can see from the total number of FTEs in row 16, the whole department gained just over 53. You can also sort the information in ascending order to find out which department received the largest cut.

	A	B	C	D
1	**2006 Operating Budget Corporate Summary**			
2		**2006**	**2005**	
3		FTE's	FTE's	Difference in FTEs
4	**Community & Protective Services**			
5	- Long Term Care	559.35	567.20	(7.85)
6	- Housing	65.40	68.40	(3.00)
7	- Employment & Financial Assistance	602.00	604.00	(2.00)
8	- Deputy City Manager	22.00	23.00	(1.00)
9	- By-law Services	146.40	146.40	0.00
10	- Emergency Measures Unit	5.33	5.33	0.00
11	- Fire Services	990.00	988.76	1.24
12	- Public Health	448.00	438.00	10.00
13	- Cultural Services & Community Funding	104.70	87.70	17.00
14	- Paramedic Service	439.00	420.00	19.00
15	- Parks & Recreation	936.30	916.60	19.70
16	Total			53.09
17				
18				

Fig. 4.6

From the illustration, we can see that Long Term Care suffered the deepest cuts, while Parks & Recreation was the big winner.

Multiplication and Division

Multiplying and dividing cells is done in much the same way. You start the formula with the 'equals' sign: '=', then enter cell references, using the symbol '*' to multiply two cells, and the symbol '/' to divide them.

Basic Percentages

Division comes into its own with one of the other basic math skills used by journalists, calculating percentages.

For some reason, journalists often find themselves befuddled by the simple percentage. On the one hand, like their readers, they intuitively understand what a percentage does. It expresses the relationship between a portion of a population—of people, trees, tests—and the population as a whole, in terms of how many of the sub-population there are for every 100 of the overall population. But while journalists understand what percentages do, they often haven't a clue how to calculate them.

Luckily, the formula for working out a percentage is dead simple. It is most easily expressed as the part (or sub-population) divided by the whole (or total population), multiplied by 100. Excel makes it even simpler, by multiplying by 100 for you when you click on the percentage format icon.

Let's take a look at a basic percentage calculation, using a slice of an inspections database from WorkSafeBC.

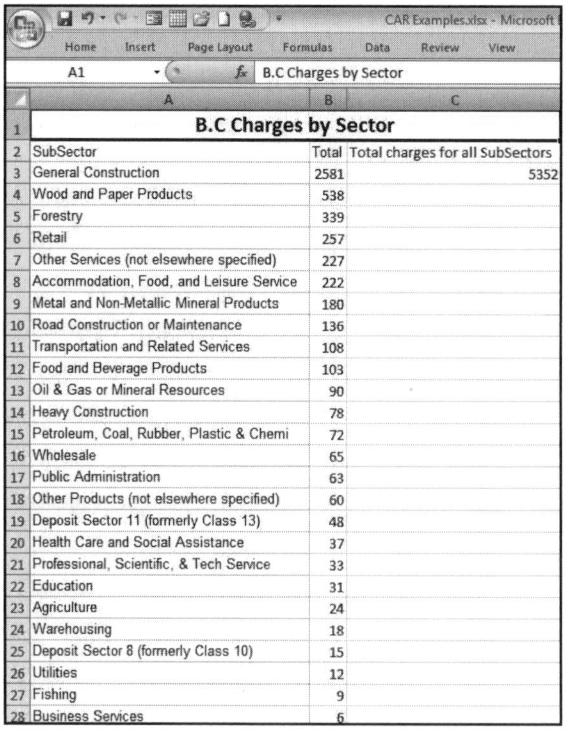

Fig. 4.7

The illustration contains the charges for workplace safety violations that WorksafeBC inspectors have laid against employers between 1995 and 2005. The total number of

⚠ TECH TIP

By default, Excel creates what's called 'relative' cell references in formulas. That means that the cell references change as you copy the formula from one cell to another. For example, '=A2+B2' written in cell C2 will change to '=A3+B3' if copied into cell C3. Sometimes, though, you want to lock part or all of a cell reference in a formula so no matter where you copy the formula, that original column, row, or cell will be used. You do this by entering a dollar sign: '$' before either the column letter or the row number, or before both. Locking the column letter will keep the formula locked on that column, locking the row number keeps the formula locked on that row, while locking both locks the formula on that cell. When locked, cell references are said to be 'absolute'.

charges for each subsector is stored in column B. Cell C3 contains the total number of charges for all subsectors combined

Let's take the first subsector, General Construction. First of all, we'll create a new column and call it Percent of Total Inspections. If we wanted to know its percentage of the total, we would simply divide the value in B3 by the value in C3: '=B3/C3'. Hitting 'Enter' will give us the resulting number, which we convert into a percentage.

While we want the references in column B to change, we want the reference in column C to remain constant, so that each value in column B will be calculated as a percentage of cell C3 (5352). To do this, we will anchor cell C3 as explained in the tip above: '=B3/$C3'.

Now that the value in C3 is locked in place, we're free to copy the formula for the rest of column D.

	D3			f_x =B3/$C3	
	A	B	C	D	
1	**B.C. Charges by Sector**				
2	SubSector	Total	Total charges for all SubSectors	Percent of Total Inspections	
3	General Construction	2581	5352	48%	
4	Wood and Paper Products	538		10%	
5	Forestry	339		6%	
6	Retail	257		5%	
7	Other Services (not elsewhere specified)	227		4%	
8	Accommodation, Food, and Leisure Service	222		4%	
9	Metal and Non-Metallic Mineral Products	180		3%	
10	Road Construction or Maintenance	136		3%	
11	Transportation and Related Services	108		2%	
12	Food and Beverage Products	103		2%	
13	Oil & Gas or Mineral Resources	90		2%	
14	Heavy Construction	78		1%	
15	Petroleum, Coal, Rubber, Plastic & Chemi	72		1%	
16	Wholesale	65		1%	
17	Public Administration	63		1%	
18	Other Products (not elsewhere specified)	60		1%	
19	Deposit Sector 11 (formerly Class 13)	48		1%	
20	Health Care and Social Assistance	37		1%	
21	Professional, Scientific, & Tech Service	33		1%	
22	Education	31		1%	
23	Agriculture	24		0%	
24	Warehousing	18		0%	
25	Deposit Sector 8 (formerly Class 10)	15		0%	
26	Utilities	12		0%	
27	Fishing	9		0%	
28	Business Services	6		0%	
29					

Fig. 4.8

With the value of C3 locked in place, we have been able easily to calculate the percentage of the total for each industrial sector. General Construction comes out way ahead of anything else.

Percentage Change

Calculating percentage changes is also easy, but don't let the simplicity fool you. Knowing how much things have increased or decreased can lead to great stories. Let's revisit the City of Ottawa's budget for the Community and Protective Services department.

We have the department's net expenses for the years 2005 and 2006 and want to tell people by what percentage the expenses have either risen or fallen. Following the usual steps when performing calculations in Excel, let's label a new column. This one we will call 'Percent change'.

We'll put our formula in cell D5. To calculate a percentage change, we subtract the new figure from the old, then divide the result by the old. The formula looks like this:

$$=(NEW-OLD)/OLD.$$

Applying the formula to the table results in:

$$=(C5-B5)/B5.$$

The first part of the formula goes in brackets, which tells Excel to perform that calculation first—the subtraction to work out the change—before dividing by the original value to calculate what percentage the change is of the original value.

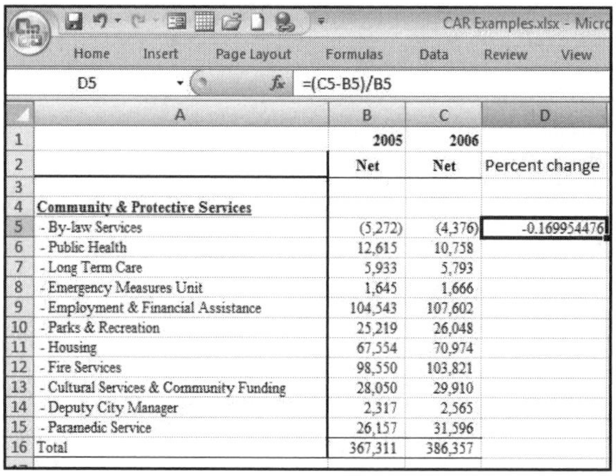

Fig. 4.9

The resulting number needs to be reformatted as a per cent. Right-click on the cell to obtain the shortcut menu and choose the 'Format Cells' option. You'll notice that we have the option of selecting Decimal places. It's usually a good idea to select one or two, mainly because the difference between two or more percentages may be miniscule. Having the decimal places makes sorting and ranking easier. Select 'OK'.

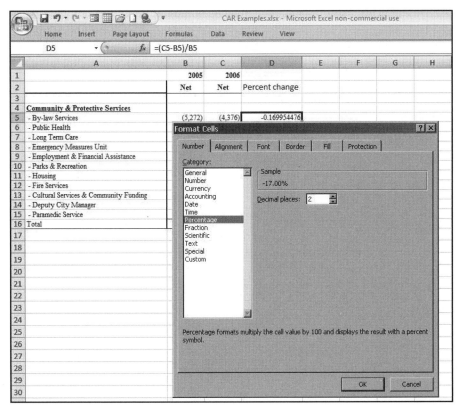

CAR Examples.xlsx - Microsoft Excel non-commercial use
Home Insert Page Layout Formulas Data Review View
D5
=(C5-B5)/B5
2005 2006
Net Net Percent change
Community & Protective Services
- By-law Services (5,272) (4,376) -0.169954476
- Public Health
- Long Term Care
- Emergency Measures Unit
- Employment & Financial Assistance
- Parks & Recreation
- Housing
- Fire Services
- Cultural Services & Community Funding
- Deputy City Manager
- Paramedic Service
Total
Format Cells
Number Alignment Font Border Fill Protection
Category:
General
Number
Currency
Accounting
Date
Time
Percentage
Fraction
Scientific
Text
Special
Custom
Sample
-17.00%
Decimal places: 2
Percentage formats multiply the cell value by 100 and displays the result with a percent symbol.
OK
Cancel
Fig. 4.10

Now, copy the formula. We learned how to sort results in the previous chapter, so let's re-arrange the order in the 'Percent change' column from lowest to highest to find out which area of the department suffered the deepest cuts. Remember, Excel indicates a negative number by using brackets.

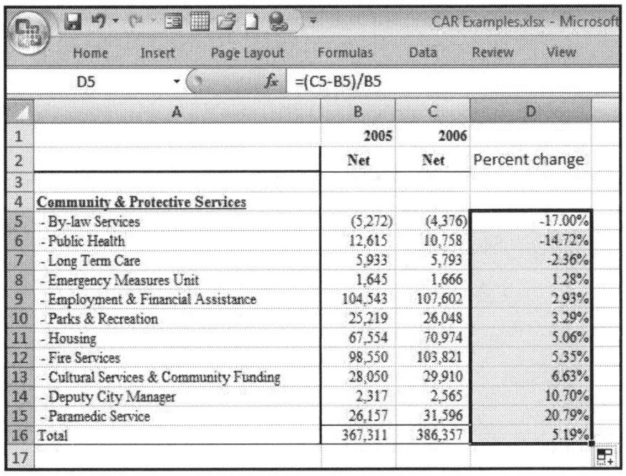

CAR Examples.xlsx - Microsoft
Home Insert Page Layout Formulas Data Review View
D5
=(C5-B5)/B5
2005 2006
Net Net Percent change
Community & Protective Services
- By-law Services (5,272) (4,376) -17.00%
- Public Health 12,615 10,758 -14.72%
- Long Term Care 5,933 5,793 -2.36%
- Emergency Measures Unit 1,645 1,666 1.28%
- Employment & Financial Assistance 104,543 107,602 2.93%
- Parks & Recreation 25,219 26,048 3.29%
- Housing 67,554 70,974 5.06%
- Fire Services 98,550 103,821 5.35%
- Cultural Services & Community Funding 28,050 29,910 6.63%
- Deputy City Manager 2,317 2,565 10.70%
- Paramedic Service 26,157 31,596 20.79%
Total 367,311 386,357 5.19%
Fig. 4.11

As you can see, the cuts were the deepest in By-Law Services. Paramedic Services received the largest increase.

Multiplying the Power of Formulas with Functions

If your formulas contained only basic operators such as the 'plus' sign, '+', for addition or the 'minus' sign, '–', for subtraction, your fingers would soon be numb from all the typing. For instance, if we wanted to add a large number of cells, you'd have to list each cell and put in plus signs. To calculate the average of the values in a number of cells, say (A1:A5), you'd have to build a formula such as this:

$$=(A1+A2+A3+A4+A5)/5$$

Not much fun, and hardly better than a calculator. Luckily, Excel has an array of 340 time-saving functions that run the gamut from simplifying operations such as these, to working out complex statistics. As journalists, we will be interested in just a few, particularly the SUM, AVERAGE, MEDIAN, MINIMUM, and MAXIMUM functions.

They are written the same way. First the '=' sign to indicate a formula, then the function name, then an open parentheses, followed by the cells to be included in the calculation, and finally a closed parentheses.

Hence, we can write such formulas as:

$$=SUM (A1:A5)$$

and

$$=AVERAGE(A1:A5)$$

Similarly, you can determine other results, such as the maximum value '=MAX(A1:A5)' in the range, or the minimum value '=MIN(A1:A5)' in the same manner.

The results of two functions can also be used within a larger formula. For example, you can write:

$$=SUM(A1:A5)-SUM(B1:B8)$$

The result of the second sum function would be subtracted from the first.

Excel even gives you help entering the functions. Say that you wanted to use the SUM function. Once you type the '=' sign and then the letter 'S', you'll see a drop-down menu shown here.

⚠ **TECH TIP**

When typing a formula using a function, the colon symbol, ':', is used to indicate all of the cells between two references. In the above example of A1:A5, the colon represents the 'range' of cells from A1 to A5, inclusive. Using a comma indicates the opposite, that the cells between the two references are not included. So '=SUM(A1,A5)' would add up only those two cells. '=SUM(A1:A5,A9:A14)' would add up everything from A1 to A5 and everything from A9 to A14, but not the cells between A5 and A9.

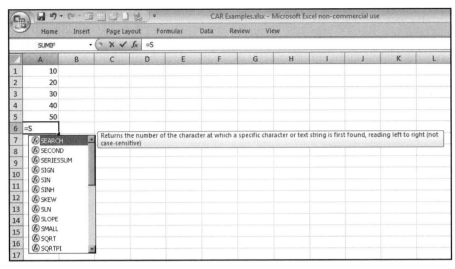

Fig. 4.12

You can see that the menu gives you a selection of functions that begin with the letter 'S'. If you type the next letter, in this case 'U', the list in the menu is shortened to match functions that contain those two letters. If you want to have Excel 'autocomplete' the entry in the list, use the arrow key to highlight the entry. Now double-click.

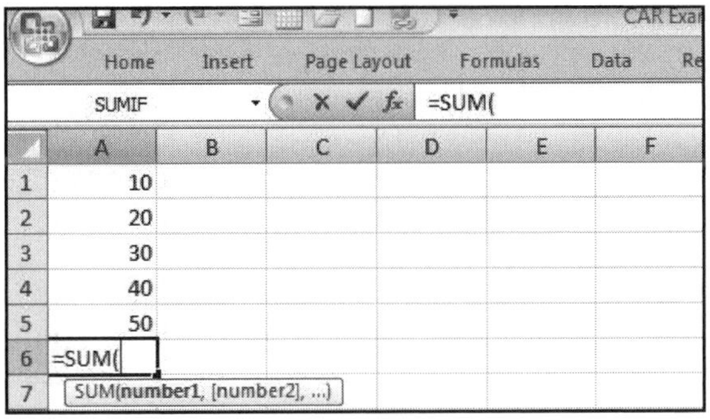

Fig. 4.13

Now you can go ahead and type the cell range 'A1:A5' between the brackets and then close the parenthesis.

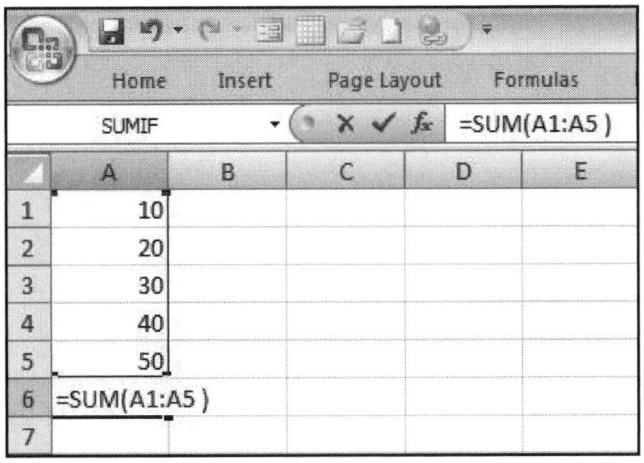

Fig. 4.14

Select the 'Enter' key. You will get an answer in the cell: '150'.

Table 4.1
Commonly Used Functions to Perform Basic Calculations

Function: **Average**
Syntax: =AVERAGE(cell address to cell address)
    Example: =AVERAGE(A1:A20)
    What it does: Calculates the average of the cell range you've identified.

Function: **Sum**
    Syntax: =SUM(cell address to cell address)
    Example: =SUM(A1:A20)

Function: **Count**
    Syntax: =COUNT(cell address to cell address)
    Example: =COUNT(A1:A20)

Function: **Median**
    Syntax: =MEDIAN(cell address to cell address)
What it does: Given that 'median' is defined as 'the middle value', that's what this function will do. In the case of the salaries table, this would give us the figure that sits in the heart of the range.

Function: **Mode**
    Syntax: =MODE(cell address to cell address)
    Example: =MODE(A1:A20)
What it does: This is the most frequent value contained in your range.

Function: **Maximum**
    Syntax: =MAX(cell address to cell address)
    Example: =MAX(A1:A20)
What it does: This allows you to pick out the largest value out of a range of variables that is unsorted.

Function: **Minimum**
    Syntax: =MIN(cell address to cell address)
    Example: =MIN(A1:A20)
What it does: Here, we have the reverse of maximum with the ability to find the smallest value.

Function: **AVERAGEIF**
    Syntax: =AVERAGEIF(RANGE, CRITERIA, OPTIONAL RANGE TO AVERAGE)
    Example (from Figure 4.29): =AVERAGEIF(C2:C19, "*Vice President*", D2:D19)

Function: **SUMIF**
    Syntax: =SUMIF(RANGE, CRITERIA, OPTIONAL RANGE TO AVERAGE)
    Example (from Figure 4.29): =SUMIF(C2:C19, "*Vice President*", D2:D19)

Function: **COUNTIF**
    Syntax: =COUNTIF(RANGE, CRITERIA)
    Example (from Figure 4.29): =COUNTIF(D1:D20, "*Vice President*")

In AVERAGEIF and SUMIF, the RANGE argument is the range of cells that will be used to set the criteria for the calculation, the CRITERIA argument sets the actual criteria, and the optional RANGE TO AVERAGE argument defines which actual numbers should be averaged. If this third argument is omitted, RANGE will be averaged. The CRITERIA can be a number, text, expression or cell reference; the text and expressions can be used in conjunction with wildcards, in this case an asterisk with the expression "Vice President", which gives us all the employees who have a "Vice President" in their job title.

    COUNTIF has only two arguments, the RANGE to count and the CRITERIA to apply. Since all you are doing is counting rows in the datasheet, no third argument is required. For more on these and other functions see the Excel help article 'List of worksheet functions (by category)'. Additional material is also posted on the companion website at www.oupcanada.com/CAR.html.

⚠ **TECH TIP**

AVERAGEIF, SUMIF, and COUNTIF can be used to find key information for your stories. For instance, in the Ontario salary disclosure data (Figure 4.29) you can use AVERAGEIF to limit your calculation to those earning a certain amount (more than $1,000,000) or to those occupying a certain position (a vice-president). The formula for the latter criterion would be <=(C2:C19, "*Vice-President*", D2:D:19.>.

Using the MAX and MIN functions, the same process can be repeated to obtain the Average of the numbers in the same range, as well as the largest or smallest value.

Excel also includes a shortcut called 'Autosum', represented by the large Greek Sigma icon. If you click in a cell below or to the right of a range of numbers, Excel will automatically pick a range to add up and propose a formula using the SUM function in the cell you chose. It will stop as soon as it finds a blank cell, but you can edit the range Excel chooses. Click 'ENTER' and the formula will add up the cells as if you had entered it yourself. You can use 'autosum' to pick several other functions as well.

Ratios

As Sarah Cohen points out in her book *Numbers in the Newsroom*: 'Most of the math we use in the newsroom revolves around ratios of some kind: A percentage, a percentage difference, a rate or a value per person. . . . So, cut most of the numbers you deal with down to size by learning to think in simple ratios. Don't try to think in terms of 1 million people. You can't picture it or write clearly about it. Instead, think in terms of 1 out of 285 people.'[6]

We examined percentages, perhaps the most common of ratios, earlier in this chapter. But other ratios you may use include rates per 1,000 or rates per million. These are often used to express the frequency with which diseases occur in a population, or with which accidents occur. In investigating infrequent highway enforcement, for example, *The Hamilton Spectator* calculated how many speeding tickets were handed out per million kilometres driven, and found rates highest on safe sections of highways, and lowest on dangerous stretches where enforcement was actually most needed.[7]

The CBC's investigative unit did similar calculations for its two series on workplace safety. Workplace safety is almost all about numbers: there are premium rates; accident rates; the number of days off the job, and so on. After obtaining databases from workers' compensation boards and ministries of labour (you can learn more about negotiating for databases in Chapter 8), it was Phil Harbord's job to study the data, and find ways to calculate numbers that would drive the stories.'By pasting the results of multiple Access queries into Excel, we were able to create simple row divisions to calculate ratios or percentages. This approach had the added advantage of enabling easy translation into graphs and pie charts. Also, Excel allowed us to colour-code and format the results much more easily than using complex Access reports.'[8]

Dying for a Job examined some of the major issues facing workers in the New Economy. Two of the main findings: that workers in the health care industrial sector were anywhere from five to 12 times more likely to file a claim for violence than workers in any other industrial sector such as those that include the police. In the follow-up series, *Out of Sync*, different data were used to demonstrate that despite these risks, workers in non-traditional industrial sectors such as health care were less likely to be inspected than workers in traditional sectors such as manufacturing or construction.

The key to comparing workers in different sectors was the use of ratios, which allowed Harbord to level the playing field. Let's take a look at a table of inspection results for British Columbia from 1994 to 2005.

BC - Traditional vs Non-Traditional Inspection Visits per 1000 Workers

Visits per 1000 workers

	Average All Years	1995	1996	1997	1998	1999	2000	2001	2002	2003	2004	2005
Visits												
Non-Traditional	56730	7684	6296	5071	4675	5611	6165	5188	4998	3746	3276	4020
Traditional	260546	38315	34730	30703	26595	28305	23641	22325	16129	11958	12058	15787
Workforce												
Non-Traditional	13255	1021.1	1045.1	1057.2	1056.2	1110.2	1125.1	1123.7	1155.4	1157.5	1193.8	1228.1
Traditional	6084.4	493.7	490.3	506.6	499.9	495.6	514.9	486.2	486.9	516.1	546	558.2
Visits per 1000 workers												
Non-Traditional	4.28	7.53	6.02	4.80	4.43	5.05	5.48	4.62	4.33	3.24	2.74	3.27
Traditional	42.82	77.61	70.83	60.61	53.20	57.11	45.91	45.92	33.13	23.17	22.08	28.28
Ratio Non-Traditional to Traditiona	0.10	0.10	0.09	0.08	0.08	0.09	0.12	0.10	0.13	0.14	0.12	0.12

Fig. 4.15

Using the labour force figures from Statistics Canada gave Harbord the denominator, a base for his calculations when comparing non-traditional sectors to traditional sectors. The inspections data came from WorksafeBC, the agency responsible for all aspects of BC's workplace safety. Harbord was able to take the total inspections for each year for traditional and non-traditional sectors and figure out the rate of inspections per thousand workers using additional workforce data obtained from Statistics Canada. In 2005, for instance, there were 3.27 inspections conducted in non-traditional sectors for every thousand workers. The result is obtained by dividing the value in M5 (the total number of inspections for that year) by the value in M8 (the total number of BC's non-traditional workers for 2005). The result, 3.27, is located in cell M11. When that figure is compared to the 28.28 (M12) visits per thousand workers for the traditional sector, it becomes evident that workers in the non-traditional sectors such as health care have far less chance of being inspected than those in the traditional sector.

Similar calculations came in handy for the *Ottawa Citizen*'s Glen McGregor for his *Rapid Fire* series, which examined some disturbing questions about gun ownership in Canada. He obtained the database that contains seven million records from the federal gun registry. One of the fields contained the postal code of the person who had registered the firearm.

But, wary of protecting privacy, the RCMP, which maintains the database at the Canadian Fire Arms Centre, refused to hand over the entire postal code, lest it be used to identify individuals. The officials compromised by releasing the first two characters of the postal code.

This database still proved to be useful because the first character indicates part or all of a province, and the second character identifies specific areas within the larger zone. For instance, the zero character in the second position represents a rural address, which then allowed him to figure out per capita ownership rates in rural areas compared to urban areas.

Better still, characters other than the zero specify *certain* urban regions. Once he had all the data for his analysis, McGregor used Excel to come up with the numbers that drove much of the six-part series. 'Excel's value for CAR projects is that it will put your data into context. It will let you see the trends, how numbers compare with other numbers. If you massage your data with Excel, you'll start to see what your stories are.'[9]

For this project he figured out the gun ownership per thousand people by dividing the number of registered guns—column E—by the population for the area identified by that postal code—column B—then multiplying by 1,000. He also used the 'INT' function to round off the number to the nearest integer.

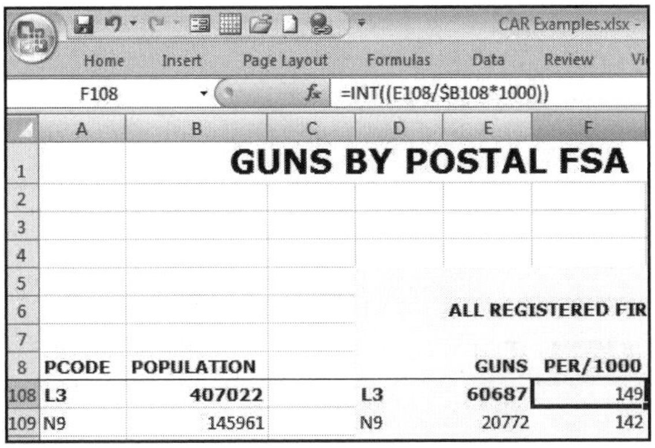

Fig. 4.16

McGregor was particularly interested in the region identified by the first two letters of the postal code: L3. In that urban area, part of the 905-region in and around the Toronto area, there were 6.7 registered guns per 1,000 residents at the time the story was published on 11 February 2007. Using a newsgroup, he was able to locate gun owner Dave Copping, and his story began like this:

> Dave Copping has a dream for his daughter.
>
> He doesn't imagine her playing hockey for Team Canada or earning a rich professional-sports contract.
>
> Instead, he hopes that seven-year-old Kenzie, who has Down's syndrome, will one day fire a gun at a bull's-eye in the Special Olympics.
>
> 'She's a bright little thing', Mr. Copping said. 'I honestly think, given the chance and the right training, she could probably do very well at it.' Although there is currently no target-shooting event in the Special Olympics, Mr. Copping thinks that could change and allow his daughter to compete in the sport he loves.
>
> Amid the manicured lawns of Newmarket, Ont., Mr. Copping's passion for guns and shooting is not as atypical as it might first appear.
>
> While the per-capita rate of gun ownership in Canada is highest in rural areas and lowest in large cities, Mr. Copping is among the vast block of suburban gun owners who fall somewhere in the middle. They are the Firearm Fathers among the Soccer Moms, the suburbanites who shoot for fun, not on the farm.
>
> In the area where Mr. Copping lives, there are 149 guns for every 1,000 people—three times the rate of nearby Toronto (50 guns per 1,000 residents), and well ahead of Montreal (85 per 1,000) and Ottawa (101 per 1,000).[10]

Ranking

Rankings or indexes are ways in which we can assign importance to our numbers based on the criteria we give them. 'Rankings cause no end of trouble in a newsroom. Whether we do them ourselves or publish those created by others, they still cause complaints,' writes Sarah Cohen. 'They are land mines in the news. Readers and sources complain that they're "just an opinion" and don't mean anything.'[11]

The dirty little secret is that these complaints are absolutely correct. The indexes, whether they measure the 'livability' of a place or the 'quality' of a school, are just opinions.'[12] In his situation, McGregor used the ranking for his own background information. The system allowed him to see that the Yukon had the highest per capita ownership of registered guns. It also allowed him to compare various urban settings.

Ranking is a function that allows you to sort the results in the order that you determine desirable. In McGregor's case, the areas with the greatest number of guns per residents received the highest rankings. The syntax for the ranking formula is as follows:

=RANK(celladdress_where_the_ranking_begins,
$Start_cell_range$:End_cell_range, the_number_
that_begins_the_ranking_begins)

- Start Range should be the cell where your data starts. Anchor the letter in the cell address with dollar signs.
- End Range should be the last cell of your data. Anchor with dollar signs.
- Order is either a 1 (the smallest value will get assigned #1) or a 0 (the largest value will get assigned a #1)[13]

McGregor used a '0' to give the largest per/1,000 value—880—a ranking of number 1, which turned out to be the Yukon. 'It's hard to do mathematical or statistical analysis on stuff that comes out of a database', says McGregor. 'But Excel's fantastic at that. If you want to do per capita calculations and rankings, like we did on this table, it's great.'[14]

If you don't want to use the 'RANK' function, there is a simpler way to go. Let's use the Ontario salary disclosure, also known as the 'sunshine list' data, as an example.

Instead of using the 'RANK' function, you can simply sort the column of interest, which in this case is the salaries in column D. Custom sorting the column from highest to lowest puts Tom Parkinson at the top, the former CEO who was forced out after questions about his use of corporate credit cards, and who earned a salary that raised eyebrows, especially given the fact that it had skyrocketed during the years he was in charge.[15]

Now we want to add a new column in which to rank the salaries. We will insert a new column A in which to place the rankings. Create a new title, 'Rank'. Type the number '1' into cell A2, and '2' into A3. Highlight both A2 and A3. Double-click on the narrow cross at the bottom right corner of cell A3 and you'll obtain sequential numbers all the way down to the bottom of the column. You'll notice that the rankings correspond to the Row numbers in the worksheet. So, you might be tempted to ask, 'Why go to all the bother of ranking?' The answer is simple. This table can be sorted in any number of ways to produced different results. The new 'Ranking' field allows you to have a permanent record of the highest salary earners, which comes in handy, particularly when you revisit the worksheet at a later date.

One thing to keep in mind is that this 'quick and dirty' method of ranking doesn't take duplicate values into consideration. While the 'RANK' function will give two duplicate numbers the same rank, then skip the next sequential number altogether, simply sorting will give two identical numbers sequential ranks.

Working with Dates

Sometimes you will need to do analysis based on dates in your data.

In the City of Ottawa budget we were able to calculate the percentage increase or decrease in spending from year to year. In WorkSafeBC's inspections database, we saw how inspections evolved during a period of several years. But it's not only during years that trends emerge.

You can also find trends by calculating the length of time between dates within a specified time period, be it months or years. For instance, in the chronology of events into the death of the Englishtown ferry worker that we examined in the last chapter, it might be helpful to know the length of time that had elapsed between Daniel LeBlanc's fatal accident and the ministry's seemingly inexplicable decision to get rid of the tractor LeBlanc was using to clear the snow before it could be examined by ministry officials investigating the mishap.

Or, the length of time between two dates could help in judging the effectiveness of inspections into restaurants, workplaces, and slaughterhouses. However, before delving into these areas, we need to have an understanding of how Excel handles numbers.

Working Out Differences between Dates

To Excel a date is just a number, starting with '1' representing 1 January 1900. If we fast-forward to our century, 15 June 2008 is simply '39614' in sequence from that '1'. This system allows Excel to calculate the number of days between two dates because it simply subtracts one number from another:

$$=(B1-A1)$$

Hours and minutes with dates are represented by decimal values.

If we wanted to calculate the number of days between 1 January 2007 (39083) and 22 January 2007 (39104), the answer would be 39104 − 39083 = 21. This formula counts every day between the two dates. To include only work days (leaving out weekends), use the NETWORKDAYS function as in this formula:

$$=NETWORKDAYS(start\_date, end\_date)$$

The formula's name derives from the calculation of the number of 'net' working days between two dates. To make it easier to visualize, let's take a look at the formula.

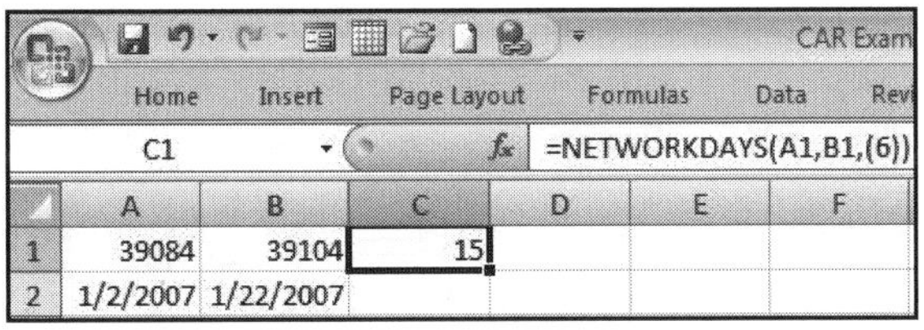

Fig. 4.17

Another useful date function to consider finds out the actual day of a particular date. This comes in handy for narrative purposes. For instance, 22 January 2007 may be one of the days in your chronology. You can quickly find out the day by using the 'WEEKDAY' function, which returns a number between 1 and 7 where each number corresponds to a day of the week, beginning with '1' for 'Sunday'. Returning to the date in our chronology, we can enter the formula '=WEEKDAY(cell_address)', which in this case is '=WEEKDAY(A1)'. Our answer is '2', which represents 'Monday', the second day of the week. You can get the same result with a little bit of formatting on cell B1.

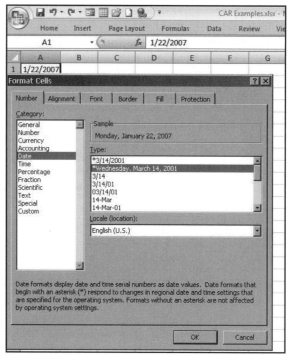

Fig. 4.18

As you can see in Figure 4.18, Excel gives you the option of displaying the day along with the date. Although this shortcut comes in handy, it's just as easy to use the 'WEEKDAY' function and, what's more, the results provide a greater variety of options when it comes to sorting and filtering the information in the table.

⚠ TECH TIP

It's important to know whether a date is formatted as a number or as text after you have imported the table from the Internet. If numbers (dates are really just numbers formatted by Excel to appear to the user as dates) are displayed on the left side of the cell that means Excel is reading them as text. If the numbers are on the right side of the cell, then it is seeing them as numeric. Date functions won't work on text entries, and if you try to sort numbers entered as text, they will sort in alphabetical order, with 10 coming before 2, with 20 before 3, and so on.

If you are entering dates into a cell, Excel recognizes a number of formats, which are listed in the Excel 'Help' system. Excel does not recognize any of the following date formats:

June 15 2007
Jun-15 2007
Jun-15/2007

Instead, it interprets these entries as text. This is why it is extremely important that you be certain that Excel recognizes your entries as dates, not text.

Summarizing Information

Pivot Tables

Pivot tables group elements in your data together and summarize information using totals and subtotals. Let's take the example of contributions to candidates who ran in the 2004 and 2006 federal elections.

The table has four columns: political_party; election_year; class_of_contribution; and monetary. We could use filters to create subsets of this table, such as contributions individuals gave to the Liberal Party in 2004. We can also filter for certain monetary values, and calculate totals and averages. But a pivot table allows you to do many of these calculations at the same time. So let's create one and walk through the steps. Go to the 'Insert' section of the ribbon and click on the 'Pivot Table' option.

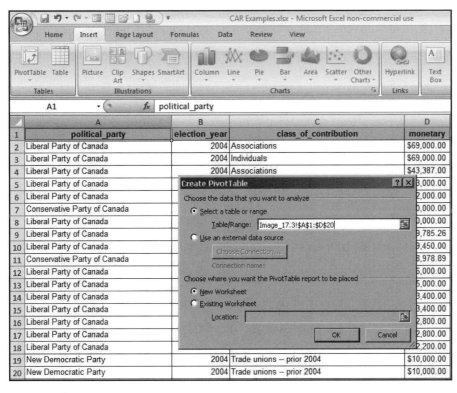

Fig. 4.19

Next, you'll get a dialogue box called Create Pivot Table. You'll notice that the table's entire range ($A$1:$D$54525) that goes beyond this illustration is highlighted. The dollar signs ($) are there simply to 'anchor' the two extreme cells—A1, and D54525—in the range. Towards the bottom of the dialogue box, you have the option of choosing to display the pivot table in a new worksheet, or the present one. We'll choose new worksheet and hit 'ENTER'.

The worksheet is divided into three sections: the Pivot Table Field List on the top, right side; the box containing the areas for the four fields, and the area on the left side for the pivot table itself. Now we're going to set up the actual layout for the pivot table by either clicking on and dragging the

TECH TIP ⚠

In older versions choose 'Pivot Table' and 'Pivot Chart Report' under the 'Data' menu to start the Pivot Table Wizard.

field names to one of the four boxes, or right-clicking on each field name and choosing one of the four boxes from the shortcut menu. Either technique is fine. So let's add the 'political party' to the 'Report Filter box; 'election year' to the 'Column Label' box; 'class of contribution' to the 'Row Labels' boxes and 'monetary' to the 'Values' box.

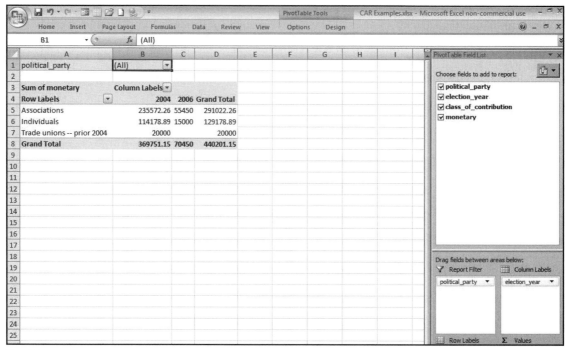

Fig. 4.20

When the field names are added to the boxes, the actual pivot table is created on the right side of the worksheet. Already, we can see how the table allows us to look at many values at once. The class of contributions such as associations and businesses are under the 'Row Labels' in Row number 4, and we'll be able to summarize the values of their contributions for the two election years 2004 and 2006: i.e., the 'Column Labels' in Columns B and C. Column D contains the Grand Total of the class of contributions for the two years. You'll find the political parties in the drop-down menu in cell B1. Right now, the pivot table is giving us the results for all the parties. Filtering for each party will give us different summaries.

From what's in the pivot table so far, you can already see the advantages. The table has calculated the total contributions received by all parties for both federal elections. To do this using the regular table would have taken us many steps.

Now, let's say we want the totals for the Liberals. No problem. Just click on the arrow on the left side of column B1.

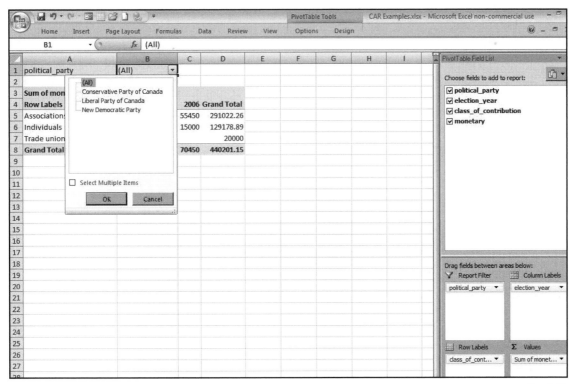

Fig. 4.21

Choose 'Liberal Party of Canada'. Select 'OK'.

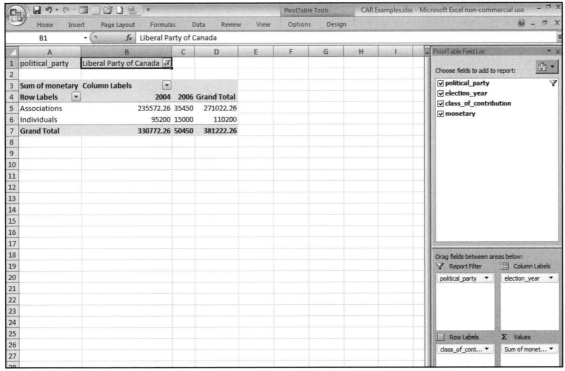

Fig. 4.22

The totals have been adjusted for the Liberals, allowing us to compare different contributions from one year to the next. But because it's a pivot table (the term 'pivot' means that you can literally rotate your table to examine it from different perspectives), we can look at the data from a different perspective: that of a certain class of donor. In order to choose our donor, click on the icon to the right of cell A4. De-select the categories by double-clicking on the box to the left of the 'Select All' option. Once all those boxes are devoid of check marks, choose the one you want, say, 'Individuals'.

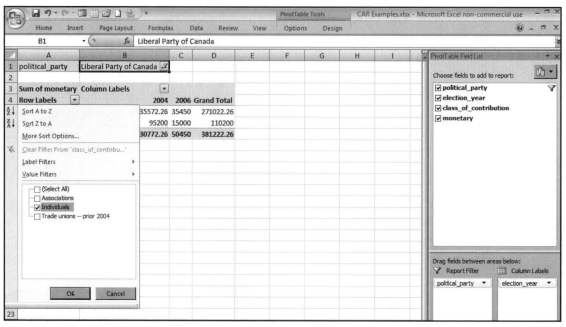

Fig. 4.23

Select, 'OK'. Now we have a table that filters for the individual donations to the Liberals and adds them up for 2004 and 2006. To convert the numbers to currency, select all the values in B5, C5, D5, B6, C6, and D6, right-click on any cell in the selected range and choose 'Format Cells' from the shortcut menu. Then select the 'Currency' option from the dialogue box.

Select 'OK', and readjust the size of the columns to get rid of the hash marks (###) and to make room for extra dollar-sign characters.

The pivot table also allows us to perform calculations on the values, using functions such as 'Average' and 'Max'.

Subtotals

Excel can also calculate subtotals within columns of numbers. For example, if you're studying campaign contributions and want to find out how much money each party received in a given year from a given constituency, you can use the subtotals feature to get your answer. You must first sort your worksheet because Excel inserts the subtotals whenever a value in a specified field changes.

Let's take campaign contributions the political parties received in British Columbia during the 2006 election. Because we want to insert the subtotals at the bottom of each grouping of political parties, we'll have to sort Column A in alphabetical order.

We're ready to begin. On the 'Data' ribbon, you'll find the 'Subtotal' option in the 'Outline' section. Clicking on 'Subtotal' brings up a dialogue box.

The Subtotal dialog box offers the following choices:

- **At each change in:** This drop-down table displays all the fields in the table. In this case six: the ID; Political Party; Class of Contribution; Monetary; Election Year; and Province.
- **Use function:** 'Sum' is the default, but you can choose from 11 functions.
- **Add subtotal to:** This also shows all the fields or columns in the table. You have the option of placing a check mark beside the field or fields that you want to subtotal.
- **Replace current subtotals:** By un-checking the box you can remove any subtotals that may have been present before.
- **Page break between groups:** It allows you to select whether Excel puts a line between each group for which the subtotals are produced.
- **Summary below data:** By default, Excel places subtotals in the column that contains the data on which the calculation was performed. If the box is checked, then Excel places the subtotals above the data.
- **'Remove all' tab:** If you want to start over, or have made mistakes, clicking on this button allows you to remove all the subtotal formulas.[16]

In this example, we want Excel to calculate the subtotals for each political party, and place the corresponding results in the 'Monetary' field. In the 'At each change in' box, choose 'Political Party'; since we want to add the totals, select the 'SUM' function in the 'Use function' box; in the 'Add subtotal to', select the 'Monetary' field because that's where you want the results to appear; and, finally, activate the 'Page break between groups' option. Make sure your choices are correct.

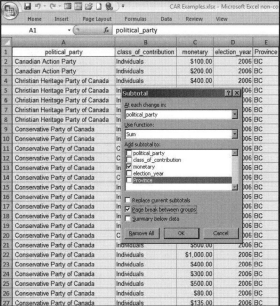

Fig. 4.24

Select 'OK'. You can see that Excel has created a new label in the 'Political Party' field that indicates the 'Grand Total'. The actual figure is located in the 'Monetary' field. Scrolling down the worksheet will give you the results of the Liberals, New Democrats, the Greens, and others.

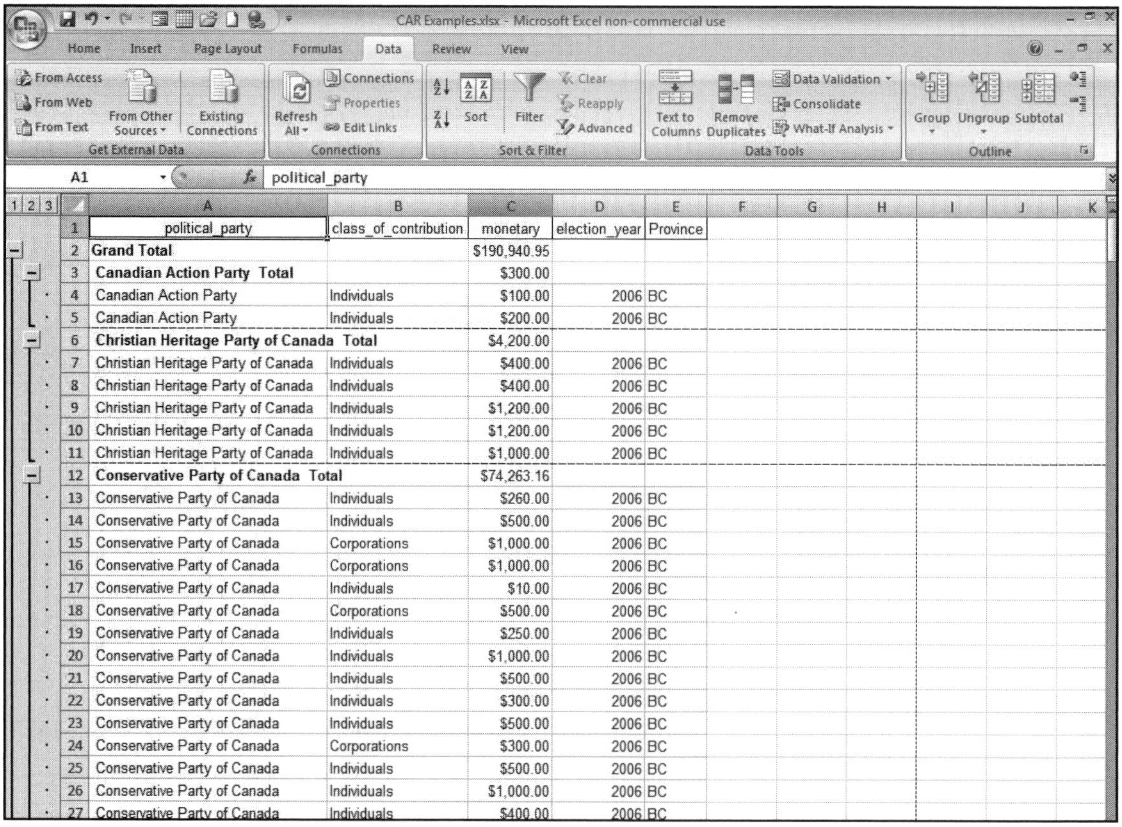

	A	B	C	D	E
1	political_party	class_of_contribution	monetary	election_year	Province
2	**Grand Total**		$190,940.95		
3	**Canadian Action Party Total**		$300.00		
4	Canadian Action Party	Individuals	$100.00	2006	BC
5	Canadian Action Party	Individuals	$200.00	2006	BC
6	**Christian Heritage Party of Canada Total**		$4,200.00		
7	Christian Heritage Party of Canada	Individuals	$400.00	2006	BC
8	Christian Heritage Party of Canada	Individuals	$400.00	2006	BC
9	Christian Heritage Party of Canada	Individuals	$1,200.00	2006	BC
10	Christian Heritage Party of Canada	Individuals	$1,200.00	2006	BC
11	Christian Heritage Party of Canada	Individuals	$1,000.00	2006	BC
12	**Conservative Party of Canada Total**		$74,263.16		
13	Conservative Party of Canada	Individuals	$260.00	2006	BC
14	Conservative Party of Canada	Individuals	$500.00	2006	BC
15	Conservative Party of Canada	Corporations	$1,000.00	2006	BC
16	Conservative Party of Canada	Corporations	$1,000.00	2006	BC
17	Conservative Party of Canada	Individuals	$10.00	2006	BC
18	Conservative Party of Canada	Corporations	$500.00	2006	BC
19	Conservative Party of Canada	Individuals	$250.00	2006	BC
20	Conservative Party of Canada	Individuals	$1,000.00	2006	BC
21	Conservative Party of Canada	Individuals	$500.00	2006	BC
22	Conservative Party of Canada	Individuals	$300.00	2006	BC
23	Conservative Party of Canada	Individuals	$500.00	2006	BC
24	Conservative Party of Canada	Corporations	$300.00	2006	BC
25	Conservative Party of Canada	Individuals	$500.00	2006	BC
26	Conservative Party of Canada	Individuals	$1,000.00	2006	BC
27	Conservative Party of Canada	Individuals	$400.00	2006	BC

Fig. 4.25

At the very top of the 'Monetary' column is the total of all the contributions. Right under that total is the figure for the Canadian Action Party. The totals for each political party are located at the top of each section Excel has used the lines to delineate. You can collapse the sheet and show just the subtotals or just the grand total by clicking on the small 2 or 1 on the left side of the sheet. Clicking 3 restores the normal view.

If you prefer a summary format, you can use a pivot table to produce subtotals. Choosing 'Pivot Table' will take you to a new worksheet.

As was the case in the 'Subtotal' dialogue box, the 'Pivot Table Field List' box on the right side of the worksheet lists all the field names. We want to group by 'Political Party'. To make this easier, click and drag the field names into the 'Row Labels' box in the 'Pivot Table Field List'. 'Political_party' is to become the column label, so place that field in the 'Column Label' box. 'Class_of_contribution' goes in the 'Row Labels' box. And, finally, we want to sum the values, so drag the 'Monetary' field into the 'Values' box. To ensure we have the proper calculation, click the arrow at the top right side of the 'Values' box. From the drop-down menu, choose the 'Value Field Settings' option. From the dialogue box, choose 'SUM'.

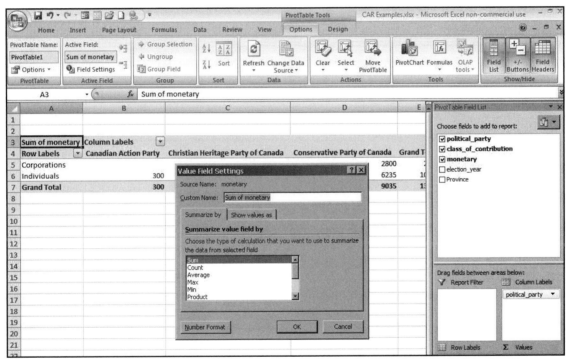

Fig. 4.26

The pivot table uses the 'General' number formatting. But in order to perform our calculations, we need to shift over to the table on the left and reformat the values as 'Currency' by selecting the range of cells that contain the values each party received from corporations and individuals, right-clicking on any cell within that range to obtain the shortcut menu, choosing the 'Format Cells' option, and then 'Currency'. We don't want any decimal places.

Select 'OK'. To hide the Pivot Table Field List on the right, click anywhere within the pivot table on the left, or click the 'X' on the top right corner of the 'Pivot Table Field List' box.

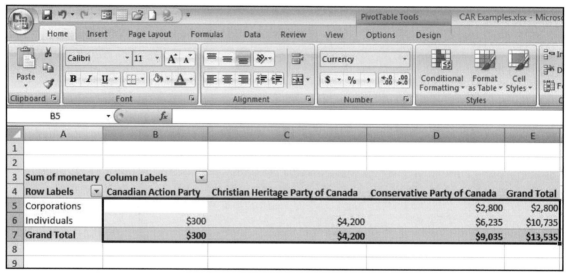

Fig. 4.27

The presentation is different, but the results are similar to our subtotal calculations earlier in the chapter. Row 7 contains the Grand Total for each party. But, as an added bonus, there are also totals for donations by individuals and corporations. The last column—Grand Total—gives us the totals for the contributions corporations and individuals made to each party, as well as the final sum of all the contributions to all parties. Because the pivot table allows you to use filters to look at a myriad of combinations (corporate donations to the Liberals and Conservatives; individual donations to both parties, etc.), you may find it a better option than simply doing the subtotals in the same worksheet. Once you have the combinations that you like, you can copy and paste them into a separate worksheet.

Working with Strings and Text

Concatenation

Importing data from the Internet can be messy. Values and text that you may have preferred to remain together may be located in separate fields, making it to difficult to sort and filter. One way to solve this problem is to join contents of certain fields. Excel uses the ampersand (&) as its concatenation operator. Concatenation is another way of describing the process in which you combine the contents of two or more cells. Again, let's use the Ontario salary disclosure table.

	A	B	C	D
				CAR Examples.xlsx - Microsoft Excel non-commercial use
		A1	*fx*	Surname
	Surname	Given Name	Position	Salary Paid
1	Surname	Given Name	Position	Salary Paid
2	PARKINSON	TOM	President/Chief Executive Officer	$1,560,900.85
3	HANKINSON	JAMES F	President & Chief Executive Officer	$1,480,804.01
4	CHARLEBOIS	PIERRE R	Executive Vice President & Chief Operating Officer	$1,015,540.32
5	DICERNI	RICHARD	Executive Vice President, Corporate Secretary	$923,499.96
6	ROBINSON	WILLIAM	Senior Vice President, Nuclear Programs & Training	$901,634.48
7	SMITH	GREGORY	Senior Vice President, Nuclear Generation Development & Services	$897,316.96
8	TWOMEY	JAMES	Executive Vice President, Fossil	$776,029.44
9	MURPHY	JOHN D	Executive Vice President, Hydro	$733,116.24
10	MITCHELL	THOMAS	Chief Nuclear Officer	$707,647.84
11	BURPEE	JAMES R	Executive Vice President, Corporate Development	$609,972.56
12	HANBIDGE	DONN W	Senior Vice President & Chief Financial Officer	$581,603.35
13	COLEBY	JOHN	Senior Vice President, Pickering A	$555,559.92
14	BOLAND	BRUCE	Senior Vice President, Corporate Affairs	$505,603.28
15	LONG	FREDERICK	Vice President, Financial Planning Corporate Finance	$496,738.52
16	SUMMERS	BETH	Chief Financial Officer	$474,166.14
17	D'ARCEY	MYLES	Senior Vice President, Customer Operations	$471,016.50
18	GOLDIE	TOM	Senior Vice President, Corporate Services	$467,990.40
19	FORMUSA	LAURA	General Counsel And Secretary	$462,272.60

Fig. 4.28

The names of the employees are located in separate fields. Let's say that you wanted to combine the names located in columns A and B into a new column. Our first step is to insert a new column, which will become C. To insert the new column, highlight column D, double-click on the mouse and choose the option 'Insert' from the shortcut menu. Excel inserts new columns to the left. Call the column 'New Name'.

Activate the second cell in column C (C2). Excel uses an ampersand (&) as its concatenation operator. As is always the case with formulas, you begin with an equal sign to signal to Excel that you are about to perform a calculation. What we want to do is join or concatenate the contents of columns A and B in column C. Press 'Enter' and adjust the size of the column so the 'Whole' text string appears.

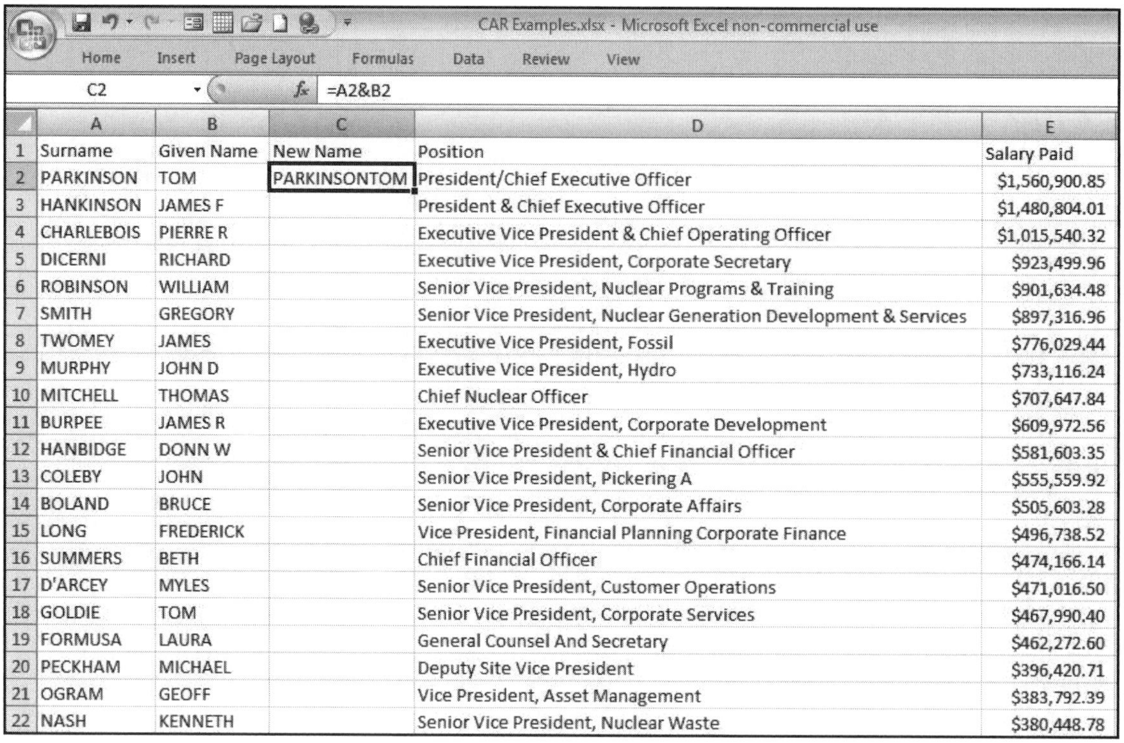

	A	B	C	D	E
	C2	▾	*fx* =A2&B2		
1	Surname	Given Name	New Name	Position	Salary Paid
2	PARKINSON	TOM	PARKINSONTOM	President/Chief Executive Officer	$1,560,900.85
3	HANKINSON	JAMES F		President & Chief Executive Officer	$1,480,804.01
4	CHARLEBOIS	PIERRE R		Executive Vice President & Chief Operating Officer	$1,015,540.32
5	DICERNI	RICHARD		Executive Vice President, Corporate Secretary	$923,499.96
6	ROBINSON	WILLIAM		Senior Vice President, Nuclear Programs & Training	$901,634.48
7	SMITH	GREGORY		Senior Vice President, Nuclear Generation Development & Services	$897,316.96
8	TWOMEY	JAMES		Executive Vice President, Fossil	$776,029.44
9	MURPHY	JOHN D		Executive Vice President, Hydro	$733,116.24
10	MITCHELL	THOMAS		Chief Nuclear Officer	$707,647.84
11	BURPEE	JAMES R		Executive Vice President, Corporate Development	$609,972.56
12	HANBIDGE	DONN W		Senior Vice President & Chief Financial Officer	$581,603.35
13	COLEBY	JOHN		Senior Vice President, Pickering A	$555,559.92
14	BOLAND	BRUCE		Senior Vice President, Corporate Affairs	$505,603.28
15	LONG	FREDERICK		Vice President, Financial Planning Corporate Finance	$496,738.52
16	SUMMERS	BETH		Chief Financial Officer	$474,166.14
17	D'ARCEY	MYLES		Senior Vice President, Customer Operations	$471,016.50
18	GOLDIE	TOM		Senior Vice President, Corporate Services	$467,990.40
19	FORMUSA	LAURA		General Counsel And Secretary	$462,272.60
20	PECKHAM	MICHAEL		Deputy Site Vice President	$396,420.71
21	OGRAM	GEOFF		Vice President, Asset Management	$383,792.39
22	NASH	KENNETH		Senior Vice President, Nuclear Waste	$380,448.78

Fig. 4.29

Double-click on the small solid square at the bottom of C2 in order to repeat the formula for the remaining cells in the column, and then re-adjust the column's width once again.

But we can see a slight problem: there is no space between the first and last names, making the content virtually impossible to decipher. To fix it, all we have to do is tell Excel to insert a space. Whenever a piece of text or value is inserted using a formula, Excel requires that it be placed between quotation marks. In this case, our character is a space, which is placed inside quotation marks: " ". Now, we must insert this new criterion into the formula, which now becomes:

$$=A2\&\ "\ "\ \&B2.$$

With this syntax, we are saying, 'Take cell A2, add it to cell B2, and then use a space—located between the set of double quotation marks—to separate the two bits of text.' We have re-activated cell C2 and amended the formula in the Formula Bar.

There is now a space between 'Parkinson' and 'Tom'. However, before we copy the formula for the entire column, we need to insert a coma between the last and first name to make it even easier to read. As was the case with the space character, we have to place a comma and a space between two quotation marks, resulting in this formula:

	A	B	C	D	E
1	Surname	Given Name	New Name	Position	Salary Paid
2	PARKINSON	TOM	PARKINSON , TOM	President/Chief Executive Officer	$1,560,900.85
3	HANKINSON	JAMES F	HANKINSON , JAMES F	President & Chief Executive Officer	$1,480,804.01
4	CHARLEBOIS	PIERRE R	CHARLEBOIS , PIERRE R	Executive Vice President & Chief Operating Officer	$1,015,540.32
5	DICERNI	RICHARD	DICERNI , RICHARD	Executive Vice President, Corporate Secretary	$923,499.96
6	ROBINSON	WILLIAM	ROBINSON , WILLIAM	Senior Vice President, Nuclear Programs & Training	$901,634.48
7	SMITH	GREGORY	SMITH , GREGORY	Senior Vice President, Nuclear Generation Development & Services	$897,316.96
8	TWOMEY	JAMES	TWOMEY , JAMES	Executive Vice President, Fossil	$776,029.44
9	MURPHY	JOHN D	MURPHY , JOHN D	Executive Vice President, Hydro	$733,116.24
10	MITCHELL	THOMAS	MITCHELL , THOMAS	Chief Nuclear Officer	$707,647.84
11	BURPEE	JAMES R	BURPEE , JAMES R	Executive Vice President, Corporate Development	$609,972.56
12	HANBIDGE	DONN W	HANBIDGE , DONN W	Senior Vice President & Chief Financial Officer	$581,603.35
13	COLEBY	JOHN	COLEBY , JOHN	Senior Vice President, Pickering A	$555,559.92
14	BOLAND	BRUCE	BOLAND , BRUCE	Senior Vice President, Corporate Affairs	$505,603.28
15	LONG	FREDERICK	LONG , FREDERICK	Vice President, Financial Planning Corporate Finance	$496,738.52
16	SUMMERS	BETH	SUMMERS , BETH	Chief Financial Officer	$474,166.14
17	D'ARCEY	MYLES	D'ARCEY , MYLES	Senior Vice President, Customer Operations	$471,016.50
18	GOLDIE	TOM	GOLDIE , TOM	Senior Vice President, Corporate Services	$467,990.40
19	FORMUSA	LAURA	FORMUSA , LAURA	General Counsel And Secretary	$462,272.60
20	PECKHAM	MICHAEL	PECKHAM , MICHAEL	Deputy Site Vice President	$396,420.71
21	OGRAM	GEOFF	OGRAM , GEOFF	Vice President, Asset Management	$383,792.39
22	NASH	KENNETH	NASH , KENNETH	Senior Vice President, Nuclear Waste	$380,448.78

Fig. 4.30

Press 'Enter'. That's better. Now that we're happy with the results, let's once again repeat the formula for the rest of the column. We have retained the order of the names, allowing us to sort the new column alphabetically in order to locate a specific individual.

Splitting Text Fields Using the Wizard

The opposite of joining cells is splitting them. Although there are many functions for manipulating fields with text and numbers, journalists just beginning to use Excel can, and should, use some of the program's built-in routines to do the job. Tables, whether they've been downloaded from the Internet or e-mailed as an attachment or burned onto a CD, may not come in a form suitable for the kind of analysis you want to do. For instance, you might receive a table that contains fields with too much information that makes it virtually impossible to filter and sort in any meaningful way. Sorting and filtering is best done when there is one piece of information—an annual salary figure, a date, a first name, a last name, etc.—in a field. To illustrate this point, let's examine the contributions data from Elections Canada.

	A	B	C	D
1	Name of contributor	Name of candidate/ Political party/ Electoral district	Date received	Class of contributor/ Pa
2	105361 Alberta Ltd.	Kenney, Jason / Conservative Party of Canada / Calgary Southeast	Jan. 14, 2006	Corporations / Part 2b
3	1054578 ALBERTA LTD	McLellan, Anne / Liberal Party of Canada / Edmonton Centre	Dec. 11, 2005	Corporations / Part 2b
4	107302 Alberta LTD (R.A.J. Saunder)	Rajotte, James / Conservative Party of Canada / Edmonton--Leduc	Jan. 20, 2006	Corporations / Part 2b
5	1093097 Alberta Ltd (Sammy Sahota)	Hanger, Art / Conservative Party of Canada / Calgary Northeast	Jan. 12, 2006	Corporations / Part 2b
6	1126688 AB LTD President-Robert Yeung	Hawn, Laurie / Conservative Party of Canada / Edmonton Centre	Jan. 16, 2006	Corporations / Part 2b
7	1136802 ALBERTA LTD. (CRAIG HUTTON)	Storseth, Brian / Conservative Party of Canada / Westlock--St. Paul	Jan. 4, 2006	Corporations / Part 2b
8	1188964 Alberta Ltd. (Niel Peacock)	Thompson, Susan / New Democratic Party / Peace River	Jan. 3, 2006	Corporations / Part 2b
9	2030617 Ontario Limited (Dipak Roy)	Obhrai, Deepak / Conservative Party of Canada / Calgary East	Jan. 21, 2006	Corporations / Part 2b
10	217770 Holdings Ltd. (Robert Rycroft)	Given, Bill / Independent / Peace River	Dec. 28, 2005	Corporations / Part 2b
11	217770 Holdings Ltd. (Robert Rycroft)	Given, Bill / Independent / Peace River	Jan. 1, 2006	Corporations / Part 2b
12	313894 Alberta Ltd (Frank Biegel)	Warkentin, Chris / Conservative Party of Canada / Peace River	Jan. 9, 2006	Corporations / Part 2b
13	35BB Holdings Ltd.	Obhrai, Deepak / Conservative Party of Canada / Calgary East	Jan. 23, 2006	Corporations / Part 2b
14	389502 Alberta Ltd. (William Choy)	Ambrose, Rona / Conservative Party of Canada / Edmonton--Spruce Grove	Jan. 9, 2006	Corporations / Part 2b
15	410141 Alberta Ltd. (Papu Sidhu)	Hanger, Art / Conservative Party of Canada / Calgary Northeast	Dec. 23, 2005	Corporations / Part 2b
16	499503 Alberta Ltd. (Dennis Tink)	Given, Bill / Independent / Peace River	Dec. 12, 2005	Corporations / Part 2b
17	519176 Alberta Ltd. (Doug King)	Benoit, Leon / Conservative Party of Canada / Vegreville--Wainwright	Jan. 4, 2006	Corporations / Part 2b
18	564609 Alberta Ltd (Joe Knoblach)	Warkentin, Chris / Conservative Party of Canada / Peace River	Jan. 12, 2006	Corporations / Part 2b
19	593605 Alberta Ltd Alex McDonald)	Warkentin, Chris / Conservative Party of Canada / Peace River	Dec. 13, 2005	Corporations / Part 2b
20	619658 Alberta lltd (Rod Dueck)	Warkentin, Chris / Conservative Party of Canada / Peace River	Dec. 30, 2005	Corporations / Part 2b
21	67 STREET LIQUOR STORE	Mills, Bob / Conservative Party of Canada / Red Deer	Jan. 23, 2006	Corporations / Part 2b
22	693702 AB INC president-David Starko	Hawn, Laurie / Conservative Party of Canada / Edmonton Centre	Jan. 22, 2006	Corporations / Part 2b

Fig. 4.31

As you can see, there's too much information in column B: 'Name of candidate'; 'Political party'; 'Electoral district'.' We need to put the 'Name of candidate,' 'Political party', and 'Electoral district', into separate columns. Doing so gives us more options for filtering and sorting. Because this is so easy to accomplish using Excel's 'Text To Columns' option, there's really no need to use any other method. Before using that command, we have to take one important step. Since we're going to be creating two new fields for 'Political party', and 'Electoral district' we need to insert two new columns to the right. So, highlight column C, 'Date', and insert two new columns. Remember that Excel inserts new columns to the left. We now have two blank columns with which to work.

Scroll to the left to find column B and highlight it. Next, go to the 'Data' section on the ribbon, choose the 'Data Tools' tab, and select the 'Text to Columns' option.

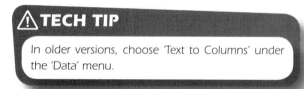

⚠ TECH TIP

In older versions, choose 'Text to Columns' under the 'Data' menu.

Clicking on the 'Text to Columns' icon will give you a series of dialogue boxes that walk you through the process. The first dialogue box asks you to select either the 'Delimited' or 'Fixed Width' options. From our discussion in the previous chapter, we already know that we're dealing with a delimited file: that is a file, whose columns of information are delimited—separated—by a character of some kind, in this case a forward slash: '/'. Generally speaking, you want to choose the 'Delimited' option. Select 'Next'.

In this case, the delimiter is not a 'Tab' or 'Semicolon', but a forward slash or division operator. That option is not on the list. So we have to select 'Other', and type the slash, '/', into the box to the right. Don't worry about the 'Text' qualifier. Select 'Next' and 'Finish', then resize the new cells, C and D. The table is in much better shape for analyzing and you were able to whip it into shape in a few easy steps.

You can also use string functions, including LEFT and RIGHT to split a text field. For example, if you needed to slice the postal code off an address and place it in its own field, you could use the RIGHT function to extract just the seven characters at the right end of the string (the first three characters of the code, the space in the middle, and the last three). After inserting a new column, the formula would be:

$$=RIGHT(cellreference,7)$$

The numeral '7' tells Excel to extract seven letters, starting from the far right end of the cell you referenced. Like other formulas, this one can be copied and pasted into other cells to extract an entire column of postal codes.

We'll deal in detail with string functions when we discuss Microsoft Access in Chapter 6. Look in the Excel 'Help' file for more details on how to use them in a spreadsheet worksheet.

Cleaning with the TRIM Function

With an increasing number of websites containing data that can be downloaded, it helps to know a little bit about cleaning; without proper cleaning, accurate analysis is impossible. So, it's worth the effort. The phrase with which you will become familiar the deeper you get into computer-assisted reporting is 'All data is dirty.' And this is often true for data that you pull off a website maintained by federal institutions, including Elections Canada or Health Canada. The 'dirt' refers to the fact that the text and values in the tables may be incomplete. Names may be misspelled, cells may be empty because the information was late in coming or never got filled in, and values may be placed in incorrect cells. The cells may also have extra spaces in them, which can cause problems when you want to filter, sort, or perform calculations. Let's take an Elections Canada table as an example.

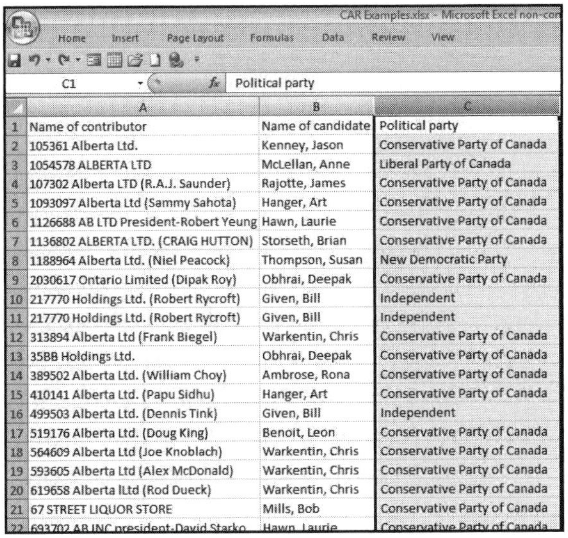

Fig. 4.32

In column C you will notice a space on the left before the names of each political party. Excel will sort anything with a blank leading character before any other entry, no matter what letter follows the blank, therefore, it's best to get rid of the space. To perform this task, Excel uses the 'TRIM' function, which looks like this:

$$=TRIM(celladdress)$$

Let's create a new column for political parties, and then type '=TRIM(celladdress)' into the first cell in the new column. Hit 'Enter'. You can see that the space before the Conservative Party of Canada is now gone. Repeat the 'TRIM' function for the rest of the column.

Rename the new column and you've solved your problem with extra characters. But before we can work with the new party names in the column that we're calling 'New Political_Party' there is one problem we have to solve. The new column is storing the formula that has created the cleaned-up name—not the actual name itself.

In order to work with the text inside the cells in the 'New Political Party' column, you must get rid of the formula and replace it with the actual values in the column. To do this we will use a feature called 'Paste Special'.

Select the column, then copy it. One way to copy is to use the keyboard combination Ctrl + C. Now right-click to get a context-sensitive menu, and choose 'Paste Special'.

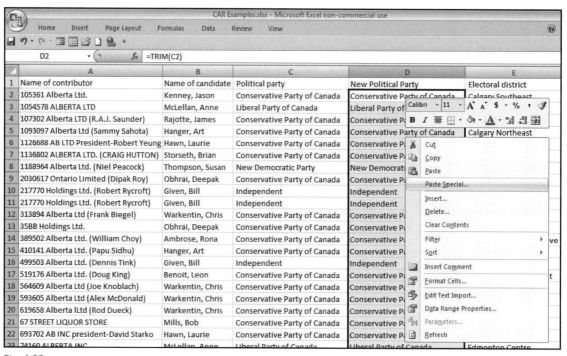

Fig. 4.33

In the dialogue box, select 'Values' in the 'Paste' section. This will cause Excel to paste the actual values into the column in place of the formulas. You can paste onto the same column, thereby replacing the formulas with values.

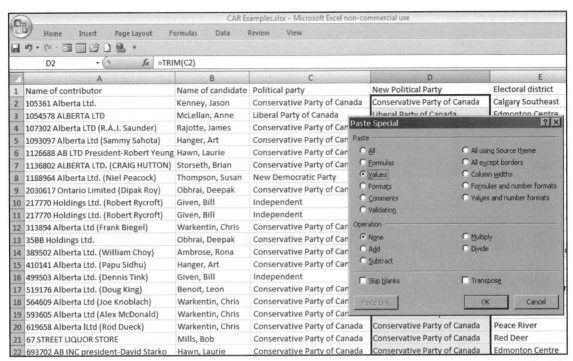

Fig. 4.34

Select 'OK'. Notice when you activate cell D2 you see an actual name—Conservative Party of Canada—in the formula bar rather than the formula '=TRIM(C2)' as was the case in Image 4.28. You can now delete column C that contains the untrimmed names.

Cleaning

The 'CLEAN' function is another handy tool. Not only do columns of data from the Internet often have leading and trailing spaces, but they can have a number of unprintable characters that can play havoc with formulas. 'CLEAN' removes all the non-printing characters or 'garbage' characters that can appear when importing certain kinds of data. The syntax is the same as with 'TRIM':

=CLEAN(range of cells)

Find and Replace

We can also do quite a bit of cleaning without using functions. A handy method is the 'Find and Replace' feature, which works exactly as it does in a word processor. For example, we can use this option to clean up a column of dollar amounts formatted as text with commas. In order to use functions or to do any calculations, these numbers must be reformatted as currency. But Excel won't let us do that until we get rid of the commas. Let's use 'Find and Replace'. You can get to it either by going to the 'Home' ribbon and

TECH TIP

'Paste Special' is versatile indeed. You can use it to make many routine changes to your data. You can select and copy a worksheet and, using the 'Transpose' option in the 'Paste Special' dialogue box, swap the rows and columns. If you have a column of 'numbers' that are actually text, you can often convert it to actual numbers by first placing the number '1' in an empty cell, and selecting and copying it, then highlighting the column of text-format numbers and choosing 'Multiply' from the paste special dialogue box.

TECH TIP

In older versions, you will find 'Replace' under the 'Edit' menu.

then to the 'Find Select' option in the 'Editing' tab at the far right side or by selecting a cell and use the Ctrl + f key combination.

We want to 'find' the comma and 'replace' it with nothing. Beside the 'Find What' option, we'll put a comma. Then select the 'Replace' tab, to make the 'Replace With' portion of the dialogue box appear. We want to get rid of the comma by placing it with nothing. So, do not put anything in the bar next to 'Replace With'. Leave it empty. Select the 'Replace' tab at the bottom left side of the dialogue box just once to make sure that we're doing it correctly.

We're on the right track. Once the comma disappears from the original number, then Excel can reformat the value as currency. Now, you're free to select the 'Replace All' tab. Success! You'll notice all the numbers are justified to the right, meaning that Excel considers them numbers that can be reformatted as currency.

Making Logical Comparisons with the 'IF' Statement

An 'IF' statement is a bit of logic stolen from the world of computer programming. A basic 'IF' statement consists of three arguments, as they are known.

1. What we're going to measure as being true or false
2. What to do if it's true
3. What to do if it's false.[17]

The simplest way to write the formula is: =A1<A2. We're using the logical comparison operator '<' This instructs Excel to return 'TRUE' if the value in cell A1 is less than the value in cell A2. Otherwise, it returns 'FALSE'. This is a useful function if you want to identify key records in your table. Let's take another look at the federal elections contributions.

The table lists candidates for the 2004 and 2006 federal elections in alphabetical order, and the campaign donations they received during those two contests. What if we wanted to determine which candidates raised more money in 2006 compared to 2004? Doing it manually is an option, but keep in mind this is a screenshot of a table that contains thousands of rows of information. Using an 'IF' statement allows you to perform the task in seconds. Here's how it works.

The columns of interest are C and D. What we actually want to determine is this: if the value in column C (2004) is less than the value in column D, then return a 'TRUE'; if the value in column C is greater than the value in column D then return a 'FALSE'. Let's put this formula in column E:

$$=C2<D2$$

and press 'Enter'.

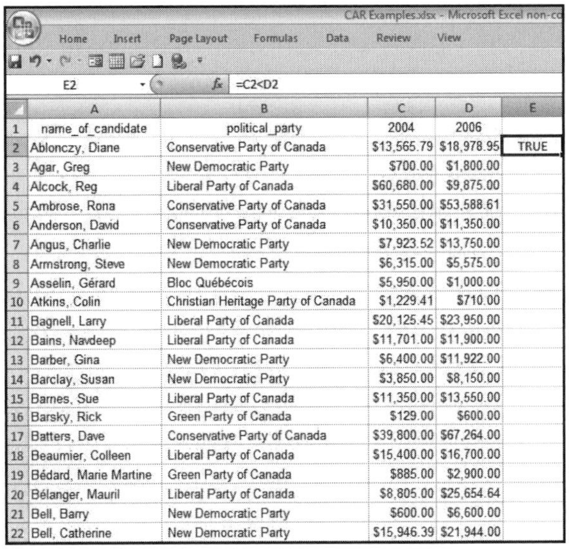

	A	B	C	D	E
1	name_of_candidate	political_party	2004	2006	
2	Ablonczy, Diane	Conservative Party of Canada	$13,565.79	$18,978.95	TRUE
3	Agar, Greg	New Democratic Party	$700.00	$1,800.00	
4	Alcock, Reg	Liberal Party of Canada	$60,680.00	$9,875.00	
5	Ambrose, Rona	Conservative Party of Canada	$31,550.00	$53,588.61	
6	Anderson, David	Conservative Party of Canada	$10,350.00	$11,350.00	
7	Angus, Charlie	New Democratic Party	$7,923.52	$13,750.00	
8	Armstrong, Steve	New Democratic Party	$6,315.00	$5,575.00	
9	Asselin, Gérard	Bloc Québécois	$5,950.00	$1,000.00	
10	Atkins, Colin	Christian Heritage Party of Canada	$1,229.41	$710.00	
11	Bagnell, Larry	Liberal Party of Canada	$20,125.45	$23,950.00	
12	Bains, Navdeep	Liberal Party of Canada	$11,701.00	$11,900.00	
13	Barber, Gina	New Democratic Party	$6,400.00	$11,922.00	
14	Barclay, Susan	New Democratic Party	$3,850.00	$8,150.00	
15	Barnes, Sue	Liberal Party of Canada	$11,350.00	$13,550.00	
16	Barsky, Rick	Green Party of Canada	$129.00	$600.00	
17	Batters, Dave	Conservative Party of Canada	$39,800.00	$67,264.00	
18	Beaumier, Colleen	Liberal Party of Canada	$15,400.00	$16,700.00	
19	Bédard, Marie Martine	Green Party of Canada	$885.00	$2,900.00	
20	Bélanger, Mauril	Liberal Party of Canada	$8,805.00	$25,654.64	
21	Bell, Barry	New Democratic Party	$600.00	$6,600.00	
22	Bell, Catherine	New Democratic Party	$15,946.39	$21,944.00	

Fig. 4.35

Now, repeat the formula for the entire column. We have identified all the candidates (TRUE) who have raised less money in 2004 compared to 2006. Or, put a different way, 'TRUE' identifies those candidates who managed to increase their corporate donations in 2006. But what if we wanted to substitute different words for 'TRUE' and 'FALSE'? For instance, 'YES' if the candidate raised more money in 2006 and 'NO' if the case was the opposite. To do this, we would introduce the word 'IF' to the formula, using the syntax: '=IF(criteria, "yes","no")'. In other words, if the value in column C is less than the value in column D, then return a 'YES', if it's the opposite return a 'NO'. You can see that the comma separates the argument and each argument—YES and NO—is enclosed in double quotation marks. Let's use our formula in column F.

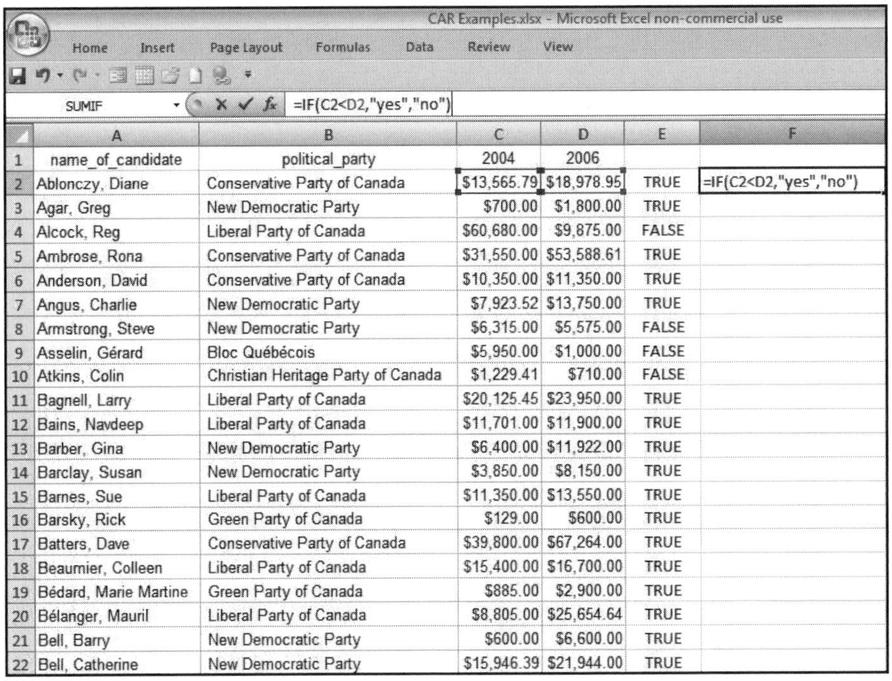

	A	B	C	D	E	F
1	name_of_candidate	political_party	2004	2006		
2	Ablonczy, Diane	Conservative Party of Canada	$13,565.79	$18,978.95	TRUE	=IF(C2<D2,"yes","no")
3	Agar, Greg	New Democratic Party	$700.00	$1,800.00	TRUE	
4	Alcock, Reg	Liberal Party of Canada	$60,680.00	$9,875.00	FALSE	
5	Ambrose, Rona	Conservative Party of Canada	$31,550.00	$53,588.61	TRUE	
6	Anderson, David	Conservative Party of Canada	$10,350.00	$11,350.00	TRUE	
7	Angus, Charlie	New Democratic Party	$7,923.52	$13,750.00	TRUE	
8	Armstrong, Steve	New Democratic Party	$6,315.00	$5,575.00	FALSE	
9	Asselin, Gérard	Bloc Québécois	$5,950.00	$1,000.00	FALSE	
10	Atkins, Colin	Christian Heritage Party of Canada	$1,229.41	$710.00	FALSE	
11	Bagnell, Larry	Liberal Party of Canada	$20,125.45	$23,950.00	TRUE	
12	Bains, Navdeep	Liberal Party of Canada	$11,701.00	$11,900.00	TRUE	
13	Barber, Gina	New Democratic Party	$6,400.00	$11,922.00	TRUE	
14	Barclay, Susan	New Democratic Party	$3,850.00	$8,150.00	TRUE	
15	Barnes, Sue	Liberal Party of Canada	$11,350.00	$13,550.00	TRUE	
16	Barsky, Rick	Green Party of Canada	$129.00	$600.00	TRUE	
17	Batters, Dave	Conservative Party of Canada	$39,800.00	$67,264.00	TRUE	
18	Beaumier, Colleen	Liberal Party of Canada	$15,400.00	$16,700.00	TRUE	
19	Bédard, Marie Martine	Green Party of Canada	$885.00	$2,900.00	TRUE	
20	Bélanger, Mauril	Liberal Party of Canada	$8,805.00	$25,654.64	TRUE	
21	Bell, Barry	New Democratic Party	$600.00	$6,600.00	TRUE	
22	Bell, Catherine	New Democratic Party	$15,946.39	$21,944.00	TRUE	

Fig. 4.36

Hit 'Enter' and repeat the formula for the entire cell F.

If you are happier with the 'YES' and 'NO' criteria, just eliminate column E. You could also replace the 'YES' and 'NO' with numbers, which would allow you to count the number of candidates who raised more money in 2006, or calculate the figure as a percentage of the total number of candidates. In this case, you would click inside the formula and replace the 'YES' with the number '1' (the number you would count) and no with the number '0.' Hit the 'Enter' key to activate the formula, which should then be repeated for the rest of the cells in column E.

Error Values

Entering formulas into Excel is far from an exact science.

Far too frequently we make errors either by keying in the wrong information or by using incorrect functions. If there are errors, sometimes Excel displays a hash mark (#), a signal that your formula is returning an error value. In other cases, Excel doesn't allow you to enter an incorrect formula.[18] For instance, if you attempted to enter the formula '=A1*(B1 + C2), Excel won't allow you to complete the task because of the missing parenthesis. After informing you of your error, Excel in its wisdom will propose a correction, which is usually accurate.[19] These examples contain error values that may appear in a cell that contains a formula. Table 4.1 lists other common error values.

Table 4.2[20]
Excel Error Values Explained

Error Message	Explanation
#DIV/O!	The formula attempts to divide by zero. This also occurs when the formula attempts to divide by an empty cell.
#NAME?	The formula uses a name that Excel doesn't recognize. This can happen if you delete a name used in the formula or if you misspell a function.
#N/A	The formula refers (directly or indirectly) to a cell that uses NA function to signal unavailable data. The error also occurs if a lookup function does not find a match.
#NULL!	The formula uses an intersection of two ranges that don't intersect.
#NUM!	A problem occurs when, for example, you specify a negative number where a positive number is expected.
#REF!	The formula refers to an invalid cell. This happens if the cell has been deleted from the worksheet.
#VALUE!	The formula includes an argument or operand of the wrong type. An operand refers to a value or cell reference that a formula uses to calculate a result.

Displaying the Information

The work doesn't end once you have crunched all the data, and identified trends. You still a need to depict the information in a manner that conveys your findings. Being able to depict the information can also help you spot new trends that may have gone unnoticed. For these key reasons charts—the visual representation of numeric values[21]—come in handy. Though Excel offers many choices, we'll focus on two of the most popular—pie charts and column charts.

When the CBC's Investigative Unit was near the end of its data analysis for the workplace safety series Out of Sync, it became obvious that the numbers in tables would mean very little if they weren't represented visually on cbc.ca, the network's website. Listeners could visit the site to read an explanation about the series, check out the numbers, and study charts, such as this one:

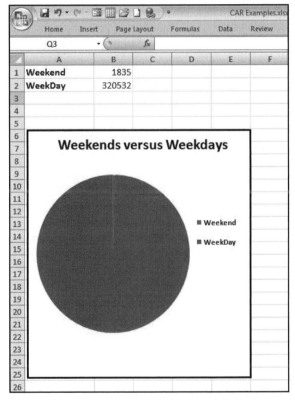

Fig. 4.37

Pie Charts

This pie chart depicts the total number of visits inspectors paid to workplaces during week days and weekends in BC for a ten-year period beginning in 1995. The numbers depicted in the chart are in B2 (WeekDay), and B1 (Weekend). It is evident from the numbers that there were fewer inspections during the weekends, but the disparity really comes to life when it is visually demonstrated in the pie chart.

Pie charts are most effective when using limited data, and the charts should be used with a small number of data points or 'slices'. If the chart contains too many slices, it becomes difficult to interpret.[22]

⚠ TECH TIP

Through their visual impact, charts, and tables are used to communicate a specific message that may not be evident from a straightforward explanation of the numbers in an Excel table. Using the wrong chart could actually lead to more confusion than clarification. So it's important to get it right, which means spending time to experiment with different styles from the choices Excel provides in its library of charts. Before using the result as a graphic for print, television, or the web, test it on colleagues to see how they react. If they're confused, then you probably have a bit more work to do. If they get it right away, then you've succeeded.

Column Charts

Column charts are different from pie charts in that they display data in vertical columns. The height of each column corresponds directly to each value. The column chart also has two axes: one vertical; the other horizontal. The vertical or 'Y' axis usually contains the values in your analysis; the horizontal or 'X' axis usually contains the 'data series' or the length of time over which your trend takes place.

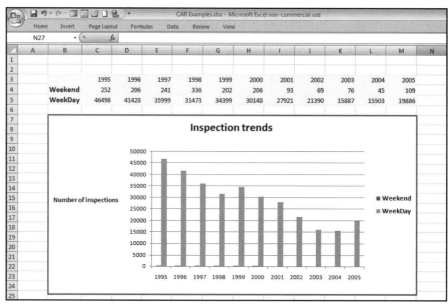

Fig. 4.38

If we return to our workplace safety example, we can see that the values in number of inspections for the weekends and weekdays are displayed in a table, and below, a column chart. It's easy to see which depiction conveys the most information.

The column chart in Figure 4.38 allowed the CBC to convey more information about inspections in BC, and how the inspections for each category play out over time. The weekend inspections are barely perceptible compared to the weekdays, represented by the tall columns. Still, we can see that over the ten-year period, the barely perceptible columns disappeared from view, meaning the province's inspectors were largely absent from worksites on the weekends. There was a similar downward trend for weekday inspections, especially during the years between 1999 and 2004. That trend line led to the questioning of officials with WorkSafeBC. It blamed the diminishing number of inspections on budget cuts; to save money, the province had reduced the number of inspectors. When

BC resumed hiring, the number of inspections began climbing, but not to the 1995 levels, when, interestingly enough, there were fewer workplaces in the province.[23]

Producing Pie Charts

Charts are relatively easy to produce, especially now with your understanding of how Excel's functions use cell ranges when performing tasks such as calculating values. Excel uses those same ranges of cells for its visual depictions. Let's stick with the BC's workplace safety example and the simplest chart, the pie chart.

We can see the inspections numbers over a ten-year period beginning in 1995 for weekdays and weekends, 320,532 and 1835, respectively. From that we will make a pie chart that will give people an idea of the disparity between the two categories. Highlight the columns you want expressed as a chart—in this case the entire table—go to the 'Insert' area of the ribbon, go to the 'Chart' section, click on the downward arrow below the 'Pie' icon. The drop-down menu will provide many options. Choose one right below the '2-D Pie' subhead.

Once you've chosen that option, Excel will give you the result on the same worksheet. Leave it there for now, though you do have the option of choosing a separate worksheet for the chart. Usually, this is a good idea, especially if you want to print the chart. But in this case the table and chart are small enough that they can co-exist on the same worksheet without creating any visual confusion.

TECH TIP ⚠

In older versions, click on the 'Chart Wizard' icon on the standard toolbar.

Excel has placed the pie chart in the middle of the worksheet. For this screenshot, we used the option for moving the pie chart, by simply clicking on the image. Once the cursor turns into a cross, you're free to drag the chart and deposit it anywhere on the worksheet—in this case, right below the table.

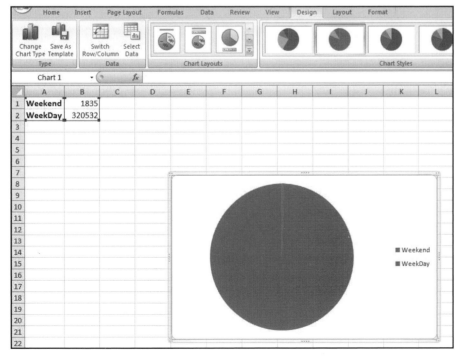

Fig. 4.39

Notice that the labels in column A are placed to the right of the pie chart in a 'legend' that consists of text that identifies the values, or colours, in the pie chart. The nice thing about creating charts in Excel is that the program provides many options for adding and editing titles. We don't want to do too much to this chart, because it does a good job of depicting the disparity between weekend and weekday inspections. But we will add a title.

Before making the addition, we have to make room at the top. To do this, left-click on any white space adjacent to the pie chart to produce what's called a plot area. This will allow you to reduce the size of the pie chart, to make room at the top.

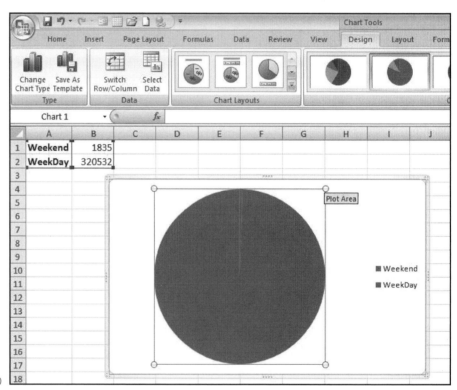

Fig. 4.40

Place your cursor on any of the circles at each end of the box. When the cursor turns into a double arrow, drag it downwards and to the left in order to reduce the size of the pie chart. The cursor now turns into a cross. Place it in any white space between the outer portion of the pie and the boundary of the plot area. You can now reposition the pie chart to the centre of the box.

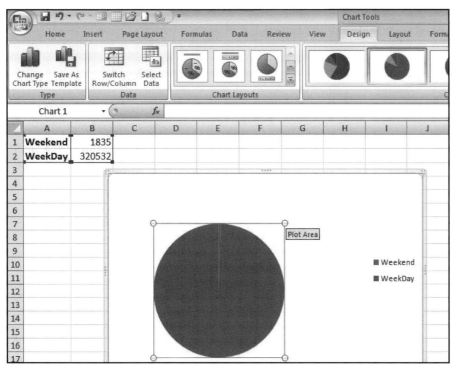

Fig. 4.41

To obtain the chart title, make sure you're in the 'Chart Tools' area (the area on the ribbon is automatically highlighted when you click on the pie chart). Go to 'Layout', the 'Chart Title' in the Labels portion of the ribbon; click on the 'Centred Overlay Title' option.

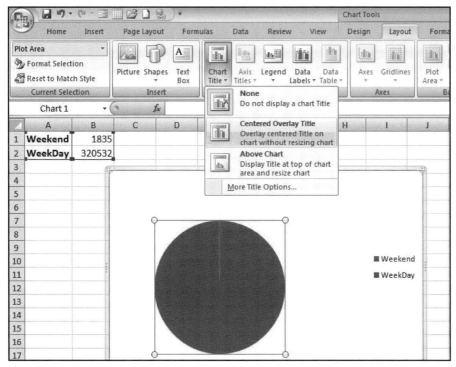

Fig. 4.42

Clicking on that option will produce a title box in which you can type a new title in one of two ways. Just begin typing and you'll notice the result in Excel's formula bar. Or, you could double click on the actual title box, which places the cursor inside.

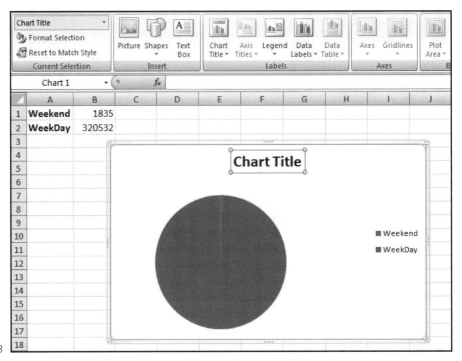

Fig. 4.43

Using either method, you're free to type your new title.

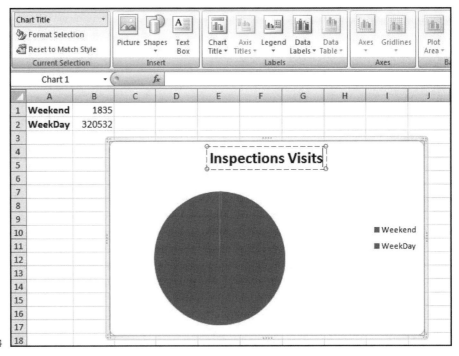

Fig. 4.44

Your work is done. The chart has a title and a legend. It is easy to see the disparity between inspections on the weekends and weekdays.

Producing Column Charts

Column charts are more flexible than pie charts in that they not only can compare variables, but depict how those variables behave during the course of a specified period. As we saw earlier in this chapter, the column chart allows us to track inspection patterns during the course of ten years. Here's how we construct the chart. We can start with three rows: Row one contains the dates; row two tracks inspections on the weekends for each of those dates; and row three contains weekday inspections. Before choosing the column chart, we have to highlight the entire table. Next, click on the 'column' icon. Choose the chart type you prefer.

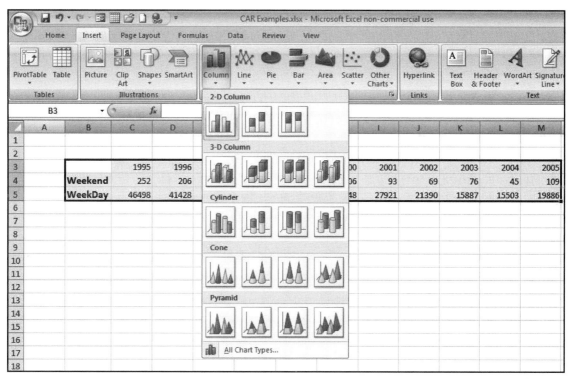

Fig. 4.45

The legend defines the variables in rows two and three. The horizontal or 'X' access has the dates contained the first row. To get our title, let's shrink the size of the chart using the same technique described for the pie chart, and then insert the title block.

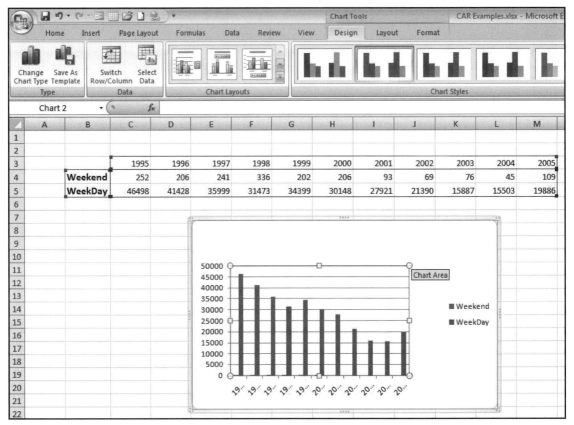

Fig. 4.46

There are many more elaborate methods you can use to create charts with even more detail. For instance, the chart is not limited to titles, legends, and labels for the axes. You can add free-floating text to bring attention to certain parts of the table, vary the number of axes and have charts within charts.

Bringing It All Together

This chapter has introduced us to Excel's starring role, as a math wizard. We've also learned how to use a few text manipulation tools to join and split fields of information. By now, you likely have a pretty good idea why a spreadsheet is such a powerful tool for journalists.

In the next two chapters we'll learn about the spreadsheet's cousin, the database manager.

Five Stories You Can Do

1. Obtain your city's budget for the last five years, and type the expenditures, and revenues (or locate and paste from the Internet). Figure out which departments have the largest increases, and which user fees went up most.

2. If you work in Ontario, go back to the salary disclosure information. Paste in this year's information for your local hospital(s), then paste in the information for last year for the same hospital(s) beside it. Edit to ensure the right names match up—people do come and go, after all—and use the percentage change formula to figure out who got the largest pay increases.

3. Get the latest census numbers, by census tract, for your municipality, in Excel format. Get the numbers for the previous census as well. Work out which neighbourhoods have seen the largest changes in population, the most new immigrants arrive, and which have the largest proportions of men, and of women.

4. Obtain numbers for different crimes in each of your police service's patrol districts. Get the latest population data from Statistics Canada. Work out the rate for 1,000 residents for different crimes in each patrol district.

5. Get incidence rates for different diseases for each of the health districts in your province (available from Statistics Canada). Enter or copy and paste the information into Excel. Find out how your municipality stacks up for different ailments. For which is your municipality worst or near worst? For which is it the best?

Chapter 5

Making the Move to Database Reporting
Fred Vallance-Jones

What We'll Cover

- Fundamentals of databases and Microsoft Access.
- Simple filtering and sorting.
- Writing basic queries, including math queries.
- Queries using more than one table.

> More than 80,000 travellers have been put at risk over the past five years when airplanes came dangerously close together in Canadian skies, according to never-before-released federal aviation data.
>
> Between 2001 and 2005, there were more than 800 incidents in which planes got too close to each other, according to Transport Canada data—about one incident every two days. Sometimes, they come within seconds of crashing.[1]

These chilling words opened an exhaustive, two-week examination of air safety in Canada by the *Hamilton Spectator*, the *Toronto Star*, and the *Record* of Waterloo Region in June 2006. The series broke new ground for aviation reporting in Canada, and told readers about the part of aviation they rarely see: planes straying dangerously close to each other, dozens of mechanical incidents and emergency landings, and pilots dead-tired in the cockpit. It was an eye-opener, even for the reporters who worked on it. Recalled Tamsin McMahon of the *Record*:

> I think what stuck out the most for me was the number of times pilots, ground crews, and controllers made serious mistakes, And passengers were so often none the wiser. At the same time, I was also amazed at how often pilots were able to land planes safely that had experienced serious mechanical problems. Planes seemed to land just fine despite being filled with smoke, or with faulty landing gear, or experiencing depressurization.[2]

The series won an Ontario Newspaper Award, and was named the best investigative report of 2006 in the annual investigative journalism awards competition sponsored by the Canadian Association of Journalists. It was awarded a Citation of Merit in the prestigious Michener Award competition.

The series was possible for one main reason: the reporters had access to a computerized database of more than 50,000 aviation incidents across Canada over a period of

12 years—a database obtained by the *Spectator* after a four-year struggle with Transport Canada, the country's aviation regulator. The *Spectator* invited the *Star* and *Record* to join the investigation. The aviation exposé was a classic example of database reporting, one of the most powerful CAR tools available to journalists. McMahon explained:

> Broadly, the database helped identify trends that weren't readily apparent and tested subjective comments against objective data. It helped to spot issues that even government or industry hadn't identified. It challenged Nav Canada's claim that losses of separation were on the decline. . . . Likely all of the stories would have been less informed, less authoritative, and less precise without the data.'[3]

The series prompted nearly immediate change, with Transport Canada moving to pass key safety improvements that had languished for years. Now, collision-warning devices are mandatory on most commercial planes, and there are tougher rules for landings in bad weather.

The aviation series was one of several major investigative stories published in Canada in 2006 using government databases. Others included a *Toronto Star* exposé on charity fundraising, the CBC series on workplace safety discussed at length in Chapters 2 and 3 (the two spreadsheet chapters), and the *Edmonton Journal* series on dirty restaurants discussed in Chapter 1.

Data analysis allows reporters to gauge how money is being spent, how effectively a program is being administered, or how well public health and safety is being protected. The basic techniques are not difficult to master.

In the last two chapters, we learned about spreadsheets. For many purposes, Excel is all you will ever need to do simple data analysis. But spreadsheet programs are limited in their capacity to work with large amounts of data.

Many database tables contain much more than 1 million records, which means that if you wanted to work with the data in Excel, you'd need to split it into more than one sheet. Such a division would make analysis awkward. Spreadsheets cannot query data in the way databases can, and they cannot easily join data contained in separate tables, which makes tedious the creating, managing, and analyzing of anything more than simple lists.

Most reporters doing CAR eventually gravitate to database programs.

The Way Databases See the World

At first glance, databases can seem impenetrable. A screen full of rows and columns appears daunting. But, conceptually, they are quite simple.

Databases reduce complex real world events, and descriptions of people and things in that world, to what some have called a 'two-dimensional world'[4] of rows and columns. A big part of learning to use databases effectively is grasping how that happens. By understanding how data is gathered and stored, you will start to see the connection between the rows and columns on the screen and the real world events they represent.

One of the simplest ways of conceptualizing a database and its tables is that they are the end product of people's filling out forms. Unless data is gathered automatically—an example might be weather readings fed from automated stations—it probably comes from a form or questionnaire. That form could be printed on paper or displayed on a computer screen.

A simple example is the work of a municipal health inspector. Each time she visits a restaurant to inspect the kitchen, she fills out a form that records *standardized* details of what she found. She identifies herself by entering her inspector number in the specified location on the form. Similarly, she fills out the name and address of the establishment, the date of the inspection, and the time she arrived and left. She records any violations by ticking off specific choices on the form. Finally, if she has any additional comments to make, she records them in a specified location.

In this way, every piece of information has its place.

The structure of the database mirrors the structure of the form into which the information originally was entered; the database information will be transcribed from the forms either manually by a data-entry clerk or automatically when the inspector submits an onscreen form or runs a paper form through a computer scanner.

The database program places the information into a table that has a columns (called 'a field'), for each of the pieces of information on the form. When all of the information from the form has been entered into the database, it will comprise one row of the table (called 'a record').

All databases are essentially the same in that they take real world events or things, break them into component pieces of information, and store the pieces in tables. Once you understand this, it is much easier to make the reverse journey. If you understand what the database records, you can reconstruct the event or thing by reading through the record, and see how the data relate to the real world.

Of course, databases do not just store information. What they really do best is analyze it. So, using a database program, you can count up, say, how many inspections took place at a particular restaurant, how many violations the restaurant has had, how many violations it has had in comparison to other restaurants, and how that has changed over time. When you obtain the database, it is almost as if you had followed along with the inspectors, making notes every time an inspector visited an establishment. By reading a record, picture what must have occurred on the inspection, and by focusing on the most interesting records, you can start to see a story.

Relational Databases

Years ago, computer scientists needed to find a way to make the storage of data in a database program as efficient as possible. Data storage—which in those days meant big reels of magnetic tape—was expensive, as was computer time and memory. They also knew that the more often the same information had to be entered, the more likely it was that errors would creep in. So they came up with the concept of a relational database.

In a relational database, information is divided up into separate tables in order to minimize the amount of data that must be entered and stored.

In the simple example of the restaurant inspection database, there would likely be separate tables, one containing the basic information about each restaurant, one with information about each inspector, and one recording the details of each inspection. These would be tied together with common ID numbers to link the data so it could be combined for viewing and analysis.

Much less work is required to maintain the database because the only thing that needs to be entered after a new inspection is the information about the inspection. The other information about the restaurants and inspectors only needs to be updated when it changes. This way, duplication is avoided, and there is much less chance of mistakes such as misspellings because basic information isn't being entered repeatedly.

The subject of database organization, or normalization, is far too complex to get a full airing here. If you would like to know more, there are many books available on database theory. But suffice it to say a well-organized database is an efficient database. When you obtain databases from governments, they may contain dozens and dozens of tables.

Data Sources

For now, what you need to know is that data generally can come from two sources. You either build the database yourself or you obtain an existing database from a government, business, or other source.

Journalists build their own databases when they want to take advantage of the power of a database program to systematically record information and analyze it. For example, it would be much easier to analyze voting records of city councillors if details of each vote were entered into a database. By querying the database, a reporter could quickly find out how many times each councillor voted with or against the mayor, how each councillor voted on different classes of issues, and how often each councillor was absent. If the reporter continued to update the database, it could provide an easy source of ongoing stories. We will deal in detail with building your own database in Chapter 6.

Journalists obtain databases for much the same reason they obtain paper documents. They want to see inside a story and get beyond handouts. In fact, you won't go too far wrong if you think of databases as electronic documents. Developing CAR skills gives you the means to read and understand these documents.

Existing databases can come from many sources, but those most frequently used come from governments. This is partly because the means exist to obtain them, namely, access to information laws that compel governments to hand them over. We elect governments to act in the public interest. A great many of their activities at the federal, provincial, and municipal levels involve the regulation or overseeing of a wide range of activities that intersect with the public interest, such as the preparation of food in restaurants, the operation of airlines, or fundraising by charities. Governments directly engage in other activities, from policing to health care to gambling, and where any repetitive, systematic activity takes place, be it laying criminal charges, awarding hospital construction contracts, or operating lotteries, a database is bound to be recording it all.

Introduction to Access 2007 and an Overview of the Interface

Several desktop database systems are available, including Corel Paradox, Filemaker Pro, and Microsoft Access. More powerful database server systems include Microsoft SQL Server, Oracle, and MySQL.

We will discuss primarily Microsoft Access, and in particular, Microsoft Access 2007. We made this choice because of its wide acceptance in newsrooms across North America, because of its ease of use and because of its relatively modest cost. In Chapter 6, we introduce you to MySQL. While not as easy to use as Access, MySQL can handle enormous databases with millions of records, which Access cannot. Furthermore, it is free, which is a big advantage for those with a limited software acquisition budget, and it can run on Mac OSX.

As with anything specialized and technical, databases come with their own set of terminology. Go deeply enough, and it can become dense and difficult to penetrate, but the basics are easy

> ### TECH TIP ⚠
>
> Either of the current and previous versions of Access will get the job done, but with the 2007 version, Microsoft introduced changes to the onscreen user interface. Log on to <www.oupcanada.com/CAR.html> for a tip sheet with cross references between Access 2007 and earlier versions.

enough to understand. Here is a short glossary of some of the key terms we will use in this chapter:

database   A database is, broadly speaking a systematic electronic collection of information. That is the definition with which most people are familiar. In Access, a database has a more specific definition. It is a file containing all of the tables, queries, forms, and other objects related to a particular project. You can also divide a project into several databases.

object   A piece of an Access database. The term is borrowed from the physical world. In construction, a warehouse might contain a number of different kinds of objects used to build houses: lumber objects, nail objects, and hammer objects. Similarly, an Access database contains tables, queries, forms, and reports. As with the construction warehouse, there can be many objects of each type. You can see your objects in the 'Navigation Pane' visible on the left side of the screen or in the 'database window' in earlier versions of Access.

table   A table is where the information in a database is entered and stored. It is arranged into rows, called 'records', and columns, called 'fields'. A database may contain many tables.

record   A row in a database table. A record contains all of the information about one instance or example of what is being recorded in the table. For example, if a table records inspections of restaurants, a record will contain the information about one inspection. Unlike many Excel Worksheets, there is no set order for the records in a table. They can be sorted endlessly without affecting the integrity of the data.

field   A column in a database table. A field contains a single element of the information that is being recorded. In a restaurant inspection database, fields might include the date of the inspection, an ID code for the inspector, an ID number for the restaurant, and the outcomes for various items being inspected.

primary key   A geek term that, for our purposes, refers to a field in a database table that is used to link to another table, and in which the values never are repeated. You can read a great deal more about primary keys in any book on database theory.

query   A query is a question put to the database to extract desired information. Queries are written in a simple computer language called Structure Query Language that is understood by database programs. It is usually known by its initials, SQL. One of the reasons Access is so user-friendly is that it hides the writing of SQL behind an easy-to-use query 'grid'. We will explore SQL in Chapter 6.

form   An Access form is an electronic form in which a user enters information to add, modify, or delete records, or to run pre-defined queries. Forms are most commonly used to cut down on tedium and the potential for errors when entering data in your own database, but they can also be used to create simple search applications so other journalists can access data without having to learn the details of the program.

record layout   Sometimes also called a data dictionary or the data elements, the record layout lists each table, the names of all of the fields in tables, the field lengths, and the data types. It is an invaluable guide to the information contained in a database.

ribbon   As in Excel 2007, the 'ribbon' is the wide bar across the top of the window with a variety of icons to perform different operations. Several ribbons are available, each selected by clicking on the ribbon's tab. In some situations, additional ribbons will appear with command buttons applicable to the context in which you are working.

Office button   In Microsoft Office 2007 applications, the large, round icon at the top left corner of the screen that provides access to basic operations, such as opening, saving, and printing files, found under the 'File' menu in earlier versions.

A Cautionary Note about the Access File Format

Microsoft Access has long used a file system that has significant advantages and short-comings. As we noted earlier, Access creates a single database in which resides everything you create on a project. In Access 2007 this file has the .accdb extension. Older versions used the .mdb extension.

The advantage of this system is that everything is in one place; all of your tables, queries, and other objects are right in front of you. The disadvantage is that *because* everything is in one file, if the file is damaged or corrupted you can lose everything. We don't really need to explain what that could mean if you have worked on a database for days or weeks.

Access includes a repair utility that will try to fix a corrupted file, but our experience on previous versions suggests this will fail as often as it succeeds.

So, to avoid disaster, you should back up your database file frequently, certainly as often as you make significant changes, or at least once each working day. Just make a copy of the .accdb file. Another good idea is to keep a backup copy on another hard drive, on a CD, or on a DVD in case your hard drive crashes.

The Access file format has changed over the years, as Microsoft has added new features to the program. Older versions cannot open newer file formats, but the newer versions can open the older formats, or convert them to the new. Access 2007 can convert back to the Access 2002–3 and Access 2000 formats, so if you are stuck with a database written in a newer format than what your version supports, you can ask whoever is giving you the data to convert it for you. While Microsoft offers a 'compatability pack' to allow earlier versions of Excel to open the Excel 2007 format, this was not available for Access files when this book went to press.

An Access database can hold up to about 2 gigabytes of data, which is enough for small to medium-sized projects. In practice, you don't want to get too close to the 2-gigabyte limit as the program gets sluggish as it approaches this ceiling.

The Data

In this chapter we use the same data as the *Spectator*, the *Toronto Star*, and the *Record* for their award-winning series on airline safety: Transport Canada's Civil Aviation Daily Occurrence System, or CADORS, database. You can download the demonstration data in text format, and a complete record layout, from <www.oupcanada.com/CAR.html>. You will find instructions for importing text files into Access below in this chapter. Of course, you will need a copy of Access 2007, and a PC to run it on. Access is not available for Apple MacIntosh machines but can run on the virtual Windows desktop environment made available by the Mac application Parallels.

When you open Access 2007, you will see a welcoming screen.

Fig. 5.1

First, you need to decide whether to work with a new or an existing file. The key choices are 'New Blank Database', 'Open Recent Database', and 'More'. 'New Blank database' permits you to open a new Access database file with no objects in it, and save it onto your hard drive. This is what you ordinarily will do when you receive new data and need to import it, or if you want to create your own database (see Chapter 6, below).

⚠ TECH TIP

Older versions of Access present the same choices in slightly different format and wording.

Access provides a list of the most recently used databases, and your can click on the 'More . . .' icon to search your file system for a database previously saved that does not appear on the list. This is what we will do.

The CADORS data used in this chapter is available for download from the companion website. Ensure that you download that data in the version designed for Access. It is already in an Access database 2002 format so you can open it in any of Access 2002, 2003, or 2007. Download the zipped file, unzip it, and save the file in a folder on your hard drive.

On the welcoming screen, click 'More' and navigate to the folder where you saved the CADORS database. Double-click on the file name, and the database will open in Access, so long as you have Access installed on your machine.

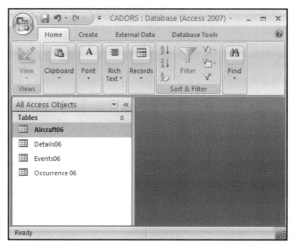

Fig. 5.2

At this point, the Navigation Pane contains only the tables, because we have not created any other objects in the database.

The CADORS database is made up of four tables. Transport Canada keeps the data back to 1993 (prior years' data is in a different, archived system). In order to keep the file size reasonable, we are using just the 2006 data.

⚠ TECH TIP

Older versions of Access use a different user interface called the 'Database window'. Tabs on the left allow you to switch between different types of objects. The names of the objects themselves appear in the main part of the database window.

The main table in the database is the 'Occurrence 06' table, which contains all of the basic information about each aviation incident. Each incident is identified by a unique code called the

CADORS number. This is used to connect the incidents to the data in the other tables. There is one record per incident.

The 'Aircraft06' table contains information about the aircraft involved in each incident. If more than one aircraft was involved in an incident, a record for each aircraft appears in the table.

The 'Events06' table contains brief descriptions of the types of incidents. If an incident involved more than one event type, there will be one record in the table for each type.

Finally, the 'Details06' table contains an expanded description of each incident. Sometimes, these descriptions are updated, and each update is entered as a new record.

In this database, there is either a one-to-one or one-to-many relationship between the 'Occurrence 06' table and the other tables. This means that for each record in the 'Occurrence 06' table there is one or more records with the same CADORS numbers in the related tables.

If you double-click on one of the table names, you will see the table in what Access calls 'Datasheet View'. For a table with many fields you will see only a few of the fields at a time. Scroll bars on the right side and bottom of the table allow you to move across and up and down the table. The keyboard shortcuts Ctr + Home and Ctrl + End will take you to the very top and very bottom of the table, respectively. The 'Occurrence 06' table looks like this when first opened in 'Datasheet' view.

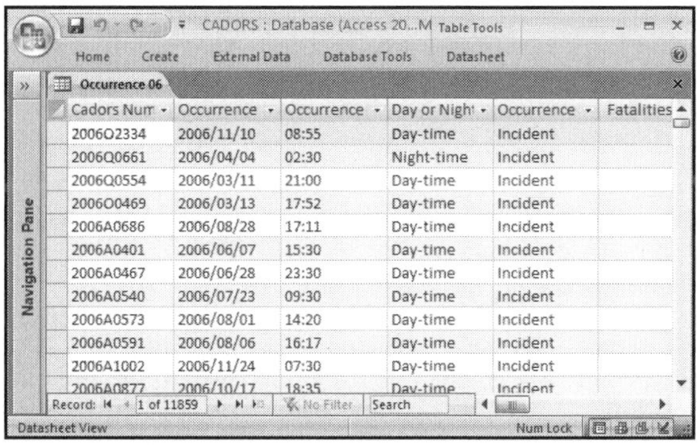

Fig. 5.3

We don't explain every feature you see on the screen. Instead, we stick to the functions journalists use most often. In order to fit as much of the relevant part of a screen image on the printed page, we will hide features such as the ribbon and Navigation Pane when they are not relevant to the explanation.

Seeing your Table in Design View

You can see a summary of the fields in a table and their data types by clicking on the 'View' button, which you see at the top left of the screen when the 'Home' ribbon is selected.

When you click on 'View'>'Design View', a screen appears that looks like this. Notice that a new, context-sensitive 'Design' ribbon appears at the top right of the screen.

TECH TIP ⚠️

In older versions the View button is located on the table 'Datasheet' toolbar. If you don't see it, open the 'View' menu and click 'Toolbars'.

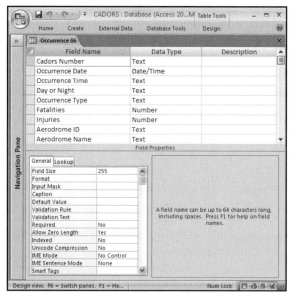

Fig. 5.4

For now, we are concerned with the Field Name, the Data Type, and some of the information contained under the General tab at the bottom of the screen.

The 'Field Name' category is self-explanatory. Field names in Access can be up to 64 characters long and unlike many database programs can contain spaces. You had best keep your field names as short as possible to save time typing them out later.

In Access, as in any database system, and in Excel, data of several different types may be recorded: text, numeric, and so on. Specifying the kind of data both tells the computer how to process the information and saves storage space and memory. Access has several data types, which in summary are:

- **text fields**   Can contain any character, including numbers, but numbers will be treated by the program as characters; so, if you sort a field, the number 1234 will come before the number 2. Text fields can be up to 255 characters long. It is the most common field type.
- **number fields**   These fields contain numbers on which you can do math. They are treated by the program as numbers. Number fields come in several varieties, indicated beside 'Field size' under the general tab. Normally, you will choose 'Long integer' if you want numbers without decimal places, and 'Double' if you want decimal places. You can control the number of decimals for a double type under the General tab.
- **currency fields**   Currency fields are a special type of number field displayed with a dollar sign and having two decimal places.
- **autonumber fields**   A Long integer type of field that counts up from 1 every time a new record is added to the database. If you add an autonumber field to an existing table that you are importing, the records will be numbered sequentially from 1. *If you delete a record*, Access will discard and *not reuse* the number that was in the autonumber field for that record.
- **yes/no fields**   A field that contains only one of two values, yes or no/true or false. This field type is useful whenever there are two choices or when something either is or isn't true.
- **memo fields**   A specialized text field that can hold thousands of words (up to about 64,000 characters).

- **date/time fields**   This type is self-explanatory. You can change how a date is displayed by going to 'Field properties' and under the 'General' tab clicking on 'Format' and selecting 'Date/Time' field. A small arrow will appear, which you can click to be given a drop-down menu with a variety of display options.

You can make a great many more changes to the default way that Access displays fields.and handles data in fields. They vary according to the data type. You make the changes in the 'Field Properties' sheet at the bottom of the table's Design window.

Taking an Initial Look at Your Data

The big moment arrives. A disk chock-full of data from a government agency arrives on your desk. You're euphoric, but you need to know better how the data is structured, and what is in the fields. It's time for a little exploration. Some authorities refer to this as 'interviewing' your data.

Begin by examining table structures in Design view. Take note of their data types. Make sure that fields in different tables that are meant to be joined (see the section on multi-table queries later in Chapter 5) are of the same data type to avoid error messages later.

> **TECH TIP** ⚠
>
> You can change the data type of any field in the table Design view. Just make sure before you convert from one data type to another that you won't lose data. If you convert a field from the Text type to a Number type, for example, any entries that contain text characters will be deleted. Similarly, if you convert to a Date/Time field type, any incompatible data will simply disappear. Access will warn you if that is about to happen, and give you the opportunity to cancel the change.

When you have done this, return to the Datasheet view by clicking View/Datasheet view.

Next, open each of the tables in turn, spending some time learning about the data in detail. While you are reviewing the tables, consider:

- What kind of data is in each table? In each field?
- How do the tables relate to one another? What field(s) are used to link them?
- Are there any codes in the database table for which you do not have the plain-language meanings? If so, you may have to go back to the source of the data for clarification.
- How many records are in the table? You can always see that number in the Record Counter at the bottom of the window. The Record Counter also will tell you where you are in the table in relationship to the first record.
- Are the fields consistently filled in, or are some blank some or most of the time? Fields with a lot of blanks, or null values, may be less useful for analysis because you don't know if the ones that are filled in are truly representative of the big picture. Sometimes fields are added to tables, and then not used all of the time or by all who enter data.
- Is the data in the fields spelled properly and are the spellings consistent? If not, you may need to clean the data before it is useful for analysis. To a database, Montreal is a different place from Montréal. We cover data-cleaning in Chapter 6.
- Are number fields actually in a number format? If not, are they tainted by any non-number characters. If so, you'll have to either leave the field in text format, or get rid of the non-numeric characters before changing the data type. You can use 'Search and replace' to do this.
- What period of time does the data cover (of course, our aviation data covers only 2006)?
- What might you be able to find out by analyzing the data? Make some notes on this. What kinds of queries might you run? Begin to make a list.

- Are there fields you would like to add to the database to make it more useful? For example, do you need to add a year field to make querying by year easy?
- Is there anything you don't understand? You may need to contact the agency that provided the data for explanations.
- Is there unfamiliar terminology in the database? If so, you will have to do some research.

Once you have gone through this process, you will already have a much better understanding of the data than when you started. As with anything journalistic, you may also have a lot of new questions.

If you aren't working with the data, you can still obtain the record layout from <www.oupcanada.com/CAR.html> to view the fields.

Getting Started with Analysis: Sorting and Filtering

Just looking at data only takes you so far. You want to start identifying some of the patterns. The most basic analysis you can do is sorting and filtering, similar to the parallel features in Excel.

One extremely common way of sorting is to organize data by date so it is possible to scan through a portion of the data to see what was happening at a particular time or to consider the chronological order in which events occurred.

We will sort the 'Occurrence06' table in order of occurrence date.

To do this, open the table in Datasheet View, and select the occurrence date field by clicking on the field name. Now, click on the small arrow beside the field name. You will be offered two choices, either 'Sort Oldest to Newest' or 'Sort Newest to Oldest', as in Figure 5.6.

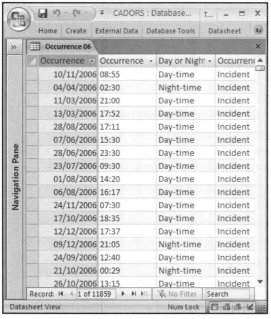

Fig. 5.5

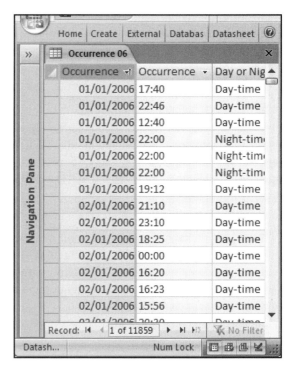

Fig. 5.6

The same thing can be accomplished by clicking on the 'A to Z' or 'Z to A' buttons on the 'Home' ribbon. We will sort from oldest to newest (A to Z). You should get the result shown in Figure 5.6. You can now scroll through the data in chronological order.

Now, let's suppose you want to see only incidents that happened in or near Port Alberni, British Columbia. Scroll to the right in the table until you see the fields for aerodrome, aerodrome name, and occurrence location. The first two are essentially the same, one merely being the standard letter code for the airports, the other the name written out. The third field gives the location more precisely, stating, for example, if an incident occurred a certain distance from a location. We will use both the second and third fields.

To begin filtering, click the small arrow beside the 'Aerodrome Name' field. The 'Sort/Filter' dialogue will pop up again. You will see a series of check boxes representing each of the unique entries in the field (the choices you will be given here vary depending on the content of the field).

The next step is to click on '(Select All)' at the top of the list, which will remove all of the check marks. Now, scroll down the list until you find Port Alberni (Alberni Valley Regional), which is the entry for Alberni Valley Regional Airport. Click in that check box.

TECH TIP ⚠

In older versions, the sort buttons are on the Table Datasheet toolbar. You can also move the cursor to the head of a field until an arrow appears and right-click to bring up a menu from which the type of sort you want can be selected.

TECH TIP ⚠

In journalism, size really does matter. While spreadsheets and databases can sort fields in either ascending (smallest to largest) or descending (largest to smallest), you will find the vast majority of your sorts are in descending order. That's because reporters usually want to know the biggest, most frequent or most expensive thing: the largest tax increase, the drug that has killed the most people, the biggest polluter, or the most generous political donor. By sorting in descending order, we put the biggest on top. Exceptions include sorting a table or query by date, when we may want to use ascending order.

TECH TIP ⚠

Older versions of Access do not include the small arrows to start filtering. Filter options are found by clicking 'Filter' under the 'Records' menu.

Fig. 5.7

Click 'OK', and you will now see only incidents that occurred at or near Port Alberni's airport, two incidents in all.

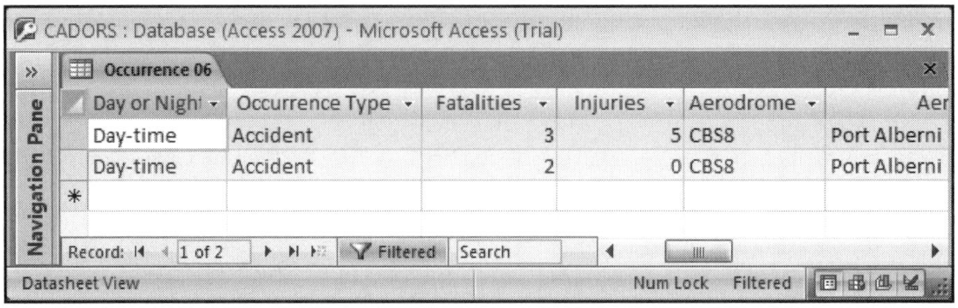

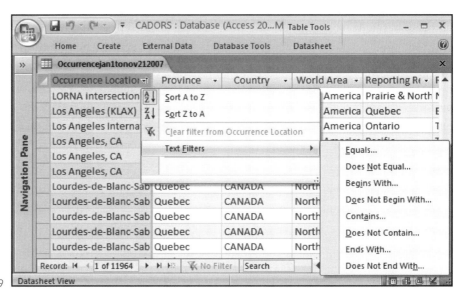

Fig. 5.8

You can now scroll from side to side through the results, to see all of the fields. To return to the entire datasheet, click on the 'Filtered' button at the bottom of the window.

You can create a filter that searches for specific words or numbers within a field. To begin, click on the small arrow beside the 'Occurrence Location' field. Now, click on 'Text Filters', which will bring up a list of choices.

Fig. 5.9

The list of choices is self-explanatory, so we will pick 'Contains'. This brings up a small dialogue box labelled 'Custom filter.' Enter 'Port Alberni' in the text box.

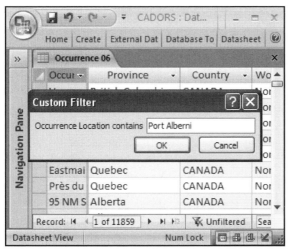

Fig. 5.10

Click 'OK', and the records will be filtered. As you will have noted from the 'Text Filters' list, you can also specify that the word begins or ends the field, or is exactly the same as what is contained in the field. Finally, you can specify that the word *not* be in any of these locations.

If you are working within a table or query result and want to filter quickly based on the contents of a field you are looking at, use your mouse to highlight and 'select' the portion of the field contents that you would like to use as the filter criteria, then click on the 'Selection' button, the icon of a funnel with a lightning bolt, located on the Home ribbon. You will be given the choice of filtering for records that contain or do not contain the content you have highlighted. Here, the selection filter has been activated to filter on the word 'Quebec', selected in the 'Province' field.

Fig. 5.11

Access also provides options for filtering using Forms. These are similar to writing queries, but not as flexible or powerful. If you would like to learn how to use these types of filters, see the topic 'Filter: Limit the number of records in a view' in the Access 2007 'Help' file.

Moving to the Next Level: Writing Queries

The real power for data manipulation in Access, and all databases, comes from their ability to run queries. In Access you can write a query to extract data from one or more tables. You can also extract data from an existing query that you have saved.

We'll divide this discussion into two parts. First, we will consider queries that simply filter and sort data. They allow you to see what is in the database, the order in which events occurred, and to focus on specific parts of the data that are particularly interesting.

Second, we will discuss queries that summarize data, and do math. These kinds of queries let you answer questions such as how much, how often, and how many.

The beauty of Access is that you will never have to learn a word of SQL if you don't want to do so. Almost all queries can be written in the query grid. Learning SQL at some point is a good idea because it will give you a better understanding of what the program is doing, but for starters, working with the grid works well.

To begin writing a query, switch from the 'Home' ribbon to the 'Create' ribbon. Do this by clicking on the 'Create' tab at the top of the Access 2007 window. Now, click on the 'Query Design' button to bring up a new dialogue box in which you can select the tables (or queries) you want to include in the query.

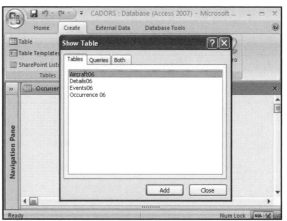

Fig. 5.12

For now, we will choose 'Occurrence 06'. Select it with the mouse, click 'ADD', and close the dialogue window. A new 'Query' design window will open and the Design ribbon will open. The screen looks like this:

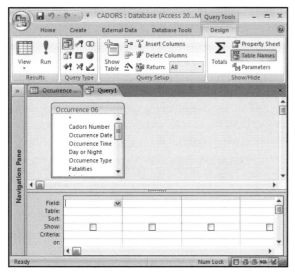

Fig. 5.13

You probably will spend more time in this screen, with this ribbon, than just about anywhere else in Access. From left to right, the most commonly used elements are:

- The 'View' button allows you to toggle between views. The main ones we are concerned with are 'Design View' and 'SQL View'. 'Design View' shows you the Query grid. 'SQL View' shows the underlying SQL statement that Access creates for you. Another choice is 'Datasheet View', which has about the same effect as clicking on the 'Run' button.
- The 'Run' button, the one with the big red exclamation point, executes the query to make the query result—sometimes called a 'view'—appear.
- 'Query Type' allows you to choose between different types of queries. Most of your queries will be 'Select' queries, the default choice. Other types include 'Make Table' queries, which create a new table containing the query result in your database; 'Append' queries, which add data to an existing table; 'Update' queries, which allow you to change information in your query; 'Delete' queries, which allow you to delete all or part of a table, and 'Union' queries, a specialized type that joins together the output of two queries.
- The 'Show table' button has a big yellow plus sign. Clicking it will bring up the 'Add Table' dialogue box you saw when you first created the query.
- Adjacent to the 'Show Table' button you will find buttons to add or delete rows and columns from the query grid. Next to these are the 'Return' button, which allows you to limit the number of records displayed when you run the query.
- The 'Totals' button adds a line to the query grid needed for mathematical queries, while the 'Table Names' button toggles the Table Name line in the Query grid on and off.

TECH TIP ⚠

In older versions the 'Run', 'Show Table', and 'Totals' icons are found on the 'Query Design' toolbar, which appears when a query is in Design View. Once open, the 'Query Design' grid is the same in all versions.

⚠️ **TECH TIP**

Unlike some other database programs, Access doesn't care if you enter text in upper- or lower-case letters. 'APPLE' means the same to Access as 'apple' or 'Apple' and text will be sorted without reference to case. The same goes for object names, which can interchangeably be in upper- or lower-case letters. There are workarounds to make Access case-sensitive when needed. For example, the Microsoft website article 'Sort records in case-sensitive order' <office.microsoft.com/en-us/access/HA100627601033.aspx> explains how to use Visual Basic for Applications Code to sort records in a case-sensitive order (upper case before lower case).

The simplest queries are similar to the sort and filter functions we have already tried. They return a portion of the table, based on criteria that we enter, and sort the results in a desired order.

Let's put something in the Query grid we opened earlier. We'll use a query to do the same work as the filter we used before to find incidents that occurred near Port Alberni. We want to see all of the fields in the table, but only some of the records.

There are three ways to move a field into the query grid. The first way is to double-click on the field name in the small 'Table' box in the upper portion of the Query design window. The second way is to click and drag the field name from the box to the first empty column on the left side of the grid. The third way is to click in the top row of the first empty column, and select the field name from the list that appears. Using whichever way you find works best for you, add the asterisk from the top of the Query list to the first column of the grid. The asterisk stands for all fields in the table. Add the aerodrome name field to the second column. To limit your query just to incidents at or near the Port Alberni airport, enter "Port Alberni (Alberni Valley Regional)" in the criteria line below the aerodrome name field in the grid. Enter it exactly as you see it here, and include the double quotation marks. This is what the grid should look like:

Fig. 5.14

Now, click on the 'Run' button. The results—the same two records we filtered before—should appear.

We can also sort the results. Click on the 'View' button to return to 'Design View'.

Since we are showing all of the fields in the result, we need to add the field we would like to sort on. Move the 'Occurrence Date' field into the Query grid. Click on the 'Sort' line under the 'Occurrence Date' field, and pick 'Ascending' from the list as in this illustration.

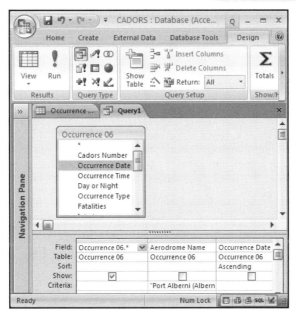

Fig. 5.15

Now, when you run the query you will notice that the occurrences are sorted by date. You can sort on multiple fields in the same query. Access will sort the fields, starting from the left and moving to the right. The records will be sorted on the leftmost field first, followed by the next sorting field to the right, and so on. A good example of sorting on more than one field is first sorting on last name, then on first name. If there are several Smiths in the 'last name' field, they will be sorted further by first name. If you have a 'middle initial' field, you can further sort any identical last-name/first-name combinations by middle initial.

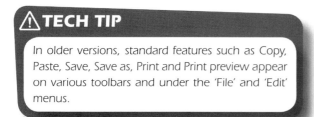

⚠ TECH TIP

In older versions, standard features such as Copy, Paste, Save, Save as, Print and Print preview appear on various toolbars and under the 'File' and 'Edit' menus.

Database Logic

Database programs use what is called Boolean logic, named after a nineteenth-century English mathematician, George Boole (1815-64), noted for writing an algebraic system of reasoning. It uses words such as 'AND', 'OR', and 'NOT to build logical statements to extract data from tables.

Let's start with 'AND'.

Suppose we wanted to see only accidents at or near Port Alberni in which more than two people died. To find this, add the fatalities field to the Query grid of your existing Port Alberni query. Now, in the criteria line under the fatalities field, type in >2.

Adding a second criterion directly to right of the first requires that both be true for records to be returned. In other words, one condition is true AND another is true.

If you run the query now, only one of the incidents will be displayed. This accident, involving a Sonic Blue Cessna Caravan, became the focus of a major story in the *Spectator-Star-Record* series.[5]

Another Boolean logic word is 'OR'. It will return records if one 'OR' the other condition is true.

To set up an 'OR' condition in the Query grid, place the second criterion one line down and one or more columns to the right of the first. This illustration shows a query that finds incidents in Port Alberni in which people were killed or injured:

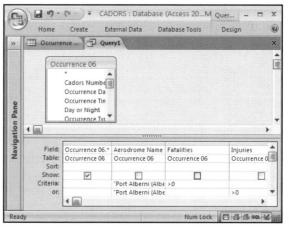

Fig. 5.16

You may wonder why the name of the airport is repeated twice under the 'Aerodrome Name' field. This is because each criteria line in the grid is read separately by Access. If you did not repeat the aerodrome name in the second line, the query would return records where people were killed *and* the incident occurred at Port Alberni airport, plus all records where people were injured, at any airport. By entering the name of the Port Alberni airport in the second line, the query returns all records where the incident occurred at Port Alberni and people were killed, as well as all records where the incident occurred at Port Alberni and people were injured.

You will notice that there are numerous blank criteria lines below the first. This allows you to cascade a series of 'OR' conditions, each being placed one row down and one or more columns to the right of the last. It is possible to create quite complicated-looking queries, such as this one, which would find injury incidents at one of three airports.

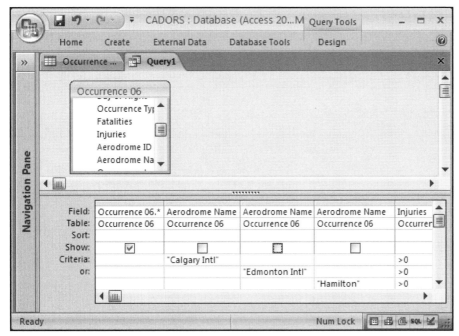

Fig. 5.17

Notice that the little 'Check' box has not been selected under the 'Aerodrome Name' columns. If this were not done, the query result would include three extra aerodrome name columns, all with exactly the same information in them. By unchecking the boxes, the columns affect the query's output, without being visible in the result.

By the way, the same result can be obtained by writing in the 'OR's, as in this example:

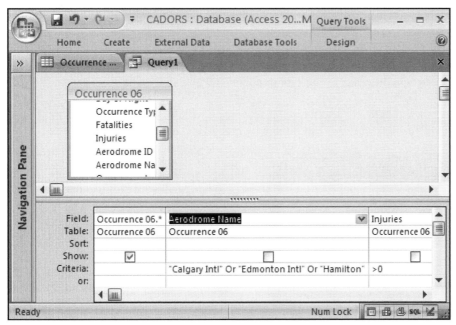

Fig. 5.18

Both this and the previous constructions will produce exactly the same result. Some users might consider the second to be more elegant.

If there are a great many possible alternatives, you can use the 'IN' operator instead of 'OR'.

The syntax for 'IN' is:

$$IN(``x",``y",``z")$$

This is the same query using 'IN':

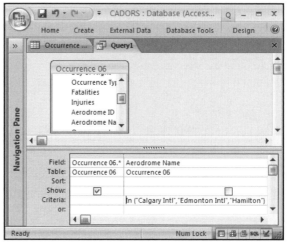

Fig. 5.19

One Program, Many Operators

As you might expect, you can use a number of different operators in the criteria line of the Query grid. So far, we have used '=' and '>'. Any time you enter a text string in the criteria line and don't specify an operator, = is assumed.

Other operators include:

>= Greater than or equal to. Example : >= 10
< Less than. Example: <10
<= Less than or equal to. Example: <= 10

Between x and y   This operator allows you to select a range of values. Example: 'Between 10 and 20.' This is the same as >=10 and <= 20.

TECH TIP

The 'OR' and 'AND' operators can be confusing. 'OR' will return all records where either condition you set is true. It increases the number of records displayed. 'AND' will return only those records where both conditions are true. It reduces the number of records displayed.

Like   Used with wildcard characters, 'like' is used to find words or letters within a text string. The * wildcard stands for any number of characters, the ? wildcard stands for one character, and # stands for any digit. For example: 'Like "*Smith*"' will select any record that has 'Smith' somewhere within the field. 'Like "Smith*"' will find any record where the entry in the field begins with 'Smith'. 'Like "Montr?al"' will find both 'Montreal' spelled in English, and 'Montréal' spelled in French. Furthermore, you can specify a range of characters using square brackets. 'Like "[cd]art"' will find 'cart' and 'dart'. 'Like "[b-d] art"' will find 'Bart', 'cart', and 'dart'. 'Like "[1-10000] Wilson Street"' will find any address on Wilson Street between 1 and 10,000.

Access also uses the 'NOT' logical word. Placing 'NOT' before any logical statement in the criteria line will reverse its meaning. For example, 'NOT like "*Toronto*"' will find all records where 'Toronto' is not in the field.

'Not equal' has a special short form, <>, created by typing the 'less than' and 'greater than' signs in succession. It is followed by either a number or a character string (enclosed in quotation marks).

In summary, you can write simple queries that limit either the columns displayed (by picking certain columns and not others) and/or limit the rows displayed (by using the criteria line). When using the criteria line, you can use a variety of operators, and the logical words 'AND', 'OR', and 'NOT'. You can also sort the output on one or more fields. Finally, by clicking off the 'Show' box under any field, you can eliminate that field from the query result, while still using the field to affect the output of the query.

Summary Queries Using Mathematical Operations

Some of the most important findings in database investigations come from queries that summarize data, and help reporters reach conclusions about the big picture. When the *Spectator*, *Toronto Star*, and *Record* reporters were working on their series on aviation safety, they did dozens of summary and mathematical queries. They counted the number of incidents of each type each year, calculated numbers of mechanical incidents per year, and summed up fatalities and injuries. The lead paragraph that begins this chapter started with a query that counted up the number of loss-of-separation incidents involving different types of passenger aircraft. A little more math in Excel, and the reporters were able to estimate the number of passengers aboard the planes.

To do these kinds of queries in a database, you need to understand a concept called 'grouping'. It can be a little confusing at first, but once you get the hang of it, you'll become a math query whiz. Grouping is exactly as it sounds. When Access groups on a field, the resulting output is a list of all the unique entries in that field. So, if a table has 14 records with 'Ottawa' in a city field, 17 with 'Toronto', and 23 with 'Halifax', the result of grouping them would be a list with one 'Ottawa', one 'Toronto', and one 'Halifax'.

Grouping can be combined with counting, summing (addition), and other mathematical functions to produce subtotals.

When grouping is combined with counting, Access produces the same list of all of the unique values in the grouped field. But it also provides a second column with a list of how many records had each city in the city field. For the above example, the output would be:

Group	Count
Halifax	23
Ottawa	14
Toronto	17

When grouping is combined with addition, the same thing happens. The result includes a list of all of the unique values in the grouped field, and a second column containing the summed values of a second field. You can also group on more than one field. Access will then group on every unique combination of the two fields.

The simplest query using grouping produces a list of all of the unique values in one or more fields. To begin, start a new query. Click on the 'Totals' button on the 'Query Design' ribbon, to make the 'Total' line appear in the grid. The 'Totals' button is labelled with its name, as well as the Greek sigma character, which looks like a stylized capital letter 'E' and is used in math to designate summing. You will recall the same character is used for the 'Autosum' button in Excel.

Your Query grid screen should look like this:

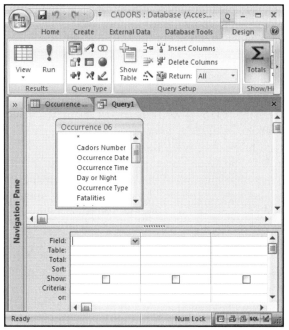

Fig. 5.20

To create a query that groups on one field, drop that query into the grid. We will choose the 'Province' field. Notice (Figure 5.21) that the 'Total' line says 'Group By'. It will do that by default. You can also enter mathematical instructions here, as we will show in a moment. Now, click on the 'Run' button in the 'View' ribbon, and you get this result: Figure 5.22.

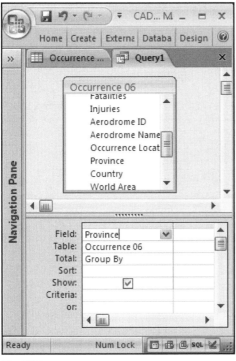

Fig. 5.21   Fig. 5.22

You begin to see the power of queries. This simple query has reduced thousands of province entries down to a list of 13 provinces, and territories. In database language, Access has grouped on the 'Province' field.

Moving from simply grouping to grouping and counting, or grouping and summing, is only a matter of adding one more field to the Query design.

Return to Design View. Move the 'Cadors Number' field into the second column of the grid. Now, click in the 'Totals' line under the new field, and change 'Group By' to 'Count'. In the last query, we didn't choose a sort order, Access automatically sorted in ascending order. For this query, we want to see which provinces had the largest numbers of reported aviation incidents, so we will click in the 'Sort' line under the 'Cadors Number' field, and choose 'Descending'. Figure 5.24 is the query, ready to run; Figure 5.25 is the result of the query after clicking 'Run':

⚠ TECH TIP

When Access counts, you select a field on which to do the counting. But this is only a means to an end. What you actually are doing is counting records in the table. In this case, Access is counting aviation incidents, because each record represents one incident. Always count on a field you know is never blank ('null', in computer lingo). If you choose a field that is sometimes blank, Access will miss counting the records with blank entries.

Your count will end up inaccurate. It is best, therefore, to count on a key field such as Cadors Number, which you know will always contain a value. If you prefer, you can create a counting column by entering COUNT(*) in the 'Field' line of the grid, then change GROUP BY to EXPRESSION in that column of the grid. This will explicitly count all rows in the table, regardless of whether they contain NULL values.

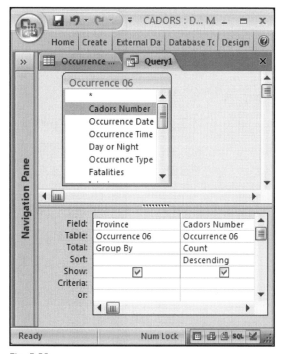

Fig. 5.23

Fig. 5.24

As you can see, the number of incidents in each province and territory declines roughly in order of their population, although the Northwest Territories in particular appears significantly over-represented, possibly reflecting the dependence of the Far North on aircraft to move people and goods.

Any mathematical query can be fine-tuned to operate on only some of the records in the table. This is done by adding criteria, as we did before in our simple queries.

For example, by adding the 'Fatalities' field and entering '>0' in the 'Criteria' line, we can count fatal accidents by province.

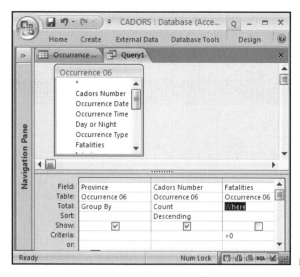

Fig. 5.25

Notice that under the 'Fatalities' field, we need to change 'Group By' to 'Where'. By doing this, we ensure that Access doesn't create a new group—you can call it a subtotal if you like—for every unique combination of number of fatalities and province name. By changing it to 'Where', you are telling Access to use that field to set a condition for the query, without including the field itself in the grouped output.

In the last two query results, you will have noticed one row where there was nothing under the 'Province' field. This is because the 'Province' field includes blank values. The blank line is telling you the number of records where the name of the province wasn't entered. You can eliminate this line by entering 'is not null' in the 'Criteria' line under the 'Province' field in the grid.

Other mathematical queries are structured in the same way. You group on one or more fields, and then enter one or more fields on which to do the math.

Let's figure out the total number of fatalities for each province. We'll simply modify our existing query. If you like, save your count query before doing so. Now, delete the 'Cadors Number' field from the grid by highlighting the column and hitting the 'Delete' key. Under the 'Fatalities' field, change 'Where' to 'Sum'. Finally, under the same field, eliminate '>0' from the 'Criteria' line so we will be able to see which provinces had no fatali-

TECH TIP ⚠

Not all empty field entries are null. It is also possible to have what is called a 'zero-length string' in a field. You type a zero-length string by entering two quotation marks with no characters or spaces between them. A zero-length string will be counted by Access, unlike a null value. The fact the two look exactly the same is another reason never to count on a field with blanks. The result is unpredictable if you don't know which records have null values and which have zero-length strings. If you want to prohibit zero-length strings in a field, you can set 'allow zero length' to 'no' under 'field properties' in table 'Design' view.

ties. Make sure the check box in the 'Show' line under the 'Fatalities' field has a check mark, so you will see the output. Finally, sort the 'Fatalities' field in Descending order. Rename the query, if you like, by clicking the 'Office' button and choosing 'Save As'. Figure 5.26 is what your finished query should look like and Figure 5.27 is the result:

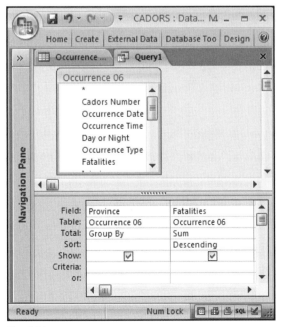

Fig. 5.26

Fig. 5.27

Access offers several other choices for calculations, which you choose by picking from the list that appears when you click on the 'Totals' line:

- **Avg**   Calculates the average value in a number field. For example, you could calculate the average number of injuries by province using the 'injuries' field in the 'occurrence' table.
- **Min**   Displays the smallest value in a number field or the first entry in alphabetical order in a text field.
- **Max**   Displays the largest value in a number field, or the last entry in alphabetical order in a text field. You could use 'Max' to find the largest number of people to die in a Canadian aviation accident in 2006.
- **StDev**   Calculates standard deviation, a statistical measure, in a number field.
- **Var**   Calculates variance, a statistical measure, in a number field.

Creating a Top Values Query

If you want to find the top or bottom values in a numerical or date field you can run a 'top values' query. To do this, create a query as usual, containing at least one field with text, and one with numerical or date data. The query can either be a basic select query or a math query, except that *only* for the field in which you want to find the top or bottom values, select ascending or descending order. Now, pick one of the preset values, or enter you own value, in the 'Top values' list box on the query Design ribbon.

When you run the query, it will return only records that satisfy the top value criterion you have set. The query in this illustration will return only the incidents in the 'Occurrence 06' table with the top five numbers of fatalities.

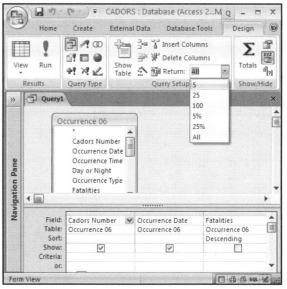

Fig. 5.28

This is the result:

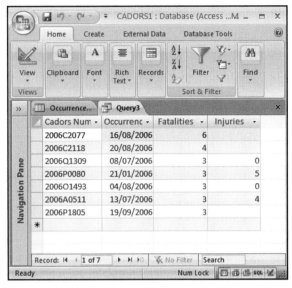

Fig. 5.29

Crosstab Queries

Access can also create what is known as a 'crosstab query'. This is short for 'cross-tabulation' and is similar to Pivot tables in Excel that we learned about in Chapter 4. Crosstabulation is exactly the same as grouping on two fields, but instead of displaying both fields along the left side of the window (or right, as it moves your fancy) one is displayed along the side, and one across the top. Let's look at both versions. Figure 5.30 shows a query that counts injury incidents, and groups them on the combination of the 'Province', and 'Day or Night' fields.

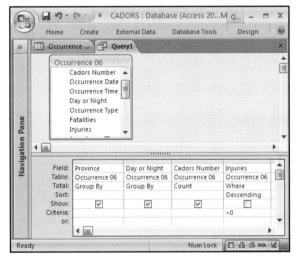

Fig. 5.30

When you run your query, the result looks like this:

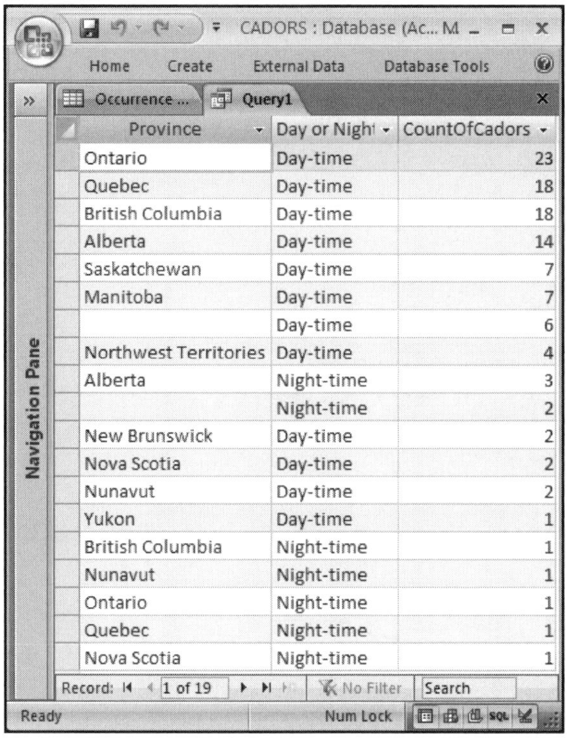

Province	Day or Night	CountOfCadors
Ontario	Day-time	23
Quebec	Day-time	18
British Columbia	Day-time	18
Alberta	Day-time	14
Saskatchewan	Day-time	7
Manitoba	Day-time	7
	Day-time	6
Northwest Territories	Day-time	4
Alberta	Night-time	3
	Night-time	2
New Brunswick	Day-time	2
Nova Scotia	Day-time	2
Nunavut	Day-time	2
Yukon	Day-time	1
British Columbia	Night-time	1
Nunavut	Night-time	1
Ontario	Night-time	1
Quebec	Night-time	1
Nova Scotia	Night-time	1

Fig. 5.31

By reading down the one column, you can see that there are more such occurrences during the day than during the night, probably because more flights, and especially more flights by small private planes navigating by the pilots' eyes alone, take place during the day. But wouldn't it be nicer to be able to view the results as two columns, one for Daytime, and one for Night-time? That is what the crosstab query will do.

> **⚠ TECH TIP**
>
> In older versions, you can switch between query types using the 'Query' menu or the 'Query Type' icon on the Query Design toolbar. The icon looks like two overlapping tables and has a downward-pointing arrow to select the query type.

To convert this query to a crosstab, click on the 'Crosstab' query icon in the Query Type area of the Design ribbon. It is the icon at the very centre of the group and, like other icons, holding the mouse pointer over it for a couple of seconds will make a description appear.

Switching to crosstab type will add a new line to the query grid, labelled, appropriately enough, 'Crosstab'. Under the 'Province' field, click in this row and select 'Row Heading'. Under 'Day or Night', select 'Column Heading', and under 'Cadors Number'—the field we are using to count—select 'Value'. Remove any sorts from the 'Sort' row to avoid getting an error message.

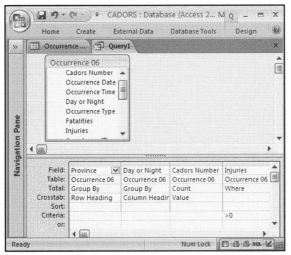

Fig. 5.32

This is the result when you run it:

Province	Day-time	Night-time
	6	2
Alberta	14	3
British Columbia	18	1
Manitoba	7	
New Brunswick	2	
Northwest Territories	4	
Nova Scotia	2	1
Nunavut	2	1
Ontario	23	1
Quebec	18	1
Saskatchewan	7	
Yukon	1	

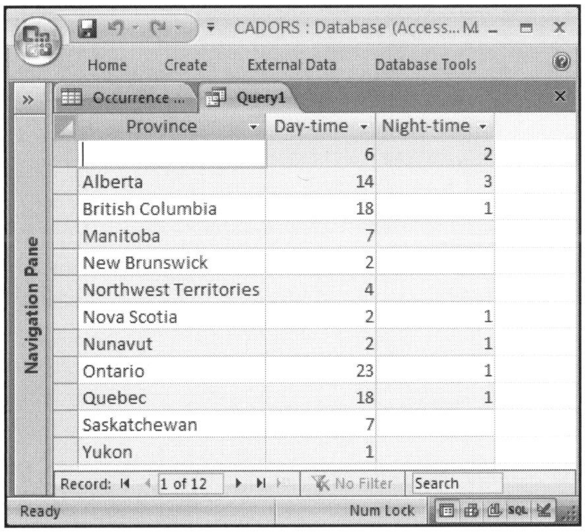

Fig. 5.33

We will save this query to use again.

The 'Crosstab' query will create a column for each unique value in the 'Column Heading' field. This result has only two columns because the 'Day or Night' field has only two possible entries. One frequent use of 'Crosstab' queries is to produce results that show sums or counts by year.

Queries Involving More than One Table

All the queries we have created so far have used only one table. But the principles we have learned can be applied to multi-table queries. As we noted earlier, the CADORS database contains four tables: 'Occurrence', 'Events', 'Aircraft', and 'Details'.

Queries involving more than one table are created in the same way as queries involving a single table, except that we add more than one table to the grid. Start a new query, and add both the 'Occurrence' and 'Events' tables to the grid. Next, we need to establish a relationship, or 'join condition', between the tables. In other words, we need to tell

Access how to join them. If you forget to define a relationship, you will end up with a Cartesian join, where every record in every table joins itself to every record in every other table. This produces a runaway query with meaningless results *that may well crash your computer.*

Luckily, creating a join condition in Access is easy. In the 'CADORS' database, the field that joins all of the tables together is the 'Cadors Number'. Each Cadors number appears only once in the 'Occurrence' table, but can appear many times in the other tables depending on how many related records there are. If you are unsure why, please refer to the discussion of relational database design above, p. 116.

Telling Access to join on the Cadors number is easy. Using your left mouse button, click on 'Cadors Number' in its table box at the top of the grid and hold and drag with the mouse to the same field in the other table, e.g., the 'Events06' table illustrated below. Let go, and a line will appear between the two to indicate the join.

If you are using the same related tables over and over, you can create a permanent relationship between them that Access will remember each time you open the database. Typically, this is not necessary for a journalistic project, but you can find details on how to do this in the Access 2007 'Help' file topic 'Create, edit, or delete a relationship'.

> ## ⚠ TECH TIP
>
> Sometimes, you will need to join tables with more than one field. For example, postal codes might be broken into two fields, one containing the first three characters, the other the last three. Both fields would have to be joined to create a unique join. If you joined only, say, the first three characters, every code with the first three characters in one table would be joined with every code with the same first three characters in the other table, even though most wouldn't really be related.

Once you have joined the linking field(s), you can create queries, mixing and matching fields from the two tables, using criteria, and sorting, as if you were working with one table. The fields you select from each table will be joined together horizontally based on the join condition(s) that you set. Because the principles behind single-table and multi-table queries are essentially the same, we won't run through each type of query again. Instead, we will simply present a couple of examples.

For the first, using the join we have established between the 'Events06' and the 'Occurrence 06' tables, we will build a query that shows how many incidents have occurred at each airport, where the event is a conflict between two aircraft—two planes getting too close to one another—sorted by the number of occurrences, but only where the airport name is not blank and where the count of the number of incidents is at least 10. In other words, we will draw from much of what we have learned before.

Notice that we also are renaming the centre column using an alias: 'Events' becomes 'Incident type'. Aliases are alternative field names you can assign in a query. You create an alias by typing the new name, followed by a colon, then by the original name, in the field line in the query grid. This is what the query looks like in the grid. You can follow the illustration to recreate the query:

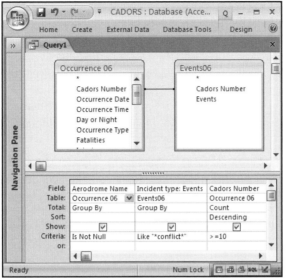

Fig. 5.34

This is what it looks like when it is run:

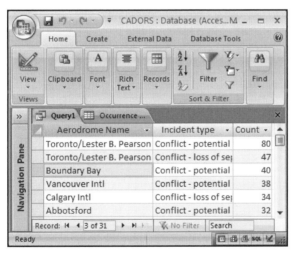

Fig. 5.35

⚠ TECH TIP

When there is a great deal of information in one field or you want to see better when you are entering information directly into the 'field' line of the query grid, you can open the zoom box. This is a separate window with plenty of room to read a long entry or enter a complex expression such as those we discuss in chapter 6. You open the zoom box by using the keystroke combination Shift + f2.

You can also change the vertical height of each row and the width of each field by dragging the boundary between the field names at the top of the table, or the boundary between the records at the far left of the table.

Enterprise Matches

Journalists can take advantage of the ability of Access and other database programs to join records between tables. You are not restricted to joining tables that were intended to be joined. Indeed, you can match any tables that have fields with the same entries. In 2002, the *Hamilton Spectator* matched a large table of political contributions in Ontario with a table of participants in the newly privatized energy market, revealing that companies who would benefit from the policy had been major contributors to the Progressive Conservative party, then in government, and to the Energy Minister.[6]

Other Queries that Change Your Tables

Until now we have focused on 'Select' queries, which help us analyze data. At times, we want to change data, by adding new records to a table, changing existing records, deleting records, and making entirely new tables. We can do these things using 'Action' queries.

Append Queries

In this exercise, we will add records from a table called 'Newoccurrence' to our 'Occurrence 06' table using an 'Append' query. Begin by starting a new query in 'Design' view, and adding the 'Newoccurrence' table. Click on 'Append' in the 'Query Type' area of the 'Design' ribbon. You will be prompted for which table to which you would like to append the data.

Fig. 5.36

Choose the 'Occurrence 06' table, click on the 'Current database' radio button, and click 'OK'.

The 'Append To' query grid looks like the regular grid except that it adds an 'Append To' line that contains the names of the fields in the receiving table where the data will be appended.

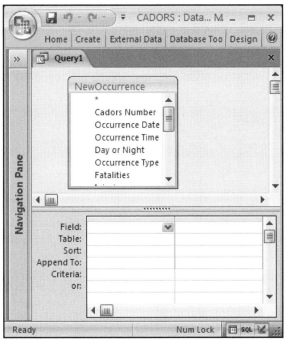

Fig. 5.37

Next, add the fields that you would like to add to the other table. In this case, we want to add all of the fields, so move the asterisk into the 'Query' grid. Do this only if you know all of the field names and the data types in the appending and receiving tables are identical. Otherwise, move the field names into the grid one at a time. If any of the field names in the table you are appending from are different from those in the destination table, you will have to manually pick the field that will receive the records by changing the field name in the 'Append To' line of the grid.

Open the 'Design' ribbon and click 'Run'. You will be asked if you would like to append the records and the number of records being appended will be noted. Click 'YES' and the records will be added.

Make-Table Queries

Sometimes, you will want to make the output of a query into a new table. You may want to provide a portion of the table to someone else, or make a separate copy of part of your data to run further queries. Either way, the process is simple.

Again, start a new query in 'Design' view, and click on the 'Make-table query' icon in the 'Query Type' area of the 'Design' ribbon. You will be prompted to name your new table. Now, design a query as you would any other, until the result is the new table you want. When you run the query, you will be asked if you would like to paste xx number of records into a new table. Answer 'Yes', and the new table will be created.

Update Queries

An 'Update' query is used to change data in an existing table. Create a new query, add the 'Occurrence 06' table, and click on the 'Update Query' icon in the 'Query Type' area. You will notice that parts of the grid are labelled differently. The 'Field' line is the same as in the conventional grid, but here you will add only the fields you wish to change plus any fields you wish to use to limit which records are updated. We will pick the

'Aerodrome ID' and 'Aerodrome Name' fields. We will then use an Update query to correct the entry 'Brandon Muni' in the 'Aerodrome Name' field, replacing it with 'Brandon municipal'.

In the 'Update To' line under Aerodrome Name, we will enter 'Brandon municipal'. In the 'Criteria' line under 'Aerodrome ID', we will enter 'CYBR', thus:

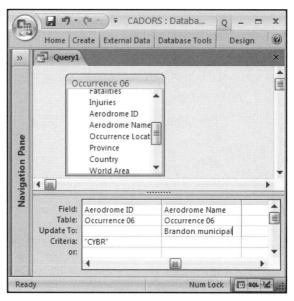

Fig. 5.38

This simple query asks Access to update the 'Aerodrome Name' field to 'Brandon municipal', replacing whatever was in the field before with the new entry, but only when the aerodrome ID is 'CYBR', which stands for Brandon Municipal Airport.

When you click 'Run', you will be told how many rows you are about to update. When you click 'OK', the table will be updated with the new information.

You can also use an 'Update' query to populate a new field you have added to the table in 'Design View'. Update queries can become quite complex, sometimes involving more than one table, and can be combined with advanced tools such as string functions to update fields in almost any way you like. We will return to 'Update' queries in the next chapter.

Delete Queries

The final type of query we will deal with here is also the most dangerous. A 'Delete' query removes records from the table that meet the criteria you set. It works like a 'Select' query in reverse. First, you start a new query; next, add the table you want to delete from; and then add the field or fields that will control the deletion. Enter into the 'Criteria' line the terms that will limit which rows will be deleted, in this example, Like "*Toronto*". This example query, *which we do NOT suggest you run*, deletes records from the 'Occurrence 06' table where the occurrence location contains the word 'Toronto'.

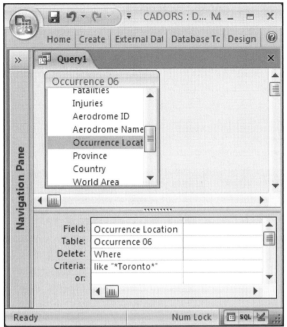

Fig. 5.39

When you run the query you will be warned you are about to delete records and told how many. Once you click 'Yes', the deleted records will be irretrievable—another reason why you make backups.

> ## ⚠ TECH TIP
>
> Before you run a query that will change the structure or contents of your table, it is a good idea to create a backup copy. Do this by running a 'Make-Table' query, and including all fields. You can also copy a table by right-clicking the table name in the Navigation Pane, clicking 'Copy', then right-clicking again and clicking 'Paste' (or using the keyboard shortcut Ctr + v). You can now choose to copy just the table structure, which will create a copy with no data, or choose to copy the structure and the data, or choose to append the data into an existing table. You will also need to enter the name of the new table or the table you would like to paste into.

You can also delete records and columns manually in Access, by clicking at the left end of a field or at the top of a field. Any of the normal delete methods in Windows will then delete the record or field. You will get an 'Are you sure?' prompt before the delete is completed. Once deleted, the record or field is irretrievable.

⚠ **TECH TIP**

Access 2007 has a security feature that will sometimes block you from running Action queries that change your data. This feature is new to this version of the program. To ensure you can run these queries, click on the 'Office' button and 'Access Options'. Click the 'Trust Centre' tab and 'Trust Centre Settings'. Make sure the 'Show the Message Bar in all applications when content has been blocked' radio button is selected. Click 'OK'. Close and reopen your database. When it reopens, you will see a security warning at the top of the screen, just below the ribbon. Click on 'Options' and ensure the 'Enable this Content' radio button is selected. Click 'OK', and you will be able to run Action queries.

Importing Data and Exporting for Further Analysis

Sometimes you will be lucky, and you will receive data for your database project in Access format. All formats since Access 2000 can be opened directly in the current version. If the data is in Access 1995 or 1997 format, you will have to convert it upon opening it, as Access 2007 can't work directly with these earlier formats.

Other types of data have to be imported into or linked with Access. You can access any of the needed 'Wizards' by clicking on the 'External Data' ribbon.

The most common types of files that you will import are Excel worksheets, delimited text files, and fixed-width text files. As we discussed in Chapter 3, a delimited text file is a file containing data in which the field boundaries have been replaced by a delimiter, often a comma or tab, and each row is in a new line. The field names will often be in the first row. A fixed-width file separates the fields with spaces instead to create evenly arrayed columns of information.

We will walk through the process of importing a delimited text version of the 'Occurrence06' table. The other imports work in much the same way; the Access program guides you through the process.

Begin by clicking on the tab for 'External data' ribbon, and clicking on 'Text file' in the import area. That will bring up this dialogue box:

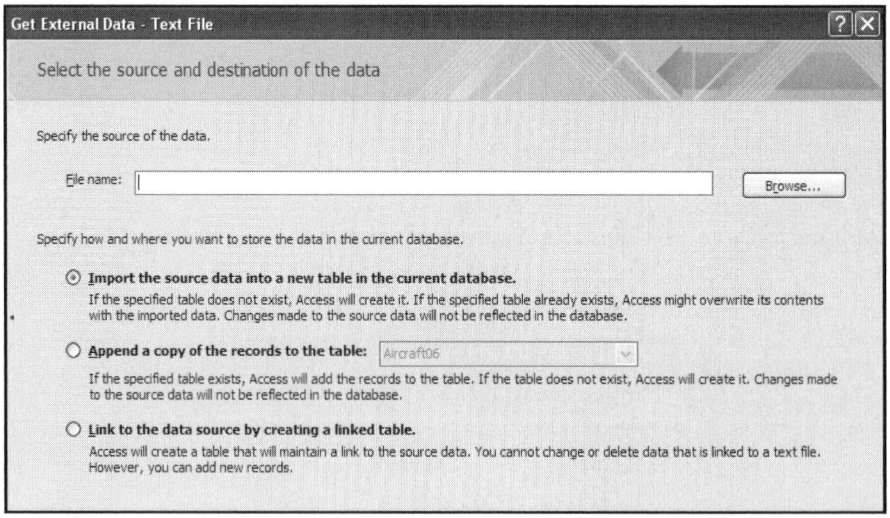

Fig. 5.40

Here you are given three choices: to import the source data into a new table, to append the source data to an existing table, or to link to the file. When you link to a file, you don't import the actual data into your database, but instead create an ongoing link to it. It creates a mirror of the file in your database. When the external file changes,

TECH TIP ⚠

In older versions, click on 'Get External Data/ Import' under the 'File' menu to begin the same import process.

your mirrored copy changes with it. This is in contrast to what happens when you import a file. An imported file remains a static copy of how it looked at the time of importing into your database.

For now, select 'Import into a New Table', and click on the 'Browse' button to open up a standard 'File open' dialogue box. Navigate through the directories on the hard drive until you find the file you wish to import. Click 'Open' and you will be returned to the above dialogue box. Click 'OK', and the import text 'Wizard' will open. It looks like this:

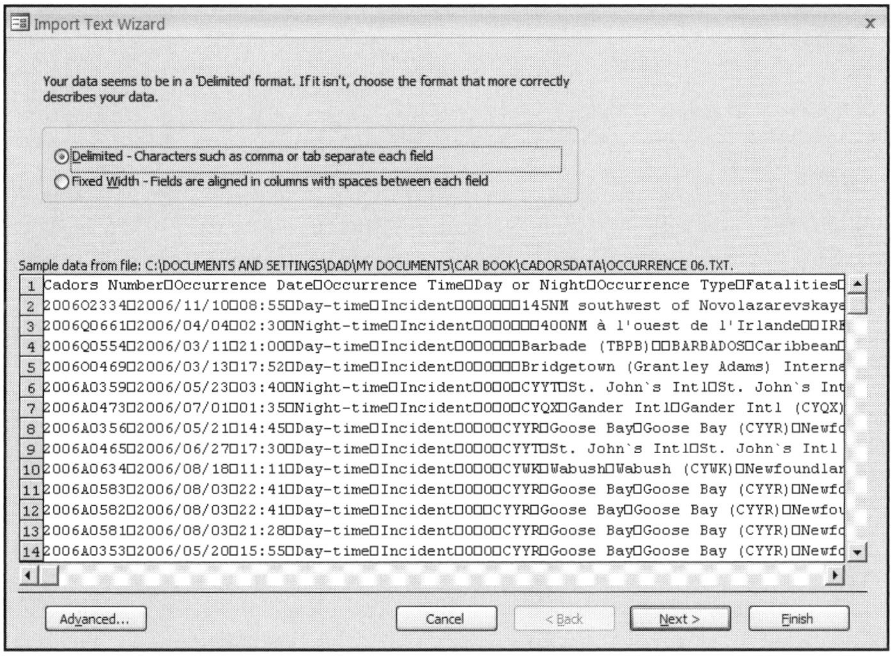

Fig. 5.41

Access will often 'guess' accurately which type of file you are trying to import. In this case, we want 'delimited'. Make sure the 'Delimited' radio button is selected. You will see a sample of the data in the text file in the area below. When you are satisfied, click 'Next'. On the next screen, pick the type of delimiter used in the file, in this case 'Tab'. Also, if the field names are contained in the top row of the text file, click on the 'First Row Contains Field Names' check box. If the file uses a text qualifier—single or double quotation marks that enclose each text field—open the 'Text Qualifier' list and select the type of qualifier. Clicking 'Next' brings up a screen on which you can specify the data type, and if you like, change the name, of each field.

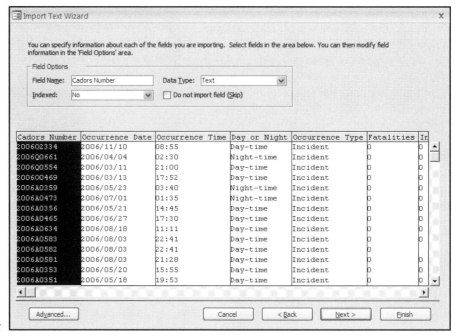

Fig. 5.42

To confirm or change the settings for any field, click on the field name, and fill in the options. You can decide not to import a field, and you can choose to index any field.

When you are sure you have set the fields correctly, click 'Next' to bring up the next screen.

⚠️ TECH TIP

An index in a database table is similar in concept to an index in a book. It is a pointer to the data contained in a field, which allows the program to run queries based on that field more quickly. You should consider indexing any field you will use frequently in queries. For more information on indexes, see the topic 'Create and use an index to improve performance' in the Access Help system.

Earlier in the chapter we mentioned the concept of a primary key. This screen allows you to specify an existing field as the primary key, to allow Access either to add an autonumber field to the table to function as the primary key, or to do without a primary key altogether. Once you click 'OK', you will be prompted to confirm the name of the table that will be created in your database.

When you click 'Finish', Access will again prompt you, this time asking if you would like to save the import steps. If you choose to do so, Access will remember all of the choices you made. Any time you would like to import the same file again, click on 'Saved imports' on the 'External data' ribbon.

That's it. You have imported the file and can begin working with it. It will appear in the 'Tables' list in the 'Navigation Pane'.

Exporting Data

Just as Access can import data, it can also export data. You may find yourself using this ability frequently, to send text copies of data to other journalists or to another computer you use, or to convert to Excel format to do further calculations.

In the 'Export' area of the 'External data' ribbon, click on the 'File format' to which you would like to export. A new dialogue box will pop up asking you to specify where the exported file should be saved. When you click 'OK', you will be offered further options depending on the file type you have chosen. For 'Export to text', for example, you will be asked whether you would like to save as a delimited or a fixed-width file. The choices are essentially the opposite

TECH TIP ⚠

In older versions choose 'Export' under the 'File' menu.

of those offered when you import. At the end of the process, you will be offered the chance to save your export steps in case you should choose to run the export again.

Access Reports

Access contains powerful features for creating reports. Reports present raw or summarized data in a more attractive format than the usual Datasheet view. They are used typically to provide summaries to supervisors or colleagues who do not work with the data. They can also be used to create simple html reports for posting on the Internet. Reports have limited application in computer-assisted reporting and a detailed discussion of them is beyond the scope of this book. However, one advantage of reports is their ability to show individual data records and totals for numerical fields at the same time.

In the aviation database, we can use this feature to show a list of incidents at airports, with the dates and times, whether the incidents occurred during daytime or night-time, and the numbers of injuries and fatalities. We'll use the report 'Wizard', which simplifies the creation of a report. To begin, click on the tab for the 'Create' ribbon, then click on 'Report Wizard'. This will bring up the Report Wizard dialogue box.

1. The first step is to select the fields we want to see in the report. Use the small arrow (>) to move fields from the 'Available Fields' box to the 'Selected Fields' box, as shown here:

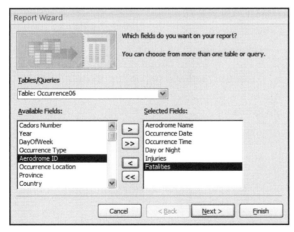

Fig. 5.43

The small arrow (<) pointing back to the 'Available Fields' box is used to remove fields. The double arrows (>>) add all of the fields or (<<) remove them.
Click 'Next'.

2. In the next step, you can select fields for grouping. This is the same grouping concept that we saw in queries, except now the grouping takes place on the report. When you choose to group on a field, each unique entry

TECH TIP ⚠

In older versions, choose 'Report' in the dropdown list accessed from the 'Object type' icon.

in that field will appear as a new header with the remaining fields shown in detail below. We will group on 'Aerodrome Name', as in this image:

Fig. 5.44

The 'Grouping Options' button gives you the option of grouping on the entire contents of the field, or on just the first or first few letters or each name.

Click 'Next'.

3. The next step allows you to sort on one or more of the other fields. We will sort by 'Occurrence Date', in ascending order.

   If we click on 'Summary Options' we can now choose to do some simple math on one or more numerical fields. In this case, we'll sum the injuries and fatalities fields. We'll also calculate the percentage of all injuries and fatalities for each aerodrome. This is what the dialogue looks like when it is completed.

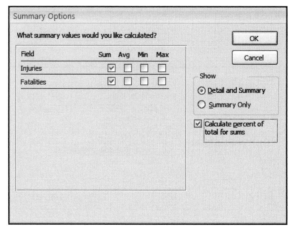

Fig. 5.45

Click 'OK' and 'Next'.

4. The next two screens allow you to manipulate how the reports will be laid out and are self-explanatory. Clicking through them brings you to the last step where you name your report and choose to either 'Preview' it, or change its design.

5. We will choose to preview our report, and click 'Finish'. This shows a portion of the report, with the incidents in Port Alberni, and the associated totals and percentages:

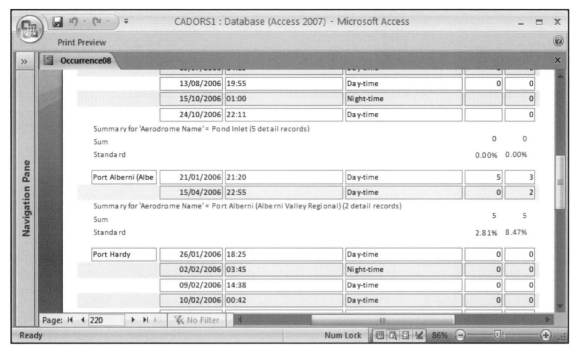

Fig. 5.46

If you right-click on the tab with the report name, you can switch to 'Design' view and modify the design of the report. You can move, resize, and delete any of the report's elements.

For more information, go to the Access 'Help' menu, and look for topics using the keyword 'reports'.

Bringing It All Together

In this chapter, we have gone over most of the basic tools you need to get up and running to analyze databases using Microsoft Access. You now know how to obtain and import a database, manipulate it using filter and sort, and analyze it with queries. You also know how to add, update, and delete data in a table, as well as how to make a new table using a query. Finally, you have learned the rudiments of creating Access reports. In the next chapter we will cover more advanced database techniques.

Five Stories You Can Do

1. Obtain a copy of your municipality's pet-licensing database. In this perennial story, reporters see which names and breeds are most common in their city or town. An excellent starter story.
2. Get your local fire department's calls database. Query the database to find out where fires are occurring, what is causing them (where are the arsons taking place in your community?), and how long it takes firefighters to reach them.
3. Do the same with the ambulance calls database for your area.
4. Obtain your local public health department's database of restaurant inspections. A blockbuster story wherever it has been done, reporters typically query to find out

which restaurants have had the most violations, whether inspectors are meeting legal requirements for inspection frequency, and whether poor operators actually face sanctions.

5. Download Health Canada's adverse drug reaction data from <www.hc-sc.gc.ca/dhp-mps/medeff/databasdon/extract_extrait_e.html>. If the link printed here doesn't work, go to <www.oupcanada.com/CAR.html> where you will find the current link as long as the data remain available.) Do your own analysis of which drugs are causing severe reactions, and find people in your community who have suffered as a result.

Advanced Database Techniques

Fred Vallance-Jones

What We'll Cover

- Building your own database.
- Using date and other functions to update tables, and in queries.
- Manipulating and cleaning data.
- Analyzing large databases in MySQL.
- Writing queries directly in structured query language.

In the last chapter, we explored the basic features of Access that you will use most often. This chapter is about the specialized skills you need to conquer the challenges that you will face as you embark on more complex data projects. Some of these more difficult tasks include:

- Building your own database to analyze information not available in electronic form.
- Dividing up data in a table into smaller chunks to make analysis easier. For example, you may have a single date field, but would like to add a year field so you can easily write queries to count a number of events per year. Or, you may need to divide up an address field into street number and street name fields so you can sort first on street names and then on the street numbers.
- Doing calculations based on the contents of existing fields. This could involve calculating the time elapsed between two dates or the percentage change between two fields.
- Correcting large numbers of misspelled words in key fields and eliminating duplicate records to make accurate, complete analysis possible.
- Using Excel to do further analysis of results obtained from database queries.
- Analyzing databases too large for a desktop database such as Microsoft Access.

Building Your Own Database

Our discussion of databases has dealt mostly with data sets, such as the aviation database, that are obtained from government agencies. But sometimes, a ready-made database will not be available. Those are the times when you consider building your own.

When the *Toronto Star* investigated doctor discipline in Ontario, there was no database available detailing who had been disciplined, why, and what penalty had been assessed. So the paper teamed up with students at the Ryerson University School of Journalism to build its own database of 141 disciplinary cases, using public records from the College of Physicians and Surgeons of Ontario. The leadoff story found a medical complaints system 'cloaked in secrecy'.

> Data on those cases, compiled by *The Star* using the college's public records, reveal a disciplinary system that typically hands out lenient penalties, rarely revokes licences, can take years to render decisions, and puts doctors on higher legal footing than complainants.
>
> *The Star*'s data show that 111 doctors have been found guilty of offences ranging from fraud, drugging, and sexually assaulting patients, and missed diagnoses, some causing death. Of those, 34 received the college's maximum penalty—licence revocation. The majority of sanctions handed out were suspensions averaging less than three months or reprimands, usually with some conditions, such as cash fines, additional training or letters of apology. Ontario's college took an average of three years to reach those decisions—tied with Manitoba as the slowest medical disciplinary system in Canada.[1]

A similar situation arose when the *Hamilton Spectator* needed a database of election contributions to Ontario's political parties. No such database readily existed, but contributions information was available in Microsoft Word files on the Elections Ontario website. The paper downloaded hundreds of reports for provincial parties, riding associations, and individual candidates, then extracted the information into a single table. The resulting database was used in numerous stories and made available to the newsroom for future enquiries about contributions. As new contributions were made public, they were added. The data were also used by the *Spectator* and the *Toronto Star* for a major investigation that showed how the contribution rules could be manipulated to maximize contributions from large corporate contributors.[2]

> Ontario political parties routinely circulate hundreds of thousands of dollars in political contributions through local ridings, maximizing the money they can legally raise from large donors. Taking advantage of a loophole in Ontario's Election Finances Act, the parties can, in an election year, legally collect as much as $25,000 from donors instead of the normal $15,000 limit set out in the act. The extra money is initially given to the party. It splits the one donation into as many as five, of $2,000 each, and transfers the money to five riding associations. The associations, in turn, send the money back to the central party. The manoeuver enabled the Progressive Conservatives to raise nearly a million dollars extra in 1999 and 2000. The Liberals, doing the same thing, raised an extra $72,000 in 1999.[3]

In 2007, the *Ottawa Citizen* uncovered an eerily similar financial arrangement involving the federal Conservative Party. The 'in-and-out' system was used to send central party money to ridings during the 2006 federal election. The money was then used to buy advertising that was nearly indistinguishable from national ads. In all three cases, the analysis and stories that followed would not have been possible had the reporters not built their own databases.

You will develop a better understanding of when to build your own database after you have worked with data for a while. As your understanding grows of how data is stored and can be analyzed to develop stories, you will see many possibilities for database stories.

But you will also discover that in some cases, no databases exist, or that it would be faster and more efficient to build you own. Building a database can be as simple as copying and pasting html pages from Microsoft Internet Explorer into Excel, then importing the tables into a database application such as Access for further, more detailed analysis. The *Spectator* has been doing this for years with the annual Ontario 'sunshine' list of public-sector salaries greater than $100,000. On other occasions, you will have to enter information from paper records by hand, as the *Star* did for 'Medical Secrets'.

Designing the Database

Once you have identified the data you want to use, the first step is to design the database and its tables. You have a distinct advantage when you build your own because you can control exactly what you enter. Because you have a good sense of the analysis you want to do before you begin, you can tailor the fields to your needs.

Examine your source information carefully and consider what is most important about it. Say, you wanted to build a database of zoning-variance decisions at city hall, based on minutes of meetings of the planning committee. A variance is an authorization to build something not normally permitted by the zoning bylaw. Your purpose is to analyze how many variances are being allowed, who is getting them, how this may have changed over time, what kinds of developments are being allowed by means of variances, and whether the committee members tend to vote as a bloc or to divide their votes.

These are some of the fields you might include in your table(s):

- An ID number for the decision;
- The date of the hearing;
- The date the decision was made;
- The name of the developer or proponent;
- The type of developer or proponent (e.g., individual or corporation);
- The type of application, whether for a variance or other exception to the usual rules;
- The type of development (e.g., new homes, commercial building, etc.);
- The address of the development, probably as separate fields for street number, street address, and community;
- The dollar value of the development;
- The outcome;
- Whether the requester was told to come back with more information;
- The number of votes in favour;
- The number of votes against.

Once you have decided what you would like to include in the fields, you need to decide what the field data types will be. In the above examples, you would want to enter the dates in date format, the dollar value in a currency or number field, the outcome in a yes/no field (assuming the only possibilities are 'approved' or 'not approved'—if a third possibility is 'deferred' you could use a text type), the numbers of votes in number fields, and the remaining information in text fields.

Flat File or Relational?

The fields we listed above could easily be accommodated in one flat-file table. Except for the proponents, little else is likely to be repeated, and it is unlikely you will be building a table large enough to warrant separating this information into different tables.

But what if you also wanted to analyze how different councillors voted, and how their votes changed according to proponents, types of developments, and so on? If you wanted to stick to a flat file, you could simply add a field for each councillor, and enter their vote there. But what if you wanted to be more sophisticated in your analysis, and also determine how groups of councillors from richer and poorer areas voted? At this point, you would want to consider a relational structure for your database (see Chapter 5 for a more complete discussion of relational database design).

A logical approach would be to create a table of councillors and a separate table of councillor votes. The councillor table would have one record per councillor and would likely include last and first name fields for each councillor, the area or ward each represents, whether the councillor represents a richer or poorer area (however you would define this), and perhaps some 'boiler plate' information such as city-hall and home telephone numbers. These would likely all be text fields. The table would have a councillor ID number field to relate it to the others.

The vote table would include the detailed information on how councillors voted. You could create one record for each vote by a councillor, with the table containing a field for the decision ID from the main table, the councillor ID from the councillor table, and a text field for the vote itself (e.g., Yes, No, Abstained, Absent).

With this setup, you could then build queries to analyze the vote from many angles, while keeping the data entry manageable.

Creating the Tables

Once you have mapped out the database and table designs, you can create the actual tables. In Access you will need to create a new blank database. Once you do so, and the database opens, Access 2007 automatically creates a generically-named 'table 1.'

On either the 'Datasheet' or 'Home' ribbons, click on the 'View' button. Access will prompt you to give your table a more useful name. Once you do so, you will be switched to table 'Design View' (additional tables can be created by clicking 'Table' on the Create ribbon).

> ⚠ **TECH TIP**
>
> In older versions you create a new table by clicking on one of the 'Create-table' options in the Database window.

In 'Design View', Access will have automatically created the first field, an autonumber field, which it presumes is the primary key for the table. If you would like to use that as your ID field, go ahead and keep it, although you may wish to rename it. You can now proceed to add the remaining fields. The 'Design' ribbon provides you with a number of tools to toggle a field on and off as the primary key, to insert and delete fields from the

> ⚠ **TECH TIP**
>
> It is important when naming tables and other objects, as well as when naming fields, not to use any of Access's reserved words or characters. Reserved words and characters , such as 'SUM', 'AND' and '#', are used as part of Access's internal language. If you use them for names or in text strings not surrounded by double quotation marks, Access may interpret them as command words or characters and generate an error. You can read more about this in Microsoft website articles 'List of reserved words in Access 2002 and in later versions of Access', found at: <support.microsoft.com/kb/286335/> and 'Special characters that you must avoid when you work with Access databases', at: <support.microsoft.com/kb/826763/>.

design grid, and to index fields. You are familiar by now with the 'Design' ribbon. It is illustrated below as we continue to work with the 'Occurrence 06' table.

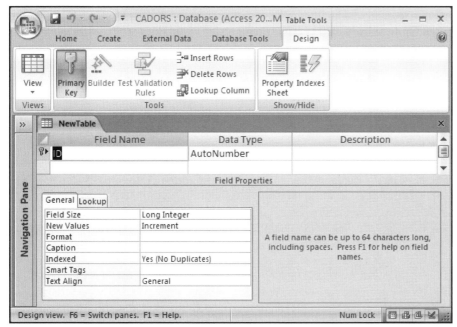

Fig. 6.1

Adding your fields is a simple matter of filling in the form. In the lower window you are also presented with a number of ways to restrict what can be entered in the table, such as setting validation rules or creating input masks. We are not covering these here, as these typically are used more by businesses who will have many people entering data. The Access Help system provides detailed information on how to use these features, which are common to the 2007 and earlier versions.

When you are done, save the table and click on 'View' to return to 'Datasheet View'. You can create additional tables by clicking 'Table' on the 'Create' ribbon.

Adding Data

In Access, you have two choices for adding data. One is simply to open the table in 'Datasheet View' and begin to type in values. For many smaller projects, this method will be perfectly adequate. For more involved data-entry projects, you may want to create an Access form. Go to the Access 'Help' file under 'Create a Form' for detailed information on how to create a form to use in adding information to a table. Access will do all the work for you of linking your form to your table. Any changes you make in the form will be reflected in the original data table.

Building a Table Month by Month with Updated Data

One of the great advantages of building your own database is that you can add data as more information becomes available. The example we used in Chapter 5 of a city hall reporter routinely updating a list of votes is a good one. In Access, simply open your table(s) or form(s), and begin adding to the database.

Other Ways of Building Databases

You won't always have to enter data manually. Sometimes, the raw material for your database already exists in electronic form—just the wrong electronic form. Chapter 10 has detailed information on how to extract data from Adobe's pdf files, from Microsoft Word, from formatted reports, and from searchable databases online. Whatever method you use, once you are done you can begin analyzing the data using the methods you learned in Chapter 5, and the remainder of this one.

Splitting Existing Data in Tables

In an ideal world, every database would contain all you need to analyze it for journalistic purposes. But in reality agencies don't build their databases with reporters in mind. They have their own record-keeping and reporting requirements and end-users rarely work with raw data the way journalists do. Database administrators develop pre-set reports that employees run periodically to extract specific information they need to do their jobs.

When you receive a database, you generally are faced with the task of figuring out how to analyze it yourself, and that often will mean modifying the data by adding fields that don't exist in the database as kept by the agency.

The need to create a new field usually comes as you begin the process of reviewing the database, and considering the analysis you want to do. The first step is to create an empty column or columns to contain the value or values you want to add. The next is to start an update query and use string functions to extract part of an existing field to insert in the new field. The existing field may be in the same table, or in another table.

Typically, you will be working with Access functions. We will examine two types, date functions and string functions.

Date Functions

When the *Hamilton Spectator*, the *Toronto Star*, and the *Record* of Waterloo Region were analyzing the data for the joint air safety project we talked about in Chapter 5, the reporters needed to add fields for incident year and incident month to the occurrence table. These fields were needed so they could easily analyze trends over several years, and see if certain mechanical failures were related to cold winter weather.

The answer to the problem was Access date functions. These are exactly as their name suggests. They manipulate an existing date field in order to extract a portion of the date, either as part of a query, or to populate an entirely new field. They are quite similar to the date functions we looked at in Chapter 4 on advanced Excel. The main ones with which we are concerned are:

- YEAR function   Extracts the year from a date field, either in date format or formatted as a date in a text field.
- MONTH function   Works in the same way to extract the month.
- DAY function   Works in the same way to extract the day.
- WEEKDAY function   Extracts the day of the week as a number from 1 to 7.
- WEEKDAYNAME function   Used in conjunction with WEEKDAY, returns the name of the day of week.
- MONTHNAME function   Used in conjunction with MONTH, returns the name of the month as text.

The first four work in pretty much the same way, returning a number that represents the year, month, day, or day of the week. The fifth function returns the names of the days of the week as text.

The YEAR function is entered like this:

YEAR([NAME OF DATE FIELD])

It doesn't matter whether the date field is an actual date/time type, or if it is a text field containing a date. As long as Access can recognize the field as containing a date, it should be able to extract the year. It works as well on January 14, 2004 as it does on 2004/01/14. The field doesn't even have to have a consistent date format so long as the entry is a recognizable date.

Let's walk through this task, using the 'Occurrence06' table.

First, open the 'Occurrence 06' table in 'Design View', and in the top of the 'Design' grid, highlight the row where you would like the new field to be inserted. In this case, the 'Occurrence Time' row will be selected in the 'Occurrence 06' table Design grid.

TECH TIP ⚠

Before you do anything to alter the structure of a table, by adding fields or changing data types, you should make a backup of the original, unaltered table. That way, if you make a mistake that results in your losing data, you can always revert to the original. Either make a copy of the table within your database or, even better, make a backup of the entire database file. Right-click on the 'Start' button and choose 'Explore.' It allows you to explore the files on your computer. Right-click on your database file and choose 'Copy', or click on the 'Office' button and choose 'Manage/Back Up Database'.

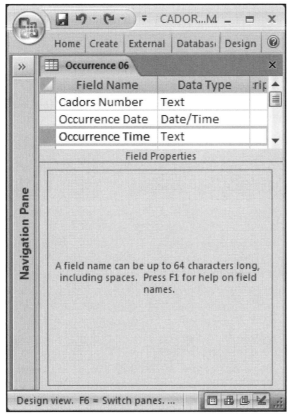

Fig. 6.2

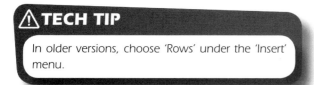

⚠ TECH TIP

In older versions, choose 'Rows' under the 'Insert' menu.

To add the new field, click 'Insert Rows' on the 'Design' ribbon, *or* right-click on the selected field name and choose 'Insert Rows' from the menu that appears.

When the new field has been added, the 'Occurrence Time' field will be shifted down one row. Now, give your new field a name and choose a data type. The type you choose depends on what you are extracting. In this case, we will choose a 'Number/longer integer' data type and call the new field 'Year' before saving the table structure.

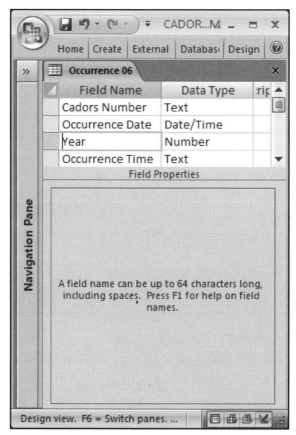

Fig. 6.3

The next thing you need to do is start a new query in 'Design View'. Remember that you do this by opening the 'Create' ribbon and choosing 'Query Design'. In the 'Query Type' portion of the 'Query Design' ribbon, choose 'Update'. Now, bring the new 'Year' field into the Query Design grid.

The basic syntax for the year function is 'YEAR (a date Access can understand)'. The part within the parentheses is what is called an 'argument' in computer talk. No, it's not going to put up a fight. An argument in this context is an instruction to the program of what to have the function do. In this case, you are telling Access to apply the function to the date contained within the parentheses.

Of course, feeding Access each date would be tedious and time-consuming. So the program allows you to give it the name of the field instead, enclosed within square parentheses. In this case, you end up with the function written as 'YEAR([occurrence date])'.

⚠ TECH TIP

Square brackets are Access's way of knowing that a word or words are the name of a field (or table). They can be used not only in functions or calculated fields, but in the 'Criteria' line. Like quotation marks, you can sometimes do without square brackets around field names, but if you use them, you ensure Access understands that what you have entered is a field name. When you use a field name in a function or calculation, Access replaces the field name with the actual contents in that field in each record.

Enter 'YEAR([occurrence date])' in the 'Update To' line of the query you have created, under the new 'Year field', as in this illustration:

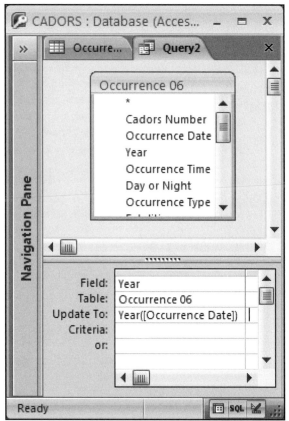

Fig. 6.4

After running the update query, go back to the table in 'Datasheet View'; you should see that the 'Year' field now contains the year, extracted from the 'Occurrence Date' field, as in this illustration:

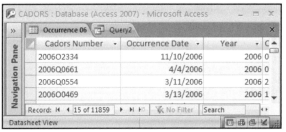

Fig. 6.5

We are not going to demonstrate the month, day, and weekday functions here, because they work identically to the year function. Just insert 'MONTH', 'DAY', or 'WEEKDAY' in the place of 'YEAR' before the brackets.

The 'WEEKDAYNAME' function is a little different in that it produces text instead of numbers, and because it needs to be fed a number representing the day of the week in order to produce the written-out version. You can provide that number, however, by using the 'WEEKDAY' function to first extract the day of the week from a date, then using that as an argument for the 'WEEKDAYNAME' function. This is the basic syntax for 'WEEKDAYNAME':

Weekdayname(a number from 1 to 7 representing a day of the week).

The number within the brackets can be a number, or it can be another function that returns a number, more particularly in our case, the 'WEEKDAY function, as in:

Weekdayname(weekday([date field name]))

Okay, let's try it with the 'Occurrence 06' table.

In 'Design View', add a new field to the table, after the 'Year' field, called 'dayofweek'. Make it a text field.

Now, start a new query in 'Design View'; make it an 'Update Query'; and bring the new 'Dayofweek' field into the grid. In the 'Update To' line, enter this expression:

WEEKDAYNAME(WEEKDAY([OCCURRENCE DATE]))

With all the parentheses, this may seem a little hard to follow, so let's tear it apart into its component parts. Inside the outer set of parentheses you find the weekday function, used in exactly the same way as the 'YEAR' function discussed above. If it were used by itself it would return a number from 1 to 7, with '1' representing Sunday and '7', Saturday. Actually, you can make '1' represent any starting day of the week by adding a second argument to the function. WEEKDAY(date,1) would make the first day Monday. WEEKDAY(date,2) would make it Tuesday, and so on.

The result of the 'WEEKDAY' function within the innermost set of parentheses is that a number from 1 to 7 is returned. This then becomes the argument for the 'WEEKDAY-NAME' function, which then translates that number into the day of the week written out. This is what the query should look like before you run it:

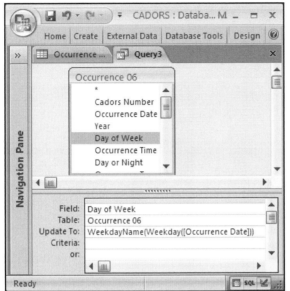

Fig. 6.6

If you go to the 'Occurrence 06' table, the new 'Dayofweek' field should now have the days of the week as seen here:

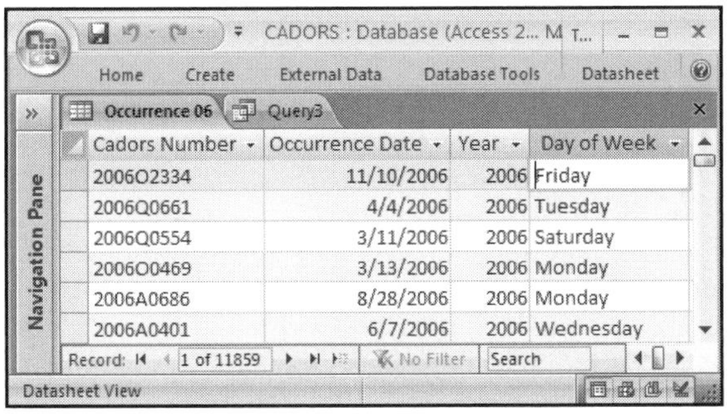

Cadors Number	Occurrence Date	Year	Day of Week
2006O2334	11/10/2006	2006	Friday
2006Q0661	4/4/2006	2006	Tuesday
2006Q0554	3/11/2006	2006	Saturday
2006O0469	3/13/2006	2006	Monday
2006A0686	8/28/2006	2006	Monday
2006A0401	6/7/2006	2006	Wednesday

Fig. 6.7

Working Out the Number of Days between Two Dates Using DateDiff

A common challenge faced during database analysis is working out the time that elapsed between two dates. As long as they are in different fields, this is not difficult. Access has a function called DateDiff made just for this purpose. It is really easy to use, so long as the two fields are both in date/time format. The basic syntax is DATEDIFF(Interval,date1,date2)

The interval is the units in which you would like the difference to be stated. Access offers a number of choices, but the ones you will most commonly use are yyyy for year, m for month, and d for day, always set in double quotation marks. If you are working out a time difference of only a few hours, you can also use h for hour, n (m is already used for month so n is used instead) for minute, and s for second.

For this example, we will work with a table of Ontario Liberal Party contributions, available through the website <www.oupcanada.com/CAR.html>.

In the table, both the deposit date of the contribution and the date it was reported to Elections Ontario are recorded:

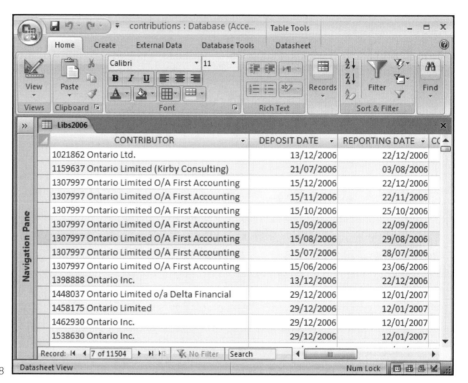

Fig. 6.8

Using the 'DATEDIFF' function, we can work out the number of days that elapsed between the two, to see how promptly the party reports money it receives.

Again, we will add a new field to the table, and call it 'days_elapsed'. We will make it a long integer, number type. We will then start an 'Update' query, and add the new field to the grid. Now, in the 'Update To' line, enter this expression: DATEDIFF("d",[deposit date],[reporting date]). The query should look like this:

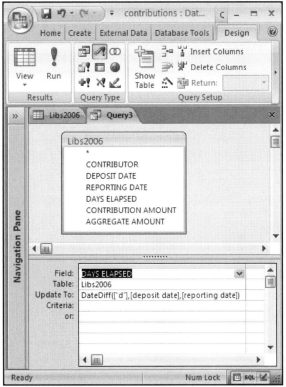

Fig. 6.9

When you run the query, the field is updated:

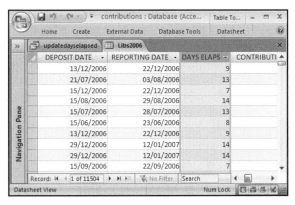

Fig. 6.10

Using String Functions to Update Fields

Just as date functions allow you to extract portions of dates, string functions allow you to extract portions of text fields. They are a little more complicated, because you have to tell Access where to look in a text field to find the part to extract, but otherwise, they are entered and used in much the same way.

The key string functions are 'LEFT', 'RIGHT', 'MID', 'INSTR', and 'INSTRREV'. Used singly or in combination, they allow extensive manipulation of text in fields.

Let's look at how each function works.

'LEFT' starts at the beginning of a text string, and extracts a specified number of characters going to the right. The basic syntax is:

LEFT(text string, number of characters to extract).

'RIGHT' begins at the end of a text string, and extracts a specified number of characters going to the left. The basic syntax is:

RIGHT(text string, number of characters to extract).

'MID' begins at a specified point within a string, counted from the left, and extracts a specified number of characters to the right of that point. The basic syntax is:

MID(text string, number of characters from left where portion to be extracted begins, total number of characters to be extracted).

'INSTR' is different from the others in that it returns a number representing the position in a string, as counted from the left, of a character you specify. It usually is used in combination with one of the other string functions. The basic syntax is:

INSTR(text string, 'character to report position of').

A variant is 'INSTRREV', which starts looking for the specified character(s) from the right side, although it still returns a number representing the position counted from the left.

'LEN' returns a number representing the full length of a text string. The basic syntax is: LEN(text string).

In each case, you can substitute a field name, enclosed in square brackets, for the text string.

The simplest use of string functions is to slice off a few characters at the beginning or end of a field using the 'LEFT' or 'RIGHT' string functions. For example, in the 'Occurrence 06' table, left([Cadors Number],4) would extract the first four characters of the Cadors Number, the year in which the ID was created (Note that you wouldn't use this to create a year field because some 2006 incidents were entered after December 31 and have Cadors numbers starting with 2007).

Usually, though, reporters want to do something a little more complicated, and most often it involves splitting an existing text field into two or more parts. In order to divide a text field, you need to do two things. First, identify a character that can be used to mark the splitting point and, second, write an expression to accomplish the split.

In a table of 2005 Progressive Conservative Party donations in Alberta (again, available for download from <www.oupcanada.com/CAR.html>, there is a single field for the contributor. It is good practice, though, to have separate fields for first and last names to make querying by last name, or first name, easier. This is what the table looks like before we make any changes:

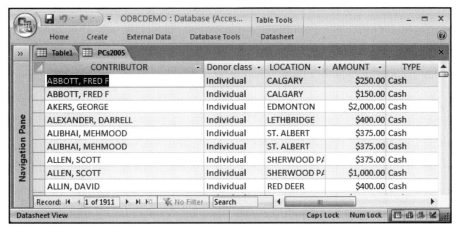

Fig. 6.11

The first step is to create new fields. Switch to table 'Design View' and add text fields for last and first names. Your table should end up looking like this:

Fig. 6.12

Now, start a new 'Update' query. We will write a string function in the 'Update To' line under the last name field. This is the expression to enter:

LEFT([CONTRIBUTOR],INSTR([CONTRIBUTOR],',')-1)

Again, this may seem confusing at first, so we'll divide it into its component parts, this time from the outside in. The 'LEFT' function takes two arguments, in this case, the name of the field that contains the text string, and the number of characters to be extracted starting from the left end of the string. But the number of characters varies in the name field, depending on how long the last name is. So, we use the 'InStr' function to count the number of characters from the left end of the string to the comma, and return that as a number. But since the comma is actually one character further along than the end of the name, we subtract one. The result is an expression that neatly slices off the last names. This is what the query looks like when it is finished:

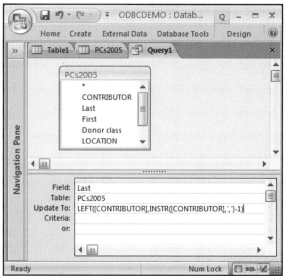

Fig. 6.13

Extracting the first names is almost as easy. Start a new 'Update' query, bring the first name field into the grid, and enter this expression in the 'Update To' line.

Right([CONTRIBUTOR],Len([CONTRIBUTOR])-InStr([CONTRIBUTOR],',')-1)

If the first expression seemed complicated, this one may seem positively baffling. But, again, the trick is to slice it into its component parts. Again, the foundation is a function, in this case 'RIGHT'. We already know that 'RIGHT' extracts a specified number of characters starting at the right end of a text string, and going backward. It takes two arguments, the name of the text string from which the characters are to be extracted, and the number of characters to be extracted.

The number of characters to be extracted is returned by this part of the expression:

Len([CONTRIBUTOR])-InStr([CONTRIBUTOR],',')-1

The first part uses the 'LEN' function to calculate the entire length of the string. The second half uses the 'InStr' function to work out the number of characters from the start of the string to the comma. As in the expression we used to extract the last name, we subtract one from that result. Since the number returned by the 'InStr' function is subtracted from the total length of the text string in the field, what's left is the remaining length of that string. That number is then fed into the 'RIGHT' function to provide its second argument. The result is that the first name is neatly sliced off, and placed in the first name field. By the way, the reason the '–1' is in this expression is because the contributor field has a space after the comma. If there were no comma, you wouldn't need to subtract one from the number returned by the 'INSTR' function.

This is what the query looks like when it is finished:

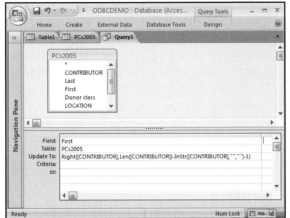

Fig. 6.14

Here is what the table looks like after this sequence of queries has been run.

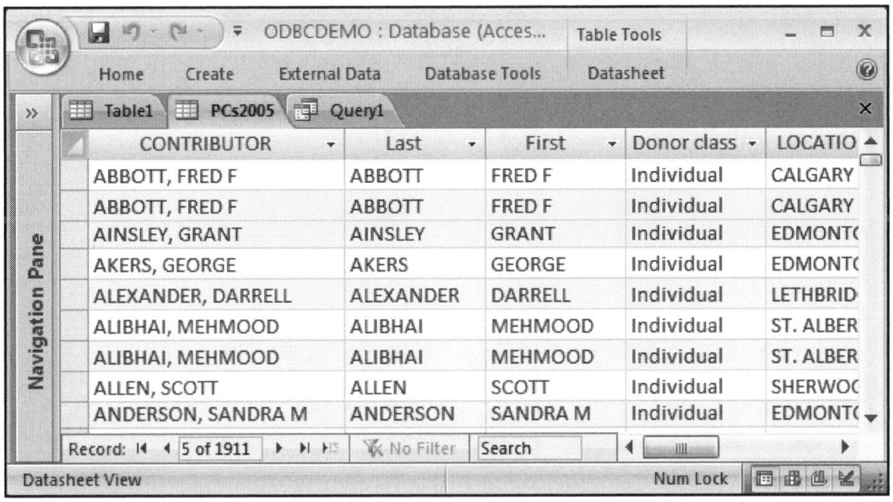

Fig. 6.15

This may seem rather complicated right now, but once you have done this a few times, it will become much easier. The key thing to remember is that you can use 'InStr', which returns a number representing the position of a character in a string, to provide the second argument for the left function. For the 'RIGHT' function, you need to use 'Len' and 'InStr' together in order to provide the number of characters to extract counting back from the end of the string.

Sometimes you will need to extract some text from the middle of a field. This is where the 'MID' function comes in. As with the other functions, it can be used in combination with 'InStr' to find and extract text that begins with a common character, word, or phrase.

During the air safety investigation, the team from the *Spectator*, *Toronto Star*, and *Record* received data from the Transportation Safety Board of Canada that did not include the registration number of an aircraft involved in an incident or accident. It was needed to write queries counting incidents associated with individual aircraft.

⚠ **TECH TIP**

If you want to split up an address field, with entries such as 123 Any Street, you can use 'Search and Replace' to replace each instance of '0 followed by a space' with '0 followed by a comma', each instance of '1 followed by a space' with '1 followed with a comma', and so on. This works because the only place you should find those combinations is at the end of the street number; it always ends with a number and is followed by a space. With 10 Search-and-replace operations, you will have inserted a comma between the end of every street number and every street name. You can then use the same expressions we looked at above to populate fields for street number and street name. You would likely create the new street number field as a text field, then change it to a number field after populating it.

The registration number was contained only in a narrative field that was part of a static portable document file (PDF) file. We'll deal with getting data out of pdfs in Chapter 10, but for now suffice it to say the reporters first extracted data from pdf files into an Access database. A large memo field dubbed 'EVERYTHING' held information from several fields. From there, they used the 'MID' function to extract the registration number or numbers. Here is an example of what the 'EVERYTHING' field contained:

> A98FOO46 INCIDENT REPORTABLE 18-Aug-1998 SPOKANE
> WASHINGTON 49:OON Registration Make/Model Operator Fatal
> **C-FKCK** AIRBUS/A320-200 AIR CANADA 0 Longitude 121:OOW
> Serious Minor 0 0 Summary: Serious Minor 0 Fatal Ground Injuries: 0
> 0 Total Injuries (air + ground): A98FOO46: DUE TO A ROUGH RIDE
> AT FL370, THE CREW OF THE AIRBUS 320 REQUESTED A DESCENT
> TO FL310. DURING THE DESCENT THE CREW NOTICED THAT
> THE CABIN WAS INDICATING A RATE OF CLIMB OF +6500 FEET
> PER MINUTE AND INCREASING. THE RAPID DEPRESSURIZATION
> DRILL WAS CARRIED OUT WITH THE CABIN RATE OF CLIMB AT
> +8000 FPM, AND THE CABIN ABOVE 14,000 FEET. THE PASSENGER
> OXYGEN MASK DEPLOYED. THE EMERGENCY DESCENT WAS
> COMPLETED AND CONTROL OF THE CABIN PRESSURIZATION
> WAS REGAINED AT 16,000 FEET. THE FLIGHT CONTINUED TO
> VANCOUVER AND THE AIRCRAFT LANDED WITHOUT FURTHER
> PROBLEM. THE OUTFLOW VALVE WAS DEFECTIVE AND REPLACED.
> THE #1 CABIN PRESSURE CONTROLLER AND THE OXYGEN
> GENERATORS WERE ALSO REPLACED.[4]

As in many such instances, the key to extracting the registration lay in finding a pattern in the text of the field that was consistent from record to record. Luckily, the registration number, at least for Canadian aircraft, was always the letter 'C' followed by a dash, and four more letters. Further examination of the field, however, showed that the combination 'C- with four following characters' sometimes appeared in other contexts, particularly for dates in December, which would be written as 18-DEC-1997. However, the registration number was always preceded by a space, which allowed the registration numbers to be differentiated from the dates in December. This is the function the *Spectator*'s reporter devised:

Mid([EVERYTHING],InStr([EVERYTHING],' c-')+1,6)

Again, it looks complicated, but really it's not. Looking from left to right, we begin with the 'MID' function. It takes three arguments—the string being searched, the position where the first character should be extracted, and the number of characters to be extracted from that point. In this example, the first argument is the field called 'EVERYTHING'. The second argument, where to begin extracting, is provided by the 'InStr' function, which finds the character string 'space c-' and reports back how many characters from the left it is. We add one' to that because we don't want to extract the space itself. The third argument is the number '6', because we know that the registration including the dash is always six characters long. This is how the query looks in the grid:

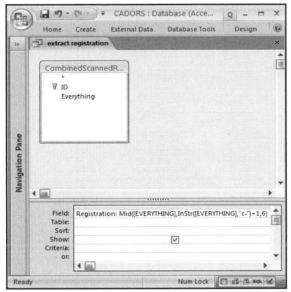

Fig. 6.16

The query produces a list of the registration numbers, neatly extracted. As with all such expressions, it can be written either in the 'field' line of the grid, for a Select query, or in the 'Update To' line in an Update query, assuming you have created a new field.

Some incidents involved two aircraft, which presented a problem because the above expression grabbed only the first registration number. The answer was to run a second expression using the 'InSTRrev' function. 'InSTRrev' does exactly the same thing as 'InStr' but it starts the search from the end of the string. If there is a second registration number, 'InStr' rev gets to it first. ('InSTRrev' is available only in Access 2007.)

This example illustrates an important point. The key to using string functions is creativity. Once you are familiar with how each function behaves, and you gain some practice in using it with text, you can mix and match functions very precisely to extract what you need to do your analysis. Unless you have had some previous experience with text-extraction expressions, perhaps from working with a text manipulation language such as PERL, you will likely find this somewhat challenging. But as your experience grows, you'll find that writing such expressions in Access becomes second-nature.

Putting Two Fields Together

Access is just as adept at putting strings together as it is at splitting them apart. Computer types refer to the process of adding two strings together as 'concatenation', and in Access (as in Excel), the ampersand—'&'—symbol is the operator that does it.

The simplest operation joins the contents of two fields together, either in a 'Select' or 'Make table' query, by writing an expression in the field line of a Selection query, or the 'Update To' line of an Update query.

The syntax is the same in both cases:

$$[\text{FIELD 1}]\&``\ ''\&[\text{FIELD 2}]$$

You may wonder why there is a space surrounded by double quotation marks, thus " ". You add this is to ensure that there is a space between the end of the contents of the first field, and the beginning of the contents of the second field. Unless a trailing space exists in the first field, or a leading space in the second, the two would simply be scrunched together. You could put other characters, or even whole words, in quotation marks between the two fields, or before, or after.

You can combine the concatenation operator with the string functions we discussed earlier. For example,

$$\text{LEFT}([\text{FIELD1}],\ 4)\&``-''\&\text{RIGHT}([\text{FIELD2}],\ 3)$$

would create a new string made up of the leftmost four characters of the first field, an n-dash, and the rightmost three characters of the second field.

Using Functions in Query Columns

Throughout this section, we have presented most of the functions in the context of updating new fields added to a table. But all of these functions also can be entered in the 'field' line of an ordinary 'Select' query to return the extracted content as part of a normal query result. Such 'on the fly' functions are quite commonly used by reporters. If you save the query, you can run it again whenever you need to do so.

Let's try it using the 'Occurrence 06' table and the 'YEAR' function.

Start a new query in Design view, add the 'Occurrence 06' table, and bring the 'Aerodrome Name' and 'Occurrence Date' fields into the 'Query' grid and click on the 'Totals' button to make the query into a math query.

Next, edit the entry in the 'Field' line for the 'Occurrence Date' field so it reads: 'Year([Occurrence Date])'. Give this field the alias 'Year'. Add 'Is Not Null' in the 'Criteria' line under the 'Aerodrome Name' field to exclude null values. Finally, type: 'Count(*)' in the 'Field' line of the empty third column and change 'Group By' to 'Expression'. Sort this count column in 'Descending' order and give it the alias 'Incidents'. This is what the query should look like when it is finished:

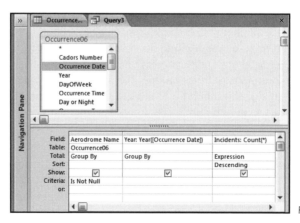

Fig. 6.17

This is the result:

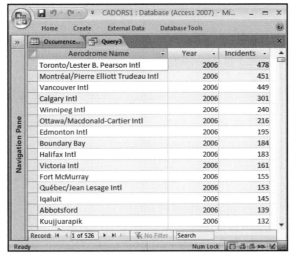

Fig. 6.18

By using the 'YEAR' function in a query, we have been able to quickly create a query that counts up the number of incidents per year by airport. You could also set up the query as a crosstab, using 'Year' as the column header. See Chapter 5 for details on creating crosstabs.

Creating Queries with Calculated Columns

You also can do math within fields, by creating 'calculated' fields. You do this by entering a formula, not dissimilar to the formulas you used in Excel, into the 'Field' line of the query grid. Reporters often do this in order to derive a new value based on existing fields in a table or query.

Calculated fields can be used for many purposes, such as calculating percentages and other rates.

Data Cleaning Using Update Queries and String Functions

An expression among those who work with databases is, 'It's not a question of whether your data is dirty, but of how dirty.' The aviation data we have been using in the last two chapters is a perfect case in point. If you open the Aircraft06 table, you will find that the names of aircraft operators are not entered consistently. 'Air Canada' is entered several different ways, as are 'WestJet' and many other operators' names. In order to analyze the data by airline, you would need first to clean up the operator field and the owner field, both of which can contain the airline name.

You could go through the table and make the fields consistent by editing them one by one, but you can do it much more quickly by making a cleanup table, and then using an 'Update' query to do a batch cleanup. But let's take a step back.

The first thing you need to do—as part of your initial review of the data—is to see if and where you have dirty data. The easiest way to do this is to run a 'Group By' query on each field, and sort the results in ascending order. A quick scan over the list will show you if you have more than one spelling of each name. When you do that with the 'Operator' field you can see two different types of entry for 'Air Canada'—one with and one without the number 5262. Once you have determined that data in one or more fields is dirty, you need to create a cleanup table for each dirty field.

Start a new query in 'Design View', and make it a 'Make Table' query. Next, bring the 'Operator' field down into the grid, and add the 'Totals' row by clicking on the Greek Sigma character on the 'Design' ribbon. Sort the field in ascending order.

In the next column to the right in the grid, in the 'Field' row, enter:

CLEAN_OPERATOR: " "

Make sure you include the colon and the two double quotation marks that follow. 'Clean Operator' is an alias that will become the name of the new field, and the pair of double quotation marks tell Access to create the field with a zero-length string.

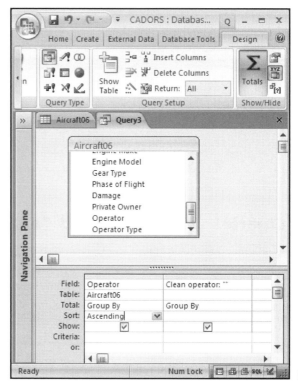

Fig. 6.19

When you run the query you will create a new table with one example of each entry in the original, dirty field, and an empty field, ready for the matching, clean values.

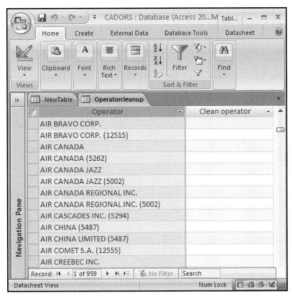

Fig. 6.20

This is where the tedious work begins. You will now need to enter manually clean values for any of the entries where there is more than one spelling, or where there is one entry but the spelling is incorrect. Do this in the 'Clean operator' field. Don't worry about fixing those entries where there is one correct spelling.

If there are a great many spellings to enter, you can also run an 'Update' query on your cleanup table, putting the clean spelling in the 'Update To' row, and using a 'LIKE' expression in the 'Criteria' line, under the dirty field. For example, you could update the 'Clean operator' field to 'Air Canada' by putting 'Air Canada' in the 'Update To' row under 'Clean operator', and entering:

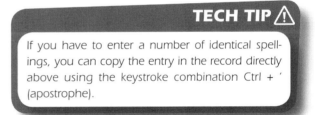

TECH TIP ⚠

If you have to enter a number of identical spellings, you can copy the entry in the record directly above using the keystroke combination Ctrl + ' (apostrophe).

LIKE "*Air Canada*" And Not Like "*Jazz*"

in the criteria line under operator. The latter half of the expression is necessary because Jazz is a separate airline, even though it has Air Canada in its name.

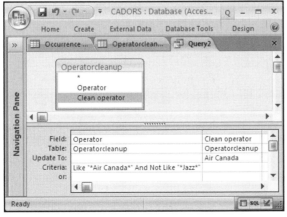

Fig. 6.21

When you have finished manually entering clean spellings, create an 'Update' query and update the remaining rows of the 'Clean_operator' field with the contents of the original 'Operator' field, the ones you left as is. You only need to add one field, 'Clean Operator', to the grid. In the 'Update To' line enter '[Operator]' so the contents of the 'Operator' field will be copied into the 'Clean Operator' field before you run the query.

In the 'Criteria' line under the 'clean_operator' field, enter: = ""(equal sign followed by two double quotation marks) to ensure only those records that still have a zero-length string are updated. You will now have a cleaned-up field that contains a single consistent spelling for each operator.

This done, it is time to clean up the original table. Remember, *always* make a copy of your original table before you start altering its structure of contents. Now, go to table 'Design View', and insert a new text field in the 'Aircraft' table, immediately after the 'Operator' field. In this case, we will call it 'Clean operator'. Now, start a new 'Update' query, and add both the 'Aircraft06' table and your cleanup table. Draw a join line between the (dirty) operator field in the two tables.

Bring the 'Clean operator' field you just created in the 'Aircraft06' table into the query grid.

In the 'Update To' line, enter the name of the clean field in the cleanup table. In our example, it is 'clean_operator'.

This is what the query will look like when it is finished.

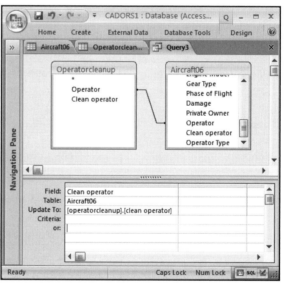

Fig. 6.22

You will notice that the name of the table 'operatorcleanup' is enclosed in square brackets before a dot, followed by the name of the field 'clean operator', also in square brackets. This is because the 'Clean operator' field exists in both tables, so it is necessary to differentiate the two by adding the table name. When doing this, the table name must always be entered first, in square brackets, followed by the field name. Now, run the query. The 'clean operator' field in the aircraft table will be populated with the entries in the cleanup table so each misspelled name is adjacent to the cleaned up value.

As we mentioned earlier, cleanup of the 'Aircraft06' table is complicated by the fact there is also 'Private Owner' field, and in some cases the name of the airline is entered there. You can use the same method we have just used on the 'Operator' field to clean up the 'Private Owner' field. You would probably want to use the same spellings as you used in the 'Clean operator' field for consistency. Ultimately, queries looking for airlines might have to look for the airline name in either field using an 'OR' query to find a name in either one.

Eliminating Duplicate Rows

Another important data-cleaning task is getting rid of duplicate records in a table. In an ideal world, there wouldn't be duplicates. But the reality is that sometimes you will find the same entry twice and, to make matters worse, sometimes a few of the fields will be filled in differently. In order to analyze a database accurately you need to find a way to eliminate duplicates.

The simplest way to find duplicates is to create a query containing all of the rows in a table. (Don't use the asterisk.) Add in the 'Totals' line; group on all of the fields; then add a field to the end of the query on which to count. Sort the count in descending order. If you get any counts greater than one, you know you have duplicated rows.

To get rid of them, first run a 'Make-Table' query to create a new table with one each of the duplicated rows. The query can be the same as the above query, except in the 'Criteria' line under your count column, enter >1. This will eliminate any rows that are not duplicated.

Next, start a 'Delete' query, adding both the original table and the table you just made. Join on enough fields to ensure only identical records in the two tables are matched.

Add the asterisk (indicating: all fields) for the main table to the grid. Now, run the query. The duplicated records will be deleted from the main table. Now, run an 'Append' query to add the records (now not duplicated) from the table you created back to the main table.

Further Complications

In some cases, you will find duplicated rows where some of the fields are filled in differently so one record is not fully identical to the other. This is a nasty situation for a couple of reasons. First, you will have to find out why it happened. Second, you have to find a creative way to get rid of duplicates and make sure the information in all of the fields is correct and complete.

There is no right way to do this, but one method that can work is to go to 'Design View', and add a new 'Yes/No' field to the table. Save the table.

Next, run a 'Make-Table' query similar to the one we used in the last procedure. This time, add only the fields that are common between duplicated records. It may just be a matter of grouping on one key field such as an ID. Again, add a 'Count' column and sort in descending order of the count.

When this has been done, run an 'Update' query on the main table that updates the 'Yes/No' field to 'YES' in any case where the count was greater than one. Again, include the table you just made in the 'Update' query, and join on a sufficient number of rows to join all the duplicates.

From here, you can run a query on the main table that selects only those records where the 'Yes/No' field that indicates duplicates contains a 'yes' or 'true' value.

At this point, you likely are going to have to manually delete and edit records. The agency that released the data may be able to give you assistance in identifying which records should be deleted, in which case you may be able to run a 'Delete' query using criteria.

Trimming

As with Excel, Access has three functions designed to slice leading and trailing spaces off records. Such spaces are unnecessary, and can make querying inconsistent and difficult. The 'LTRIM' function will remove leading spaces, the 'RTRIM' function gets rid of trailing spaces, and 'TRIM' eliminates both. The syntax is:

TRIM(text or field to be trimmed)

The safest way to do this is to add a new field to the table beside the one you are trimming. Then, create an 'Update' query, adding the new field to the 'Query' grid. In the 'Update To' line, type in:

TRIM([FIELDNAME])

'FIELDNAME' is the name of the field you want trimmed. When you run the query, the field entries, minus the leading and trailing spaces, will be inserted in the new field. Once you are sure it has been done correctly, you can delete the old field, if you like. Many CAR practitioners like to keep the old field so they have the original data should they wish to revert to it.

Replacing Text

While Access has a 'Search and replace' feature similar to that in word processors, it also has a feature that will do large-batch searches and replaces as part of 'Update' queries.

Simply start an 'Update' query, add the field in which you would like to search and replace, and enter an expression in the 'Update To' line using the 'REPLACE' function. The basic syntax is:

REPLACE([fieldname], "text to replace", "text to replace it with").

This works faster than 'Search and replace', but doesn't offer a failsafe chance to cancel the 'Replace' operation. The advantage of doing it in a query is that you can save the query so you can run the 'Search and replace' again later. This saving strategy would useful if you were regularly adding data to the table that needed to be modified in the same way.

Analyzing Very Large Databases with MySQL

MySQL is an industrial-strength database system used by some of the world's largest companies to run critical systems. It is sophisticated software, and can handle very large databases that would make Access choke and crash your computer. For example, when the *Hamilton Spectator* had to analyze 12 million Drive Clean emissions tests in 2004, the reporters turned to MySQL for the job.

While the examples in this book will focus on using MySQL on a PC running Microsoft Windows, the program will also run on a MacIntosh with the OSX operating system and under Unix.

MySQL is open-source software (although a commercial version is available), which means you can download and use it at no cost. If you are so inclined, and skilled, you can participate in the ongoing development of the program. Most users will just want a copy to run.

We aren't going to cover installation issues here, because the program is constantly changing, and installation procedures may change with it, and vary by operating system. Very generally, though, you will find downloadable versions of the program designed to run on Windows, Mac OSX, and Unix machines. The web site is <www.mysql.com/> and as of this writing, the free version was found under the 'developer zone' tab. In early 2008, Sun Microsystems, Inc., which also markets the Java programming language, acquired MySQL AB, maker of MySQL. Sun said it would continue to offer an open-source version of MySQL (Blog entry by Sun president Jonathan Schwartz, 26 Feb 2008 at http://blogs.sun.com/jonathan/).

You will also find uncompiled program code that you can download and compile yourself, but most readers of this book are unlikely to want to go that route.

The compiled, binary versions usually install without any difficulty, and you will be led through a series of options to configure the server for your particular needs. Unless you expect to have many users—and most won't—make sure you choose the option for a smaller number of server connections.

At the time of this writing, the version you will want to download is called MySQL Community Server. The paid version that comes with support is called MySQL Enterprise. You can usually find solutions to any problems you are having on one of the online MySQL forums or in the excellent documentation. It runs more than 2,000 pages and covers most issues exhaustively.

The current version of MySQL as this book goes to press is MySQL 5.0. You should download and install a copy of the MySQL Query Browser, a graphical utility for entering commands and viewing the results. More on that in a moment.

MySQL Basics

Unlike Access, which you start, run, and eventually close after you have finished your work, MySQL is a 'server program'. It runs all of the time in the background, unless you specifically halt the process. You send commands to the server, using MySQL's command line utility, a graphical utility such as the MySQL Query Browser, or another database program linked to the server. The server then returns the results.

For the purposes of this discussion, we will use the Query Browser. From within the browser you can create tables, populate them, build and run queries, and export query results as text or as Excel files.

To begin, let's take a look at the functions in the Query Browser itself. After you start the program, you will get a screen titled like this:

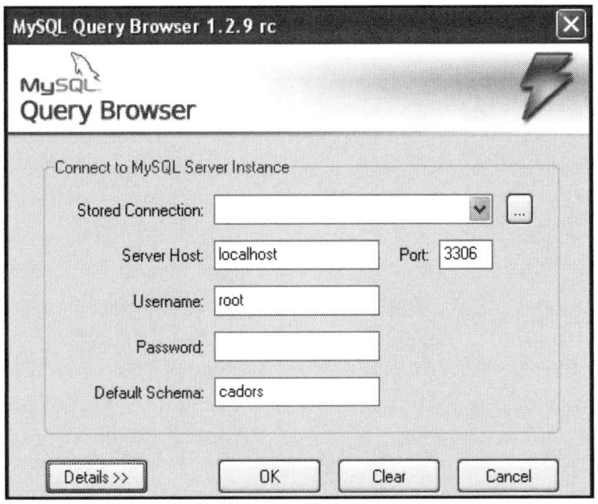

Fig. 6.23

If your MySQL server is running on the same machine where you are running the browser, the server host should be 'localhost'. If it is running on a remote machine on a network, you will need to find out from an administrator what to type here. For servers running on your local machine, the username will usually be 'root' and the port '3306' unless you specified other settings when you configured your server. If you specified a server password, you will need to enter that as well. Finally, the default schema is the name of the database you intend to query, in this instance, 'cadors'. You can change this once you are in the browser. You can leave empty the box labelled 'stored connection'. Once you click 'OK', you will get the query browser screen.

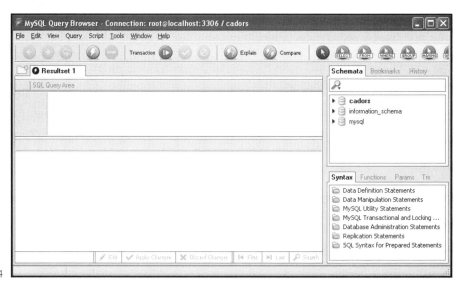

Fig. 6.24

The key components of the interface include:

- The 'SQL query area' at the top of the screen, where you enter not only query statements, but also commands to import data and change settings for the MySQL server itself.
- An area below the query area where query results are displayed. You can create additional query and result areas by clicking on the 'FILE/New Resultset' tab.
- The 'schemata' area to the right, which displays the available databases, the tables within them, and any views you create (see later section on 'Views'). Clicking on the small arrow beside a table name displays all of the fields in that table. If you click on the 'History' tab, you will see a list of all the queries you have run in the current session.
- A table editor. Right-clicking on a table name brings up a menu that allows you to edit the table structure, as well as to create a new table, or drop (delete) an existing one.
- Various navigation and query execution icons. The 'Run' button is the round green icon with the lightning bolt and runs the query currently written in the query area. The 'Forward' and 'Back' icons, similar to those on a web browser, allow you to go back and forth between the queries you have run during the current session.
- The round, blue icons to the upper right of the screen allow you to 'build' SQL queries. The program's documentation available at MySQL.com provides more details on how to use these 'Build' buttons. We will write our queries directly using the SQL query language. More on that later.

- One of the most useful features is the small 'Syntax' box on the lower right, where you will find a quick reference to SQL syntax, string functions, and other commands available within MySQL. It can forestall forays into MySQL's humungous manual.
- The 'File' menu also contains commands to save queries, and to export the results to Excel, html, and comma-delimited text files, among other types.

Creating a Table

In order to analyze data, you first have to get it into one or more tables. Unlike Access, in which the process of importing data as easy as running a 'Wizard', the process is a little more involved in MySQL. You first need to create the table structure to take the data. If you are importing a text file, you need to know what the fields are supposed to be called, and what kind of data is in each field.

Have a look at the text file in a text editor to confirm the field structure. If it is a file of up to a few megabytes, a word processor such as Word or Open Office will suffice. If it is a very large file, you can use a specialized text editor such as Vedit (http://www.vedit.com/). It is specifically designed to allow you to open files of almost limitless size and costs about $100 to download.

Only once the table is created do you actually import the data.

> **TECH TIP** ⚠
>
> Later in this chapter we will discuss how to use Access as a front end to MySQL. When you do so, you can use the Access table export function to move a table directly from Access to MySQL, without first needing to create the table structure. This means you can import or link a text file into Access using its Wizard, then in turn export it to MySQL. This method is limited, of course, by the table and database size limitations of Access. But without regard to the amount of data you can still create an empty table in Access, export it to MySQL, then populate the table using the 'Load Data Infile' command (discussed later in this chapter).

MySQL Data Types

MySQL supports a range of field types similar to those of Access, but they often have different names. Here are the types you will use most often:

- **VARCHAR**   A text type that can hold up to 255 characters in older versions of MySQL, and more than 65,000 in newer versions. When you create a 'VARCHAR' field, you must state the maximum number of characters you want the field to be able to hold. This is done as a number in brackets after 'VARCHAR': e.g., VARCHAR(25).
- **Boolean**   Similar to a yes/no field in Access. 0 is false, 1 is true.
- **Integer**   Similar to a long integer in Access, a whole number ranging from -2,147,483,648 to 2,147,483,647. If you don't need negative numbers, you can designate the field as 'unsigned' and double the size of the positive numbers you can store.
- **Bigint**   A really big integer, ranging from -9,223,372,036,854,775,808 to 9,223,372,036,854,775,807.
- **Double**   As in Access, a number type that allows decimal places
- **DATE**   For dates from 1 January 1000 to 31 December 9999, displayed in format YYYY-MM-DD. Dates must always be in the year, month, day order or you are liable to get an error message.
- **Datetime**   A date/time combination with the same range of dates as in the date field. Displays in the format YYYY-MM-DD HH:MM:SS
- **TIME**   A time in HH:MM:SS

This is only a brief overview of MySQL data types. The MySQL documentation includes an entire chapter on data types, so if you want to know more or use some of more specialized types, that is the place to look.

Once you know what data you have, what fields are contained in it, and what the data types should be, you can proceed to create a table.

If you are working in the 'Command' line, you use the create-table syntax. The table editor in the Query Browser, however, lets you do it by filling in a form.

We will start the process of creating a new table by right-clicking on the name of our database, in this case CADORS, in the small window at the top right of the Query Browser, and picking 'Create New Table'. That brings up another dialogue box. Here, you can give your table a name, and start adding fields (and assigning data types to them). You also have the option of creating indexes. The first table we will create and populate is the occurrence table that we used in the previous sections on Microsoft Access. Note that in this section, this table name does not have a space within it as the table in Access did. This conforms to normal table-naming conventions. Using the Table Editor, enter the following field names with these data types. Include the numbers in brackets where indicated. The maximum length of each 'VARCHAR' field must be declared. Make sure the 'Column Details' tab at the bottom of the table editor screen is selected.

CadorsNumber, varchar(10)
OccurrenceDate, date
OccurrenceTime, time
DayorNight, varchar(12)
OccurrenceType,varchar(10)
Fatalities, integer
Injuries,integer
AerodromeID,varchar(6)
AerodromeName,varchar(50)
OccurrenceLocation,varchar(100)
Province,varchar(30)
Country,varchar(25)
WorldArea,varchar(25)
ReportingRegion,varchar(25)
ReportedBy,varchar(75)
TSBOccurrenceNumber,varchar(10)
TSBClassOfInvestigation,varchar(1)
AORNumber,varchar(10)

When you enter the primary key for a table, in this table the 'CadorsNumber', make sure you tick off the 'Primary Key' checkbox. This will automatically create an index for the field. You can also specify that a field not be allowed to be null—or empty—and set a default value for the field (such as 0).

Your table editor screen should look something like this when you are finished:

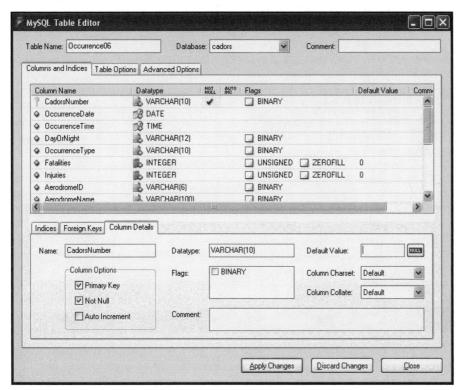

Fig. 6.25

Notice that the only field we are insisting cannot be null is the 'CadorsNumber'. In the others, we are allowing for the possibility that the occasional record may have left a field blank.

When you are satisfied you have entered all of the information correctly and completely, click 'Apply Changes'.' That will bring up a confirming dialogue so that you can double-check the information you have supplied. Once you have made sure your input is correct, click 'Execute'. The table will now be created in the database and will appear under the database (Schema) name on the right of the Query Browser. If you get an error message, go back and check that you have not made any mistakes in entering the information.

Adding Data to the Table

We are now ready to put data in our table. In this case, the 'Occurrence06' table is contained in a delimited text file. [The table is named differently from the way it was named in Access, so no space between the word and the number is correct.] You can download the text file version of the data from the book's website, <www.oupcanada.com/CAR.html>.

The easiest way to add data is to use the LoadDataInfile command. You type the command into the top box of the Query Browser window.

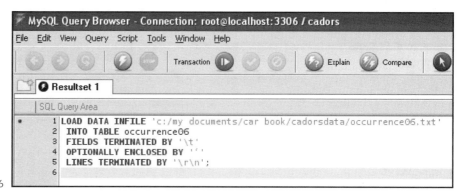

Fig. 6.26

This is the command:

LOAD DATA INFILE 'c:/path to file on your drive/occurrence06.txt'
INTO TABLE occurrence06
FIELDS TERMINATED BY '\t'
OPTIONALLY ENCLOSED BY '""'
LINES TERMINATED BY '\r\n';

⚠ TECH TIP

MySQL can be a fussy creature at times, but we can live with that because of its raw power. One of its complications is that the server can be set to run a number of different SQL modes. We won't get into modes in detail here, but it is a good idea before you run your 'LOAD DATA INFILE' statement to enter a command to change the mode setting to one which will not be too picky about what data it allows to be added to a table. In particular, the server has what are known as 'strict' modes, which will abort the data-loading operation if there is a single field in one record containing data the program deems out of the normal range, for example, trying to enter a null value in a number field. Try entering this command in the query area: SET GLOBAL SQL_MODE='ANSI';

For more on MySQL modes go to <dev.mysql.com/doc/refman/5.0/en/server-sql-mode.html>.

Let's walk through this command, because you will use it often. The first line invokes the 'Load data infile' command, and tells MySQL where to find the file. Type the directory path to the file (the location where you have saved the file on your computer's hard drive) within single quotation marks.

The second line tells MySQL where to put the data. It must be an existing table. In this case, we are using the table we just created.

The next line tells MySQL what the delimiter is. In this case, it is a tab, represented by the symbol \t in single quotation marks.

The optionally enclosed statement tells MySQL that text fields may be enclosed in double quotation marks.

The last line tells the program what it should expect to find at the end of each record. In this case, because the file was created on a Windows machine, the lines end with a carriage return, expressed as \r and a line feed, expressed as \n. In some other operating systems, only the carriage return will be required.

If the first line of the text file contains the field names, you will need to strip them off so they don't end up in the table. You can do this by adding one extra line to the command:

IGNORE 1 LINES.

MySQL will then ignore however many lines you stipulate.

⚠ TECH TIP

'LOAD DATA INFILE' imports data with Porsche-like speed, but we found some annoying behaviours. For example, the program also rejects dates not in year/month/day format. One workaround would be to import such a field into a character field, then use string functions to populate a date field with a date in the correct order. The files available for download at <www.oupcanada.com/CAR. html> have date fields in the proper format.

Viewing Your Table

One you have successfully imported your data, you can view it in the Query Browser in much the same was as you do in Access. By double-clicking on the table name (on the right side of the screen) you run a query to open it in the large, lower window, as in this illustration:

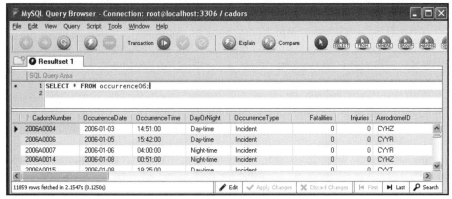

Fig. 6.27

You will notice that the automatically generated query is written in SQL, which you need to write queries in MySQL (unless you set up an Access front end, as we explain how to do later).

Introduction to SQL

Whether you want to learn to write SQL queries in Access or are working with MySQL, you will discover that SQL is a powerful way to access and manipulate data.

One of the advantages of learning SQL is that once you know it, you can use it to write queries in almost any database program, and while there are small differences in the SQL used in different programs, the basics are the same. In fact, SQL is governed by international standards to ensure the core language is consistent.

An SQL statement is made up of several parts. For readability, you normally write each part on its own line, although you can write one long statement if you like. Throughout this introduction, we will refer to the 'SELECT' line, the 'FROM' line, and so on, as a way of differentiating the different parts of the statement. SQL can be a deep and involved subject, and there are many third-party books that get into great detail on its intricacies. This section is, by necessity, only an overview, but it contains all of the commands you need to run the queries and commands journalists need.

The Parts of an SQL Statement

You begin with the statement 'SELECT', followed by the fields you will include in the query, separated by commas. As in the grid, an asterisk stands for all of the fields in the table. You also enter math, string, or date functions here.

The next part begins with 'FROM', and is a list of all the tables being used by the query.

The third part begins with 'WHERE', and sets the criteria you will use to limit the rows returned by the query. You also state any join conditions here if there is more than one table in the query. If there is no 'WHERE' clause, all rows are selected.

The fourth line, which is required if you enter math functions in the first line, is the 'GROUP BY' statement. Here, you state which fields you wish to group on.

'HAVING' works much like the 'WHERE' line, but rather than limiting the rows that are selected, it places limits on which groups will be displayed.

The last line, which is optional, is the 'ORDER BY' statement. Here, you state the fields you wish to sort on and whether the sort will be in ascending or descending order.

SQL also allows subqueries, which are essentially queries within queries.

With that basic rundown, let's write our first SQL query. Because it requires SQL, we present the queries in the format best suited for use in MySQL. But the queries also will run with little or no modification in Access. Where there are significant differences, we will note them. One major difference between the two programs is that field names containing spaces must be enclosed by square brackets in Access, but single quotation marks in MySQL. For these queries, we are using the field names adopted for the import of the aviation data into MySQL. These query names, following proper database conventions, do not have any spaces. Finally, MySQL is case-sensitive for text strings in the 'WHERE' clause, which Access is not.

Those provisos stated, let's try a basic query in SQL. In MySQL, write them in the query area of the 'Query Browser'. In Access, start a new query in 'Design View', but don't add any tables. Switch to SQL view, and you will get an empty window that looks like this.

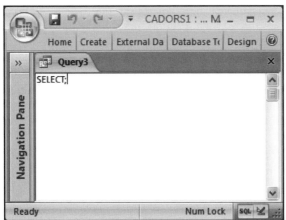

Fig. 6.28

We'll begin with a query to extract some fields from the 'Occurrence06' table of the air incidents database, while setting some 'WHERE' criteria.

SELECT Occurrencedate, Occurrencelocation, dayornight
FROM Occurrence06
WHERE dayornight = 'day-time'
ORDER BY Occurrencedate asc;

This is what it looks like in the Query Browser with the result appearing below.

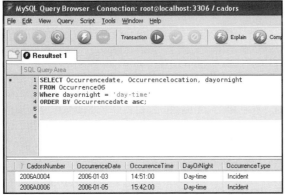

Fig. 6.29

The 'WHERE' line in an SQL query can include any of the criteria types we talked about in Chapter 5, including any of the operators such as LIKE, >, <=, and BETWEEN. (See Chapter 5 for a rundown of these operators.) Text used in the 'WHERE' line must be surrounded by quotation marks, while numbers must not be. In most database programs other than Access, including MySQL, the ? and * wildcards used with 'LIKE' are replaced by an underscore _ character for a single character and a percentage sign % operator for more than one character. Let's take a look at a 'LIKE' query written using those symbols (incidentally, Access 2007 will allow you to use those wildcards, but they cannot be combined in the same query with the Access-specific wildcards).

SELECT * FROM Occurrence06
WHERE occurrencelocation like '%Montr_al%'
ORDER BY occurrencedate asc;

The 'ORDER BY' statement does not require the trailing 'asc' to sort in ascending order, but if you want to sort in descending order, you must write 'desc'.

Boolean Logic Words in SQL

As in the Access Query grid, you can use the Boolean logic words 'AND', 'OR', and 'NOT' in SQL queries. For example, the above query can be modified to find incidents where the occurrence location contains 'Montreal' or 'Toronto'.

```
SELECT * FROM Occurrence06
WHERE occurrencelocation like '%Montr_al%' or occurrencelocation
like '%Toronto%'
ORDER BY occurrencedate asc;
```

The following query finds the same incidents, but only those that occurred in August:

```
SELECT * FROM Occurrence06
WHERE (occurrencelocation like '%Montr_al%' or occurrencelocation
like '%Toronto%')
and month(occurrencedate)= 8
ORDER BY occurrencedate asc;
```

The first part of the 'WHERE' line is enclosed in brackets to avoid confusion. The 'OR' condition placed in brackets forms the first half of the 'AND' condition that follows.

The query can be modified yet again to exclude injury incidents:

```
SELECT * FROM Occurrence06
WHERE (occurrencelocation like '%Montr_al%' or occurrencelocation
like '%Toronto%')
and month(occurrencedate)= 8 and not injuries >0
ORDER BY occurrencedate asc;
```

Again, note that the 'OR' statement is placed in brackets, so that the program will understand the part following and is to be applied no matter which city is selected.

The placement of 'NOT' may seem unusual, but it is always placed before the first words of the clause it modifies.

Calculations and Concatenations

Any calculated fields or concatenations (joining fields together) must be stipulated in the 'SELECT' line. They are written as if they were fields, with commas separating them, and can be combined with field names. Similarly, you can enter string functions in the 'SELECT' line, again separated by commas. Let's write a query that includes all of these. Again, write it exactly as it appears here.

```
SELECT Province, OccurrenceDate, Right(AerodromeID,3)
AS Airport,
CONCAT_WS(' ','fatalities:',fatalities,'injuries:',injuries) AS
Casualties, DateDiff(Now(),Occurrencedate) AS Elapsed
FROM Occurrence06
WHERE Province='Ontario'
ORDER BY 4 DESC;
```

Okay, that's a bit of mind-bender. So let's tear this apart, starting with the 'SELECT' LINE.

The first column being selected is the 'OccurrenceDate' field. That is followed by an expression that extracts the last three characters of the 'Canadian Aerodrome ID' field into a second column. The third column uses the CONCAT_WS string function to join together the word 'fatalities' followed by a colon with the contents of the 'fatalities' field, and the word 'injuries' followed by a colon with the contents of the 'injuries' field. 'CONCAT_WS' means 'concatenate—join together—with separator'. The First argument within the parentheses, the space within single quotation marks, is the separator, or value that is inserted between everything else being joined. As in other functions, commas separate the arguments. Finally, the last column is a calculated column, using the 'DATEDIFF' function to work out the time that has elapsed since the occurrence date to the current date. The current date, represented by now() is stated first, then the earlier date. Some of the columns are given aliases, which are preceded by the word 'AS'.

The 'FROM' line indicates that only one table, 'Occurrence06', is being used.

The 'WHERE' line limits the results to records where the province is Ontario.

The' ORDER BY' line sorts the result in descending order of the fourth column.

This is what the results look like when you run the query:

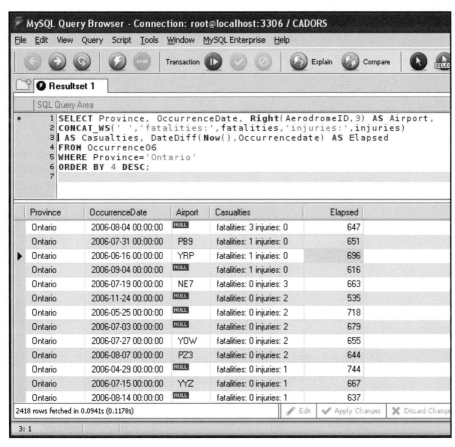

Fig. 6.30

This is one of those cases where an Access query would be written substantially differently. In the third column, which concatenates several elements, instead of using 'CONCAT_WS' you would simply write 'fatalities: '&[fatalities]&' injuries:

'&[injuries] AS Casualties. The separating spaces are simply included within the strings to be joined while Access uses the '&' sign for concatenation. The other difference is in the 'DATEDIFF' function. In MySQL it works out the number of days between two dates, and the current date is stated first, the reverse of Access. See the discussion of 'DATEDIFF' earlier in this chapter for the full Access syntax.

The Distinct Operator and Distinctrow Operators

When you work with the Access query grid, you can create a query that returns one of each unique entry in a field or every unique combination of several fields by adding the 'Totals' line and grouping on the field or fields. When you work in SQL, you can use the 'DISTINCT' and 'DISTINCTROW' operators to do the same thing. 'SELECT DISTINCT (PROVINCE)' will return a list of the provinces in the province field.

Related to distinct is 'DISTINCTROW'.

The next query selects all records in the 'Occurrence06' table where there are matching rows in the aircraft table. But even though this is really a one-to-many match, with more than one aircraft often involved in an incident, as long a we don't actually select any fields in the aircraft table, the query returns just one row for each CADORS number in the aircraft table. The query looks like this:

```
SELECT distinctrow a.*
FROM Occurrence06 a, Aircraft06 b
WHERE a.cadorsnumber=b.cadorsnumber
ORDER BY a.cadorsnumber asc;
```

You will note that this query joins two tables. We will discuss that more a little later in the chapter.

Math Queries

Creating a math query in SQL is easy. You use the same math functions as in the Query grid, and put them in the 'SELECT' line. You use the 'GROUP BY' line to declare which fields to group on.

This query will count how many incidents there are of each type in the database, grouping by event type, and sorting in descending order of the count:

```
SELECT Events, COUNT(*) as NumberOfIncidents
FROM Events06
GROUP BY Events
ORDER BY 2 desc;
```

This is a similar query, this time counting the number of incidents in each province and limiting the results to incidents in January using the WHERE line:

```
SELECT Province, COUNT(*) as NumberOfIncidents
FROM Occurrence06
WHERE month(occurrencedate)=1
GROUP BY Province
ORDER BY 2 desc;
```

Writing a query to do addition follows the same pattern. This query adds up all fatalities in British Columbia and Alberta, grouping them on whether they occurred during the day or at night.

```
SELECT Dayornight, Sum(Fatalities) as Fatalitiestotal
FROM Occurrence06
WHERE Province='British Columbia' or Province='Alberta'
GROUP BY 1
ORDER BY 2 desc;
```

Using the 'IN' operator, this could also be written as:

```
SELECT DayorNight, Sum(Fatalities) as Fatalitiestotal
FROM Occurrence06
WHERE Province in('British Columbia','Alberta')
GROUP BY dayornight
ORDER BY 2 desc;
```

The 'HAVING' Clause

'HAVING' is similar to 'WHERE', except that it establishes conditions for groups.

It is needed, because the 'WHERE' clause in an SQL statement can refer only to individual fields. 'HAVING', on the other hand, can limit output based on groups. It is the same effect you get when you enter a criterion under a math function in the Access query grid. This is the same query we looked at a moment ago with the 'HAVING' clause added to limit the output only to the time of day when there are more than 5 fatalities.

```
SELECT Dayornight, Sum(Fatalities) as Fatalitiestotal
FROM Occurrence06
WHERE Province='British Columbia' or Province='Alberta'
GROUP BY 1
HAVING Fatalitiestotal > 5
ORDER BY 2 desc;
```

Here is the result with the query visible in the upper window:

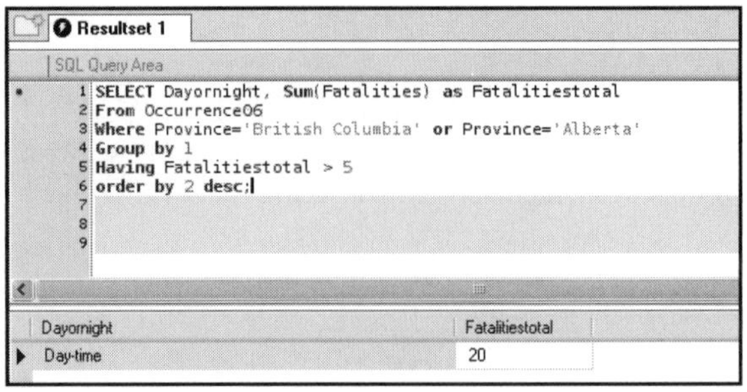

Fig. 6.31

Joining Tables in SQL

Once you have mastered the basic SQL syntax, joining two tables is easy. Let's construct a query to link up each incident with the aircraft that were involved. This is the syntax:

SELECT Occurrence06.occurrencedate, Occurrence06.occurrencetime, Occurrence06.aerodromename, Aircraft06.aircraftmake, Aircraft06. aircraftmodel
FROM Occurrence06, Aircraft06
WHERE Occurrence06.cadorsnumber= Aircraft06.cadorsnumber
ORDER BY Occurrence06.occurrencedate asc;

Scanning over the query, you can see the key differences between a query of one table and one that joins two tables.

In the 'SELECT' line, you will notice that the table name is now added to each field name, with a period joining the two. This is not absolutely necessary unless the field name is in both tables, but it is good to get into the habit of declaring the tables this way. Beyond that, it lists fields as in a single-table query.

In the 'FROM' line you now list all of the tables in the query.

The join condition is actually declared in the 'WHERE' line by simply stating that TABLE1.FIELD1=TABLE1.FIELD2.

This query can be written more easily if you give the tables alias names. This is how the query looks with aliases added. Note that they are declared in the FROM line.

SELECT A.occurrencedate,A.occurrencetime,A.aerodromename, B.aircraftmake, B.aircraftmodel
FROM Occurrence06 A, Aircraft06 B
WHERE A.cadorsnumber=B.cadorsnumber
ORDER BY 1 asc;

The aliases don't actually change the names of your tables, but instead exist only for as long as it takes the program to process the query.

Of course, you can also join more than two tables. The pattern is the same, except that in the WHERE line, you need to state a join condition for each pair of tables, joined together with ANDs. This query joins the 'Occurrence06', 'Aircraft06', and 'Events06' tables to find incidents and aircraft involved in incidents in which there was a near-collision between two aircraft:

SELECT a.Cadorsnumber, a.occurrencedate, a.aerodromename,
b.aircraftmake, b.aircraftmodel, c.events
FROM Occurrence06 a, Aircraft06 b, Events06 c
WHERE a.cadorsnumber=b.cadorsnumber and a.cadorsnumber=c.
cadorsnumber
AND c.events like "%near collision%"
ORDER BY 2 asc;

This is the result as seen in the MySQL Query Browser:

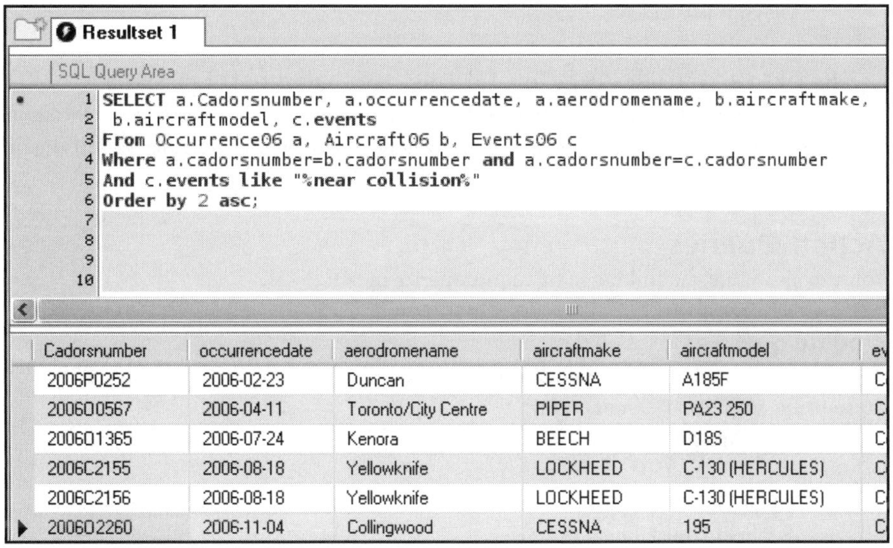
Resultset 1

SQL Query Area

```
SELECT a.Cadorsnumber, a.occurrencedate, a.aerodromename, b.aircraftmake,
 b.aircraftmodel, c.events
From Occurrence06 a, Aircraft06 b, Events06 c
Where a.cadorsnumber=b.cadorsnumber and a.cadorsnumber=c.cadorsnumber
And c.events like "%near collision%"
Order by 2 asc;
```

Cadorsnumber	occurrencedate	aerodromename	aircraftmake	aircraftmodel	ev
2006P0252	2006-02-23	Duncan	CESSNA	A185F	C
2006O0567	2006-04-11	Toronto/City Centre	PIPER	PA23 250	C
2006O1365	2006-07-24	Kenora	BEECH	D18S	C
2006C2155	2006-08-18	Yellowknife	LOCKHEED	C-130 (HERCULES)	C
2006C2156	2006-08-18	Yellowknife	LOCKHEED	C-130 (HERCULES)	C
2006O2260	2006-11-04	Collingwood	CESSNA	195	C

Fig. 6.32

Subqueries

Subqueries are literally queries within queries. The result of the inside, or nested, query (of which there can be more than one) are passed to the outside query for use as part of its SQL statement.

Subqueries can be used to produce results similar to queries that join tables, but one of the most valuable uses is to write a query that returns records that don't match between two tables. This application is more useful than it might sound at first. Suppose you had a table of traffic accidents and another of highway sections. You could use a subquery to find sections of highway where no accidents had occurred, in other words, safer sections.

This query finds all records in the occurrence table that don't have a matching record in the aircraft table, incidents which did not involve aircraft:

SELECT *
FROM Occurrence06 a
WHERE a.cadorsnumber Not In (select cadorsnumber from
aircraft06);

Union Queries

A 'Union' query is a special type of query that joins two queries together, one on top of the other. As you might expect, the two queries must output an identical number of fields, and the fields must have the same sequence of data types. This makes sense as, obviously, you cannot stack a number data type on top of a text type.

One possible use for a 'Union' query would be extract records from two separate but similar tables into one result. The basic syntax is:

```
SELECT FIELD1, FIELD2, FIELD3
FROM TABLENAME
WHERE
UNION
SELECT FIELD1, FIELD2, FIELD3
FROM TABLENAME2
WHERE
ORDER BY
```

The 'ORDER BY' clause can be stipulated only once, at the end of the query.

A 'Union' query can also be used to combine two or more queries run on the same table. This produces a result that is the equivalent of specifying multiple conditions in the 'WHERE' line of a query.

Action Queries

You can also write the full range of action queries in SQL.

Update queries

As in the Access query grid, you can update the information in one or more fields. You do so using an 'UPDATE' statement.

The basic syntax is:

```
UPDATE TABLENAME
Set fieldname1='new value'
Where fieldname2='criteria you set'
```

This query would insert the new value in the field you specify whenever the condition in the where statement is satisfied. You can use the full range of operators (=, like, in, >, >=, <,<=, Between) in the 'WHERE' line, as well as the Boolean logic words, 'AND', 'OR', and 'NOT'. You can set as many 'WHERE' conditions as you like.

As in the Query grid, you can use a second table to update the first. The following SQL query has the same effect as the cleanup table we discussed in the section on data-cleaning:

```
UPDATE aircraft06, cleanuptable
Set aircraft06operator=cleanuptable.clean_operator
WHERE event06.operator=cleanuptable.operator
```

The query will run faster if you index the 'Operator' field in both tables. You can add indexes in the table editor.

Delete queries

Delete queries follow much the same pattern.

For example, this query would delete all records from Occurrence06 with fatalities:

```
DELETE from Occurrence06
Where fatalities >0;
```

Adding Data

You can add data to a table using the 'INSERT' statement. This is the equivalent of an 'Append' query in the Access query grid.

The basic syntax is:

> INSERT INTO TABLENAME (FIELD
> NAME1,FIELDNAME2,FIELDNAME3)
> SELECT FIELDNAME1,FIELDNAME2,
> FIELDNAME3
> FROM tablename2;

TECH TIP ⚠

Always be careful how you write 'Delete' queries, because you can easily and irretrievably delete all of the records in the table. Once deleted, they cannot be recovered. Always make a backup of your database files before running either a 'Delete' or 'Update' query.

The field names inside the brackets of the insert statement are optional but are generally a good idea unless you are appending records with the identical field structure. Explicitly stating both the fields being appended to and the fields being appended ensures you put the right data where you want it.

The following query would add all of the contents of a table called newoccurrence to the 'Occurrence06' table:

> INSERT INTO Occurrence06
> Select * from newoccurrence

And this query would insert three fields:

> INSERT INTO Occurrence06(cadorsnumber, occurrencedate,
> occurrencelocation)
> Select cadorsnumber, occurrencedate, occurrencelocation
> FROM newoccurrence.

Making New Tables from a Query

As in the Access query grid, you can create a new table using the output of a query.

The syntax differs between Access and MySQL. Here is how you would create a new table called newoccurrence in Access:

> SELECT * into newoccurrence
> FROM Occurrence 06;

[Note that here the table name is in the form used in the Access database.]

The rest of the statement can use any of the features of a standard SQL query, including joins and subqueries.

In MySQL, you use a variant of the 'Create table' syntax. The following MySQL query has the same result as the above Access SQL query:

> CREATE table newoccurrence
> SELECT* from Occurrence06

Again, except for the 'Create table' statement at the top of the query, the remainder of the query can use any of the features of a standard SQL query, including joins and subqueries.

Creating Views and Exporting Results in the MySQL Query Browser

In Access, you can save your queries and run them again whenever you like. MySQL can do the same thing, in two ways. Once you have written a query in the MySQL Query Browser, you can save an SQL query by clicking on 'Save As' under the 'File' menu. You can then open and run the query anytime you like. The browser merely saves your SQL script.

You can also create 'Views,' which are much the same as saved queries in Access in that they can be used as the basis for subsequent queries. To create a View, write and run an SQL query, then click on the 'CREATE' button in the top right of the Query Browser window. That will bring up this dialogue box in which you enter the name of the View you wish to create:

Fig. 6.33

The View will then appear along with the table names on the right side of the browser screen. You can now use it in new queries or open it to run it any time you choose.

Creating a Connection to MySQL from Microsoft Access.

While the MySQL Query Browser provides ample features to write and save queries, create views, and export query results, if you are familiar with Microsoft Access, you may prefer to create a direct connection between Access and MySQL. This allows you to use the familiar Access Query grid to write and save queries within an Access database to run again later.

Before you can do this, you will need to download, and install the MySQL Connector/ODBC from <MySQL.com/products/connector/odbc/>. We assume you are working under the Microsoft Windows operating system, as that is where Access runs. Once you have installed the MySQL Connector/ODBC you will need to go to the Windows 'START' menu and select 'Control Panel'. Double-click on 'Administrative Tools' > 'Data sources (ODBC)'. That will bring up the ODBC data source administrator, which looks like this:

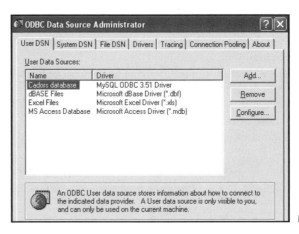

Fig. 6.34

Choose the 'User DSN' tab if you will be the only user using this connection. If more than one user on the machine will use the connection, choose 'System DSN'. In either case, click on 'Add', scroll down the resulting list, and choose MySQL ODBC (version number) driver, as in this illustration:

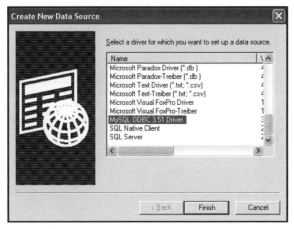

Fig. 6.35

Click 'Finish' to bring up this window:

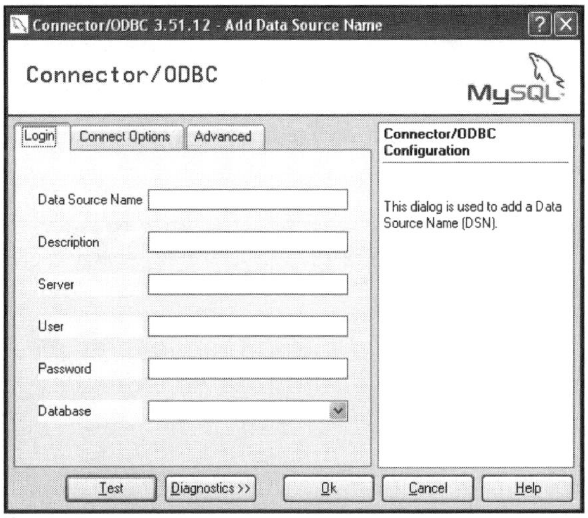

Fig. 6.36

Enter whatever name and description you like in the first two fields.

Next, enter the server name. If you are running the MySQL server on the same machine on which you are working, this normally will be 'localhost'.

Enter the username and password you set when you configured your MySQL server (the same username and password you enter when you start up the MySQL Query Browser).

Assuming you entered a valid user name and password, the database field should automatically be populated with the names of the database(s) to which you (the user) have access rights. Pick a database name. Click 'Test' to ensure the connection works.

Finally, click 'OK' to complete the connection. From this point, it is simply a matter of linking to the data tables from within Access.

To do this, create a new database, or open an existing one.

Next, open the 'External Data' ribbon and click on 'More/ODBC' database, as in this image:

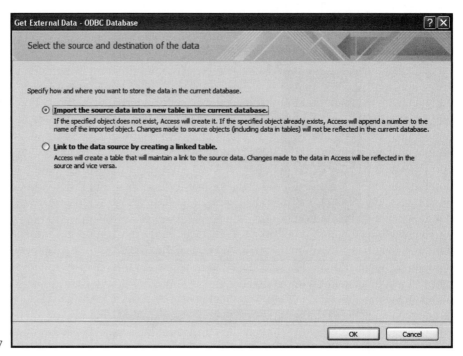

Fig. 6.37

On the window that opens, click on the 'Link to Data Source' radio button. Click 'OK' to bring up this window:

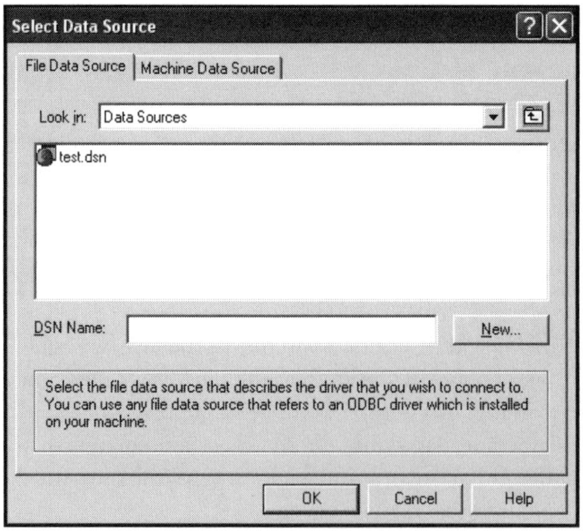

Fig. 6.38

Click on the 'Machine Data Source' tab, and select the name of the data connection you created earlier.

Click 'OK', and you should now see a list of the available tables in the MySQL database. Choose the table or tables you wish to use, and click 'OK'. You can now query the MySQL database from the familiar Access environment. One thing to keep in mind is that because you are passing queries to the MySQL server, certain Access-specific SQL language may fail.

Once you have created an ODBC connection, you can also use it to export tables from an existing Access database to the MySQL database. To do so, open the Access database, open a table, then pick 'Export/more/ODBC database' on the 'External Data' ribbon. Access will then ask you to pick a name for the table in the MySQL database, with the default being the existing table name in Access. Click 'OK', choose your ODBC data source, and then click 'OK' again. Your table will be exported. Note that the export will fail if a table of that name already exists in the MySQL database. This method of transferring tables from Access to MySQL can be used as a workaround for transferring tables to MySQL without first having to build the table structure manually. You need to be alert to a couple of caveats, however. First, you may find that the data types need to be adjusted in MySQL. As well, indexes will not be exported. You will need to recreate any indexes in MySQL or the MySQL Query Browser.

> **TECH TIP** ⚠
>
> In older versions, choose 'Get External Data/Link Tables' under the 'File' menu. When the 'File' dialogue box opens, navigate to the directory location of the ODBC data source, and choose ODBC databases under 'Files of type'.

Bringing It All Together

In this chapter, we have explored some advanced functions in Microsoft Access, learned about the SQL query language, and learned the basics of the MySQL Community Server. With the techniques you have learned in this chapter and Chapter 5, you will be able to handle just about any database task that comes your way. But where to find data? That is the focus of Chapter 8.

Five Stories You Can Do

1. Get your provincial government's highway construction contract database. Query the data to find out who is getting the contracts, and how much they are being paid. Do some traditional sleuthing to find out about the biggest players' track record for quality and staying on budget. Do any of the firms have ties with the government?

2. Obtain political contribution information for your local municipality, at the provincial level, or from Elections Canada for federal donations. Who is giving the most and to whom? What influence might they be gaining by doing so?

3. Download the latest data from the National Pollutant Release Inventory from <www.ec.gc.ca/pdb/npri/>. Who are the biggest polluters in your area? What are the most common substances released into the air, water, or earth environment in your area? Which areas of town are most affected? Do some research on what those substances can do to people, as well as to animal and to plant life, then go and talk to the people in the affected areas.

4. Obtain a copy of the bridge-maintenance database for your municipality, or from your provincial highways department. Which bridges are the oldest? Which ones are in the poorest condition? Are the bridges getting the repairs they need, or is the work being deferred?

5. Get updated aviation occurrence data from Transport Canada or the Transportation Safety Board of Canada and analyze safety trends in your area. Which incidents occur most often? Which aircraft are involved? Are there problems with ground equipment or navigation aids?

Chapter 7

Mapping Your Way to the Story
Fred Vallance-Jones

What We'll Cover

Fundamentals of mapping and ArcView.

- Working with map layers.
- Working with projections.
- Working with non-map data.
- Creating thematic maps.
- Geocoding.
- Buffering.
- Drawing new map features.

'Seeing is believing.' 'A picture is worth a thousand words.' These are the worst sort of clichés, but they perfectly capture the principal advantages of using mapping software as a reporting tool. Mapping programs take geographical information and project it onto a map. Therefore, journalists now can plot out where crimes are taking place in a city, and place them in relation to other features, such as schools and neighbourhood income. They can map out which properties in a coastal region are most prone to rising sea levels from global warming. And they can show, rather than simply tell, readers how a city voted in a mayoral election.

That's exactly what the *Hamilton Spectator* did in the fall of 2006. Readers could see voter turnout patterns with much greater clarity than if they had been described in words alone.[1]

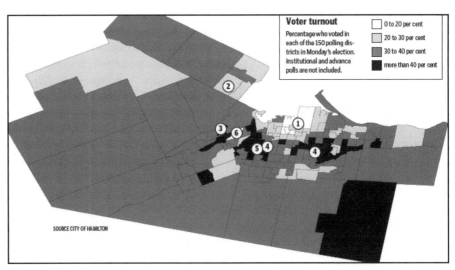

Fig. 7.1

Mapping also can be used for large, investigative projects. It was an important part of the *Toronto Star*'s landmark 2002 series 'Race and Crime', which looked at inequitable treatment of blacks by the city's police force.[2]

Matthew Cole is a GIS specialist with the *Star*, and worked closely with the reporters on the story. 'All of the Police records had a Division and Patrol Area (subset of Division), so we were able to map the distribution of crime at these levels', Cole wrote. 'We did this by the type of crime, by the suspect's 'skin-type', and by the police treatment of the suspect (arrested and jailed over night, let go at the scene, taken to the station and released, etc.).'[3] The series went on to win a National Newspaper Award, the Michener Award, and the CAJ's Computer-Assisted Reporting Award.

The merging of data and maps in GIS has made possible an entirely new kind of 'spatial journalism' reporting that looks at the relationships between things that can be defined by their place on the face of the earth, whether that be populations of people, things that we build, or natural features and hazards.

When Hurricane Andrew slammed into south Florida in 1992, damage from the storm's savage winds topped out near $35 billion, based on year 2000 construction costs. Yet the damage was far from uniform. Areas battered by the highest wind speeds didn't necessarily have the worst damage. Steve Doig and an investigative team at the *Miami Herald* wanted to know why.

'I was one of those who that morning stumbled out of the wreckage of my own home with half my roof gone,' Doig said. 'My home was supposedly built under the toughest building code in the nation, so how was my house and all these other ones down in my area so badly damaged by this thing?'[4] Doig, the paper's computer-assisted reporting specialist, used Atlas GIS, an early mapping program, to compare a map showing when homes were built in Dade county with another that showed the severity of damage throughout the area. The results were startling. 'The real smoking gun that I found was the single finding that the newer the house, the more likely it was to be destroyed, and that really was the only true smoking gun I have had in my career. It was "wow" when that first came out of the data.'[5]

Builders had blamed God, but it seemed they had themselves to blame. Reporters sifted through wreckage with construction engineers, and went on to uncover shoddy building practices, such as attaching roofs with staples instead of nails to save money. The supposedly strongest building code had been watered down during 25 years when hurricanes had not hit the area. Lighter materials, such as thinner plywood, were allowed.

Reporters also found county building inspectors were so overworked they couldn't keep up with the area's housing boom and were inspecting four times the number of homes they could do properly. 'We found instances where a roofing inspector would inspect 70 roofs in a day', Doig recalls.[6]

The team went on to win a Pulitzer Prize for its series.[7]

As with spreadsheets and databases, mastering the techniques of spatial journalism is a matter of taking the time to learn the techniques and the thinking behind them. We'll explore both in this chapter.

The Software

The two biggest players in the GIS field are MapInfo Corporation's MapInfo, and ESRI's ArcMap. Both have many of the same capabilities, but have frustratingly different ways of getting things done.

As with the spreadsheet and database chapters, we had to make a choice as to which package we use to demonstrate the various skills. We chose to use ArcMap because it is the most-commonly-used platform in North American newsrooms and is relatively easy to learn.

ArcMap comes in several graduated versions, and with each step up, more features are added. They range from the basic, and free, ArcReader, which allows you to view and query maps published using ESRI's Arc GIS Publisher extension, right up to the highest level ArcInfo, which includes high-end editing and analysis tools.

ArcView sits comfortably between these extremes, allowing for sophisticated geographic analysis and map-making at a price that is still within reach of most newsrooms and is significantly discounted for educational use.

Mapping Basics

We will begin with a few basic concepts and definitions.

A GIS is really just a sophisticated database program. In behind the pretty graphics is a world of rows and columns not dissimilar to Excel, Access, or MySQL. In fact, the information about the maps, how they should displayed, where features should be located and how they should be displayed is contained in tables. These tables can be joined to each other, allowing maps to be layered on top of each other. They also can be joined to non-map tables that contain some geographic information, such as street addresses, postal codes, or electoral wards.

GIS programs have to know where on the earth to place various objects. This is done through the use of a datum. A datum is a model of the earth's surface. There are a number of datums, each one based on a slightly different calculation of the size and shape of the earth[8] but one you will see often in North America is the North American Datum 1983, also called NAD83. Because of the differences in calculations, the datums differ slightly in their conclusions as to exactly where a particular point is located. These differences of metres are slight in the context of the whole earth, but perhaps are a little more noticeable in the context of a city neighbourhood, especially where precision is required. A datum is the basis for a map's geographic co-ordinate system, one which is based on latitudes and longitudes, and places objects according to their position on the globe.

A mapping program has to know not only where points are supposed to be on the earth, but also how to display the information. As with paper maps, the surface of our nearly spherical world has to be displayed on a flat, two-dimensional surface. Like paper-map makers, GIS programs use 'projections' to accomplish the task. Projections use geometry and mathematical calculations to take what is really a sphere and lay it out flat. Each way of doing this introduces distortions in size, shape, distance, or direction, or some combination of these. The classic Mercator projection, used for so many maps of the world on classroom walls, distorts the size of objects nearer to the poles. Greenland ends up looking larger than South America. ArcView needs to know the projection of any map layer in order to display it properly. A projection is one element of a projected co-ordinate system, which uses 'x' and 'y' values instead of latitudes and longitudes to determine the locations of various geographic features, and places objects on a flat surface.

Individual map layers are made up of features of which there are three main types. Point features represent such geographic features as cities, oil wells, and fire hydrants. They generally do not attempt to portray the actual area of the object they represent. Line features represent things that run from one place to another, such as roads, pipelines, and electrical-transmission lines. Polygon features represent geographic features that have boundaries, such as countries, provinces or states, cities, neighbourhoods, postal code or zip code areas, and so on. Together, all of the features of the same type contained in a shapefile or other map file are called a 'feature class'.

Overview of ArcView

Let's take a look at the different parts of ArcView. We assume you have installed the program on your computer and are ready to get it running.

The ArcView package is actually made up of two separate applications. The first is ArcView itself, in which you do actual map-building and analysis. The other is Arc-Catalog, which manages your various map files, allows you to establish connections with data in other database programs, export and import files to and from other formats, and allows you to create address locators, something we will explain later when we discuss 'geocoding'.

Like database programs, ArcView has a place that brings together all the different files that are being used to build a map. It is called, rather prosaically, a 'map document'. Unlike Access, the files aren't actually all stored together in one file. Instead, the map document keeps track of where each individual file is located on your hard drive. The files and other objects are listed in the table of contents area on the left side of the main ArcView window. This is what the main application window looks like when it is in what ESRI calls 'Data View'. A 'Layout View' is used to format maps for printing.

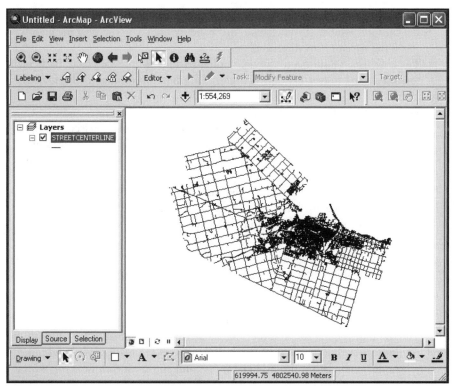

Fig. 7.2

As with any new software application, the array of toolbars and icons can seem intimidating at first. But as we have done with the other programs in this book, we'll focus on the features useful in journalism, and leave the rest to the software specialty books.

The screen can be reshaped and the various elements resized or repositioned, but in the default layout, the largest area to the centre right displays the actual map layers.

In this case, the map is the street network for the City of Hamilton, Ontario.[9]

The dark central mass is the main urban area of the city. At this magnification, the streets merge together into a blob.

Changing magnification to either 'zoom in' or 'zoom out' can be done in one of several ways.

The uppermost toolbar in this illustration is the 'Tools' toolbar. The two icons farthest to the left, the representations of a magnifying glass with either a plus or minus sign, allow you to zoom in or zoom out by either clicking on the map—the zoom will be centred on the spot where you click—or by holding the left mouse button and drawing a rectangle or square around the area of the map to which you would like zoom.

The next two icons to the right, with four small arrows pointing either towards the centre or the outside, zoom in or out, respectively, keeping the map centred on the same spot.

If you click on the 'earth' symbol further to the right, the map will zoom out so you see the entire area represented.

The current map scale—the ratio of the distance between points on your map to the actual distance on the surface of the earth—is always displayed on the standard toolbar, the one with the buttons for saving, printing, and so on. You can change this manually to any value you like, or choose one of the values from the list. The map will continue to be centred on the same spot.

Some of the other tools available, include:

- On the tools toolbar, if you click on the 'hand' symbol, you can drag the map across the screen in any direction.
- The blue arrows pointing to the right or left are like the 'Forward' and 'Back' buttons on a web browser, taking you back and forth between zoom levels previously chosen.
- Again on the tools toolbar, the small white arrow pointing upwards and to the left, with what looks like a tiny map beside it to the right is the 'Select Features' tool. When this tool is selected, you can select any line, polygon, or point feature by clicking on it. By drawing a rectangle around any portion of the map, features within that rectangle are selected.
- The icon like a tourist information sign activates a tool that allows you to click on features to see their attributes.
- The binocular icon opens the 'Find' dialogue box, which is similar to the 'Search and Find' feature in a word processor, except it finds map features.
- The icon with the tiny measuring tape and the question mark above it is the measuring tool. It allows you to measure the distance between two points on the map. The measurement dynamically appears in the lower left area of the screen.
- The 'Labelling' toolbar is fairly self-explanatory, and allows you to choose which features will be labelled on the map, and how.
- The 'Editing' toolbar contains tools for modifying existing map files.
- An important icon, on the standard toolbar, appears as a black plus sign over a yellow diamond. This is the 'Add Data' icon, and you use it each time you wish to add another table or layer to your map.

At the bottom of the table of contents you will see three tabs labelled 'Display', 'Source', and 'Selection'. The first shows you only the names of the tables or layers, along with any associated symbols; the second is similar but also shows the directory path to the files on the computer hard drive; and the third shows a list of map layers on which you can select features.

How a Map Goes Together

Now that you know your way around the main map window, let's take a look at the basics of how to put a map together in ArcView.

When you first open the program, a blank map document will open with both the map window and table of contents empty. If you think of the document as a blank canvas, you won't be too far off. From here, you can add layers to build exactly the map that you want.

For this exercise, we will illustrate the steps using map data supplied by the City of Hamilton (for reasons of copyright we cannot make it available for download), but you can use any map set that you like, including free data you can download from the Internet. See Chapter 8 on obtaining data for a discussion of map data sources.

The most common type of file you will encounter when working with ArcView is the Shapefile. In fact, whenever you seek map data from a government agency or private vendor, with the intention of using it in ArcView, try to get it in Shapefile format. This is ESRI's native format for map files. You will, of course, receive files in other formats, including Arc Interchange, a file type often used to make files available for download, and MIF files—MapInfo Interchange Format—a similar type from the MapInfo universe. ArcView, or ArcCatalog, have tools to import these formats and use them in your map documents.

For our purposes in this chapter, we will work with shapefiles.

Earlier we looked at the street map layer for Hamilton in the map window. To add this map to the blank map document, we would click on the 'Add Data' icon to bring up the add-data dialogue. It is much like a standard Windows directory tree. ArcView will default to the last directory from which you opened a file, but you can navigate to any other directory using standard Windows File navigation tools. ESRI Shapefiles have the extension .shp To add a file, click on the file name and click 'Add'.

We add the STREETCENTERLINE.shp file, which is the street network for the City of Hamilton. The file is made up of line features, and the file name appears in the table of contents. Checking and unchecking the small check box beside the name of the file toggles the image of the map in the large window on and off. If you are working with a number of layers this allows you to turn layers on and off as necessary.

Let's use the Zoom tool to look at a small part of the map in downtown Hamilton. The closer view looks like this:

> **TECH TIP** ⚠
>
> Just as some people do, shapefiles like to travel in groups. Each shapefile comes with three 'helper' files, with .prj, .shx, and .dbf extensions. These files live in the same directory as the .shp file. They contain key details the program needs in order to know the map's projection, attributes and other information.

> **TECH TIP** ⚠
>
> If you expect to go back to a directory folder frequently, you can add a connection to that folder by clicking on the 'Add Folder' icon either in the 'Add Data' dialogue box or in ArcCatalog, which is ArcView's file-cataloguing sidekick, which we will introduce later in this chapter. The 'Add Folder icon looks like this:
>
>   Fig. 7.3

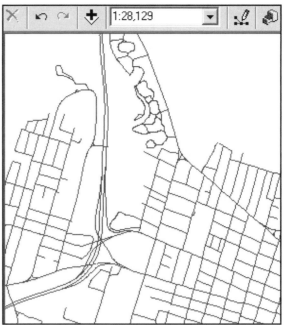

Fig. 7.4

As we discussed earlier, a map layer in a program such as ArcView actually is stored in a database-style table. The program interprets geographical information contained in the table to create the display you see in the map window.

To see the table behind any map layer, right-click on the layer's name in the table of contents, then choose 'Open Attribute Table'.

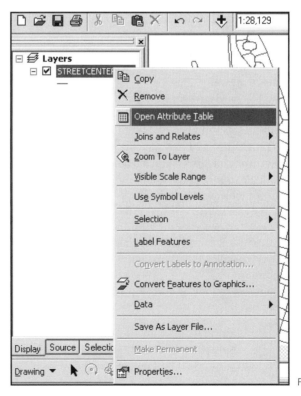

Fig. 7.5

which brings up the table, looking like this:

FID	Shape*	ID	SEGID	CLASS	TEXT_ID	FRADDL
0	Polyline	79	5491	403	1478	
1	Polyline	80	5492	403	1478	
2	Polyline	81	5493	403	1478	
3	Polyline	82	4496	403	1478	
4	Polyline	83	4497	403	1478	
5	Polyline	84	5494	403	1478	
6	Polyline	85	5495	403	1478	
7	Polyline	86	4498	403	1478	
8	Polyline	88	5496	403	1478	
9	Polyline	90	5497	403	1478	
10	Polyline	92	4502	403	1478	
11	Polyline	95	23511	403	1478	
12	Polyline	96	20576	403	1478	
13	Polyline	97	20577	403	1478	
14	Polyline	98	20580	403	1478	
15	Polyline	99	20582	403	1478	
16	Polyline	100	22620	QEW	2429	
17	Polyline	102	22658	QEW	2429	
18	Polyline	103	22660	QEW	2429	

⊞ Attributes of STREETCENTERLINE

Record: |◄ ◄ 1 ► ►| Show: All Selected Records (0 out of 17011 Selected.)

Fig. 7.6

Like other similar street files, the Hamilton street network file contains the names of the streets. To toggle the street names on and off, right-click on the table name in the table of contents to bring up the same menu we saw in Image 7.6, then click 'Label Features'. When the map is zoomed out to its greatest extent, few or any of the labels will appear, because they would be a jumble. You can make changes to the way labels are displayed using tools on the 'Label' toolbar.

Unless you are trying to plot a route to the grocery store, looking at a plain street map is probably not particularly illuminating. But the magic of mapping programs is their ability to layer additional maps upon the first.

If we click on the 'Add Data' icon, we can choose additional layers, such as this layer of polygon features representing city parks in the City of Hamilton. It layers neatly on top of the layer of line features representing streets.

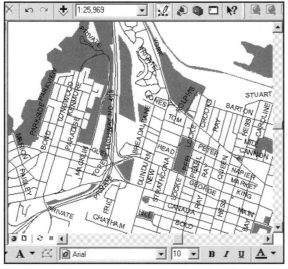

Fig. 7.7

But, we don't have to stop there. We can also add others layer, such as one containing libraries. This file, called libraries.shp, is another feature class, this time containing point features. In a few mouse clicks, we have created a map of Hamilton that shows the locations of parks, libraries, and city streets. Notice that each layer stacks over the last, and when you zoom in and out, ArcView maintains the proper relationship among each of them. All of the information about where each feature is supposed to be located on the earth is contained in the attribute tables working quietly in the background. If we were to add another map representing all of Canada, so long as the map's projection is accurately recorded, ArcView will match everything up.

But this raises an important issue. The information needs to be recorded accurately or Arcview won't be able to perform its magic. Sometimes you will need to make corrections.

Let's take a look at the projection information and how we can change it if necessary.

Working with Projections

You can view these details in two places. The first is within ArcView itself. Right-click on the layer name in the table of contents. Now, click 'Properties' to bring up the Properties dialogue box. Choose the 'Source' tab:

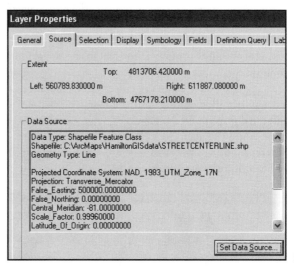

Fig. 7.8

Under 'Data Source', you can see the name of the projected co-ordinate system, and the projection type. If you scroll down, you will be able to see the geographic co-ordinate system, and the datum on which it is based.

The other way to see the same information is in ArcCatalog. We haven't looked at this companion program yet. To open it, click on the filing cabinet icon on the standard toolbar. ArcCatalog will open, and a window will appear with three tabs in the main part of the screen. The tab we want is labelled 'Metadata'. Click on it, and you will again be given three choices. This time you want to pick the 'Spatial' tab, which brings up this window:

> **⚠ TECH TIP**
>
> At the heart of every map is its geographic co-ordinate system and its associated datum. Features are placed on the surface of the earth based on their latitudes and longitudes. Every projected co-ordinate system is based on a geographic co-ordinate system.

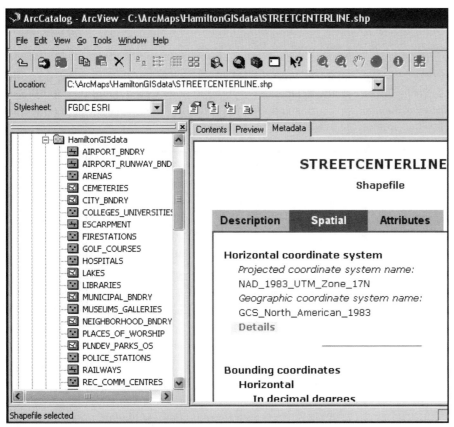

Fig. 7.9

Clicking on 'Details' (highlighted) will give you even more information.

It is important to know about maps' co-ordinate systems because different maps will not line up with each other properly if the systems contain errors. In versions 9.2 and later you can also view metadata by right-clicking on a layer's name in the table of contents and choosing Data/View/Metadata.

In some cases, you may receive map files in which the co-ordinate system information is not recorded. In other cases, you may receive different map files that contain layers with different geographic co-ordinate systems. In either case, you may need to make changes manually to make sure your maps will display properly. If you are hoping to reach conclusions based on how features relate to each other, errors could be costly indeed.

⚠ TECH TIP

As long as two layers have the same geographic co-ordinate system, ArcView will automatically change the projected co-ordinate system of a new layer to match that of one that is already open. Whichever layer you open first will determine the projection that will be used. Subsequent layers will be re-projected 'on the fly' to match that of the first layer. ArcView can do this because the program 'knows' how each projected co-ordinate system relates mathematically to its underlying geographic co-ordinate system. When projecting on the fly, the program effectively removes the existing projected co-ordinate system, then (based on the geographic coordinate system), re-projects the map. This works so long as the co-ordinate system information is recorded correctly. Projection on the fly will run into trouble if the underlying geographic co-ordinate systems are different. In that case, you will receive a warning that the maps may not align properly.

How do you change the co-ordinate system information, whether to fix a problem or simply to take advantage of a different projection? The first step is, as always, to make a backup copy of your data to ensure that if you make a fatal mistake, you can recover the file in its original state.

Once you have done so, you can make changes from within ArcView, using the ArcToolbox. The Toolbox appears as a separate window within the main map window, between the table of contents and the map itself. If it isn't displayed, click on the red 'Toolbox' icon on the standard toolbar.

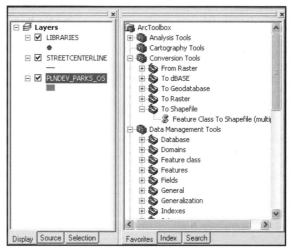

Fig. 7.10

As you can see, it looks much like a file directory tree. Scroll down to 'Data Management Tools', then open 'Projections and Transformations' by clicking on the plus sign beside that subheading.

If the problem is simply that the co-ordinate system information is not recorded in the file—this can happen fairly easily with shapefiles because the projection information is in a separate file with a .prj extension—double-click on 'Define Projection', which will bring up a dialogue box.

Click on the 'Open File' icon beside 'Input Dataset or Feature Class' and navigate the file system until you find the map for which you wish to record the proper information. For this example, we picked the communities.shp file, which has no projection defined.

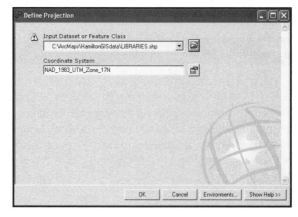

Fig. 7.11

If you click on the icon to the right of the 'Co-ordinate System' box, you get this dialogue box:

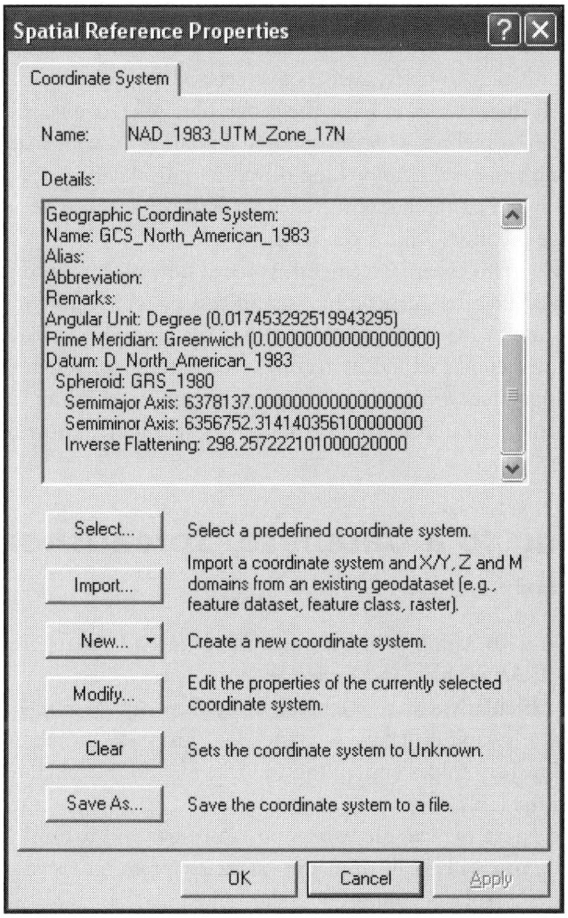

Fig. 7.12

From here, you have several choices. By clicking 'Select', you can pick from a wide range of both projected and geographic co-ordinate systems. By clicking 'Import', you can apply a co-ordinate system from another map file. You can also clear an existing co-ordinate system, leaving the file with none recorded. Whichever method you choose, once you add the correct information, the map will project properly and align with other layers. You should use 'Define projection' only when you know what the projection should be and it is missing.

You will have noticed another option, called 'Project'. You use this to change a map's projection. You will end up with a new map file, with the new projection information applied. The process is similar to the one we followed to define projections, except the resulting dialogue box has more options. We will explore re-projecting a map later when we discuss adding data from data tables containing latitude and longitude information later in this chapter.

TECH TIP ⚠

If you don't know what the co-ordinate system for a map is supposed to be, you will need to find out. This may mean going back to the agency that provided the data.

Working with Non-Map Data

As we discussed earlier, one of the most useful features of a GIS for journalists is the ability to take information from an ordinary database and display it on a map. Generally, you will need two things in the data you wish to display. The first is a field or fields that contain information tied to place, such as a street address, postal code, census tract, or electoral district. It doesn't matter what the geographic reference is, it just has to be one that can be matched somehow with information contained in your map's attribute table.

The other thing you need is some kind of value to display on the map. This can be a discreet value, such as a crime that occurred at an address, or it can be an aggregate value, such as the average income within a census tract.

Armed with these two essential elements, you can now place your data onto your map in one of two ways. The first, geocoding, is a process by which individual addresses in a table are plotted onto a map. You would use this, for example, to place crime locations on a city map. The second method is creating a thematic map, which colours in boundaries, such as census tracts, with colours representing ranges of values in the data table.

We will deal with each in turn, but before we do, let's look at how to connect to outside data.

Connecting to a Database, Spreadsheet, or Text File

ArcView can work with data files in a number of common formats, including delimited text files, Microsoft Access files, and Excel files.

Text files are particularly easy to use because ArcView can open them directly without the need to create any kind of database connection. Just click on the 'Add Data' button, navigate to the directory folder containing the text file, double-click on it, and the text file will appear in the table of contents.

If the file has a .txt or .csv file extension, ArcView will assume that the files are comma-delimited. You will recall from the earlier chapters on Excel and Access that a comma-delimited file replaces column boundaries in a database table with commas.

If the file has a .tab extension, ArcView will assume that the file is tab-delimited. A tab-delimited file uses tab stops to replace field boundaries. If you have a tab-delimited file with a .txt extension it is best to change the extension to .tab so ArcView will interpret it correctly. You can do this in the Windows explorer. Open the explorer by right-clicking on the Windows Start button, clicking Explore, by right clicking on the file name and choosing 'Rename.' If the extension is not visible, click Tools>Folder Options and click on the View tab. Make sure 'Hide extensions for known file types' is not checked off.

The program will use the first row in the file as field names.

Adding an Access File

Adding an Access file takes a few more steps. Begin by opening ArcCatalog by clicking on the ArcCatalog icon on the standard toolbar.

In the catalog tree, click on the plus sign beside 'Database Connections'. Now, double-click 'Add OLE DB Connection'. You will get this new dialogue box:

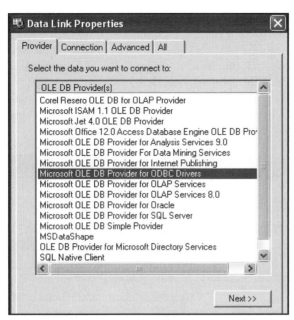

Fig. 7.13

The next step is to pick the type of connection that you need. For Access 2000, 2002, or 2003, select 'Microsoft Jet 4.0 OLE DB Provider'. For Access 2007, choose 'Microsoft Office 12.0 Access Database Engine OLE DB Provider'. Click 'Next' to bring up a dialogue box for specifying the data link properties.

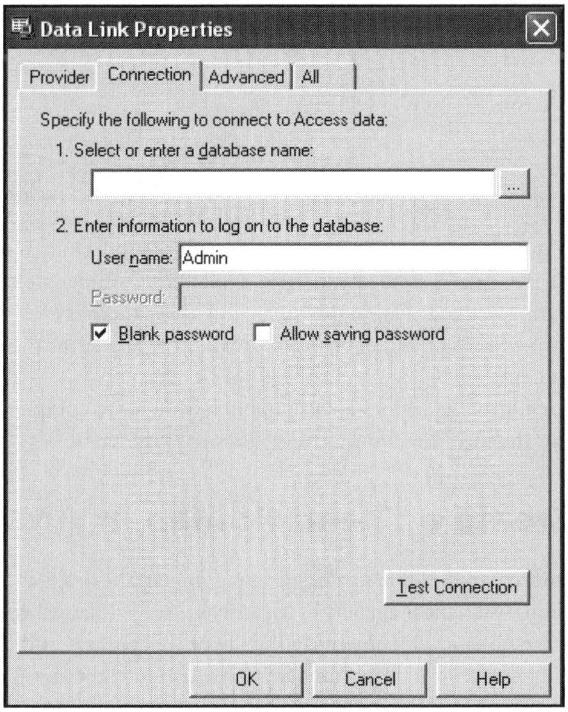

Fig. 7.14

Click on the ellipsis icon, and navigate to the directory that contains the Access database to which you wish to connect. For the purposes of this exercise, we will use an Access database of crime occurrences in Halifax.

When you have selected the file, click on 'Test Connection' to ensure it works. If not, go back through the previous steps to ensure you have not made a mistake, such as choosing the wrong OLE DB provider. If your database is password protected, enter that information as well. When you are done, click 'OK'.

You will be taken back to the main ArcCatalog window, where you can give the connection a name to better identify it. In this case, we are calling it 'Poverty', and its name appears under the contents tab.

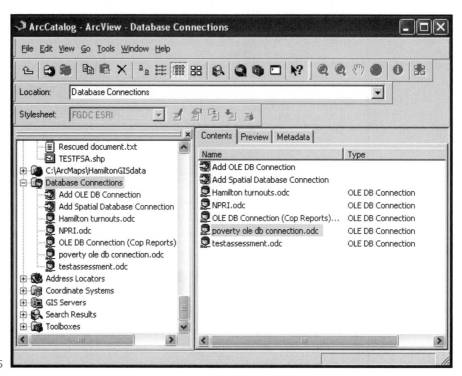

Fig. 7.15

Your connection is now ready to use. If you click on the 'Add Data' button in ArcView, you will see that the Access database is now available. Double-click on the database name, and you will see the available tables. In this case, there is only one table, called 'Poverty', which we will select and click 'Add'. It will now appear in the table of contents for the map document.

The process for adding Excel files is similar, but a little more complicated. Refer to the ArcView 'Help' for detailed directions. The end result is the same.

How to Create a Thematic Map in ArcView

One of the best sources of data for working in mapping applications is Statistics Canada, the country's national statistical agency. Statscan has a well-deserved reputation for producing authoritative statistics documenting the life of the country and its citizens.

Arguably, the agency's most important job is to conduct the national census. Every five years, 'Statscan' counts each and every person in the country and gathers an impressive array of facts about them, including how much money they make, where they work, their ethnic backgrounds, and so on. The results are crunched at different geographic 'levels', from the country as a whole, right down to blocks on neighbourhood streets. For confidentiality reasons, the closer the level gets to individuals, the more likely that some of the data will be left out or rounded off to ensure no one person can be identified.

One of the most useful levels for journalists is the 'census tract', an area about the size of a city neighbourhood whose boundaries remain about the same from census to census so changes in population and population characteristics can be followed over time. For the purpose of this exercise, we will use census tract data for the incidence of low income in the City of Halifax (used with permission). This is a Statscan measure of what proportion of people in a tract live with low incomes.

To begin, we will open a new map document and add the 'halifaxtracts.shp' file, which is a map of the census tract boundaries.[10]

Next, we need to add a file containing census information so we can build a thematic map. The census information is contained in an Access database called 'Poverty'. We create a connection to the Access database, and add the table 'Poverty' to the map document. The file contains the incidence of low income for the census tracts in Halifax.[11]

The main window looks like this:

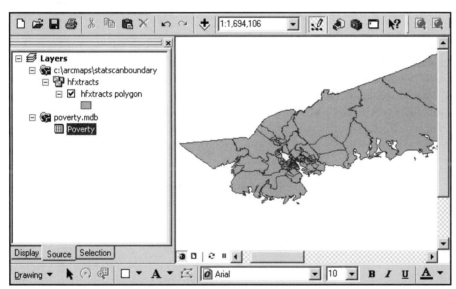

Fig. 7.16

Once the census data file has been added, right-clicking on it in the table of contents reveals a context-sensitive menu from which we can choose 'Open'.

Fig. 7.17

We can now see the 'Poverty' table and its fields.

ID^	Tract	Tract2	2	Perc_empl_inc
2	Halifax (205) 00001	205) 0.00	100	77
3	0001.00 (205000100) 00000	2050001.00	100	68
4	0002.00 (205000200) 00000	2050002.00	100	72
5	0003.00 (205000300) 00000	2050003.00	100	78
6	0004.01 (205000401) 01000	2050004.01	100	81
7	0004.02 (205000402) 01000	2050004.02	100	80

Record: 1   Show: All | Selected   Records (0 out of 86 Selected.)

Fig. 7.18

As you can see, the table includes the census tract number and the percentage of individuals living with low incomes. The next step is to create a join between the 'census tract boundaries' map and the census 'Poverty' table.

Again, right-click on the 'halifaxtracts map' table and click 'Joins and Relates', then 'Join'. You will get a dialogue box for which the required entries are relatively self-explanatory. Just think of the joins you created with Microsoft Access and you will get the idea. You need to first pick the field in the map table that will join to the 'Poverty' table, in this case, the census tract ['CTUID'] field. In the next box, add the name of the table you are joining to, in this case the 'Poverty' table. Finally, add the name of the field in the joining table that will join to the field you picked at the top from the map table. This is what the 'Join' dialogue box should look like when you have finished filling it in:

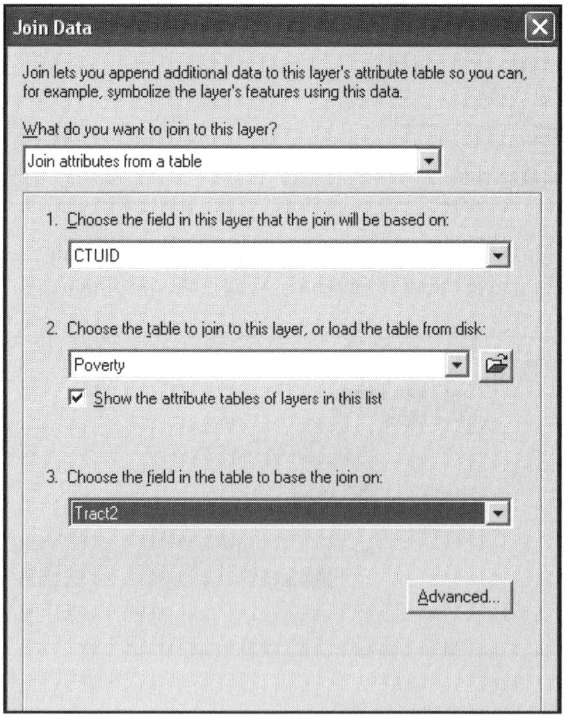

Fig. 7.19

When you are done, click 'OK'. ArcView may ask you if you wish to index a field in the non-map table. You can choose to do so, especially if the table is very large, as this will speed up performance.

Once you have established the join, you can create your thematic map. Once again, right-click on the map table name in the table of contents. Choose 'Properties,' then click on the 'Symbology' tab. Under 'Show' pick 'Quantities'.

TECH TIP ⚠

Just as in Access, the data types of the two fields must match—text (string) type to text type or number type to number type. You can see the data types by right-clicking on a table name in the table of contents, and clicking 'Properties'. For a map table, you will need to click the 'Fields' tab. For a non-map table, you will see the fields as soon as you click on 'Properties'.

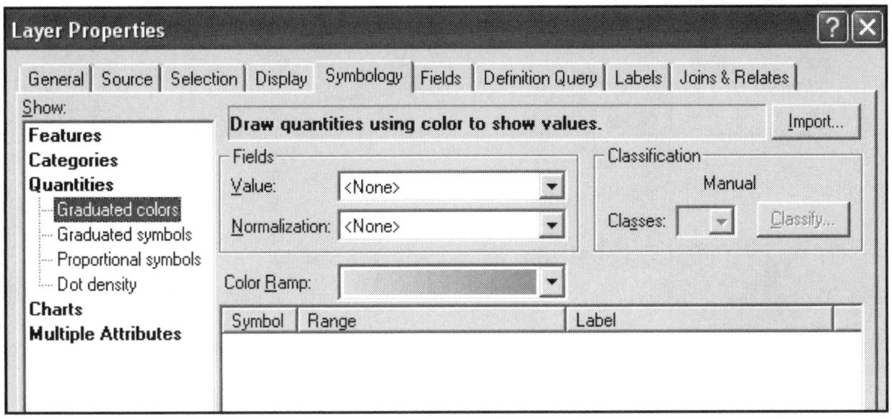

Fig. 7.20

Next, in the 'Fields' area, pick the name of the field in the non-map table that contains the numeric value you wish to plot on your thematic map. In this case, it is the 'lowincome' field.

The 'Color ramp' combo box allows you to pick the range of colours that ArcView will use on the thematic map. Under 'Classification' pick the number of different colour ranges you would like to see on the map. Then, click on the 'Classify' button to bring up this dialogue box.

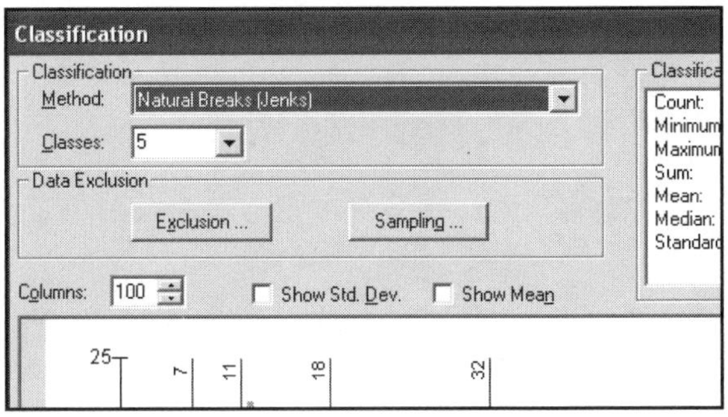

Fig. 7.21

While there are many changes you can make to the classification and we are showing only a small part of the window, the main thing you need to do is pick a method. You have a variety of choices. 'Natural Breaks', the default, creates ranges based on logical chunks of the data. 'Equal Intervals' divides the range of values into equal chunks.

'Manual' allows you to set the divisions. We will pick 'Manual' because it gives us maximum flexibility to set divisions that will make sense to our readers or viewers.

Click 'OK', and you will be taken back to the 'Symbology' dialogue.

By double-clicking on the figures under 'Range' you can change the values to those that suit you. You can edit the labels in the same way.

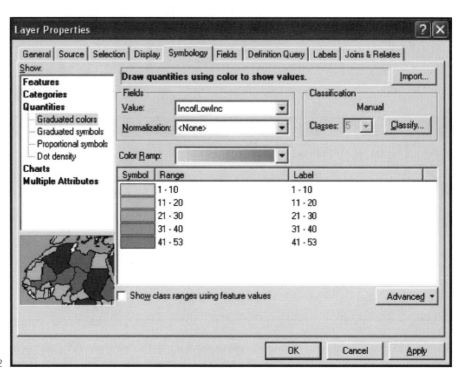

Fig. 7.22

Once you are satisfied with your entries, click 'OK', and you will see the map has now been shaded to indicate the incidence of low income in each tract. This is how the map document looks:

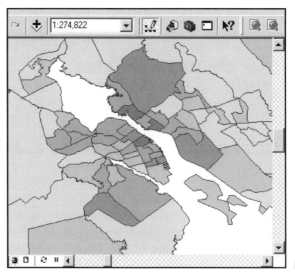

Fig. 7.23

You use the same basic steps to create any thematic map.

Under the 'Symbology' tab, you will notice you can also create other types of displays, including using symbols of various sizes to indicate changes in values within boundaries. They follow much the same pattern as we have followed here and you may like to experiment.

The thematic map we have created shows census tracts, or neighbourhoods, in the City of Halifax, coloured according to the incidence of low income. Lower income areas are seen in blue and higher income areas are seen in green. We can now use the map to analyze crime in the city. To do that, we will need to add some crime data to our map.

Geocoding Addresses

The database of crimes in Halifax, available on the companion website, was built by students in the Investigative Workshop at the University of King's College School of Journalism in the spring of 2007. The data was taken from publicly available incident reports, published by Halifax police. The students chose to classify robberies according to type, including muggings. The database is contained in a Microsoft Access database. Once the database is on our hard drive we can make a connection to it in the same way we connected to the census tract data, using an OLE connection, before clicking the 'Add Data' icon and adding the table to our map document.

Once added, the table of contents looks like this.

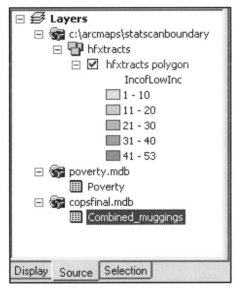

Fig. 7.24

When we open the 'Combined_muggings' table, we can view its fields. Note that it contains, along with the type of crime, either a street address or an intersection. ArcView can place points on the map using either. In some cases, there is only a street name, usually a short local street. In all cases, exact addresses are left out by the police for crimes occurring at private residences.

Geocoding is the process we use to plot such geographic points on a map. In geocoding, address ranges contained in a map's attribute table are used to add the necessary geographic co-ordinates to points contained in a non-map data table. As well as addresses, polygon features such as postal code zones also can be used to locate points, albeit with less precision.

⚠ **TECH TIP**

Just as with conventional database matches, features such as street names must be spelled properly if they are to be geocoded. If necessary, clean up the data in your non-map file to ensure that street names and types are entered properly.

To begin our process of geocoding muggings, we need to add a street map to our map document. To do this, we click on the 'Add Data' button and navigate to 'HalifaxStreets. Shp'.

The next step is to choose what is called an address locator and to establish the settings for the geocoding session. An address locator tells ArcView what it should expect to find in your non-map table's address fields so it can match them properly with the features in the map table. Once you make an address locator available, you will be able to use it in future geocoding exercises.

In version 9.1 you begin the process by opening ArcCatalog, and in the catalog tree choosing 'Address Locators', then, 'Create New Address Locator'. In versions 9.2 or later, right-click on the hard drive folder in the ArcCatalog directory tree where you would like to save the address locator. Then select New/Address Locator.

You will then be given a choice of 'Locator Styles', essentially templates of locators designed to read different types of address information. We will pick 'US streets with zone'. This locator style expects to find the whole street address in a single field, and then uses a second field to make the search more precise. In this case, we will use the zone field to specify a community within the Halifax area, so the program will be able to differentiate between streets with the same name in two different areas.

When you click on 'US Streets with Zone', you get a screen where you establish the various settings that will govern how the Address Locator is used to geocode the 'Address' field in the 'muggings' file (see below).

We navigate to the directory containing the street map file that we will use as our reference map for the geocoding. A series of fields immediately below will become available to be filled in. ArcView needs to use specific fields within the map table, including fields that indicate the ranges of addresses on the right and left side of each street. Individual addresses are not stored in the table, but rather short ranges of addresses. You also need to indicate which fields contains the zone, or community, information. This is what it looks like when filled in using our example:

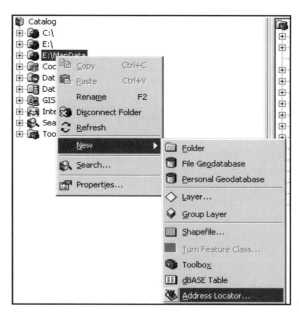

Fig. 7.25

At the top of the right side, you need to ensure that ArcView will be able to recognize the address and zone fields in the 'mugging' table.

In the 'Matching Options' area you can designate how close the match between the information in the data table and the map table must be before a point will be placed on the map. The defaults are usually a good place to start.

The 'intersections' area is used to designate the characters that can be used between two street names when the 'address' field contains an intersection, as the data in the 'muggings' table does. We used the '&' symbol. If you click on the 'X & Y co-ordinates' check box in the 'Output Fields' area, the projected locations of each geocoded point will be added to the data table that is created by the geocoding operation.

Before you finish, give your address locator a name, in the upper left, and click 'OK'. You will now see the address locator you created under the 'Contents' tab in ArcCatalog.

We are now ready to try geocoding our addresses.

Returning to ArcView we will right-click on the name of the table we are going to geocode, 'muggings', and choose 'geocode addresses'.

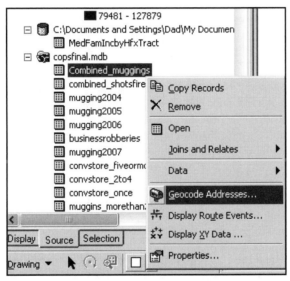

Fig. 7.26

Clicking on 'Geocode Addresses' will bring up the menu that allows you to 'Choose an address locator to use. . . .' If the address locator you want to use is not listed, click 'Add'. In version 9.1 navigate to 'Address Locators' in the directory tree, select the one you just created, and click 'Add'. In versions 9.2 and later, navigate to the hard drive directory where you created the address locator, select it, and click 'Add'. When you click 'OK', you will get this screen:

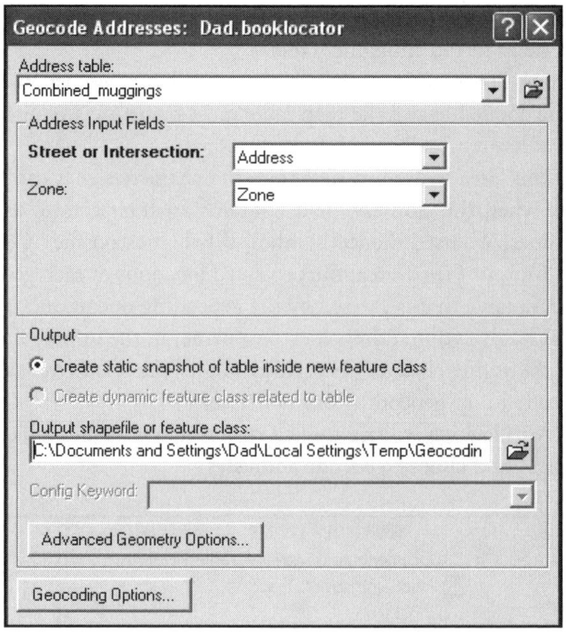

Fig. 7.27

Ensure that 'Address' table is filled in with the name of the table you are geocoding, and that the correct street name and zone fields from that table are indicated below that.

Under 'Output shapefile or feature class', indicate what name you would like to give to the copy of your data table that will be created containing the geographic information, and where you would like to save it.

Clicking 'Geocoding Options' allows you change some of the settings you set when you created the address locator.

When you click on 'OK', ArcView will show you a screen with a progress bar and begin geocoding. Depending on how many addresses need to be read in, this will take a short or long period of time. Eventually, you will see a screen that tells you how the session went.

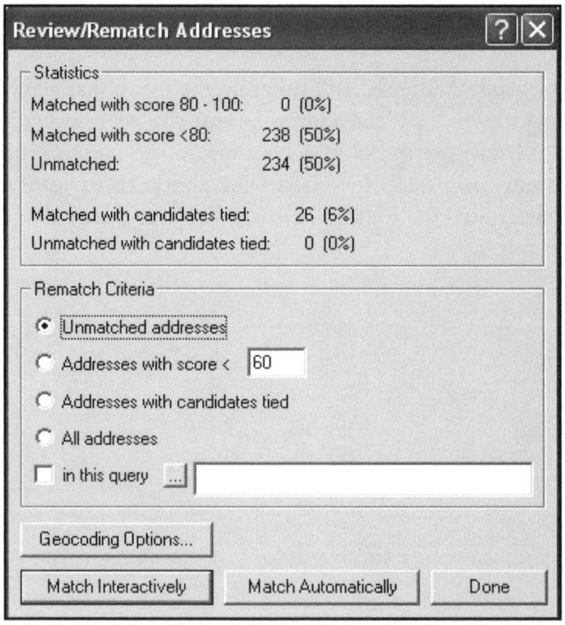

Fig. 7.28

Whenever you geocode addresses, likely some of the addresses will fail to geocode. This can be because street names are spelled incorrectly, the wrong city is indicated, or the street number in the address doesn't fit within one of the address ranges in the map table. Some streets in your data table may be too new to have been included in the map table.

If geocoding performance is poor, you may wish to return to the data table to see if cleaning up data would help increase the number of matches. Otherwise, you can either change some of the settings to require less stringent matching (which could result in incorrect matches being accepted) and click 'Match Automatically'; or, click on 'Match Interactively'.

The latter choice allows you to step through each failed match. You can now make selections to geocode more addresses manually. This is how the screen looks:

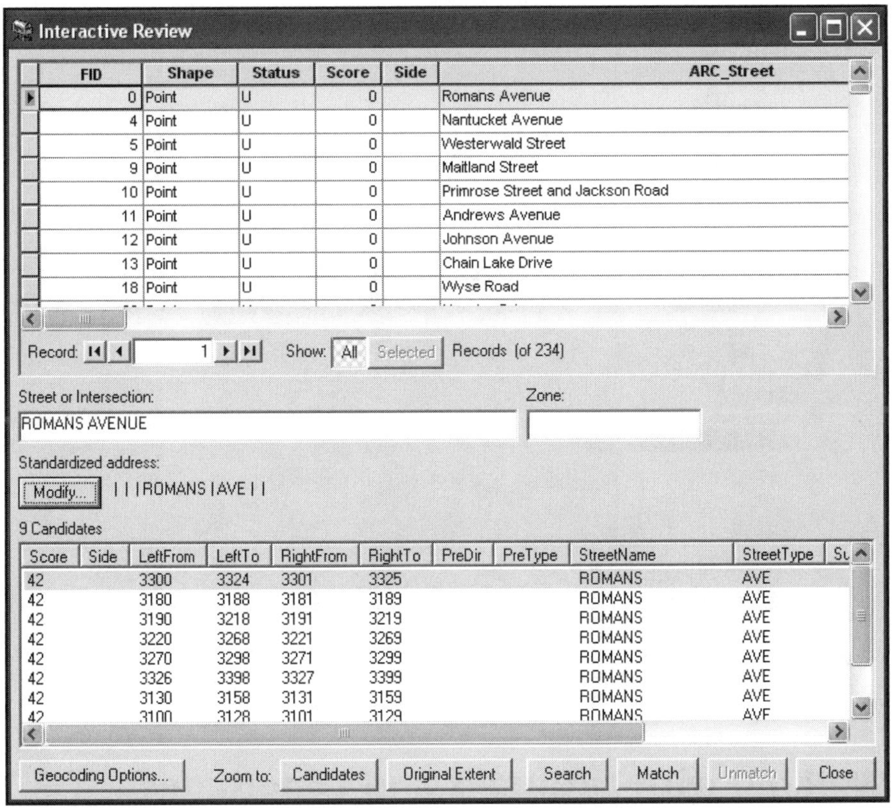

Fig. 7.29

In some cases, you will be offered a number of possible matches at the bottom of the screen. You can also modify manually the spelling of the street or intersection—make a change in what is read—or change the standardized address—in other words, make a change to ArcView's interpretation of what the input address is. The latter change is sometimes necessary when a street has the words 'North' or 'South' in its name, as in 'South Street'. ArcView will interpret the 'South' as a street direction prefix or suffix, as in 'South 22nd Street', which in this case would be wrong.

Once you have corrected as many of the addresses as possible—it may not be possible to match 100 per cent of the addresses 100 per cent of the time—click 'Close' to go back to the geocoding 'results' screen. When you click 'Done', you will see a new entry in the table of contents representing the results of the geocoding exercise. If you double-click on

⚠ TECH TIP

How close to 100 per cent you need or want to get depends on how critical it is to map every point. If your goal, for example, is to get a general idea of where muggings are concentrated, reaching a 100 per cent success rate may be unnecessary. On the other hand, if you want to show how many muggings take place on each street, missing some could throw off the true picture. Use your judgement and geocode accordingly.

the name, you can rename it something more useful. We will rename ours 'Geocoded Muggings'. If you double-click on the symbol immediately below the name, you can choose from a number of alternative symbols, sizes, and colours.

We have created a map document containing a thematic map showing neighbourhood median incomes, and locations of muggings. We can now see, much more clearly than if we simply looked at data in rows and columns, the relationship between these crimes and income. Clearly, such crimes are much more common in lower-income areas.

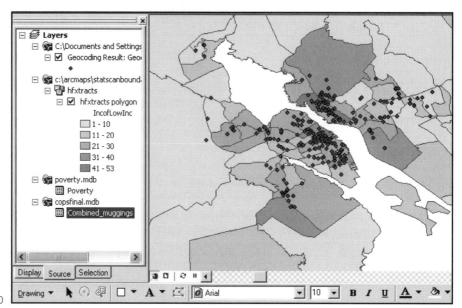

Fig. 7.30

This is only the beginning of the kind of analysis you can do with a mapping program such as ArcView.

Working with Latitudes and Longitudes

The program can also directly map points that are identified by their latitude and longitude.

Environment Canada's National Pollutant Release Inventory records the releases of more than 150 chemicals and air contaminants across Canada. A file available from the NPRI website includes the latitude and longitude of each polluting facility.

An Access database, available for download at <www.oupcanada.com/CAR.html>, contains tables showing facilities that emitted mercury into the environment in 2005. We will add a file of these facilities to our City of Hamilton maps.

Since latitudes and longitudes are proper geographic attributes, tables containing these values can be added to a map document as if they were map documents. Begin by clicking 'Tools', then, 'Add xy data'. That will bring up a dialogue box in which you can enter the file name of the table with the latitudes and longitudes, or browse through the directory tree to find it. In this case, ArcView automatically detects the latitude and longitude fields. If it does not, you can add them manually.

Fig. 7.31

In some cases, you may not know what co-ordinate system was used. In this case, we know that it was the North American datum of 1927. Click on 'Edit', then on 'Select', then pick the 'Geographic co-ordinate systems' folder. Inside the 'Geographic co-ordinate systems' folder choose 'North America', then browse until you find the appropriate system.

Now click 'Add' and 'OK'. This will bring you back to the 'Add xy data' dialogue box. If you click 'OK', you will see that dots have appeared in the main map window. You have now created a new map with point features.

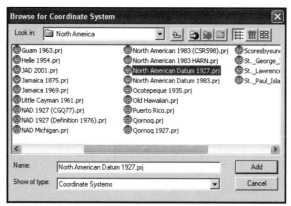

Fig. 7.32

Re-Projecting a Map File

As we mentioned earlier, adding two layers to a map document that have different geographic co-ordinate systems can lead to problems in alignment. The table of mercury emitters was added to the map document using a geographic co-ordinate system based on the NAD27 datum, creating the potential for problems with alignment with the rest of the City of Hamilton map files, which are based on NAD83. We will solve this in two steps, first by exporting the pollution layer as a new shapefile, then by re-projecting the new shapefile so that it has the same projected co-ordinate system as the City of Hamilton files.

In the table of contents, right-click on the mercury emitters layer. Choose 'Data' then 'Export' as in this illustration:

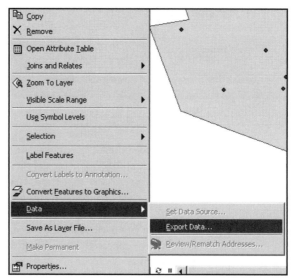

Fig. 7.33

That will bring up a dialogue box in which you can specify a location and filename for the exported file. Leave the radio button on: 'This layer's source data'.

Click 'OK', but answer 'No' to adding the map layer to the map document. We still need to re-project our new shapefile.

Click on the 'ArcToolbox' icon on the standard toolbar and click on 'Projections and transformations', then 'Feature', then 'Project'. Add the shapefile we just created to the top text box of the dialogue box that appears. ArcView will automatically choose a name for the new shapefile that will be created, but you can change it to anything you like.

Click on the icon next to 'Output co-ordinate system', and click 'Import'. We will apply the existing co-ordinate system of the Hamilton map files.

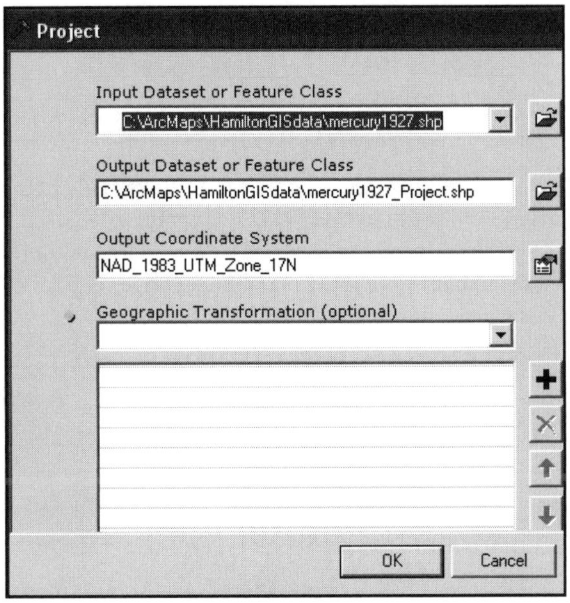

Fig. 7.34

If you were to click 'OK' now you would get an error because the new co-ordinate system is based on a different geographic co-ordinate system. So, we will pick a transformation, then click 'OK' and 'Close'.

You are now ready to do further analysis on the data.

Buffering

Start a new map document, and add the re-projected pollution file. The result will be a screen with a bunch of dots. For the dots to have some meaning, we need to put them in the context of other city features. So, we will add the files showing municipal boundaries, the Hamilton shoreline, and the Niagara Escarpment, a prominent geographical feature that slices the city in two. Now we can see that the dots representing mercury emitters all are located in the north end of the city.

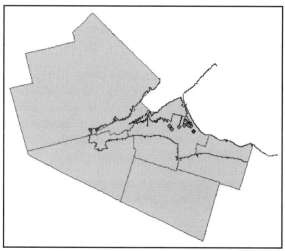

Fig. 7.35

Mercury is a potent neurotoxin that can build up in the body over time. At extreme levels, it can cause serious disease. It is particularly harmful to small children.

Let's figure out how many schools are located near mercury emitters. Emissions are at low levels, but schoolchildren would be exposed on an ongoing basis. The first thing we could do is add the shapefile showing schools.

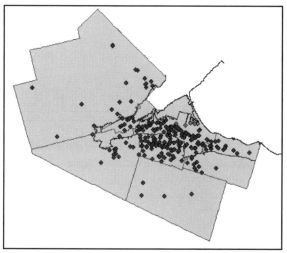

Fig. 7.36

Just by eyeballing the map, we can see that there are some schools fairly near to mercury emitters. But ArcView can do a great deal more than eyeball. We can actually run a map query to find schools within a specified distance from a mercury emitter.

To begin, click on the 'Buffer Wizard' icon. If it is not displayed—and it is not displayed by default—click on 'Tools' then, 'Customize', and click on the 'Commands' tab. Under 'Categories' pick 'Tools', then drag the 'Buffer Wizard' item to one of your toolbars. When you click on it, you get a dialogue box that allows you to choose 'The features of a layer.'

⚠ TECH TIP

By double-clicking on the symbols below the names of the maps or other layers in the table of contents, we can alter the size and/or colour of the symbols.

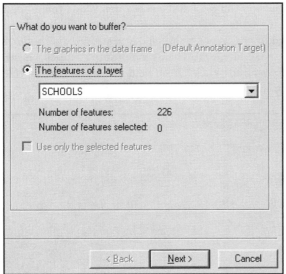

Fig. 7.37

A 'buffer' is a circle with its centre on the point being buffered. In this case, we will choose mercury emitters.

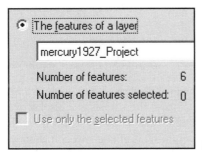

Fig. 7.38

Click 'Next', and you will get a dialogue box asking, "How do you want to create buffers?' Choose the first line, since you want to specify the distance, i.e., the radius of the buffer you will draw. We will pick '3 kilometres'.

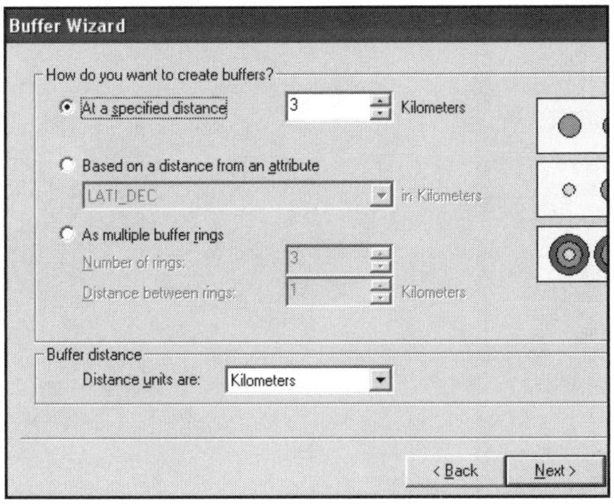

Fig. 7.39

Click 'Next' and you will get a dialogue box that allows you to specify whether common sections of the buffers will merge into each other. If you merge them, only one shapefile is created. If you do not, a shapefile is created for each buffer. Since you are creating one or more shapefiles, you also are prompted to give each a name. When you have completed the dialogue box, click 'Finish', and the new buffer shapefile(s) will be added to the map document, as in this illustration:

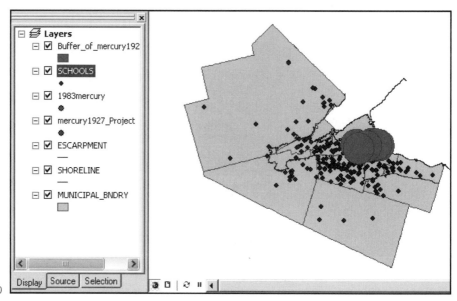

Fig. 7.40

You can modify how the map displays. For example, we will drag the schools layer to the top of the table of contents so the schools will display over the buffers. We will also change the colour of the buffer zone by double-clicking on the swatch of colour underneath the buffer file name in the table of contents and choosing the new colour. You can also choose 'Hollow', which then displays the buffer as a transparent circle outline. Your map should look something like this:

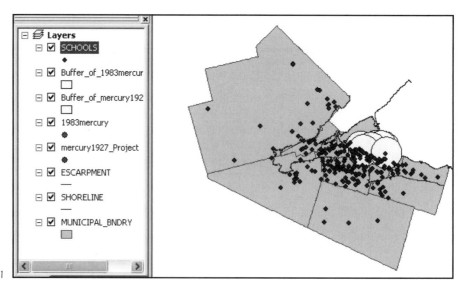

Fig. 7.41

We can now run a query to find schools within the three-kilometre buffer zones. This will allow us to move to on-the-ground reporting, to find out about the schools, the health status of students in them, and the possible impact of the nearby mercury polluters.

The first step is to click on 'Selection/select by location', to bring up this dialogue box:

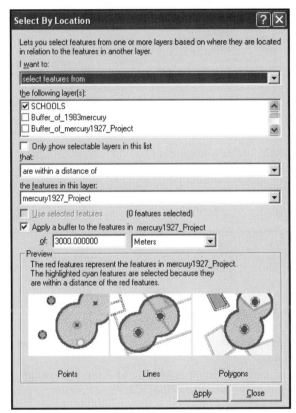

Fig. 7.42

We will fill in the dialogue box, as in this illustration, to select schools that intersect with the buffer around the mercury emitters.

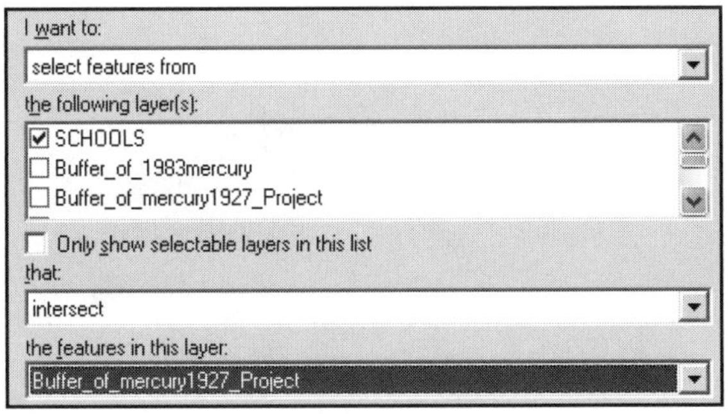

Fig. 7.43

Click 'Apply', and the features will be selected on the map. If you right-click on the schools layer in the table of contents and click 'Open attribute table', you can see the selected schools in the table, highlighted. If you click on 'Selected' beside 'Show', ArcView will hide all but the schools within the three-kilometre buffer zones, as in this image:

	FID	Shape	ID	NAME	
▶	0	Point	100	ADELAIDE HOODLESS	71
	3	Point	103	NOTRE DAME	400
	21	Point	122	WOODWARD	575
	24	Point	125	ST. MARY ELEMENTARY	209
	32	Point	133	QUEEN MARY	129
	42	Point	143	HOLY NAME OF JESUS	181
	46	Point	147	GIBSON	601
	47	Point	148	ST. HELEN	785
	48	Point	149	ST. JOHN THE BAPTIST	115
	49	Point	150	STINSON STREET	200
	51	Point	152	HIGHVIEW	104
	52	Point	153	ST. PATRICK	20
	69	Point	6	DR. J. EDGAR DAVEY	99
	76	Point	13	ST. BRIGID	24
	78	Point	15	PARKVIEW	60
	95	Point	32	PRINCE OF WALES	40
	96	Point	33	EASTMOUNT PARK	155

Record: ◄◄ ◄ [1] ► ►◄ 　 Show: All Selected 　 Records (42

Fig. 7.44

You can use the same steps outlined above to draw buffer zones around any point features and to find other point features that overlap with the buffers.

Querying by Attributes

ArcView also allows you to write queries very much like the ones you wrote in straight database applications.

In this map, again of the City of Hamilton, we have displayed all of the facilities in Hamilton that report to the National Pollutant Release Inventory.

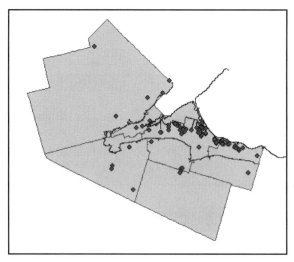

Fig. 7.45

Hamilton as it exists today is an amalgamation of six former cities, including the old urban City of Hamilton. Let's say we want to select only facilities within the former City of Stoney Creek. Begin by clicking on 'Selection/Select by attributes' as in this illustration.

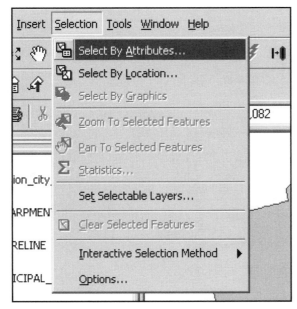

Fig. 7.46

Choosing 'Select by Attributes brings up a dialogue box that is ArcView's version of an SQL query dialogue (see Figure 7.47). By clicking on various elements, you can build a simple or complex SQL query.

In the 'layer' box, you can pick from any of the map layers that are open in the map document. In this case, we pick the file 'HamiltonNPRI'.

In the next box, you see a list of the fields. Double-clicking on the 'City' field will add it to the area at the bottom of the screen where you build your SQL syntax.

By clicking on the = sign you add the = operator to the query.

Now, manually type in: 'Stoney Creek'—ensuring that you use the single quotation marks around the string. Double quotes are reserved for use around field names.

That's it. Your query dialogue should end up like this:

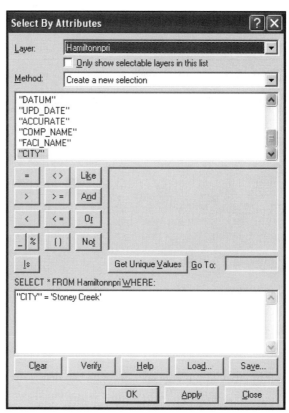

Fig. 7.47

Click 'OK', and the selected points will be highlighted on the map, as in this image:

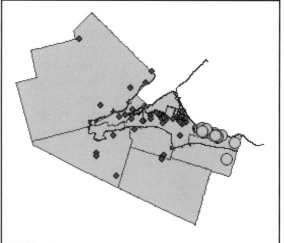

Fig. 7.48

The same method can be used to query the attribute table of any map table.

Drawing Your Own Map

Sometimes, you won't be able to get a map containing the features you need for your analysis. Fortunately, it is not difficult to create your own map containing polygon, line, or point features. We will look at creating a map containing polygons.

The first step is to create a new shapefile. Open ArcCatalog and in the catalog tree, left-click on the folder that will contain the new shapefile. On the 'File' menu, click 'New' and choose 'Shapefile'. Alternatively, you can right-click on the folder name and choose 'New', then 'Shapefile'. Either method brings up a dialogue box.

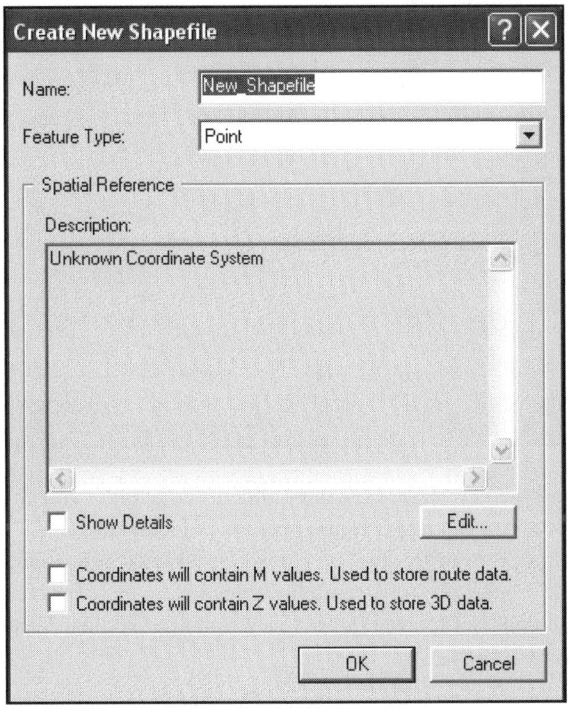

Create New Shapefile

Name: New_Shapefile

Feature Type: Point

Spatial Reference

Description:

Unknown Coordinate System

Show Details   Edit...

Coordinates will contain M values. Used to store route data.
Coordinates will contain Z values. Used to store 3D data.

OK   Cancel

Fig. 7.49

Enter a name for the new shapefile, and choose a feature type: variations on point, line, or polygon. We will choose 'Polygon'. Click on 'Edit' and you will get the now-familiar 'Spatial reference properties' dialogue box. As before, we will import a co-ordinate system from one of the existing City of Hamilton map files.

Click 'OK', and the new shapefile dialogue should look like this:

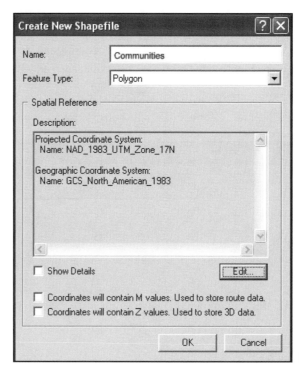

Fig. 7.50

Click 'OK', and the new shapefile will be added to the folder you chose.

Back in ArcView, you can add it to the open map document.

We are now in a position to draw new polygon features in our empty shapefile. We will use part of the 'Hamilton street centreline' file to trace these new features. Make sure that the editing toolbar is displayed (go to 'View', choose 'Toolbars', then click the 'Editor' icon and 'Start editing').

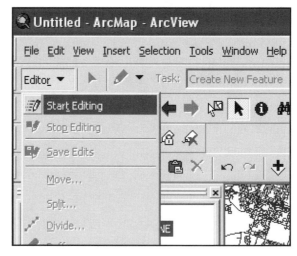

Fig. 7.51

We will pick 'Create New Feature' as the task, and the 'communities' shapefile we just created as our target. Now, you need to pick a tool to use. We will pick the 'Sketch' tool, represented by the pencil icon.

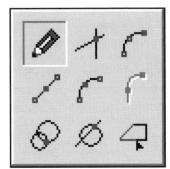

Fig. 7.52

To create new community boundaries in the 'communities shapefile', we will trace along streets in the 'streetcentreline' file. Begin at an intersection by clicking with the Sketch tool there, then hold and drag to draw a line to the first corner of your new polygon. Continue tracing until you get back to the original point. Double-click there, and the first new feature will be created on your shapefile. You can see it highlighted here:

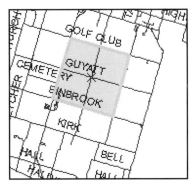

Fig. 7.53

You can continue to add new polygons until you are finished.

The next thing you need to do is modify the 'attribute' table for the shapefile to add one or more new fields to identify the features in your map. Do this by first going to the 'Editor' menu and choosing 'Stop editing'.

If you double-click on the map name in the table of contents and click 'Open attribute table,' then 'Options', then 'New field', you will get the 'Add field' dialogue box. Fill it out to add a new text field for the community name.

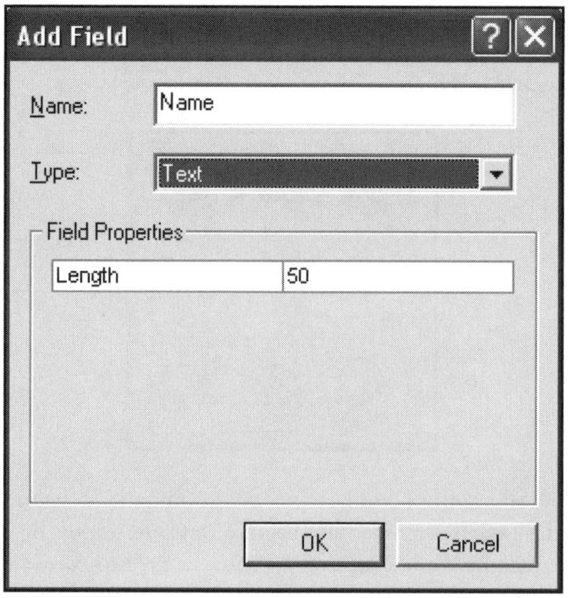

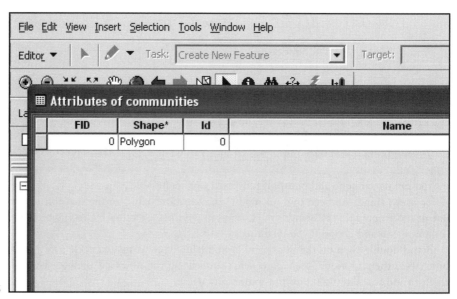

Fig. 7.54

When you are done, click 'OK' and you will see the new field has been added to the 'attributes' dialogue:

Fig. 7.55

You can now add information to the 'Attribute' table, in this case, the new 'Name' field. 'Select' the feature to highlight it, then click the 'attributes' icon on the 'Editor' toolbar—the one that looks like a miniature data table. You will get an 'Attributes' dialogue and you can now edit the 'Name' field to add a name. Do this for each of your new features, and you will have done.

You can use the same method to create any number of maps with boundaries, points, or lines that mimic those of a layer you already have. The potential is particularly great in the urban context, where there are a great many everyday things defined by boundaries, but where a ready-made map or one you can obtain easily or affordably may not be available. These could include police and fire response zones, city neighbourhoods, election polling divisions, or anything else where activity is divided up into different zones of a community.

Once you have created a shapefile and added features, you can use it in the same way as any other shapefile, including to create a thematic map.

For more details on editing in ArcView see the pdf document 'Editing in Arcmap', part of the excellent and comprehensive electronic documentation that comes with ArcView.

Publishing Your Maps

Mapping programs such as ArcView are powerful analytical tools that help you to understand better the relationships between almost anything that can be defined by its location on the earth's surface. They are, unfortunately, not ideal as graphic arts tools.

Under the 'File' menu in either 'Map' or 'Layout' view, you can choose 'Export map' to export your map to a number of graphics formats, including .jpg and .eps files.

There are limitations to this method, particularly in terms of flexibility and quality. If you can work within these limitations, these exported files may be suitable for your purposes. On the other hand, if you need high-quality vector image files for use in Adobe Illustrator or other high-end graphics packages, you may want to purchase a program called MapPublisher from Avenza Systems of Toronto, <www.avenza.com>.

The program is pricey, at close to $1,500 Canadian, but if you are working in a professional desktop publishing environment, this should not be an enormous hurdle. Lower prices are available for students. Contact Avenza for more information.

Bringing It All Together

In this chapter we have learned how to use a professional geographic information system, or GIS, to analyze and interpret map data. We have learned how to add data from non-map tables to display key attributes on our maps. And we have learned how to do simple querying, to identify patterns on maps.

Because this is merely one chapter in a book covering many areas, it is not possible to discuss comprehensively ArcView's many capabilities. There are a number of third-party books on ArcGIS that go into these and other topics in greater depth. Another excellent resource is *Mapping for Stories: A Computer-Assisted Reporting Guide*, available from Investigative Reporters and Editors. Go to <www.ire.org> for more information. In the next chapter, we will talk about how to obtain data of many types, including map data.

Five Stories You Can Do

1. Obtain the census tract maps for your municipality in shapefile format, from Statistics Canada. Also, obtain census tract level data for population in the last two censuses. Map the percentage change in population for each census tract, to see which of your municipality's neighbourhoods are shrinking in population, and which are increasing. Try mapping other variables, such as the percentage of immigrants and visible-minority groups in each tract.

2. Download the latest National Pollutant Release Inventory files from Environment Canada. Using the latitude and longitude file, map all of the polluting facilities in a new Shapefile. Add in a census tract map, as you did above, to see how many people live near the various polluters.

3. Obtain or draw a Shapefile of polling division boundaries for your next municipal election. On election night, obtain poll-by-poll results and map where the winning mayor got the most votes. Try mapping percentage turnouts in each polling division.

4. Using the Statistics Canada census tract files and the latest census data for median family income, map out the median family income for each tract. Add a layer of local parks and recreation facilities to see if poor areas have equal access to recreational services.

5. Obtain or draw a Shapefile of major natural gas pipelines in your area. Add a layer showing new subdivision development to see if once-rural pipelines are now near to people's homes.

Finding and Getting Data

Fred Vallance-Jones and David McKie

Chapter 8

What We'll Cover

- When data is likely to be available.
- Negotiating for data.
- Getting data from the web.
- Finding mapping data.

To this point, we have spent time learning how to work with spreadsheets and databases to find stories in areas such as air safety, workplace safety, and political donations. We have looked at how to use map data to produce electronic maps that help us to understand relationships between things that are located on the face of the earth. But none of this is possible without access to data.

Fortunately for those engaged in computer-assisted reporting, getting one's hands on useful data isn't nearly as hard as you might expect. In fact, some of it is there for the taking—as downloadable data sets on the Internet. Other information may not be in the form of rows and columns, but you may be able to manipulate it into that form. Still, other data may be in the form of rows and columns, but kept sealed in government vaults, necessitating negotiation or freedom-of-information requests to pry it free. Finally, some data may be available pursuant to licensing or usage agreements. This is particularly so with map data, which unlike ordinary administrative data is often a copyrightable 'work', which the creator has a right to control. Statistics Canada also releases much of its data to the media on a licensed basis, generally with a prohibition on using the data for any purpose other than researching news stories unless specific permission from the statistical agency is obtained.

Beginning the Search

The search for data usually begins with one or more questions that may be related to a story you are doing, or may start simply with an idea. How many? How much? How often? Where? These are the sorts of systematic questions that can launch you on the quest for data.

You can then ask whether a relevant database is likely to exist.

There was a time when paper records were the primary method of storing information. Forms, reports, and memos—the ongoing record of the life and activities of an organization—were created on paper then filed away for some period of time. For organizations of any size and complexity, this required the creation of record-keeping systems and the hiring of people to run them. Computers changed all that. Today, paper records are more likely to exist as backups, supplements, or summaries of electronic records.

Database systems of one kind or another have largely replaced paper-based systems for the collection of routine administrative information.

Think of all the times you have been asked to fill out a form to participate in a program, obtain a government benefit, or enter a contest. In all likelihood, information from that form ended up in a database somewhere, whether to track program participants, record benefit payments, or create a mailing list. Databases may also be fed information automatically, such as when you fill out an online form or, if you live in BC or Ontario, take you car for an emissions test.

Databases are ubiquitous. The ability to access and analyze them is essential, therefore, to a complete understanding of how agencies operate and how their programs are performing. Some journalists might ask why they would want access to raw data when summarized information can be obtained from documents or media relations officials. The answer is that those who have the power to summarize have the power to influence and control how the data will be interpreted, or what conclusions may be drawn from it. Power to spin information comes with what you control, what summaries you do, and how you present them. Even when officials have no specific intention to hide anything, those journalists deal with usually have access only to certain reports, not the raw data. Such reports, typically, are ones that officials believe will be of the broadest interest or that have been requested most often. So, when someone says, 'We don't have anything on that', he or she may well be telling the truth.

Once you get your hands on the raw data, you have the power to analyze any parameter yourself, come to your own conclusions, and come closer to the ideal of telling the whole truth.

When is a database likely to exist? Basically, anytime an agency does anything on a repetitive and ongoing basis and needs to keep track of it. Here are some examples of things that might be tracked in a database system:

- Outcomes of government inspections of almost any kind, including health or safety inspections.
- Government payments to individuals, companies, or other organizations.
- Permits or licenses issued, such as building permits, liquor licenses, gun permits, and business licenses.
- Administrative actions, such as fines and/or convictions for statutory offences.
- Incidents or accidents in fields subject to government regulation, such as transportation, the environment, or worker safety.
- Test results, such as standardized school tests or emissions-testing results.
- Readings kept on a regular basis, such as air pollution measurements.
- Complaints from the public in areas subject to government regulation.
- Administrative lists, such as employee telephone and e-mail lists.
- Records of internal expenditures in areas such as travel or sick leave.
- Records of decisions taken.

This list is by no means exhaustive. The general rule is: if an agency does something over and over again, someone is probably keeping track of it in a database.

If you believe that data exists, the next step is to verify that fact, and find out what steps will be required to obtain it.

In some cases you will be really lucky, and not only will a database exist, but it will be available for download from a government website. Almost as good, the guts of the data you need will be posted online and with some manipulation with a word processor or other tool (see Chapter 10) you can pull the data into a useable form.

More likely, the data won't be that easy either to verify or to get. Sometimes you can confirm that a database exists by reading reports, such as department annual reports or reports on specific topics, published by the agency that likely maintains the data. Tables and other statistical summaries in reports can be a dead giveaway that a database exists and has been used to crunch the summaries. You can consult online record directories such as the federal government's InfoSource. These contain long lists with descriptions of records, including electronic records.

The existence of a searchable database on a website means, of course. that the agency keeps a database containing that, and probably more, information. Don't overlook past news reports, news releases, and other secondary sources that may have mentioned the existence or creation of data sources, often by name.

It's also important to 'find everyone on your beat who asks for and uses reports created with computerized data—the end users.'[1] It's always necessary to develop good sources. These end users can also be founts of information about the kind of material that is stored, and the frequency with which is it updated.

Another tactic is to ask for a list or inventory of databases. A official's first reaction may be to say a list doesn't exist, but most agencies did compile inventories in advance of 2000, because of the fear of the Y2K 'bug'.

You might also want to think about anyone else outside the government who might be using the data and might be willing to share it. In many instances, academics may be using municipal data sets to track 'traffic' patterns.

If research of this kind doesn't do the trick, likely the next step is to contact interest groups and others who are familiar with the subject area. Such people often will be aware of minutiae, for example, which data system is used to record what. Eventually, you will want to approach the agency to inquire about the existence of a database; and how you go about this is going to depend on the circumstances of the particular case. Ideally, you want to call the section of the agency that deals with the subject matter, but in today's world of tightly controlled information, you may be channelled to the media relations department. Keep in mind that these people deal with high-level issues, and may have no idea that a database exists. It is important to be precise and clear, and insist that the person you are dealing with take the question back to those who will know.

Eventually, you will establish that a database exists; but that is not enough. You now want to know what form it is in. Here, having some technical knowledge goes a long way. If you've reached this far in this book, you've been introduced to a lot of the jargon already. You're liable to learn a lot more as you move forward.

While we are not insisting that you become a computer expert, it is important to learn the lingo necessary to find and obtain databases. So learn the nerd language for the different file formats, software, database sizes, and the difference between a fixed length and delimited file.

Don't forget, also, to find out what the database is called. It's far easier to ask for it if you can give it a name. It's also harder for officials to deny the existence of something you can name.

Having established all of this, it's time to get the data from their hard drive to yours.

Of course, getting governments to hand over data is not always easy. It can take skilled negotiation or the use of access-to-information statutes to pry it free. Later in this chapter, we will present three case studies of how reporters successfully obtained data from various agencies. The key thing to remember is the 'AND' rule. First Ask; then Negotiate; finally, Demand, using the access laws.

Journalists are surprised often at what they can get simply by talking to the official in charge, and asking her to send over a CD. For years, the *Hamilton Spectator* has received a monthly database containing all of the building permits issued in the City of Hamilton, the address, type of construction, value of construction, and so on. It began with a simple request. The Transportation Safety board similarly handed over data on reportable aviation incidents after a simple request by the newspaper to the media relations office.

When the official says, 'No', that's the time to start to give and take, to try to negotiate access to some or all of the data you need. When the *Spectator* was told by the city's transportation department in 2002 it could not have a database of traffic accidents, the paper initiated a discussion to find out why. It turned out the city's police service was blocking access. So, the paper requested and got a meeting with senior police and transportation department officials. Armed with previous orders from Ontario's Information and Privacy Commissioner, the paper's representatives were able to demonstrate that the data should be public. It was released without further fuss, without the need for a formal access request.

Only when negotiations lead nowhere should you use the powerful, but time-consuming, method of filing an access request. Even then, as you will read in the case studies, you may need all the negotiating skills you can muster. As the Canadian Newspaper Association pointed out in its 2007 freedom of information audit,[2] access requests should be a last resort.

Negotiating for Data and Using Freedom of Information

If you follow the 'AND' rule, the time inevitably will come when negotiation is necessary, through informal discussions with the people who maintain and administer the data or through the last resort: federal access-to-information and provincial freedom-of-information laws. As anyone who works with a lot of data will quickly explain, an inordinate length of time is taken looking for and negotiating for data. To make the negotiations easier, we will suggest some strategies that have yielded great results and review four case studies where the negotiations, sometimes combined with access requests, have led to great stories.

Engaging in the art of dialogue is one of the best ways to obtain data from bureaucrats who can be reluctant to co-operate. The reason the 'N' precedes the 'D' in 'AND' is because once you demand under the access laws, the process slows down and can become confrontational. This has led to protracted battles between journalists and bureaucrats. Even when you demand, you may find yourself negotiating the finer points of access anyway.

So remember the 'N', and develop your negotiation strategy.

If you've done the type of homework outlined above, you should know quite a bit about the kind of data that can be made available. In general, negotiating for data is no different from negotiating for any other record. Typically, bureaucrats will want to apply the same restrictions on release as they would apply to a formal access request, so don't be surprised if they insist on removing information, such as references to individuals, or even information that *could* be related to an individual.

As with any such process, know as you are going into negotiations what you can give up, and what you need to have. You can use your 'dispensable' fields the same way you'd use the $5,000 you know you'll give up when selling your house. They become your negotiating 'elbow room'. One of the truths of any negotiation is that everyone can go home happy if they feel they won something. 'Frequently agencies will have no problem with 95 per cent of what you're asking for, but the remaining fields can torpedo the whole deal,' writes Bob Warner in his tip sheet for the National Institute for Computer-

Assisted Reporting. 'Try to think through in advance what's essential to your project, and be openly flexible in dealing with your sources of information. Even if they're balking at giving you something like home addresses, or the precise street addresses where crimes occurred, you may be able to come up with a computer-driven solution. In a dispute over addresses, for instance, you could design a simple program to change to '00' the last two digits of each number it encounters in an address field. This would generally allow you to identify blocks but not specific homes.'[3]

This is the kind of compromise that the *Ottawa Citizen*'s Glen McGregor used when negotiating for his gun registry database. Officials would not release the entire postal code, arguing that this information could help McGregor identify individuals. Instead, he ended up receiving the first two digits of the postal code, which identified rural versus urban areas, and specific geographic areas within municipalities. Hence, he was able to determine that the Yukon had the highest per capita gun ownership in the country.

Says Carla Heggie, national chair of the Canadian Association of Professional Access and Privacy Administrators. 'It's all about communication.'[4]

Getting the Guts First

One step that often helps ease the negotiating process is to begin by asking for information about the database's structure. This is especially so with larger, more sensitive datasets. What you want is a list of fields and their data types and lengths, often called a 'record layout'. This will give you an idea of the fields and the information that they contain. If you can't get a record layout, ask for the form that inspectors must fill out when in the field, or the form that doctors and drug companies must complete when people become ill. Each category such as a name, date, time of incident, cause of incident, drug involved, etc, usually represents a field in the database. In this case, you would not be able to ask for the name, but you could ask for other anonymous details such as the time of the accident, the drug involved, whether the premises ever were inspected before, and so on. Such information would allow you to identify important trends that can drive your stories.

Once you know the fields you want, it might be an idea to ask for a sample of the database. This will reveal important characteristics about the database, such as the accuracy of the information, or fields that may be missing.

Another question you'll be asked is the time period. That is, for how far back in time do you want records. As a general rule, you should 'ask for as many years of data as you can manage. You want to see patterns over time.'[5] You may end up using only a five-year time period, but it's helpful to have as complete a dataset as possible. Usually, there's little difference in exporting a five-year time period compared to a ten-year time period. What takes time is figuring out which fields you want.

It is impossible to cover all the areas that you should consider when negotiating for data. However, in addition to the suggestions mentioned thus far, here are other key considerations to ponder.

Know the size of the database or table. Excel 2007 can store one million records, Access has a theoretical 2-gigabyte limit on a database, while other programs such as MySQL are limited mostly by the capacity of your hard drive and limitations in your operating system.

Know the law. As you will almost certainly find your requests, whether formal or informal, governed by rules set by the access statute in force in the jurisdiction in which you are making your request, take the time to get to know the law (or laws). Get to understand the exemptions to access, when they apply, and when they don't. If you are working in a jurisdiction with an information commissioner and the reports or orders are public, read them to understand how the law has been interpreted until now. Pay attention to special provisions related to electronic records. Most provinces, as well as Ottawa, equate electronic and paper records. But at least one, Saskatchewan, allows officials to refuse to release electronic records. Others go the other way, requiring that electronic records be created from databases for requesters, so long as the job doesn't strain the department's resources. As a general principle, if a record is public in paper form, it ought to be available in electronic form, although that logic has been questioned by the courts in Ontario.[6]

Know who is in charge. The person in charge isn't necessarily the one who enters the data. Rather, he tends to be the individual responsible for quality control issues—such as the integrity of the data, the frequency with which the database is updated, and so on. It's a good idea to ask to discuss your request with this person. That said, it's also a good idea to get to know the people who actually administer the data, if you can get to them. If you cultivate relationships with the line IT people, they can quickly answer technical questions to which higher-ups could take weeks or months to respond.

If necessary, follow up for details you can't get the first time around. You may not want the specific details of occurrences that you're tracking. These details are sometimes contained in large memo fields and if the fields contain personal information or other information that may be exempt from disclosure, officials may insist on editing them one by one. You will need to make a judgement as to whether pressing to get such fields is worthwhile, at least for the first round. If the data records occurrences involving individuals, officials may well press to review each record. However, there will be some instances where such a claim is absurd. For example, when the *Hamilton Spectator* requested Transport Canada's air safety database, it argued successfully that the memo field did not contain exempt information, and it was released along with the others. Even if you choose not to go after the memo field, once you spot your trend, you may want to want to request paper incident reports, or the memo field itself, for a limited number of occurrences that could become central to your story.

Be prepared to explain why you want the data. 'Granted, this is the question that makes a typical reporter grit [his] teeth', writes Ziva Branstetter in his tip sheet for the Investigative Reporters and Editors. 'But in electronic news-gathering, the reporter rarely has the upper hand. It helps to be able to describe goals that are a little more public spirited than a fishing expedition.'[7] The best approach is to divulge enough information to make your request seem less intimidating, but not enough to make the agency just shut down your request.

Try to avoid people in communications departments. Generally speaking, they know very little, if anything, about databases. They also have a tendency to raise unnecessary alarm bells when all you may be initially requesting is a record layout, or data from the agency's website. It's best to go straight to the source: the person in charge of the data; or, failing that, an officer in the freedom-of-information office who can help you obtain the data without filing a formal request.

Don't accept the argument that they can't export the data or that they're getting a new computer in another few months. Any system should be capable of exporting data. If the bureaucrat insists on sticking to his argument, ask whether a minister would have to wait a few months to have important data on her desk? A minister waiting days and days for bureaucrats to produce data? Now that would make a great story! And besides, a system incapable of exporting subsets of data would be a waste of taxpayers' money.

Don't buy the explanation that it has too much private information. The onus is on them to explain why you shouldn't have it. And, as we've already learned, it's easy for them to exclude fields if they contain personal details.

Cost shouldn't be a huge factor. Journalists always have the option of asking for a special fee waiver. Carla Heggie of the Canadian Association of Professional Access and Privacy Administrators advises that it's important to use this argument with caution. Hence, . . .

Don't use a boilerplate reason for a waiver. '"I am a member of the fourth estate and therefore doing it for the public good and I should automatically get a fee waiver for any fee application I ever put in." Well, that argument has already been tested and tried in the courts and in reviews with the commissioner. It doesn't hold water', Heggie says. 'Because in the same way that I can't make boilerplate decisions, you shouldn't make boilerplate requests for exemptions or waivers. You have to make the argument on a case-by-case basis. Some of them you're going to win, and some of them you're not.'[8]

Have a good reason for asking for a waiver. Heggie strongly suggests that journalists explain why they think it's important to have the fee waived. For instance, in the case of workplace safety, it's easy to argue that people have a right to know about dangers in their workplace; similarly, with air safety data.

Be transparent. For obvious reasons, journalists are reluctant to share information about their stories before they're aired or published. While it's never wise to totally abandon this kind of caution, it's important to be open about the nature of your request during negotiations. Explain what you plan to do with the information. Very politely explain that a database is like any other record. 'Be up front and honest', advises Heggie. 'And that way you have more credibility. You're going to get more buy-in [from the bureaucrats].'[9]

Proprietary software. In some instances, bureaucrats will attempt to deny the information by arguing that software is proprietary. But you are not asking for the software, only the data, which is just like information in a paper record.

We don't keep that in a database. This may not be true. Institutions have databases to keep track of everything, including personnel issues such as payroll. These administrative databases allow government departments to manage their affairs efficiently and keep track of huge volumes of information. On the other hand, it really could be that they don't keep databases to track certain aspects of their activities. For instance, while cities such as Edmonton, Toronto, and Hamilton use databases to track restaurant inspections, other cities such as Ottawa do not. So it's always wise to challenge assertions about information not existing in databases.

Find out if government agencies in other jurisdictions are giving out the same sort of information. This is useful information to have in anticipation of a 'No' response. You can argue that other jurisdictions are co-operating. This strategy came in handy for the CBC's investigation into workplace safety. Certain jurisdictions, such as Newfoundland and Labrador, found it easier to co-operate when they discovered that Nova Scotia and New Brunswick had agreed to hand over some of their data.

Watch out for arguments about 'programming time'. It is not unusual for agencies to send reporters large bills for computer programming or other tasks associated with the release of electronic datasets. For example, Transport Canada initially assessed the *Hamilton Spectator* a fee of several thousand dollars for the release of a copy of its CADORS air safety database. The fee was based on a provision in the Access to Information Regulations allowing for a fee of $15 per minute for CPU time. The provision dated from the act's passage in the 1980s, when processor time could still be a valuable resource. But with the arrival of personal computers on nearly every desktop, that had changed. The *Spectator* pointed out that the Treasury Board doesn't allow for any more than the *actual costs* to be charged, and Transport's bill disappeared.

The *Spectator* also won an important decision before Ontario's information and privacy commissioner that writing queries to export data did not constitute programming time, which is charged at twice the rate of other 'preparation' under Ontario's Act.[10]

Preparation fees. You should never have to pay anything more than the preparation fees allowed by the act in the jurisdiction in which you are seeking the data.

The data belongs to a private operator. More and more, institutions are turning over the maintenance of their databases to private agencies that can do the job more cheaply. But this doesn't mean the government department is off the hook. Carla Heggie points out that 'it's still government information. You have to look to the question of custody and control. And government may not have the custody, but they still have the control, and if they don't have the control, then we've got a bigger problem than access. I can't see any government in its right mind relinquishing control of their information, even if it has gone to a third party for revenue or organizational reasons.'[11] The *Spectator* obtained a database of projects under Ontario's Superbuild infrastructure program even though the data were maintained by an outside company hired for the purpose.

This whole database is considered private. This may, indeed, be a legitimate argument when it comes to some databases for operations strictly internal to the department that deals with sensitive issues. Personnel matters, such as payroll, could fall into this category. Don't be afraid to challenge the ruling, as agencies will sometimes be extremely creative in defining data as personal. When the *Spectator* sought the airline safety data, Transport Canada maintained information about incidents involving aircraft was the personal information of the pilots! Of course, the department eventually had to relent.

Is there a code book that goes with the data? As we have already learned, databases use codes and identification numbers. Without a code book, or look-up tables that come with the database, such codes would be meaningless.

Find out when you can receive the next update. It's very easy for data to become stale. That's because government departments, especially large ones, often are updating them on a daily basis. The Ontario government, for example, keeps a database of all Drive Clean emissions tests. Thousands of tests are added every day. Other databases, such as the adverse drug reactions and workplace safety datasets, may be updated less frequently, but on a regular basis. It is important to find out when the updates occur. Once you've done the hard work of negotiating for the data, doing updates should be a snap. You might consider some sort of calendar marked with the approximate dates new sources of data will be available.

I need help. Inevitably, aspects of the database will boggle the mind. Why are certain fields left blank? What is the meaning of certain categories? Am I interpreting the data correctly? What methods does the department use to check the integrity of its data? These are important questions that must be answered while working with the data. This is why it's important to give the department a heads-up that you will be coming back with questions. Be prepared to put the questions in writing, and make sure you give the department ample time—at least a few days—to respond. Don't be asking important questions just before your deadline. The more you interview or ask questions of your data, the more queries you'll have about the meaning of it all. It's also advisable to find an expert who can become a consultant. This is what the *Toronto Star* did in its award-winning 'Race and Crime' series which demonstrated that, in certain circumstances, the Toronto police treated blacks differently from whites.

How does the institution use the data? It goes without saying that journalists and bureaucrats think differently. That logic extends to the use of databases. While a bureaucracy may use a database as a lookup tool to find a piece of information or run pre-set routines to pull out specific trends, journalists are likely to do more free-form analysis, looking for various trends that the bureaucrats have never studied. While you don't want to be bound by the ways in which the department uses the data, it's important to understand the difference.

Three Case Studies

Sometimes examples best bring home lessons in an area as complex as obtaining data. Some classic, recent cases of how journalists can prevail when the going gets tough.

Race and Crime

The situation was well-known in Toronto's black community, but the news still hit like a bombshell on 19 October 2002, when the *Toronto Star* published its first of a number of stories under the headline: 'Singled out: Star analysis of police crime data shows justice is different for blacks, and whites.'[12]

Among the *Star's* findings:

- Black people, charged with simple drug possession, were taken to the station more often than whites facing the same charge;
- Once at the station, accused blacks were held overnight, for a bail hearing, at twice the rate of whites;
- Blacks were held for bail 15.5% of the time compared to 7.3% of the time for whites.[13]

The series, which went on the win the Canadian Association of Journalists Computer-Assisted Reporting award and the Michener Award in 2003, was buttressed by CIPS, the acronym for a database called the Criminal Information Processing System that the Toronto Police Services uses to record who is arrested and why. 'We could have done the series without the data', recalls Jim Rankin, one five reporters on the story and the person on the *Star* team who negotiated for the data, 'but it wouldn't have been nearly as powerful. It still would have been a good series. The data buttressed everything and made it different from what we'd been saying for years in one-of-only pieces and anecdotal stories.'[14]

Getting the data was an exercise in frustration and persistence. The idea began in 1999 after a Toronto police news release described a crime that occurred, and reported the suspect had 'yellow skin'. The police may have eventually backtracked by qualifying that characterization as an error, but the skin-colour reference got Rankin thinking. At the time, he had been covering the police beat and there was something about that characterization that didn't sit well. After asking a few questions, he discovered that the police have a database that codes skin colour: yellow for Asian; red for Native Canadian; black for black; white for white, and so on.

'That got us thinking about what kind of data they did capture', says Rankin. 'In Toronto, police had been forbidden from analyzing race-based crime stats or producing any stats since 1989 when a young police sergeant called (Julian) Fantino got himself in some hot water over some crime stats he released about Asian crime.'[15]

For about a year, they tried the informal route, attempting to negotiate with the police to obtain the data. They tried to get record layouts of the databases of interest and figure out to whom they should speak within the police force about the databases. They looked for the names of those databases to figure out which ones would be the most useful. The two that showed the most promise were a database that goes by the acronym MANIX, which is a catch-all data set the police use to track their interaction with the public, and CIPS (the Criminal Information Processing System). The informal route stalled. Fortunately, they had enough information to file a formal request.

And that's exactly what they did on 23 March 2000. The police refused to divulge anything. The *Star* twice complained to the information and privacy commission. The police force was obliged to produce lists of the kind of information contained in the databases, a necessary step to ensure that they weren't missing anything. After reviewing the list, Rankin decided that the CIPS database showed the most promise. 'The CIPS database documented arrests and charges. So we focused on that one because it seemed that there was more meat. It was definitely a larger database.'

The police denied the request. A provincial mediator was appointed to the file, and met with Rankin and an analyst from the police services to address concerns about privacy. In order to prevent any possibility of identifying individuals, some offences were re-coded into nondescript categories.

'And we had to do other things to address the privacy concerns that they had and then it took a number of months for the police analyst to come up with the programming necessary to pull out what we requested and replace specific information with non-specific information, and then in late May 2002, the police released the modified CIPS database to us at a cost of 800 dollars.'

After a lot of cleaning, and data mining, the *Star* published the series five-and-a-half months after winning the battle for the data.

For Rankin, it was a learning experience; one that taught him the value of learning everything thing there is to know about the data, co-operating, and maintaining a dialogue with the officials who maintain the data. 'The key thing to keep in mind when you're asking for other people's data, and you intend to do your own analysis of it, is: it's not going to viewed as a very pleasant proposal by the people who hold the data.'[16] 'Trying to establish a dialogue and going the informal route, that's all fine and dandy, but just know that this is what's being thought about on the other end, and so a little bit of bedside manner might go a long way. And if you can be transparent about what you're doing, and what you want to do without tipping your hand and potentially having some competitor in the media being tipped off about it, be transparent. If there are some contentious things that you think you might find in there, then bear that in mind when you're negotiating for the data. But try and be as transparent as possible. It goes a long way.'

Rankin and the *Star* suffered a setback after attempting to obtain follow-up data. The police refused to co-operate, and in 2007 won a judgment from Ontario's Divisional Court, which ruled police had no obligation to write programs to manipulate data prior to release. The newspaper is taking the case to the Ontario Court of Appeal.

'Faint Warning', and 'Collision Course'

These two cases have many similarities, so it makes sense to consider them together. Both CBC's investigative unit, and the *Hamilton Spectator*, fought for years to obtain basic public safety databases. In the case of the CBC, the team used the Access to Information Act to request Health Canada's Canadian Adverse Drug Reaction Information System, or CADRIS. In the case of the newspaper, it was a request by the *Spectator* for the Civil Aviation Daily Occurrence Reports database CADORS. Even the acronyms sound similar! In both cases it took years; five for the CBC, four for the *Spectator*, to obtain the records, and in both cases the federal Information Commissioner became involved and eventually took the matters to the federal court.

In each case, the information sought had been released in other forms before, in paper or in PDF form in the case of CADRIS, in paper and online to a specialized circle of aviation insiders in the case of CADORS. Both media organizations ended up making similar arguments that if the data was being released to some people, there was no reason the databases as a whole could not be released as well.

Both departments also made arguments about privacy, with Transport making the absurd claim that information about planes constituted the personal information of the people flying them. Similarly, Health Canada argued that even releasing the name of the city where someone had an adverse drug reaction could lead to the identification of the individual.

The key to success in both cases was patience and knowing the law. At one point during the negotiation process on the drug database, the Information Commissioner's legal counsel delivered an ultimatum to Health Canada: co-operate with the CBC and negotiate which fields can be released or be forced to hand over data.

Transport, too, dragged its feet, at one point releasing a disk with almost every field in the database removed, claiming that was all it could release under privacy laws. But the *Spectator* never gave up. Transport only gave in when the commissioner had already begun a court action.

In the summer of 2003, Health Canada finally chose to negotiate with the CBC. That fall, the CBC had about 40 years' worth of data in several tables exported into Access. The *Toronto Star* also obtained the data, and it published a series of its own a few months after the CBC's 'Faint Warning' was broadcast in early 2004.

The CBC is still at odds with Health Canada over certain fields, but that dispute was set aside to allow the request to continue. And this is an important message: don't let disputed fields hold up your request. Wage that battle at some other time. The *Spectator* also put some fields on the table as candidates for being severed, but in the end none had to be removed.

The perseverance in both of these cases led, first, Health Canada and, later, Transport Canada to publish portions of these databases on their websites, where anyone can obtain them today.

Parking Tickets

If you haven't had one, you certainly know of someone who has—parking tickets. They are annoying, and an important source of revenue for cities. Every year, municipalities hand out hundreds of thousands of tickets. Wouldn't it be interesting to find out such details as who receives the highest number of tickets, or in what areas of the city drivers are the most vulnerable for receiving these unwelcome surprises?

These are the questions that occurred to the *Ottawa Citizen*'s Glen McGregor for his series on parking tickets called 'The Hornet's Sting, Inside Ottawa's Parking Ticket System'.[17] It was also difficult getting the data, which he obtained after 10 months of negotiation. He asked for data going back to the year 2000. These data were punched into a database with their hand-held units by the bylaw officers.

Initially, McGregor was directed to a private company that handles the parking ticket data for the city. To save money, an increasing number of government departments are contracting out their data management. Frequently, when journalists ask for the data, they are told either that it's inaccessible in that it belongs to a third party, or that the data will cost an astronomical amount. McGregor was told it would cost his paper $150 an hour to have a programmer extract the data over the course of 20 hours.

During this time, he also was maintaining a dialogue with the official in the city's freedom of information office, a tactic he says came in handy because she became his ally in his fight for data. During a mediation session, the official's boss admitted that the city did have a parking ticket database. McGregor asked for a list of the fields. 'And there were fields I didn't even know existed. It was fantastic. It was a goldmine. Suddenly, I could see I could get 10 different stories out of this just by looking at these fields. . . . I didn't know that the bylaw officer who issues the ticket is not protected by privacy legislation. And one of the stories is about the guy who issues the most tickets in Ottawa. He's not going to talk to me, but it's still going to be a good story anyway. It also showed me how they code the location of the tickets. It basically gave me an outline of everything that was in the database.'[18]

But there was another problem: cost. The city wanted to charge him more than $110,000. The problem was the memo fields that contained personal information. The personal detail had to be extracted and that would take time—too much time, as it turned out.

'So I went in and met with her again and she printed out a sample of about thirty records from the database and we looked at them and said "here are the fields that are going to cause all the problems . . . they are comments fields and I don't really need them for the story I'm doing. Let's knock them out." So we knocked out all the fields that were going to cause problems, and they sent me another estimate for $240. So they did it. They sent me a disk—and a refund for $200. It ended up costing me $40, which is a lot better than $110,000. And I got just about everything I needed.'[19]

McGregor says the key to successful negotiations is being realistic. If you can't get everything you want, and you're not willing to get into a protracted battle, then how do you keep the negotiations going? 'I think you have to weigh the interests of getting the story in the paper against fighting for your rights under the (provincial) freedom-of-information law or the (federal) access-to-information law . . . . I mean, it had already taken 10 months at this point., and the other problem was that the data were getting pretty stale as well while I was doing this. So I had to go in ask them halfway through the process to change the scope of my request to update the data that can be downloaded and exported into Excel or Access.'[20]

A Final Note on Online and Other Data Sources

Obviously, any written text is going to be outdated as soon as the ink is dry, as new datasets are being added every year. For this reason, we aren't going to print a long list of data sources here. Go to <www.oupcanada.com/CAR.html> for a comprehensive, frequently updated list.

What we can do is discuss some of the principles. Generally, Internet data will come in one of several forms. One is a web page itself. Using Microsoft Internet Explorer you can select, then cut and paste, data tables from web pages into Microsoft Excel. If you like, from there, you can save the files and import them into Access or another database manager.

Another is the downloadable file. Various agencies post database files for direct download to your computer's hard drive, and import into Excel, Access, or other programs.

Then, some files aren't row and column data in and of themselves, but with a little manipulation they can be brought into that form. We'll touch more on that technique in Chapter 10 on advanced techniques.

Statistics Canada Data

One special case for access to data is Statistics Canada. As of this writing, the agency provides any of its electronic data and publications at no cost to the news media, so long as the data are one of its standard 'products', and no 'custom' data run is required. Custom data runs will generally mean charges to the media organization. Such charges can be steep, although you should contact Statistics Canada's media relations staff to ascertain what the agency may be able to do for you.

See <www.oupcanada.com/CAR.html> for a taste of what the agency has to offer.

Mapping Data

As we mentioned, map files are a special case because they represent the copyrightable work of those who made them. Until recently, government agencies regarded them as a significant source of income, and charged what the market would bear. That could be hundreds or thousands of dollars. Commercial vendors still charge large sums for street files and other basic tools.

A refreshing recent trend, however, is towards making GIS data available at little or no cost, especially to media and educational users. The Cities of Hamilton and Halifax are among those that have adopted policies to provide free access to local media. Certain federal data is provided at no cost on the Internet to anyone who wants it. Stats Can provides online access to road maps for the entire country and each of the provinces, in both MapInfo and Shapefile formats, via its geography website (<www12.statcan.ca/english/census06/geo/index.cfm>). These come complete with address ranges for geocoding. Statscan also provides provincial and city boundary maps at no charge.

Statscan sells additional levels of detail, such as census tracts, but generally will provide such data to the media at no cost.

You'll find a comprehensive list of mapping data sources at <www.oupcanada.com/CAR.html>.

Bringing It All Together

In this chapter, we have examined some of the basic principles behind accessing data from government departments and agencies. It is knowledge hard-won by pioneers in the field of computer-assisted reporting. The good news for those starting journalism careers now is that more data is available online than ever, and bureaucrats, while still reluctant, are becoming more accustomed to journalists' asking for databases. In the next chapter, we look at the writing of stories that emerge from all this data.

Chapter 9

Organizing and Writing the CAR Story

David McKie and Fred Vallance-Jones

So far in this book we have focused on finding data, downloading, cleaning it, crunching it, and analyzing it. But one of the worst mistakes a journalist doing CAR can make is to forget that she or he is a storyteller.

A real temptation among reporters and editors is to treat data analysis as if it were a substitute for traditional reporting—as if crunching data or crunching numbers in a spreadsheet were enough to generate a story ready for the front page or lead story on the newscast. Occasionally, astonishing data will come out this way, especially with daily stories that will run as sidebars or accompaniments to related stories reported in the traditional manner. A new census release, for example, may feature a story written directly from the data, with comments from a Statistics Canada analyst, and accompanied by 'people' stories that flesh out the details. A quick spreadsheet analysis of the new city budget could produce a next-day story on large increases for the police.

Much of the time you will not chart such a direct course from database or spreadsheet to completed story. More often than not, the CAR work will give you better questions to ask, paint the larger context or 'big picture', and point you more directly to the real story so you don't chase false leads. It will not excuse you from the traditional legwork, because at the end of the day you still are going to tell a story, not write a data treatise.

Too often journalists end by breaking this rule, either because of deadline pressures or laziness, but the result is the same, a boring story that nobody wants to listen to, watch, or read. The reporter inevitably struggles with the story as well, because he or she has found no compelling human element or narrative to drive the story forward. The result is a product that suits no one.

Jumping Off from the Data

Once you are satisfied that you understand what your data are telling you, and you have double- and triple-checked your results, you should be in a good position to write an initial summary of what you have found. Some reporters prefer to do this by writing an early draft of the story, so they can start to think of their findings in terms of meanings and how they could fit into a story. Others prefer to make a list of points or questions. Whichever method you choose, going through this exercise will help you distil what you have found, what questions that raises, what you still must know, what documents you may require, and to whom you will need to speak to flesh out the necessary details and provide a human face to your story or stories. This step is valid whether you are writing a one-day 'quick hit' from a Statistics Canada report or a longer-term, multi-part investigative feature.

Make this move as soon as you feel you are in a position to do so, because it is easy to become trapped in an ever-descending cycle of data analysis. Working with data can be seductive, especially if you are the type of person who really enjoys this aspect of the work. But it can be a trap. It is tempting to write dozens (or hundreds!) of queries for answers to every conceivable question, the results of most of which will remain unused.

It is far better to answer a few big-picture questions, do a few key summary queries, and start the traditional reporting phase of your work as soon as possible. Later, you will be in a far better position to know what questions you still need to answer from the data, so you can go back with targeted queries to get the details that you need.

A tremendous amount of additional reporting work needs to be done after you complete your initial data analysis. Karen Kleiss, who was the lead writer on an *Edmonton Journal* investigation into food safety, recalls all the work and her fellow reporters had to do:

> We submitted more than two dozen FOI requests and interviewed nearly 20 people, including former and current inspectors, academics, restaurant owners, and program officials. We reviewed mountains of documents detailing everything from the causes of food-borne illness to the types of disclosure systems used in other cities. We conducted a detailed review of all the prosecutor's files, where the health authority had taken restaurants to court.[1]

All in all, a compelling argument to get to traditional work as soon as possible.

Guard against Many-Layered Logic

The more you have to explain why a data finding is significant the less it will deliver to your audience. Simple conclusions work best. How many seniors died of adverse drug reactions? What percentage of cars pass their mandatory emissions tests? Which restaurant has failed the largest number of health inspections?

You tend to think of the simplest, clearest questions and issues early on in a project, when you have not cluttered your mind with detail—and at the end, when you truly understand the issues. It is when you are deep into discovering detail, that you will most likely waste time on queries that will have little use later.

One effective technique is to set a deadline for yourself to complete your data analysis. Whether that be a day, a week or a month, this technique will help to keep you focused on the essential, and avoid the tangential. You will also ensure you have time to get the meat of traditional reporting completed on time.

Knowing When There Is No Story

As important as identifying a story is being able to identify when there is no story. Not all databases are going to yield material worthy of publication, and it is an important skill to be able to identify those times.

If you find that your data results are unclear, require a great deal of explanation to demonstrate why anyone would care, and you can't imagine them pointing to a solid lead paragraph or introduction to a radio or television story, you should question whether you have a story at all. That doesn't mean that the analysis won't provide you with a solid contextual paragraph or supporting numbers, the so-called 'computer-assisted paragraph', but if you can't get excited about what you have found, probably nobody else will, either.

A crucial step in determining whether you really have a story is whether your results check out in the 'real world'. Databases are supposed to track real-world events, so if you can't find real-world examples for trends you have identified in your data, it's time to take a good step back and question whether what you have found is real at all. In that case, you may want to revisit your assumptions about the data to ensure you haven't made a big computer-assisted mistake.

Deciding How to Tell the Story

It's important to put a lot of thought and effort into how the story will be told. Far too frequently, journalists spend too little time on the storytelling aspect, assuming incorrectly that the tale will somehow write itself. This couldn't be farther from the truth. We should be thinking constantly about the story: What is it? What characters are involved? How can I develop scenes? How can the data support the action I create? These are essential questions that can't be answered at the last minute. They demand as much attention as those databases. A story that is forgotten because it's poorly written is a wasted effort.

Without strong characters—such as Wilma Johannesma, whose addiction to Ativan nearly killed her; Adam Mahn, the overnight garage worker who used his employer's emissions-testing equipment to generate hundreds of phoney test results; or Jason Burke, the Toronto-area black man who was falsely accused of dealing drugs during that city's largest summer festival—these numbers would be quickly forgotten.

By remembering these characters, the reader, listener, or viewer remembers the key numbers and trends. Hearing Johannesma's trembling voice helps us recall the fact that an increasing number of seniors are on drugs that they're not supposed to be prescribed either because the medication is dangerous or because there are safer alternatives.[2] Hearing Mahn boast about how easy it was to cheat Ontario's Drive Clean tests illustrated the vulnerabilities of the system better than any numbers could.[3] Seeing Burke's face staring angrily from the front page of the *Toronto Star* above the headline 'Singled Out', and reading his story makes us remember that during the period that the *Star* analyzed, black people charged with simple drug possession were taken to the station more often than whites facing the same charge.[4]

Finding memorable characters may not be as difficult as negotiating for and crunching the data, but without the characters your story will be much weaker. People identify with other people better than with statistics.

With this in mind, we will explore strategies and tools that are applicable to any medium: print, radio, television, online, and magazine. While there may be specific references to a particular medium, as in a discussion of a lead or an introduction, the message is the same because, ultimately, good stories contain similar elements: memorable characters, compelling details, a sense of place, suspense, and surprises. Put them all together and you get a solid narrative design, which yields a tale that will not only hold, but command your audience's attention.

'Every story is unique. It is special to its time and place', explains Carl Sessions Stepp in *Writing as Craft and Magic*, '[T]he goal is not to yoke writers to rigid formulas. Originality and innovation are hallmarks of good writing. Every assignment should be approached with imagination and treated as a one-of-a-kind opportunity.'[5]

Here are some tips on ways to achieve the magic of a great story supported by the details that serve to enhance the drama and put it into context.

Organize Your Research

Chronologies

Chronologies can provide the backbone of your research and are useful in connecting events, which for narrative purposes helps to build drama by placing significant events in close proximity. It's also important to summarize your information continually. One of the best ways is to write a synopsis that captures the essence of what you've learned up to that point. The summarizing exercise helps focus your thinking and determine holes in the argument that weren't apparent before. Summarizing 'also helps guard against over-reporting because you'll always know when you've got angles sufficiently nailed down. Perhaps most important, however, you'll be thinking about writing in the early stages, lessening the shock when it comes to actually doing it.'[6]

This may seem like a lot of front-end work, but it saves the frustration once you begin writing. 'Intensive prep work, time consuming as it is, helps you emerge from one of journalism's most daunting challenges with your sanity intact.'[7]

Interviews

Interviews represent one of the best ways for us to not only uncover key facts, but also to obtain important details for the narrative, everything from determining what the weather was like when the RCMP came to the door with news of a son's death in a workplace, to the song that was playing on the radio when a bulletin interrupted regular programming to announce that a plane had just crashed. Mining for these kinds of details during interviews will give your narrative richness and texture. The details are not just window dressing; they take people back to the scene, sharpening their powers of recollection.

It's also important to ask people about their hobbies, their likes and dislikes. Record this material into your chronology. Look at the detail in this passage from a *New York Times* investigation into crooked telemarketers who stole more than $100,000 from 92-year-old Army veteran, Richard Guthrie.

> He had lived alone since his wife died. Five of his eight children had moved away from the farm. Mr. Guthrie survived on roughly $800 that he received from Social Security each month. Because painful arthritis kept him home, he spent many mornings organizing the mail, filling out sweepstake entries, and listening to big-band albums as he chatted with telemarketers.[8]

'The way I knew about the big band thing is that I had actually asked him what type of things he bought from catalogues', recalls Charles Duhigg, the *New York Times* reporter who wrote the piece, 'and he mentioned a whole bunch of companies and . . . he said he likes to buy his big-band albums from a particular catalogue company. And then we just sort of chatted and he mentioned that he had listened to them in the morning. As I was writing that paragraph, I wanted to paint a picture. So that seemed like a good detail to include.'[9]

You can also obtain details from interviewing people who may not be central characters in your story, but have key information nonetheless. And it's also important to interview these people where they live, work, and hang out. Interviewing someone in a neighbourhood where a crime took place will help you establish the shape of the houses. Are they run-down? Talking to someone in a workplace where an accident took place will help determine if paint is peeling from the walls, or the sound the conveyor belts make when transporting the paper cups for hot and cold drinks that will be dumped into boxes and shipped off to fast-food restaurants.

'People, setting, mood, atmosphere, descriptions, locations. These are all the bits of information you can only get from being there', observes Shawn McIntosh in his tip sheet *Storytelling with Data*. 'The data may lead you to the neighborhood, the accident location, the school, or the person. Only you can paint the picture in words of what you saw.'[10]

For a more complete discussion of interviewing techniques in investigative journalism, you can refer to our book *Digging Deeper: A Canadian Reporter's Research Guide*, published by Oxford University Press Canada.

Characters

Finding characters for stories is pretty basic to storytelling. For his story on parking tickets in Ottawa, discussed in the last chapter, reporter Glen McGregor wanted to write about the parking meter that received the most action. And for that, he needed the right anecdote to make the story come alive. So he visited the area every day until he found someone. 'I finally got somebody one day', he recalls.[11] 'I happened to be there when she came out and got a ticket. The woman had been at her lawyer's because her father had just died of lung cancer and she was dealing with the will. She was having a terrible day and she comes out and there's this ticket on her windshield. So she's my lead-in for that spot that gets more tickets than any other spot in the city.'[12]

And there are other nuggets in the database. For instance, among the most highly targeted areas were parking metres next to hospitals. 'So it becomes an ethical issue. Should the city be targeting sick people? If you're going for cancer treatment, you can't afford the 13 bucks to park there every day. I talked to a woman who came out of the General Hospital who had got a ticket—she had been in a coma for three weeks! She's my lead on that story.'[13]

Award-winning CBC Radio documentary maker, Bob Carty, likens the process of finding people for his stories to auditions. First, he finds his main character—someone who possesses the characteristics that will hold the audience's understanding, attention, respect—and even affection. For Carty, the person must be articulate so that she can explain her condition or circumstance in a way that draws in the listener. The person must be introspective, capable of analyzing his own condition for contradictions. And, to a degree, the person must be likeable.

> This does mean Lily white. . . . Hamlet's not perfect. Othello's not perfect; but you 'get' them. You understand Othello's jealousy and rage. You know that at some point he's quite evil in the story, but you get him. So you have to have access to the person. I would say likeability is huge.[14]

Once the main character is in place, Carty fills out the roster with other figures he categorizes into two groups: Hinderers and helpers.

> You need hinderers because people are overcoming obstacles because that's what a story is about. So you have to find out what their quest is and who's in the way. It could be a system, another entity, a politician, a doctor, a lack of information, ignorance, lies . . . but you need to find the hinderers and helpers and make them characters in the story, too.

Helpers are the people who help tell the story on the side of the protagonist. And they're important because they give the story credibility. If you just have the one voice of the protagonist saying 'I did this and I did that', the listener can have a question about the authenticity of that voice unless it is very, very true to itself . . . and sometimes, it's very helpful to have these voices who will pitch in and corroborate and advance the story . . . .[15]

Note, also, that the 'characters' don't have to be people. The central character can be the largest polluter in your city or province, or a government department that hasn't been doing its job. With inanimate objects as central characters, it becomes important to surround them with the human beings whose lives have been affected, such as the people living downstream from a polluted river, or the whistleblower who sounded the alarm, and paid the price with the loss of his job and his dignity in tatters.

The Story Idea

Make Sure It's an Idea, Not a Topic

If you want to get an idea of the memorable imprint that CAR stories can make, talk to someone who judges them. You will remember Rob Washburn from Chapter 1 as one of the first journalists in Canada to use CAR in his work at the *Cobourg Star* in the 'nineties. He has been one of the judge's for the Canadian Association of Journalists CAR award.

The thing that I always look for is the storytelling. It's computer-assisted *reporting*; it's not computer-assisted-only reporting. . . . It's a cliché for us, but I think that it's important that people realize that it's not solely about numbers. It's about people and stories and those numbers are the infrastructure. . . . They're like the bones inside your body. You have to put the flesh, the muscle on top of it. Or else it's not there. It's not a real person. Once you've cleaned up the numbers. You've done your analysis. You've reached your conclusions. You verify your conclusions (that's always important that we reach out to experts to help make sure that we're on the right track), then we have to find the stories to tell. The stories that will illustrate what the numbers have shown. And I think that [when]you look at any successful piece of CAR that has won an award or that is highly regarded, it has those qualities.'[16]

Because many of the datasets we obtain come from government departments, many of our stories tend to be about the effectiveness of various departments in performing certain tasks. How effectively does Health Canada monitor adverse drug reactions? How effectively do provincial ministries of labour inspect workplaces? How well do municipal workers inspect restaurants? Answers to these questions lead to stories.

But it's important to distinguish between a topic and a story idea. Health Canada's monitoring of adverse drug reactions is a topic; that is, it is devoid of plot or characters. In *Writing as Craft and Magic*, Stepp relates that his students frequently bring him topics rather than ideas. As he explains it, a topic usually contains the word 'about', as in, 'I'd like to write a story about airline safety.'[17]

A story is better captured in a declarative sentence that states a thesis that will then be proved (or disproved) by the reporting. A particularly useful tool for defining a story was developed by the CBC and hinges on the use of the word 'because', as in 'seniors are dying because they are being prescribed drugs dangerous to the elderly,' or, 'airline passengers are being put at risk because planes come too close in the sky too often.' So, we need to write declarative sentences that include both the effect and the cause in order to formulate a story idea.

In developing the idea, 'the watchword for government copy is substance over process', advises Carl Sessions Stepp. 'The good stories stress the impact of government action or inaction on real people in real life. Often, government's impact is formidable. Here is a starter list of things government does or decides. Whose streets get plowed during a snowstorm? How fast do police respond to emergencies? How thoroughly are meat plants inspected? How safe are your savings? Who can own a gun, control air traffic, perform heart surgery, manufacture drugs, use lasers on your eyes? What standards are enforced for child-safety seats, airplane engines, home electrical wiring, natural gas pipelines, heart pacemakers, school bus brakes? Who oversees car dealers, nursing homes, nuclear power plants, street food vendors, foster parents? If a hurricane hits your town, who arrives for help? If you are marooned at sea, who rescues you? If you are imprisoned in a foreign country, who visits? If you work in a coal mine, clash with a harassing supervisor, or work with toxic chemicals, who enforces the rules? If you lose your job, who supplies benefits? 'Government news coverage may be boring, but government is not. The challenge: Show the impact of your story.'[18]

The story idea can also emerge out of a question, especially for issues that have a long shelf life. Upon visiting a neighbourhood, you notice that it is run-down, and dotted with decrepit buildings and crumbling roads. Your data on absentee landlords and money spent on roads and bridges points to problems in this particular part of town. People you've interviewed have spoken about a loss of hope, the loss of opportunities for young people, and the exodus to parts of the city considered to be safer. Your idea, then, might be tested as a question: Can this neighbourhood survive? Your story idea can also be tested as a prediction of what you may find: This neighbourhood is dying. 'Either way, the hypothesis, this research question, this story idea is the essential first step in focusing your work.'[19]

To Outline or Not to Outline

Once the idea is nailed down, some journalists like to create an outline that lays out how the story will unfold, the quotes or bits of dialogue that will be used, the data, and so on. The outline can be done in many ways. For instance, the CBC's Bob Carty begins with a blank piece of paper and a pencil, and he then blocks out scenes and how they connect. The eraser at the end of the pencil gets a good workout as he continually revises the structure.

Like the chronology, the outline can also help you find holes in the story that need to be addressed and will help you to assess the true strength of the characters. Determining what to leave out is as difficult as deciding what to put in. This is especially true for CAR stories using large sets of data. But with an outline, that decision becomes easier once you begin to see how all the moving parts fit together. That is why an outline is such a powerful tool. 'Their avoidance burdens either an editor, who is forced to make choices the writer should have made, or a reader, who is burdened with redundancy.'[20]

That said, rigid outlining can also be your enemy, especially in print writing, which can stray from the linear pattern particularly common in broadcast writing. Certainly, you want to make an inventory of the points you want to make, the key information, quotations that will back those points, the data you will use, and so on. But an over-organized outline can lead to a story that reads like an inventory and moves jerkily from one 'block' of information to another. Depending on your writing style, it can work better to organize your points in the approximate order you want to use them, then let what Stepp calls 'the magic' take over. In fact, some writers prefer to go over the main points they want to cover before they begin to write, and then write their first drafts almost from memory, as if telling a story to their moms. They then go back, check all the facts, correct quotations, and add supporting information they missed. This technique can lead to a story that reads much more like a story and better reflects the voice of the writer.

E-Journalism and the Use of the Web

Stories using CAR don't have to be big projects such as the ones we have used as the centrepieces here. As the *Ottawa Citizen*'s Glen McGregor demonstrated with his series on parking tickets, the stories can be more modest in scope. The trick is in knowing how to present your material in a form that makes sense. If, for instance, you have used a spreadsheet to analyze the city budget and discover that certain user fees have risen faster than property taxes, perhaps it's only appropriate to choose the user fee that has increased most, and tell stories about how the increases affect citizens. If, on the other hand, your data has uncovered a number of trends, then perhaps you want to tell many stories as part of a series.

The Internet is a storytelling tool, also. Many stories driven by CAR use the Web to maximum effect by giving readers, listeners, and viewers bonus material that enhances their understanding. In addition to a searchable database, it might be an idea to provide access to an expert who can discuss some of the findings, or to create a discussion group where people can debate the implications of the problem you've uncovered.

The Internet can allow you to make an active connection with the audience. A searchable database means that people can find out more information about the drug they're taking or the restaurant they are thinking of patronizing or not. A discussion board may allow those persons to compare notes with others. These interactive techniques are more than simply using the same content that appeared on the air or in the newspaper. For many, these techniques form the essence of E-journalism: Educate, engage, and empower.

'You watch news. You listen to news. You read news. Well, that's passive', explains Rob Washburn. 'What's possible through E-journalism is to interact. Tell me your stories, because those are valid. We do not treat our audiences as consumers, but as a community. So what we're trying to do online is build this community.'[21]

After deciding whether to roll out the series in multiple parts, you must determine how long the series should be sustained. For instance, instead of stretching the stories out all week, perhaps you have only enough strong material to last three days. So, instead of devoting the final two days to the rest of the stories you thought were groundbreaking, perhaps they would be better suited as sidebars in the paper, or online.

'Each story in a good series has substance enough to stand on its own, while being clearly identified as part of a greater whole.'[22]

The Importance of Teamwork

Not only is teamwork essential in doing the CAR work, but it's important when putting the stories together. You might need your librarian to help with the research for more background information, given that the process of reporting never really stops. Of equal importance are the other reporters and producers/editors, especially those who have expertise or beats that encompass the stories you plan to tell. After the *Toronto Star* spent the summer of 2002 analyzing the crime data, it was decided quickly to assemble a team that could produce the series for that fall.[23]

Coverage, Feedback, and Follow-up

If you've done your job correctly, people will respond in ways you've never experienced. This response cannot take you by surprise. If you tell people that cops treat blacks differently than whites, be prepared for readers willing to share their stories, or viewers who might want more information for their own legal battles or advocacy work. If you tell people that Drive Clean does a poor job preventing fraud in emissions testing, be prepared for stories from listeners about particular garages that cheated them, or for academics who may be interested in your methodology. And, most certainly, be prepared to defend your methodology and stories against the very people and institutions you have criticized.

Preparing for the fallout, whether good or bad, is an essential part of putting your story together. If you are not prepared to respond, you may inadvertently be telling people that your news organization cares enough to spend all this time and effort uncovering problems that affect their lives, but doesn't care enough to listen to what they have to say. To do this is falling into the old trap of sounding the alarm bells, then abandoning the audience once you have finally got them to pay attention.[24] This is negligence that cannot be tolerated for major investigative efforts. If you've worked that hard to gain people's attention, then wait for the feedback, pay attention, and respond.

Narrative Design

'Writing is an arrogant act, a projection of ego. *Writers expect readers to drop everything, cancel all plans, and dedicate themselves to poring over their work.* Stop whatever you are doing, and pay attention to me! This is the supreme demand, and readers deserve much in return.'[25] The criticism of arrogance that Carl Sessions Stepp makes in this passage is good and constructive. The reporter's arrogance is that of the confident storyteller who wants to engage her audience using an assortment of literary techniques. We will use the term 'narrative design', which 'refers to forming a story that presents your work in the most powerful way.' Narrative forms in storytelling include the following:

- Beginning—middle—end (Example: Life story)
- Exposition—complication—solution (Example: the System fails)
- Exposition—conflict—climax—denouement (Example: a Trial story)
- Episodic: scene–digression / scene–digression, etc. (Example: War correspondent; Travelogue)
- Order—disorder—order restored (Example: Disaster stories)[26]

If you are writing a major story or series, deciding the narrative design is one of the most important decisions you'll make. The life story with the beginning, middle, and end might fit best for someone who has experienced an adverse drug reaction, as did Wilma Johannesma in the CBC's 'Prescribed to Death' series. At the beginning, she takes Ativan to calm her nerves. In the middle of the story, she attempts to stop taking the medication but realizes she has become an accidental addict who can't stop taking the pills. Towards the end, she attempts to shed her dependence and is on the road to recovery.

The story was told in two instalments: the first was part of the original series in which listeners were introduced to Johannesma when she was in the middle of treatment to eliminate her dependency on the drug. Though we were able to backtrack to the beginning of her story and explore some of the reasons why she began taking the drug, the story didn't have an ending. That would have to wait several months later with a follow-up visit to her daughter's home on Vancouver Island where Johannesma was doing a lot better, but still in need of constant care. In telling that story, it was important to plan far in advance and signal that plan to the audience. That is, Johannesma is struggling, but she's determined to get better and we'll follow her on that journey however long it takes.

In the case of Jamie Paxton, the little girl whose birth defects were the result of her mother taking the acne drug Accutane, it made better sense to do the story as a self-contained narrative because the family had already learned to deal with her disability and had come to terms with it. So other than the facts that Dawn Paxton had unknowingly taken the drug while pregnant, rebuffed her doctor's advice to have an abortion, and then decided to sue the doctor, there was nothing left to say. What did help, though, were the pictures of Jamie on the CBC's website that accompanied the audio of the five-minute report.

Does the Story Lend Itself to a Narrative or a Harder News Story Treatment?

The story involving Wilma Johannesma was an obvious narrative, with a strong central character, drama, surprises, and an eventual conclusion. But sometimes, what you have is news to be told in a hurry. In that latter case, traditional news judgement and deadline storytelling skills take over.

For example, when the *Hamilton Spectator* did a quick turnaround story on government aircraft use by Liberal Premier Dalton McGuinty in May 2007, the paper chose the hard news approach, with this lead and second paragraph:

> Premier Dalton McGuinty has used government aircraft flights worth up to $1 million to reach destinations as close to Toronto as Hamilton and Niagara. Many of the flights—for which other users pay $2,000 an hour—were for news conferences or photo opportunities in local communities. Neither the premier nor the lieutenant governor have to pay to use the province's two executive turboprops.[27]

Because this was a political story, and the newspaper's calculation of the cost, as well as the choices of destinations, were what made the story, the hard news approach worked best. A narrative approach would have been difficult to pull off because the Premier was not available to be interviewed, and neither were the people who operated the aircraft. Further, a narrative approach would have gotten in the way of the blunt story, which touched off a raucous debate in the Ontario legislative assembly. Arguably, a narrative approach to this story would have weakened its impact.

How Will the Scenes Unfold?

When Bob Carty describes the process of blocking out a story into scenes, it's easy to imagine the work of a screenwriter or playwright mapping out the narrative with dialogue, scene settings, stage directions, dialogue, and so on. In fact, if we thought of ourselves as screenwriters or playwrights, perhaps the storytelling would come more easily. Not only do we have to know what the scenes will be, but which characters will be in them. When do we introduce the hinderers and the helpers? How do we build the conflict in the scene? An answer comes from James Neff: 'If you write scenes, they must have conflict within them. This means two characters in one setting. There must be action unfolding in real time. Your character must want something important and valuable. As a storyline, make this person face obstacles, and work to overcome them.'[28] Obtaining these elements takes planning that should take place with an editor or producer.

What to Include and Leave Out?

Just because you have analyzed countless rows of data, interviewed dozens of people, and read more documents than you'd care to remember, it doesn't mean that all that material should end up in your story. Far from it. In many instances less is more. Sometimes you need only three characters instead of five; two key numbers, instead of six. Leaving these details out doesn't necessarily mean they become lost, for we do have the Web as an important venue. The point of excluding this material is to make the characters and the data more memorable. Some of the best in the business, including Sarah Cohen of the *Washington Post*, advise people to choose the number that you want people to remember. The same goes for characters and any other important details. Remember, one of the most common criticisms of movies is that the plots are too convoluted and the characters too numerous and shallow to care about.

In 'Prescribed to Death', two key numbers helped to put Wilma Johannesma's story into context: One out of every 20 suspected deaths involving seniors that was reported to Health Canada involved a drug such as Ativan; that is, drugs that have been identified as too dangerous for seniors; and one third of Canadian seniors are on these kinds of prescription drugs.[29]

Narrative Devices

Not every story is told in chronological order as was Wilma Johanessma's. Perhaps it would be more appropriate to start from the end and work back, or start from the beginning and use flashbacks to move back and forth. Carty argues that if you make the characters memorable, the audience will stick with you whichever approach you take.

Leads and Introductions

The lead or the introduction is make or break time. If it doesn't pull in the reader, listener, or viewer, then you may have lost that opportunity to catch that person's attention. So it goes without saying that a strong opening is the key to hooking your audience. Many journalists know this but fall into bad habits or get stuck with bad editors or producers who fail to help bring their material alive.

One of the trickiest parts to crafting the proper lead or introduction is deciding what kind it should be.

Summary Lead or Anecdotal

There are occasions when your material leads to such a definitive conclusion about the behaviour of an individual or institution that you can use a lead that smacks of supreme confidence and authority: the summary or hard news lead. Examples: The mayor is wasting taxpayer's money. / The region's largest land developer is stealing money from taxpayers. / The region's most profitable medical device maker knowingly allowed its faulty product onto the market, killing hundreds. 'That is about as clearly and strongly as you could start a story. The lead is what those lawyers would call libel, per se. It is not a paragraph to be written if you harbour the slightest doubt that you could defend it in court.'[30]

It is best to use this type of lead when: there is a single, overwhelming revelation to be made; the context is already familiar to your audience; the evidence supporting the lead or introduction is unequivocal; and the story is simple enough to have few subplots and to need no chronology.[31]

The anecdotal lead, on the other hand, is a better fit when your findings are not as conclusive, or the culprit is not as clear-cut. Or when the story has many twists and turns, offering no easy conclusions. 'Remember that an anecdotal lead must move quickly to a 'nut graf:' the paragraph that tells the point of this story. This is a very important paragraph because it is also the point at which the reader decides whether or not to finish the story—if, of course, you've gotten the reader that far.'[32]

Tone

You will also leave an impression with the tone you adopt for the story. The summary lead should have an authoritative tone, which you should have the courage to stand behind. Writing with authority runs counter to the he-said/she-said formula so prevalent in today's journalism. Authority also eliminates jargon and wishy-washy language. If someone is stealing money and you have the data to prove it, then, say so. If the mayor is a crook, and you have the goods to prove it, then say so.

In its 2001 Pulitzer Prize-winning account of the failures of the child protection system in Washington DC, the *Washington Post* was able to use an authoritative tone to back up its finding that negligence led to the deaths of 229 children in the district between 1993 and 2000:

> Police officers did not fully investigate abuse reports, leaving children with violent or drug-addicted parents or relatives. Social workers did not adequately monitor neglected children. Frail newborns were permitted to go home to drug-addicted and mentally ill parents without follow-up services. Judges sent children to unlicensed foster homes, or to institutions far from the District where their care went unsupervised.[33]

There is no ambiguity in the tone. The paper's dogged CAR work gave it the right to draw conclusions that prompted an overhaul of the city's child welfare system. 'Have the courage to write with authority—that's why you're doing CAR in the first place. CAR allows you to avoid he-said/she-said reporting. It's called Precision Journalism for a reason.'[34]

More often than not, the data will force you to equivocate in a circumspect manner. In the one the *Washington Post* broke, you would let the facts tell the story. In the case of the Health Canada data, it's unclear how negligent the department may have been in monitoring its own adverse drug reaction database. So it would have been unwise to adopt a tone that prosecutes the department's bureaucrats. It's better to draw the audience's attention to the adverse drug reaction figures involving kids and seniors, juxtapose those statistics with comments from Health Canada and its minister, and let listeners and viewers draw their own conclusions about culpability and the need to reform the system.

Don't Oversell

It's one thing to explain to readers, as did the *Washington Post*, that one has uncovered the fact that 229 deaths can be blamed on negligence in the child protection system; it's another thing to blame Health Canada for deaths involving children and seniors who have succumbed to an adverse drug reaction. Why? Because Health Canada is the recorder of statistics, not the agency responsible for the conduct of those who prescribe. So the important lesson here is don't sell what you can't prove in the paper, broadcast outlet, the web, or ultimately in a court of law.

This is best accomplished by explaining the limitation of your data in the form of an explanation box, or 'nerd box'.

Explore Shades of Grey

Though we would like to think that stories are black and white, made up of good and bad guys, that is seldom the case. For example, Transport Canada had been talking to the industry for years about making improvements to air safety regulations, such as requiring collision-warning devices aboard aircraft, but after a decade, the changes had become mired in seemingly endless consultations. It's important to introduce these kinds of nuances to readers so they can ask more pointed questions of more of the players, in this case the Minister of Transport, who may have been unable to overcome the lobby from the airline industry.

Make the Numbers Meaningful

As pointed out earlier, data are like characters—too many of them can spoil the story. Be careful about the ones you choose. Perhaps the most important number in the *Washington Post* piece was the 229 children who had died.

Some of the best computer-assisted stories give almost no hint that CAR was involved at all. This is especially likely to be the case for broadcast stories because of the difficulty of accommodating more than a few key numbers in a piece. Other stories trumpet the fact in order to alert the reader to the special efforts that the outlet has made on behalf of the audience. Newspapers in particular are prone to do this, especially when the analysis has been lengthy or detailed and the results are compelling and newsworthy in themselves. In the end, though, there are only so many numbers or data results that you can cram into any kind of story. Weigh down the copy with too many and it will sink like the weight on a fishing line.

So how do you decide which numbers to include? Here are a few basic rules:

- Is the number essential to understanding either the main point of the story, or a subsidiary point? If so, you'll almost surely want to use it somewhere. These numbers will generally be pretty obvious to you.
- Does the number (or numbers) help flesh out a point in the story or provide detailed examples to help illustrate a point? You should consider using the number, or if it is a series of numbers, such as in a table, using it as a supporting graphical element.
- Is the number easy to understand? Simpler, starker numbers will have far more clout with the reader than numbers that need a lot of explaining.
- Would the reader miss the number if it were not included at all? If the answer is no, leave it out.

This winnowing process probably will bring you down to just a few numbers to include in the copy of your story, plus some supporting material to run along with it. From there, you will need to decide how to incorporate the numbers into your story.

One thing to keep in mind is that the more numbers you put into a paragraph, or a few adjacent paragraphs, the harder it will be for the reader to sort out the numbers, and understand their relevance.

Don't get stuck on the idea that your numbers need to be precise. It is far better to say 'more than 1 million,' than to say 1,246,890. Ask yourself what level of precision your audience really needs, and write accordingly. You also have to consider how certain you are of the precision of your own numbers. No data set is free of errors or dirty data, so absolutely precise numbers are a fiction anyway.

Putting Numbers into Context

It's important to tell them what you mean. Don't be afraid to summarize the meaning of the details in your story, and then use the Web site to plot out the details more systematically in charts or graphs. 'Too many investigative reporters are content to marshal their findings and parade them across the page without ever summing up, without taking the step of making clear the significance of those findings. This failure to get to the point—usually defended as 'letting the reader draw their own conclusions'—is really an abdication of the writer's first duty, namely, to be clear.[35]

One of the best ways to summarize data is provide context, to make them meaningful in a way that people can relate to. 'This is one of the single most demanding, yet single greatest sin of omission, of a lot of journalists. We need to go the extra step to make numbers make sense. Relate a number such as the amount of oil in storage to how long it would heat homes or power cars or generate electricity, if called upon in an emergency.'[36]

Also useful are comparisons. *Newsweek* ran a series on racial discrimination in mortgage-lending. The conclusion was derived from an analysis of nearly 100,000 mortgage loans. After poring over the numbers, the magazine concluded that potential African-American homeowners were rejected nearly three times as frequently as whites. As we saw in the *Star*'s examination of racial discrimination, this is a good way of comparing the rates of whites and blacks. But in its example, *Newsday* went a little further to provide context, using figures from the same dataset to help drive the point even deeper. 'The gap is so wide that a black applicant making more than $150,000 a year stands a greater chance of being rejected than does a white person making less than $35,000 a year.'[37]

Think Visually

The ability to think visually may sound odd when referring to data, but this is exactly what you should be doing. Visualizing the data helps to identify when you need a pie chart or bar graph to bring the numbers home. Thinking visually also helps you take advantage of what photographers and graphic artists can contribute. You should always be asking yourself, 'How can visuals help lighten the numerical load on a CAR story and help readers understand the data most easily.?'[38]

Checking Your Facts

It goes without saying that with all of the benefits of computer-assisted reporting comes the potential for serious computer-assisted errors. After all, unlike a reporter who took his facts from a government news release, you are responsible for your own data results. Hence, there is a compelling case to be made for careful fact-checking.

Of course, you should be verifying and checking your data results and other facts as you report, but the writing and editing process itself has great potential to introduce errors, as fact situations or results are summarized or simplified for the reader. Therefore, it is crucial to go back, before publication or broadcast, and recheck all facts, calculations, and numbers.

It is best to do this with the finished product. In broadcasting, that would mean the completed script prior to final production. Online, this would mean the material prior to posting. In print, it is ideally done with a proof of the actual page to be published, if you can obtain one far enough ahead of publication.

Go through the copy and circle each fact, spelling, number, calculation, and any other element that could theoretically contain an error. Next, go back to the original sources and check. Don't check using intermediate documents you may have created as part of your research, because errors often creep in during those middle stages. If a number or fact came from a document, go back to the original document. If you are including the result of a calculation, go back to the original data on which you based the calculation and recheck your work as well as your assumptions to ensure you didn't make a mistake. Make sure you didn't omit data or mess up a formula. Remember that your credibility is on the line for everything you say in your story; get it right.

If you find mistakes, make sure they are corrected. All of this will let you get more sleep both before and after your story is published, posted, or broadcast.

Bringing It All Together

We don't have to be great writers to tell memorable stories. What we do need is to recognize the elements of a narrative: a character whose voice on the radio will make people stop what they're doing and listen; a face on the television whose injury is so severe that we can't believe the company where the person worked could have been so negligent; a lead so stark and clear that the reader will want to stay with the story.

There are few pleasures in life more satisfying than a good read, and yet journalists tend to bore people with poor writing, which can stem from a lack of attention to narrative and literary techniques and a lack of time for polishing. Just because you have amassed all the research, doesn't mean that the story will write itself. The details have to be shaped into a compelling narrative, and that takes planning and hard work.

Narrative is especially important for stories driven by CAR. We spend endless hours negotiating for and crunching data because we want to make a difference. Telling stories that people remember and in which they can participate through the Internet will make an impression, and impact the issues to which we have committed our careers.

Advanced Techniques

Fred Vallance-Jones, Aron Pilhofer, and Jaimi Dowdell

Chapter 10

What We'll Cover

- Getting data out of pdf files.
- Scanning data from paper documents.
- Using a word processor to manipulate text for database import.
- Using Monarch software to extract data from reports.
- Scraping data from the web using Perl.
- Social networks analysis.

At times, computer-assisted reporting presents special challenges that require special techniques. Typically, they are variations of the same problem: data exists that you could use for a story, but it's not in a readily useable form. You need to convert it somehow to a format you can use.

The most common obstacles faced by reporters are: (1) data tables created in the Adobe's portable document (pdf) format; (2) data that is available only in paper print-outs; (3) data that is in a text format such as html, but not in a regularized layout you can import into a spreadsheet or database manager; (4) data that is presented in 'report' format; (5) and data that is made available only by means of an online searchable database that allows you to look up only one or a few records at a time.

There are ways to unlock all of these forms of data, and we'll examine each in turn. We'll also touch on social network analysis, a technique borrowed from the social sciences that helps identify the most connected, most powerful people in a community.

Extracting Data from PDFs

Besides the ability to recreate the exact look and format of original documents across multiple computer platforms, one of the key selling points of pdf's for distributing data is that they prevent end-users from altering or using the data in a way not intended by the creators.

Once data has been 'printed' to pdf format, it becomes trickier to get the data into a spreadsheet or database file. Anyone who has tried to use the free Adobe Reader program to copy and paste table data from a pdf to a word processor knows this only too well. All of the table formatting disappears, and the data becomes a jumble. A feature provided in earlier versions of the reader that allowed the selection of one column at a time is no longer included (but if you can find a copy of version 5, hang on to it!).

The difficulty of getting the data out depends on how the pdf was created. If it is a 'normal' pdf file, i.e., one that retains the basic attributes of the original document, you can use any one of a number of pdf extraction programs to save tables to a format you can use. If the creators have gone the next step and used Acrobat's security features to block copying, printing, or other aspects of the document, it gets a little tougher. If they have converted the document to an image, the job becomes tougher still. Nevertheless, we have ways of dealing with each of these problems.

Standard PDFs

Let's start with the standard pdf file that retains the underlying attributes of the original document. Many tools are available for extracting and reusing content from these files. Even the full version of Acrobat has some functionality in this regard, although it is hit-and-miss whether it accurately extracts tables or aligns columns correctly. We're not going to endorse any particular program, but one that works well is Able2Extract, available for download.

The program makes it almost ridiculously easy to extract data. You simply open the pdf file from which you wish to extract a table or text, select the area you wish to extract, tell the program which format you would like as output (available output formats include Excel, text, and Word files), then complete the extraction. The program does a good job most of the time, although occasionally it can make minor mistakes with alignment in tables.

Once extracted, you can work with the file in Excel, or import it from Excel into a database file for further analysis. Able2Extract can extract a single page at a time, or extract a multiple-page table. A free trial download is available that does everything the full program does, but limits the number of pages that can be extracted.

> ### ⚠ TECH TIP
>
> While today's pdf extraction technology is remarkably good, mistakes are possible. It is a good idea to scan over the results to ensure the extraction is accurate. Obviously, this becomes more difficult as the size of the file increases. One useful integrity check is to add up columns of numbers, as extracted, to see if they agree with existing totals in the original document. If they do, it is likely the numbers themselves are correct, and you may not need to check more deeply. If there are no totals in the document, you may be able to find out what the totals should be from other documents or human sources. If so much data is involved that checking over the accuracy of the extract is impractical, it may be wise to see if you can obtain the data in its original format, or another format you can import directly into Excel, Access, ArcView or other software you are using.

The program costs about $90 US as of this writing, which is on the modest end of the scale for a pdf extractor, and much less than buying the full version of Acrobat.

As we mentioned, it is far from the only player in this field. If you enter 'pdf extraction' into the Google search engine, you should be able to find others. Also, check shareware sites such as Tucows for extraction programs.

Secure PDFs

The bar gets a bit higher if you are dealing with a pdf program that has security enabled by the creator. Typically, security features disable certain capabilities, such as selecting or copying text. At the extreme, a user can be restricted to viewing only.

The first and best answer to security settings is to contact the creators of the file and persuade them either to give you the user password, which is unlikely, or to send you an unsecured copy of the pdf (or better yet, a copy of the original data file). If this sort of persuasion doesn't work, you may need to enter the data manually into Excel or a database table, or perform an OCR scan, a technique we will talk about in a moment.

One thing we would *not* recommend is the use of a security-removal utility, even though these are available for download. Not only is their use illegal in some jurisdictions, huge ethical issues are at play. If a creator has gone to the trouble of protecting content with security and is unwilling to give it to you in an unsecured format, you have to ask yourself if it is ethical to reuse that content without the creator's permission. It may depend on how 'public' the data is. For example, data tables related to a government budget or to spending estimates already belong to the public, so ethical issues involved in cracking security may not be so clear-cut. But if a private entity has provided you with proprietary information in a secured pdf file, it is, in effect, granting you a license to use its information in a certain way. Removing the security is unlikely to fall within that implied license. Cracking security puts you in an ethical and legal minefield we strongly urge you to avoid.

Image PDFs

When a pdf file has been converted into an image, you face another set of problems. An image file is just a picture of a file. The underlying attributes—the placement of letters and columns—are gone. It is similar to a digital photograph of a file, although the resolution is likely to be better in the converted file.

But don't despair, because there is a solution to this problem as well. Originally designed to extract useful text from scanned images of documents, optical character recognition, or OCR, programs also can be used to get at the data in pdf files. One particularly adept player in this market is OmniPage Pro from Scansoft. It is able to open pdf image files, along with a variety of other image formats. Once opened, the program compares the text in the pdf image with its database of known shapes of letters and numerals. It then makes its best guess as to what the text is supposed to be. Usually, that guess is very nearly perfect, these programs having been refined a great deal from their crude earliest versions.

Once the text has been 'recognized', the user is offered the opportunity to proofread suspect portions of the text by comparing the original image with the OCR result. The amount of proofreading required will vary, depending on the image quality of the original file, but one of the advantages of pdf image files is that they generally are of excellent quality, typically having been generated programmatically from the original document. In some cases, the pdfs will be scans of paper documents, in which case the quality may not be as good, and more proofreading may be necessary. There will be times when the quality will be so poor that effective OCR is impossible, but these should be rare occurrences.

Converting Paper Documents

If you obtain printouts of data tables—for example, a series of pages with lists of political contributors, and amounts given—you can use the same process to convert the paper 'data' to electronic form. The only difference is that you must first create the digital file from the paper. Sometimes you will do this if you feel it would take too long, or it would not be possible, to get an electronic copy of the file directly from the originator.

You will need a good quality flatbed scanner. Suitable scanners are not hugely expensive, and usually plug into the USB port of your computer.

The best paper documents for scanning and OCR are those with good copy quality and a reasonable text size—at least 8 points or larger. Anything that degrades the quality, such as folds in the page, loss of sharpness from too many generations of photocopying, or even coffee stains, will reduce the chances that the OCR program will be able to capture the text successfully.

Scan your documents as you would any others and save the document as an uncompressed TIFF file. This will provide the highest quality image and give you the best chance to convert the text accurately.

The actual OCR process is identical to that used to extract the image pdf's, so we won't go over it again other than to say proofreading becomes of particular importance when working with scans.

Using a Word Processor to 'Convert' a Data File to a Delimited Text File

In Chapter 3 we introduced you to delimited text files. They are used as a way to transfer data files from one user to another. But you can also create your own delimited text file as a way of taking information from an unformatted file and making it possible to import it into Excel or Access.

Because every situation is different, it's not possible to provide a recipe that works for every file. But the basic steps are the same. First, you examine the file to see what repetitive patterns exist, such as a date that always starts with the same two digits, or headers that are used repetitively. If there are carriage returns within the data that will become the end of records in the database table or spreadsheet you are aiming to create, you will want to get rid of them temporarily. An effective trick is to replace the carriage returns you want to keep—in other words the ones that will end each record—with a character combination that doesn't exist in the table, something like '%%%'. Then, replace all of the other unnecessary carriage returns with spaces. Later, you can return your unique character combination to carriage returns.

Once you have figured out the patterns and have eliminated any unneeded carriage returns, you can use the 'Find and Replace' function of your word processor to insert tabs into the text that later will be used to separate the fields in the resulting table.

Let's work through the process for a simple city building permit report.

```
Date: 2004/07/28
Permit number/type: R6f89908        Single family home
Date: 2004/07/29
Permit number/type: R6f89909        Apartment building
Date: 2004/07/30
Permit number/type: R6f89910        Institutional
```

The first step would be to replace the carriage returns that will mark the end of each record with a unique character combination. In this case, you would replace the combination of 'a carriage return followed by the word "date"' with a unique character combination—%%%%—and the word 'date'. The file would then look like this:

```
Date: 2004/07/28                    Single family home%%%%
Permit number/type: R6f89908        Date: 2004/07/29
Permit number/type: R6f89909        Apartment building%%%%
                                    Date: 2004/07/30
Permit number/type: R6f89910        Institutional
```

The next step would be to replace all of the remaining carriage returns with a space. That would produce this file.

Date: 2004/07/28 Permit
number/type: R6f89908   Single family home%%%%
Date: 2004/07/29 Permit
number/type: R6f89909   Apartment building%%%%
Date: 2004/07/30 Permit
number/type: R6f89910   Institutional

Next, we would replace the %%%% marks with carriage returns:

Date: 2004/07/28 Permit
number/type: R6f89908   Single family home
Date: 2004/07/29 Permit
number/type: R6f89909   Apartment building
Date: 2004/07/30 Permit
number/type: R6f89910   Institutional

Finally, we want to insert tabs and get rid of superfluous information. So, we would replace every combination of Date: with nothing (leave the replace line empty), and replace each header Permit number/type: header with a tab.

That would produce this result:

2004/07/28   R6f89908 Single family home
2004/07/29   R6f89909 Apartment building
2004/07/30   R6f89910 Institutional

Finally, we need to find a way to insert a tab between the permit number, and the building type. In this case, with only a few choices for building types, the easiest solution is probably to replace each building type name with a tab followed by the name of the building type. So, for example, we would replace each instance of 'Single family home' with a tab followed by 'Single family home'.

The result is a tab-delimited file such as that below, which can be saved, and imported into a spreadsheet or database. Note that we also have stripped all instances of two spaces in a row, replacing them with single spaces.

2004/07/28	R6f89908	Single family home
2004/07/29	R6f89909	Apartment building
2004/07/30	R6f89910	Institutional

By typing, at the top of the file, field names separated by tabs, you can ensure that the proper field names are included in the imported file, as in this illustration:

Permit date	Permit No.	Construction type
2004/07/28	R6f89908	Single family home
2004/07/29	R6f89909	Apartment building
2004/07/30	R6f89910	Institutional

If the imported file is not exactly what you want, you can use string functions to eliminate any unwanted characters. You can create a macro to automate repetitive steps if you have more than one file to process.

The techniques we have looked at here have the advantage of being simple, but they are also primitive. For those who want a more powerful alternative, and have the financial resources, an Australian firm called DataMystic markets a product called Textpipe Pro that has powerful tools for matching patterns and extracting data from text files. If you'd prefer to have maximum flexibility, and are familiar with Perl or PSP, you can write routines to do almost any text-extraction task. We'll look at Perl's capabilities later in this chapter when we discuss web-scraping, a technique used to process massive downloads of data from websites.

Extracting Data from a Report Using Monarch

If the data you want to use is contained in a formatted report, you can use a language such as Perl to extract data, or you can use a tool specially designed for the job. Monarch is one such tool that journalists have used for years.

A formatted report contains data laid out on a page in a predictable and repetitive way. An example with which all of us are familiar is an itemized invoice. At the top are fields containing the invoice date, customer names, customer number, and so on. Further down are fields containing details such as the item number, item name, quantity, and price. Monarch allows you to suck the data out of such a report and put it into a more traditional and useable table format.

When you use Monarch, you create 'templates' that define where to look in the report for each piece of data you intend to extract. You use what Monarch calls 'traps' to create text patterns that Monarch uses, in combination with the position of the characters on a line, to decide what to extract and what to leave out.

Once you have created all of your templates, the report will be marked up to show the data that will be extracted based on the templates.

Monarch has a variety of tools to test the template to ensure that you are capturing all of the data you want and none that you don't want. Using it can be tricky at times, especially if the report format isn't consistent. Monarch Pro can extract not only pdf reports, but a variety of text report formats, and html files.

Monarch is expensive, but it is extremely good at what it does. You will find that you can sometimes use its abilities to extract data from documents that are not strictly reports. As with other such tools, you will be amazed at what you can accomplish with a little creativity. Full details are available at <www.datawatch.com>.

Web Scraping

The web has been a boon for journalism. As a source for information, documents, and data the web has revolutionized the way we do our jobs. Documents we had to wait weeks for are now a mouse-click away. Advances in search technology has made finding the needle in a haystack almost trivial. More recent innovations like RSS, social networking, and peer-to-peer file sharing promise to make it still easier to find, filter, and share information.

But one thing has not changed since 1989 when Tim Berners-Lee conceived of what we now call the World Wide Web: The web does not come to you; for the most part, you must go to the web.

How much time do we, as reporters, spend monitoring sites for new information related to our beats? Government agencies and the private sector now routinely post news releases, reports, and other documents on their sites. Sometimes, they even let us know they've done so—usually via email or RSS.

But what about those sites that do not offer some kind of feed? And even for those sites that do, must we be limited to whatever format and structure they have set up?

These problems define why web scraping has become so popular among journalists. It is one way we can get what we what, when we want it, and in a format of our choosing. It is how we can select the web itself 'a la carte'.

Mining the Web

Viewed through the browser, the web seems like an unmanageable mess—an endless array of different designs, layouts, and technologies. But pull aside the curtains and peek at the code underneath, and you'll discover there's a lot more structure and uniformity to the web than you might suspect.

In fact, designers and developers recognize that some mutually agreed on structure must undergird the system: a single language of the web. That language is HTML. If not for these standards, a site written for FireFox couldn't be understood by Internet Explorer, and vice versa. This is a bit of a simplification. Far less agreement than there should be prevails among the various browsers—particularly when it comes to design elements. But for our purposes, there is more than enough consistency from site to site.

Why does consistency matter for 'scraping' in particular? Because there is only one way to write code to create a table of columns and rows of data on a web page. Regardless of how different tables might look site-to-site, the underlying code that tells the browser 'this is a table' will always be more or less the same.

We know it will always begin with a <TABLE> tag in the HTML code, and will always end with the </TABLE> tag. Individual rows will always begin with <TR> and end with </TR>, and each 'cell' of data within that table will begin with a <TD> tag and end with a </TD> tag. Visit a few different sites and check out the code yourself. Look for the 'View source' menu item in your browser, and then search through the HTML until you find a table.

This is why scraping works: because the structure of pages is utterly predictable, we can systematically sift through the elements of a given web page and pluck out just what we want. We can think of the web as nothing more than one enormous database. Each page is a unique record, and within each page you'll find structured data. Scraping is something like the SQL of the web.

The Process

'Web scraping' is a generic term for any automated process designed to systematically comb through websites, target certain data elements, and extract them. There are literally dozens of different approaches, including at least two off-the-shelf software packages— Kapow and Web Scraper Plus+—designed solely for this purpose.

The most powerful and flexible approach is to design a short computer program, or script, to automate the task. While that may sound like a daunting prospect for the non-programmer, it isn't. Initially you need to learn only a small portion of whatever language we're using to scrape.

It's a lot like visiting a foreign country where you don't know the native tongue: Memorizing a few key phrases can go a very long way, even if you aren't exactly sure what each and every word means. When learning to scrape you don't necessarily need to understand every detail about how a particular command or function works, just that in the right context it works.

You may find other journalism-related tasks suitable for scripting. You may even find yourself becoming quite conversant. But at least initially, only a little knowledge is essential.

How much of the programming 'phrase book' do you need to learn? First, you need to know how to tell your program to go onto the web and load a page into memory so you can access portions of it in the rest of your script. Second, you need to know how to sift through the component parts of that page and extract portions of it (called 'parsing' in programming lingo). Third, you need to be able to store that data somewhere you can get at it later, usually formatted as columns and rows for easy analysis. Finally, you need to know how to tell your script to repeat (or 'loop through') these tasks over and over.

Really, it's not much more complex than that.

The Language

But before we dive into the code, a word or two about choosing a scripting language. Scraping is possible using almost any modern programming language, including Perl, Python, Ruby, C#, Visual Basic, and so on. Although the rest of this chapter will be written in Perl (for reasons discussed below), the concepts are applicable to any language. So, don't be dissuaded from using something with which you're already comfortable.

There are, however, a few reasons Perl stands out as a language particularly suited for this purpose. Perl, which once stood for Practical Extraction and Reporting Language, was originally designed to manage, manipulate, and analyze text files. Since HTML is nothing more than formatted text, Perl is extraordinarily well-suited to the task of parsing web pages, as you'll see shortly.

But Perl's winning advantage comes from its enormous user base, which has collectively created an unparalleled library of free code (called modules), which can be downloaded and plugged into any application with a few keystrokes. The Comprehensive Perl Archive Network, or CPAN, is a repository of thousands of such modules—more than 11,000 as of this writing—that do just about anything you can imagine, and probably a few things you couldn't. It is a huge and completely free collection of incredibly useful tools, many of which make certain web scraping tasks almost unimaginably easy.

Because of modules like HTML::TableExtract, and WWW::Mechanize, which we'll get to in a minute, scraping tasks that require a line or two of code in Perl would take dozens of lines of code to accomplish in C#, Visual Basic, and other languages. No other current language has anything like it, though two newer and increasingly popular scripting languages—Ruby and Python—are getting closer. Still, as of now, Perl is far, far ahead.

There are down sides to Perl, and we would be remiss not to point them out. Perl, which was released in 1987, is among the most mature of the modern scripting languages, and it shows. The language and syntax have grown and changed considerably over the years as a result of the design philosophy, which is summed up by many devotees as: 'There is more than one way to do it.' As a result, the syntax can be inconsistent and somewhat bloated. The language is rife with shortcuts and idiomatic quirks than make Perl flexible and powerful (it is often called the Swiss Army Knife of scripting languages). But that also makes Perl fairly difficult to learn for beginners.

Perl is as loved by its fans as it is reviled by its critics. It is now considered to be a case study of how *not* to design a programming language. Python and Ruby, two languages gaining in popularity, both were designed with Perl in mind—that is, determined not to make the same mistakes. Python and Ruby are excellent alternatives to Perl, although as we've said, neither has the incredible library of resources of Perl at present. Both languages are almost certainly easier for the beginner to learn, not because the language itself is any clearer. To the rank beginner, Python and Perl will look pretty much the same: confusing. The reason they are easier is because the syntax for Ruby and Python is much more predictable and consistent, and, thus, much smaller. If Perl's philosophy is to give programmers many ways to accomplish the same task, Ruby and Python's philosophy is to give programmers only a few.

A good analogy here is the difference between German and English. Perl is a bit more like English, with inconsistent rules of grammar, an enormous lexicon borrowed from dozens of languages and as many exceptions to rules as there are rules themselves. Ruby and Python both have smaller lexicons and more predictable syntaxes. There's less to learn, in other words.

All that said, Perl is the language of choice for web scraping as of this writing, so that's the language we'll discuss.

Getting Started

We will assume readers are using a computer running the Windows operating system (either XP, 2000, or Vista). (For Mac users, all of the software mentioned below comes in Mac versions as well.) We will also assume you have sufficient security permissions to install software (if not, you may have to go to your IT department for help).

Installing Perl is fairly straightforward and, even better, is totally free. Point your browser to www.activestate.com then download Active Perl, which is free. Double-click the installer and follow the on-screen instructions. When it's finished you should have a working version of Perl on your computer (we'll test that in a minute to make sure).

Writing and running Perl scripts don't require any additional software. You can write in Notepad, UltraEdit, or any text editor you like, but a better alternative is to use a specific text editor designed for programming. Komodo is among the most popular and is available from the ActiveState website in three versions as of this writing: Komodo Edit, which is free; and the personal and professional editions, which are not free.

Komodo Edit is helpful because it will color code your scripts, making it easier to distinguish among particular commands, variables, and other elements. The personal and professional editions add more tools to help programmers identify and eliminate mistakes in their code (called 'debugging' in programming lingo).

For our purposes, the free Komodo Edit will do fine. Remember, however, that the more advanced features in the personal and professional editions can come in very, very handy. Komodo is not language-specific, incidentally. So, if you later decide that Ruby or Python is more to your liking, Komodo offers a full-featured development environment for those languages as well as many others.

Next, let's create a folder on the hard drive to hold our scripts. You can put this folder anywhere, but keep in mind that most of our applications will be invoked from the command line, so, the less typing we have to do, the better. Thus, we recommend placing the folder right on your main hard drive, here: C:\scripts.

Open the Komodo Edit, and create a new script (File->New->New File). Komodo will create a new blank Perl script for you, with just a little code already at the top. It should look something like this:

```
#!/usr/bin/perl -w
use strict;
```

We won't worry about exactly what that code means. Let's add one more line of code to the file and then save it in our scripts folder. Under the two lines Komodo inserted for you, add the following:

print "Hello World!";

Don't forget the semi-colon at the end! Every command in Perl must end with a semi-colon, or the program will throw an error. Forgetting a semi-colon and putting spaces where they don't belong are the two most common errors beginners make in Perl, so, if you get an error, those are the things to check for first.

Once you've added this line, save your file in your scripts folder (File>Save As) as 'Test. pl'. The '.pl' is what tells the system it is a Perl script. Now, let's go to the command line and see if our program works. The easiest way to do this is to click on the Start button and look for the 'Run' command (it should be on the menu to the right). Click 'Run', and in the text box type 'cmd', and hit the 'OK' button. You should see the command window open and present you with a prompt.

Probably, it will open to your system's default location (most likely, Documents and Settings). So, let's change directories to navigate to our scripts folder by entering the following command and hitting 'Return' ('cd' is the DOS command to 'change directory'):

cd C:\scripts

If you see a window that looks something like this, with a blinking cursor at the end, you're in the right place:

C:\scripts>

Type the following command and hit the 'Return' key:

perl Test.pl

You should see the following output:

```
C:\scripts>perl test.pl
Hello World!
C:\scripts>
```

If so, congratulations! You're officially a programmer. If not, run through the steps again and you'll see what went wrong. Let's go back to our script and make a change to it.

Notice two things about the line we typed in: first, the 'print' command is lower case. You'll also notice the Komodo rendered it in a purplish color in contrast with the 'Hello World!' part, which is blue.

This is a visual cue to you, the programmer. It means, in this case, that Komodo recognizes 'print' as a valid Perl statement, and 'Hello World!' as a properly formatted block of text to print to the screen.

Let's change 'print' to 'Print' (with an uppercase 'P') and see what happens. You'll notice 'Print' is no longer purple, because Komodo does not recognize it as a valid Perl command. Why? *Perl statements are lower case.* You'll also notice a red squiggly line under the statement, and if you hover your mouse over it you'll see a rather unhelpful error message. This is one of the ways Komodo indicates that it has found an error some kind.

Save your changes, then go to the command line again and run the script. You should see that same unhelpful error message in a slightly expanded form. If so, congratulations! You've made your first (of many) programming errors!

Go back to your script, and change 'print' back to lower case, save, and run it again. The squiggly red line is gone, the print command is color-coded properly and the program runs as expected.

Whether you realize it or not, you just learned a great deal about Perl and Komodo in this one little exercise. You learned how to create, save, and execute Perl scripts from the command line. You learned how Komodo helps you find and eliminate errors in your code, and you leaned one very important bit of Perl syntax: the 'print' command. As you might guess, this is the command you'll use to print to the screen, and the command you'll use later to write stored data from the pages we'll be scraping into local text files.

Not a bad start.

Beyond Basics: Fetching a Page

Before we delve too much further into Perl, let's go back to the beginning of this scraping section, and review the four techniques we need to know in order to begin scraping: fetch a page, parse a page, store information from that page locally, and repeat. This is a chapter on web scraping, after all, not on Perl programming. For those who are curious about Perl, however, a number of excellent resources are available.

⚠ TECH TIP

Learning Perl (www.oreilly.com/catalog/learn-perl4/) from O'Reilly is probably the best place to start. Also, a number of short, easy-to-read, and simple to understand tutorials are on the web. They can be found in the Perl section of the popular programming site, Devshed (<www. devshed.com>). Look for an eight-part 'Perl 101' series of articles written by Vikram Vaswani, and Harish Kamath. The website <learn.perl.org> also has links to several other articles, and books on the subject.

The first technique we need to learn is how to tell our script to go onto the Internet, locate a page, and fetch it into memory. And to accomplish this, we'll use one of those modules we mentioned earlier. The one we need is called WWW::Mechanize.

Mechanize is a module originally designed to help developers test websites. Mechanize allows you to create a virtual browser within your script, one that you can control programatically. Almost anything a normal user can do with a browser, Mechanize can mimic in your program.

Although this module was designed for web testing, it is ideal for scraping. But before we use it, we must install it from the CPAN repository, that immense library of code we mentioned before.

ActiveState Perl makes it easy to install these libraries using something called the Perl Package Manager, or ppm. Open your command prompt and type the following (note the hyphen instead of the double colons):

```
ppm install WWW-Mechanize
```

You should see some text scroll by, and you should see a note saying that the packages were installed. While we're here, let's install another module we'll use later called HTML::TableExtract. To install it, type:

```
ppm install HTML-TableExtract
```

Again, you should see a note saying the packages were installed.

Mechanize, as we said, allows us to create a virtual browser in a program. But in order to do that, we need to tell Perl first that we wish to use this module in our code, and, second, to create an instance of the browser we can control.

Clear everything we've added to the test script so far, and under the 'use strict' statement add the following:

```
use WWW::Mechanize;
my $browser = WWW::Mechanize->new();
```

This does two things. First, it tells Perl we want to use the Mechanize module, and, second, it creates a local instance of our virtual browser called '$browser'. In Perl, anything starting with a dollar sign is called a 'variable', which is programming lingo for 'container'. In this case, our container holds our virtual browser, which has a number of inherent functions. And we can tell it what to do by name. For example, $browser->get is the function we'll use to go onto the Internet and pull a web page we want to scrape into memory.

What else can our browser do? A lot. We're barely scratching the surface. If you'd like to see all the things it can do, you can view the Mechanize documentation in the CPAN repository here: search.cpan.org/~petdance/WWW-Mechanize-1.22/lib/WWW/Mechanize.pm.

Before we do that, let's look at the page we're going to be working with for the rest of this chapter. Open a browser and go to: <www.aronpilhofer.com/scrapes>. This is a page your authors have set up specifically for learning purposes, but it is not atypical. Search for name (say, 'Will'), and you'll get back results 10 at a time, which you can page through using the Previous or Next links below the HTML table.

But while paging through result sets is great from a layout standpoint, it's not so great if you want to see all the results in a single list or if you want something the search just doesn't allow you to do, like limit by a particular postal code. You could page through all the results one at a time copying and pasting each batch into a spreadsheet, but that is a tedious, laborious task. Scraping is a better, faster, and more accurate solution.

What's our goal? We're going to write a script that will automatically go to this search page, and execute a search. It will then page through the results pages, extract the results from the HTML table, and save them to a file that can be cleanly imported into a spreadsheet or database. And we'll do all this with less than 20 lines of programming code.

Go Fetch

Let's get started by telling our script to go to the Internet and fetch our page. Under the previous line of code, add the following:

```
$browser->get("http://www.aronpilhofer.com/scrapes");
print $browser->content;
```

If you run it, you should see a small chunk of HTML. This is the raw code that tells each browser how to make the page look and function. This is what the browser sees, and what our virtual browser sees.

Let's take this another step and save this page to our scripts directory. Change your print command as follows:

```
open(OUT, "> ", "c:/scripts/page.htm");
print OUT $browser->content;
close(OUT);
```

This does three things. First, it opens a file called 'page.htm' in your scripts folder. (Note the un-Windows-like forward slashes in the file path. This is a legacy of Perl's UNIX past, and while it isn't strictly necessary, it makes writing file paths much easier, and is a good habit to get into.) It then tells our virtual browser to print the content of the page not to the screen, but into our file. Finally, it closes the file.

Run it, and you should see a file suddenly appear in your scripts directory that looks identical to the target page. So, you now know how to fetch a page from the web, and save content to a file on your computer.

Now let's get to something a little more useful. We really don't want to save the search page; we want the search results. So here's where you have to start thinking creatively about getting what you want. In order to do that, you'll need to know a bit more about how the search page operates.

Go back to our scraping test page and view the source code (in Internet Explorer, look under the 'Page' menu and in FireFox it's an option under the 'View' menu).

A few important things should be noted here. First, there's only one form on the page, and the form's name is 'search.' In the form is an input field named 'q' and a 'submit' button. This is all we really need to know in order to automate our search.

Under the $browser->get statement, but before you open your local file, add these lines of code:

```
$browser->form_name("search");
$browser->field("q","smith");
$browser->submit();
```

This tells our virtual browser three things: First, to find a form on the page named 'search'. Then, to find a field within that form called 'q' and insert into it the value 'smith'. Then, submit the form.

Because there's only one form on our page, we don't absolutely have to tell the virtual browser which one to use. But it is a good habit to get into, because often there will be multiple forms on a page and in such a case you will have to tell your virtual browser which one to look at.

Run your program then open the 'page.htm' file in your scripts folder. You should see the search form and the first page of results based on the search your virtual browser just executed. Pretty cool, huh? But we're not done, because we don't really want the whole page. We just want the results of our search.

Now it's time to use our second module, HTML::TableExtract, which does exactly what its name suggests—it extract content from an HTML table. In order to use it in our script, we need to add the use statement at the top of our script. Add the following code below our first two:

> use HTML::TableExtract;

Then, we need to declare a variable, or container, so we can reference the module in our script. After the $browser->submit(); statement, add the following:

> my $te = HTML::TableExtract->new(headers => [qw(Name Address City State Zip Amount)]);
> $te->parse($browser->content);

This requires a little more explanation. The way the 'TableExtract' module works is fairly simple. Pass it a chunk of HTML, and it will find and parse any and all tables it finds there. But we're only interested in one table—our results. So, we are telling it to look for a specific table, one whose headers match the above: Name, Address, City, State, Zip, Amount. It will ignore any other tables it finds. (We know, based on browsing the source code of our search page, only one table matches this description.)

In this code, we are declaring a variable called '$te' (we could have called it anything, but '$te' we can remember is short for TableExtract) and assigned it to the TableExtract module so we can reference it later in our code. At the same time, we've told it to look for any table or tables that begin with the headers 'Name,' 'Address', and so on.

The next line tells the module to parse the results page. If you run the program now (and you should, just to make sure there are no errors), the output will not have changed, although we are quite a bit closer to our goal. By telling TableExtract to parse the page we send it, the module is working some serious magic behind the scenes, as you'll see shortly. It has broken that table up into discreet columns and rows of data, which we can then extract.

But why hasn't the output changed? While we've told TableExtract what to parse, we have not told it how to handle the rows and columns it finds. In order to do that, we need to learn the last of our critical techniques: the control loop. We'll also talk a little bit about another kind of variable, or container, in Perl: the array.

Loop the Loop

In Perl, there are many kinds of control loops, but we will work with only two: the 'foreach' loop and the 'while' loop.

TableExtract, as we said before, looks for any and all tables matching a certain criteria in HTML, and pulls out the contents of each column and row into what is called an array. The array is a list of values, either numbers or text or a combination of both. For example, the names of the authors of this book could be assigned to an array as follows:

> my @authors = ("Fred Vallance Jones", "David McKie");

This array, called '@authors', now has two elements in it, and we can access a specific element by knowing its numeric place within in the list. So, this line would print 'Fred Vallance-Jones' to the screen.

> print $authors[0];

Notice a few things here about how Perl arrays work. The first element of an array is always element zero, not one. And to access a single element of the array @authors, we use the dollar sign—$authors[0]—instead of the '@' symbol. This is one of those syntactical quirks we mentioned earlier, and is one of the many things about Perl that frustrates beginners. You don't have to know the details, just that you refer to the entire array with a '@' symbol, and individual elements of it with a dollar sign.

Let's say, instead of listing each element of the array individually, we wanted to iterate through them. This is a common scenario, since you're not always sure how many elements there are in a given array. To do that, we can use the 'foreach' loop, which is particularly useful for arrays. The syntax would look like this:

```
foreach my $author (@authors) {
print "$author\n";
}
```

The output from this code would look like this:

```
Fred Vallance-Jones
David McKie
```

The 'foreach' loop does just exactly what it sounds like. The above code iterates through each element of the array '@authors' and each time through assigns each element to the variable '$author', which we declared for that specific purpose. The '\n' in the print statement also bears some explanation. The '\n' is a special character combination (there are many more, which you will see in a minute) that tells Perl to output a newline.

So, on the first loop '$author' would be equal to 'Fred Vallance-Jones' with a newline tacked on, and on the next pass it would be equal to 'David McKie' with another newline and so forth until it hit the final element of the array. Note something else about the print line: the double quotes. If you place a variable inside double quotes, Perl will return the value of that variable (in our case, the name of an author). Single quotes, however, will not work.

Arrays and loops are very important for scraping, so if this is unclear to you at this point it might be helpful to create a new Perl script in our scripts folder called 'array.pl' within which you can experiment with loops and arrays on your own.

Objects in Motion

Now that you understand a bit about loops and arrays, let's get back to our scrape. As we said earlier, the TableExtract module will parse an HTML table into a collection of columns and rows. To access each element of the table, we need to loop through that collection one row at a time, picking out each element within the row.

TableExtract returns each row as an array, with each cell of the table being a discreet element within the array. So, in the case of our table, we can expect the first element of the row to be the contributor's name, the second will be his or her address, the third will be a city, and so on. Their order in the array will begin with zero and end with five—remember, arrays begin counting at zero, not one.

As a convenience for us, we don't have to write code to tell TableExtract to return the rows of data into a variable. It automatically does this for us using a built-in method (which is another word for a function) called 'rows', which will spit back to us an array of data for each row in the table.

So, let's add the code to our script that loops through each row, and prints each element to the screen:

```
foreach my $row ($te->rows) {
print "$row->[0]\t$row->[1]\t$row->[2]\t$row->[3]\t$row->[4]\
t$row->[5]\n";
}
```

This looks confusing, and slightly different from what you might have expected. So, let's understand what's going on here. Instead of passing the 'foreach' loop an array as we did before with the '@authors', we're passing to it a method of the TableExtract module ($te->rows) that we know will return an array containing the elements of our HTML table.

How do we know this? The documentation, for one reason. This might be a good time to have a look at how CPAN modules are documented. Point your browser to http://search.cpan.org, and search for 'HTML::TableExtract' (it should be the top result).

Scroll down the page until you see the section 'Table Methods', and find the 'rows() method' in the list. The description probably won't make a lot of sense to you, but there really is only one important part for our purposes: 'Each row returned is a reference to an array . . .'. This tells us that each call to the 'rows() method' returns an array, and because of that we can simply loop through it just as we did earlier.

Within the French braces we are printing out each of the six elements of our table, but the syntax here again is slightly different from what you might have expected, starting with the strange little arrows instead of the array notation we demonstrated above. The explanation for this is a little more complicated, and probably will confuse the issue more than clarify it. It has to do with the rather complex way the TableExtract module returns data, and is really not that important to understand in any depth at this point.

For those who do want to understand more, the answer has to do with how Perl allows you to reference and dereference complex data structures. In this case, the result of the method call is a reference to an array, which means we dereference it using the arrow notation. For more on this subject, this tutorial: <www.perlmeme.org/howtos/using_perl/dereferencing.html> will explain the concepts in more detail.

Before your head starts to spin, remember what we said before: You don't have to know *why* something works, just that it works. All that's really important to know is that when you use the 'rows() method' of TableExtract—which you will do quite often if you continue to scrape—you have to reference each element of the row using the arrow notation, rather than the standard array notation we used above.

The rest of this statement is fairly clear: We want a 'tab-delimited' file at the end of our scrape, so between each element, we're inserting another one of those special character combinations—a '\t'—which is how we tell Perl to insert a tab character. The '\n' at the end of the line is a 'new line' character, which we already learned.

Let's run our script and see what happens. If all went well, you should see something like the following results (your names may be a bit different):

```
C:\scripts>perl test.pl
William Smith    PO Box 808        New Castle        NH      03854   1000
William Smith    1700 Lincoln Street     Denver  CO    80203   500
Thomas W. Smith  323 Railroad Avenue     Greenwich     CT      06830   10000
Thomas Smith     323 Railroad Avenue     Greenwich     CT      06830   20000
Richard Smith    4001 Ella Lee Ln        Houston TX    77027   300
Philo Smith      30 Jeffrey Road Greenwich        CT   06830   1000
Philo Smith      30 Jeffrey Road Greenwich        CT   06830   1000
Michael Smith    75 Rockland Trail       Sharpsburg    GA      30277   200
Leonard Smith    401 Charlotte Street    Asheville     NC      28801   200
James Smith      1209 Glenwood Terr      Anniston      AL      36207   100
```

Fig. 10.1

We're getting closer aren't we? Just a couple steps are left and then we're ready to go. The first is obvious: We don't want to print our results just to the screen; we want to print to a 'tab-delimited' file so we can then import the data into a spreadsheet or database.

To do that, let's make a couple of changes to our script. We already know how to create an external file and 'print' something into it from Perl. (We did that at the very beginning of this chapter, remember?)

The only difference here is that we don't want to print the whole page into our external file; we only want the data elements from the table in it as we loop through each row. So, instead of printing to the screen (as we just did), we print to the file.

In order to do this, we need to make a couple of small changes. First, we need to tell Perl to open a connection to our 'external' file before we enter the loop and then put our 'print to file' statement within the loop. After the loop is finished, we need to close the connection to our external file.

Make those changes to your script (don't forget to change the name of your external file):

```perl
open(OUT, ">", "c:/scripts/results.txt");
foreach my $row ($te->rows) {
print "$row->[0]\t$row->[1]\t$row->[2]\t$row->[3]\t$row->[4]\
t$row->[5]\n";
print OUT "$row->[0]\t$row->[1]\t$row->[2]\t$row->[3]\t$row
->[4]\t$row->[5]\n";

}
close(OUT);
```

After you run the script, you should see your 'results.txt' file in the scripts directory, and you should see results that look something like this (the '>>' characters in this screen shot are tabs, which may or may not show up in the text editor you are using):

```
     ·····|····10····|····20····|····30····|····40····|····50····|····60····|····
 1  William·Smith»PO·Box·808» New·Castle» NH» 03854»1000¶
 2  William·Smith»1700·Lincoln·Street»Denver» CO» 80203»500¶
 3  Thomas·W.·Smith»323·Railroad·Avenue»Greenwich»CT» 06830»10000¶
 4  Thomas·Smith» 323·Railroad·Avenue»Greenwich»CT» 06830»20000¶
 5  Richard·Smith»4001·Ella·Lee·Ln» Houston»TX» 77027»300¶
 6  Philo·Smith»30·Jeffrey·Road»Greenwich»CT» 06830»1000¶
 7  Philo·Smith»30·Jeffrey·Road»Greenwich»CT» 06830»1000¶
 8  Michael·Smith»75·Rockland·Trail»Sharpsburg» GA» 30277»200¶
 9  Leonard·Smith»401·Charlotte·Street» Asheville»NC» 28801»200¶
10  James·Smith»1209·Glenwood·Terr» Anniston» AL» 36207»100¶
11  Harrow·Smith» 5000·Hawthorne» Little·Rock»AR» 72207»500¶
12  Dean·Smith» 7114·North·Shore·Tr.·N.»Forest·Lake»MN» 55025»100¶
13  Charles·Smithers» 570·Pauls·Avenue» New·York» NY» 10021»1000¶
14  Charles·Smithers» 570·Pauls·Avenue» New·York» NY» 10021»300¶
15  Baker·Smith»3360·E.·Terrell·Branch·Ct.·SE»Marietta» GA» 30067»250¶
```

Fig. 10.2

And Finally

There's one last step to our scrape: capturing all the results, not just the first page. Notice our search for the name 'Smith' generates 15 results, but each page contains only 10. In order to get the other five, the user must click the 'Next' link at the bottom of the page.

How do we handle this in our code? The Mechanize module's 'follow_link()' method combined with a 'do...while' loop provides a surprisingly simple solution.

The 'follow_link()' method does precisely what it sounds like: it clicks on the link we specify. There are many ways to indicate what link we want our virtual browser to click (the documentation has plenty of examples), but we are looking for one that reads 'Next' when viewed through the browser. This is the code:

```
$browser->follow_link( text => "Next")
```

Go back to our 'search' page and click through the results. Notice that the 'Next' link disappears when the last page of data is reached. That is good, because it means we can use this as an indication to our script that the final page of records has been reached. That should give us our solution, and the data we want.

But we also don't want to limit ourselves to just two pages of results, because we don't really know how many pages we'll have to click through to get all the records; but we know there will be at least one page. What we need for this particular problem is a 'do . . . while()' loop.

This control loop is different from the previous one because it will, by design, always execute whatever code is contained within it at least once.

Look back at the 'foreach()' loop in our code. There, the test comes at the beginning, when you pass an array to inside the parenthesis—in our script that's the '$te->rows()' method. But what if there were no rows of data? Then, the code between the French braces would never execute. It simply would be skipped. And that's what we want in this case. For a single page of results, 10 records or less, that's all we need for our script to work.

What if there's more than one page of results? We know we need to click the 'NEXT' link, but we don't want to do that until we've parsed the first page of data, which is why we need a loop that 'tests' at the end rather than at the beginning—the 'do . . . .while()' loop.

Let's look at the final script and our goal will probably become clearer. All we've really done is rearrange slightly the order of our commands, and wrapped the 'TableExtract' portion of the script inside our 'do . . . while()' loop.

```perl
use strict;
use WWW: :Mechanize;
use HTML: :TableExtract;

my $browser = WWW: :Mechanize->new();

$browser->get("http://www.aronpilhofer.com/scrapes")

$browser->form_name("search");
$browser->field)"q", "smith");
$browser->submit();

open(OUT, ">", "/Users/aron/scripts/trunk/working/results.txt");

do {
    my $te = HTML: :TableExtract->new(headers => [qw(Name
        Address City State Zip Amount)]);
    $te->parse($browser->content);
    foreach my $row ($te->rows) {
        print "$row->[0]\t$row->[1]\t$row->[2]\t$row->[3]\
            t$row->[4]\t$row->[5]\n";
        print OUT "$row->[0]\t$row->[1]\t$row->[2]\t$row->[3]\
            t$row->[4]\t$row->[5]\n";
    }
}
while ($browser->follow_link( text => "Next" ));

close(OUT)
```

Notice the test at the end of the loop. The loop will continue to execute as long as whatever is inside the parenthesis remains true. In this case, 'true' means there is a 'NEXT' link somewhere on the page for our virtual browser to follow.

Run the script, navigate to your 'scripts' folder, and open the 'file results.txt' in a text editor. You should see all your results, not just the first page.

And there we have it. A clean tab-delimited text file ready to be imported into Excel, Access, or any other application for analysis. Try experimenting with other search terms, ones that generate perhaps dozens or hundreds of results. Your script will loop through each page and spit out the results for you just as easily.

All that, mind you, in about 20 lines of code. Now, perhaps, you're starting to see how powerful this tool can be.

Scraping as a Last Resort

Now that we've handed you the web equivalent of a loaded gun, we think it important to say a few words about when and where to use it, and where not to.

Scraping data from a website should be a tool of last resort, not the first. It is always best to try to get the data directly from the source, either through FOI or by simply asking for it. Only after you have exhausted other means of acquiring the data should you consider scraping.

There are several reasons for this advice. First, scraping is powerful, but imperfect. Most websites do not tell you how many records are in the database behind their search page, which means you can never be certain that you've got everything. If you do resort to scraping, it's important to acknowledge in your reporting that the data may be incomplete. That doesn't mean you can't report based on the data, but you must be aware of the limitations of whatever data set you end up with in your reporting, or you'll end up doing so in the subsequent correction.

Second, scraping a website is always considered bad etiquette, and sometimes can be illegal. Just because you *can* scrape copyrighted material doesn't mean it's allowed. In fact, most websites have very specific terms of use, which often say what users are and are not allowed to do with their content. Do not ignore these warnings. If there is any question about the legality of what you're planning to do, consult your legal department before going forward.

Even if there is no legal obstacle, it is best to be mindful of other organizations' resources and bandwidth. Running a very intensive scrape in the middle of the business day, for example, is in very bad form and can often be mistaken for an attack by hackers. The organization almost certainly will see what you're up to, and may very well block your access to their website. Be mindful of this, and try to run your scripts during off-peak hours. It is also a good idea to build in a slight delay after each loop to reduce the load on the server.

That said, web scraping is among the most useful tools for any journalist, particularly as more and more information and data become available over the web.

Social Network Analysis

Who really runs the city? Who makes the big plays and pulls the strings? Who is in charge: the newly elected mayor, business owners or old, well-established families? These are questions that reporters and editors at the *Times-Dispatch* (Richmond, Virginia) attempted to answer for months. Anecdotally, they had plenty of information, but they wanted to write a story beyond what everyone thought was going on. What they wanted was a quantitative analysis of the connections in their community.

They started by thinking about who the seemingly powerful were, what they did and what might put them in a position of power. They wanted to create a central databank of relationships between individuals and organizations: how those people knew others, how they were connected. To do this they compiled a database that included more than 1,000 names and connections of people who were members of non-profit, foundation, corporate, or governmental boards of directors.

With lists of names and organizations they knew they had a start, but the information just didn't gel. They were left with finding the answer to one more question: How do you analyze a database of names and connections to unlock the secrets behind a social network?

They turned to freelance reporter Aaron Kessler, who took the data and analyzed it using social network analysis software Ucinet. Kessler used the software to narrow the field of information and display it graphically. He filtered people based on how connected they were, and was left with only those people who sat on three or more boards.

He created graphics—or maps—of the connections between those people. Each line on the map traced a relationship from a person to a board.

What was left was a visual of how the most highly-connected in Richmond knew each other—and how they shared power. The result was one overall picture of the network as a whole. 'It showed that some of these organizations were almost indistinguishable from one another because they shared the same directors. You couldn't tell where one started and the other ended', Kessler said.[1]

Other reporters at the paper took this information and used it to conduct interviews, to investigate further, and to determine the focus of the project. 'Who Runs Richmond?'[2] uncovered four individuals who wielded the most influence.

> This small, tightly knit group of leaders seems to be at the center of most decisions about what direction the region should take and in the middle of many of the changes happening downtown. The Times-Dispatch reviewed civic and corporate boards, as well as its database of contributors to local political campaigns, and found that the names of Ukrop, Armstrong and Goodwin crop up more than any others.[3]

Individuals most central to the power structure of Richmond tend to be wealthy, white males. Many had donated money to the mayor's campaign. One family in particular, the Ukrops, was prevalent. The end product included a large graphic as well as interactive, online graphics of the network so readers could view and study the network for themselves.[4]

The *Times-Dispatch*'s idea could be applied to just about any community. To get started, put yourself in a relationship state of mind. Think about the questions you have about your own community. How are people connected? What stories are hidden within those ties? Any membership, contract, or financial transaction can be translated into a relationship using social network analysis. You might want to look at campaign contributions, government contracts, non-profit board membership or corporate boards of directors.

Next, ask yourself what data you might need and what is available? Chances are, you may already have records dealing with one or more of the above categories tucked away in your newsroom. Perhaps you have already analyzed those records in Excel or Access.

Now, think visually. Think about the relationships. Not just who got the most contracts or contributions, but to whom they are *connected*. Using social network analysis, you can turn much of the same information you may already have into a format that network analysis software can read and process. (Note: For practical purposes, the explanations and examples throughout the remainder of this section will use Ucinet. Many reporters who've attempted social network analysis in their newsrooms have used software Ucinet from Analytic Technologies. You can get a free, 30-day trial download of this software and pricing information at <www.analytictech.com/>. The International Network for Social Network Analysis (www.insna.org/) has links to Ucinet and all other available software.)

Your First Network

Understanding how social network analysis might help your reporting is a little easier once you've got your hands dirty with it. Download, install, and open up Ucinet from your computer. You'll notice that like many products, this software has menu items and icons that launch applications across the top.

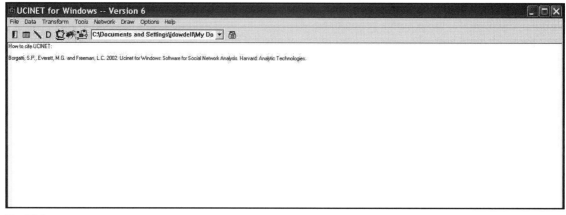

Fig. 10.3

In the next few minutes you're going to create your own network. In your work with Ucinet, it will be helpful to have a very basic file at your disposal. It may seem elementary, but creating a replica of your own personal network can be a great building block for future network analysis endeavours. Because it's all about you, you'll know what it should look like and how it operates. You'll know immediately if you've done something correctly or incorrectly.

There are several ways to get data into Ucinet. The most popular methods include creating text files, called DL files, or entering the data directly into Ucinet. For this example you will manually enter the data into the program. (For tips on making DL text files, please refer to the Ucinet user's guide.)

To get started, click on 'Data', 'Spreadsheet Editor' (you can also just click on the icon that looks like a spreadsheet). A window should open that looks similar to the Microsoft Excel interface. Just like Excel, you're going to be working with columns, rows, and numbers. The shaded areas along the left side and the top are where you'll enter names, events, organizations, etc.

Think of four or five of your friends, family, or colleagues. List their names along the left side beginning with the first cell. Now list the names—in the same order—across the top of the sheet. See figure below:

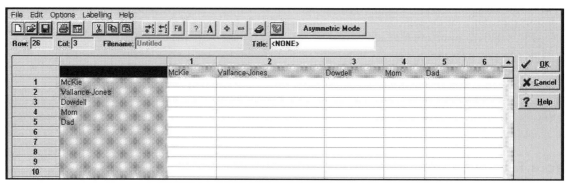

Fig. 10.4

You need to tell the software which people in this network are connected. To translate the relationships into something Ucinet can understand you're going to need to use binary numbers—zeroes and ones. A '1' means there is a connection. A '0' means there isn't.

Go through the matrix (a fancy word for the data you're using to create your network), starting with the person in row one. Look at each column. If the first person is connected to someone, put a '1' where their names intersect. (Please note that you do not put a '1' in a cell where a name meets itself. This is because someone can't 'know' him- or herself in the sense we're talking about.) See the image below:

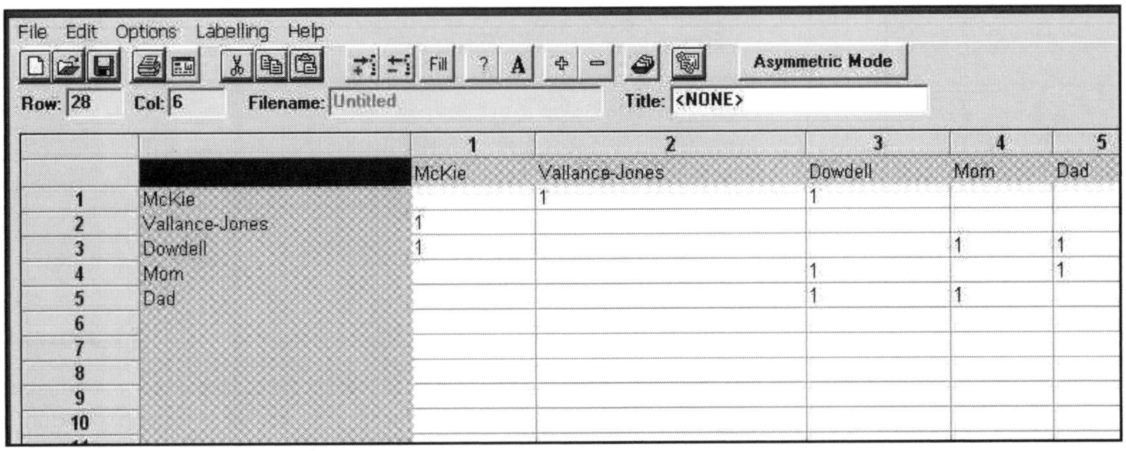

Fig. 10.5

The last step to create your own network is to fill in the remainder of the cells. Click in the very last cell of your matrix. If you used four names it'll be cell 4-4, and if you used five names it'll be cell 5-5. Click once on the 'Fill' button on the top of the spreadsheet and the remaining spaces should fill in with zeroes. Now save your network (commands: 'File', 'Save As') and click the button with the green checkmark labelled 'OK'. This will close the spreadsheet view and take you back to the general Ucinet display.

To see a graphic representation of your network, you'll need to launch NetDraw, a built-in application that draws networks. To do this, click on the menu item at the top of the Ucinet display that says 'Draw'. A new window should open. Once it does, click on 'File', 'Open Ucinet dataset', 'Network', and navigate to the file you just created.

Your network should instantly appear on the screen. See figure below:

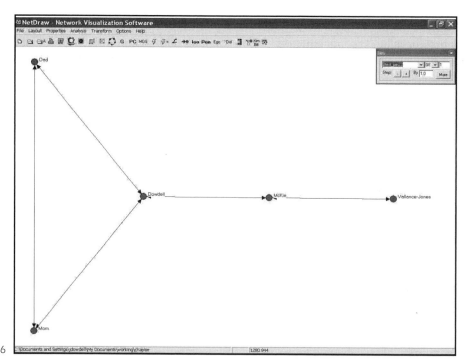

Fig. 10.6

In this view you can click on any of the names, or 'nodes', and drag them to a different spot on the screen. You can also turn off the arrowheads to get rid of some of the clutter (commands: 'Properties', 'Arrowheads', 'Visible'). This should make the checkmark next to 'Visible' disappear.

Now that you understand the most basic way to enter data into Ucinet, let's go back to the Richmond project. After reporters completed the database containing individuals sitting on more than 60 boards of directors in the Richmond area, Kessler put that network into Ucinet. Here's what the data looked like in the spreadsheet view:

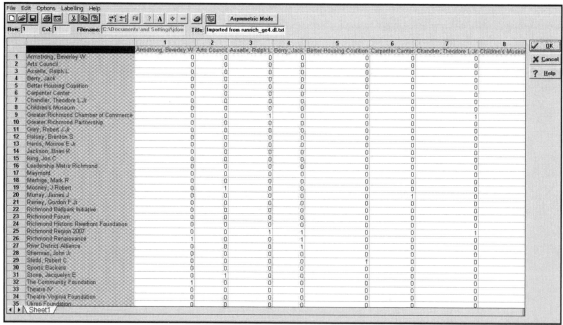

Fig. 10.7

The original network included more than 700 people. The figure below shows the entire network displayed graphically:

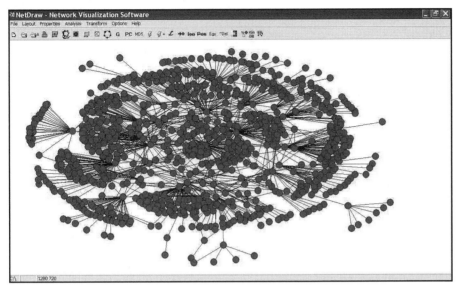

Fig. 10.8

With so many nodes, or people and organizations, involved it makes the network look messy, or what network analysts call a 'hairball'. This makes it difficult to see the details of the network and how individuals are connected. At this point in the Richmond project analysis Kessler had to make some decisions. He wanted to make the network more manageable, but didn't want to lose focus of the main goal: uncovering the highly connected individuals in Richmond.

To achieve this, Kessler decided to narrow the scope so that the network contained only the most highly connected individuals. In the end, this was shown to be people who were members of four or more boards. This fact quickly filtered out people in the network who weren't as important, at least in network terms. The figure below shows the narrowed network:

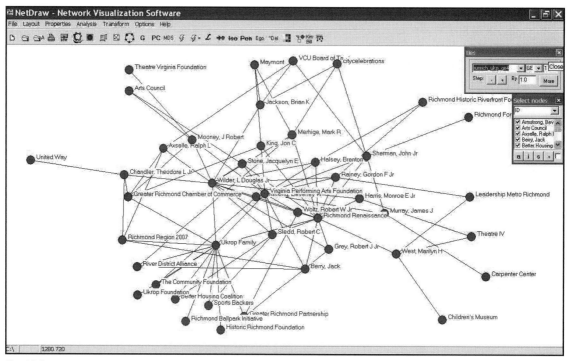

Fig. 10.9

Unlike the personal network you created, this one includes both individuals and organizations. With a network like this it's helpful to make the nodes, or circles, appear differently in the graphic so that people are symbolized one way and organizations another by using an attribute file. This is a special type of file that simply lists the actors (people and organizations) in the network and then signifies that they have certain characteristics. The Image below is an attribute file for the Richmond network:

File Edit Options Labelling Help

Row: 33 Col: 14 Filename: C:\Documents and Settings\jdow Title: Importe

		1	2	3	4	5	6
		Type					
1	Armstrong, Beverley W	1					
2	Arts Council	2					
3	Axselle, Ralph L	1					
4	Berry, Jack	1					
5	Better Housing Coalition	2					
6	Carpenter Center	2					
7	Chandler, Theodore L Jr	1					
8	Children's Museum	2					
9	Greater Richmond Chamber of Commerce	2					
10	Greater Richmond Partnership	2					
11	Grey, Robert J Jr	1					
12	Halsey, Brenton S	1					
13	Harris, Monroe E Jr	1					
14	Jackson, Brian K	1					
15	King, Jon C	1					
16	Leadership Metro Richmond	2					
17	Maymont	2					
18	Merhige, Mark R	1					
19	Mooney, J Robert	1					
20	Murray, James J	1					

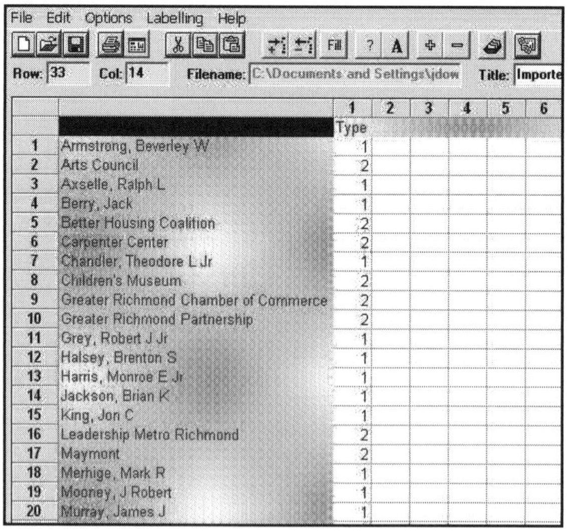

Fig. 10.10

The first column contains the names of all of the actors. The second column signifies the 'type' of actor. A '1' designates a person and a '2' designates an organization. This file must be loaded into NetDraw after the main file is opened. The 'Properties' menu allows you to change the appearance of the nodes based on their type. Attribute files don't have to be limited to people or organizations, you can get creative and use it to specify gender, ethnicity, etc. In the figure below, the people now appear as circles and the organizations appear as squares:

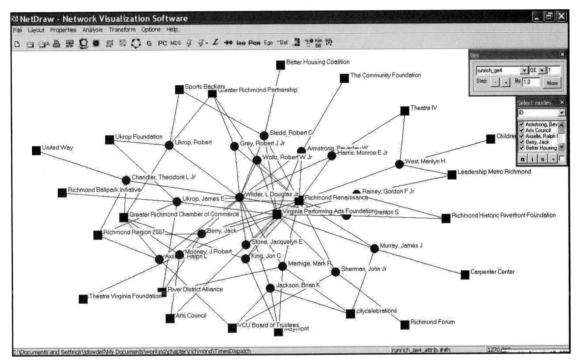

Fig. 10.11

At the heart of the network is Mayor L. Douglas Wilder, Jr. As the recently-elected leader of the community, Wilder's prominence in the network made sense to reporters. To uncover other key players Kessler measured the degree of centrality of each person in the network to see who else was highly connected. The measure of degree centrality is simply the total number of connections each person has. The higher the number of connections, the greater an individual's degree of centrality.

With this measure they discovered that a prominent Richmond family was more involved in politics and philanthropy than originally thought. Two members of the Ukrop family are present in the network shown above. With seven and five connections, respectively, James E. Ukrop and Robert Ukrop have important positions in the Richmond network. This knowledge was the basis for a number of additional analyses in Ucinet and laid the groundwork for the reporting that completed the project.

Where Do You Go from Here?

This section includes just a taste of all of the things you can do with social network analysis. In addition to different displays and analysis in NetDraw, there are many different analyses that can be done in Ucinet itself. These analyses allow you to determine who the key players are either by the sheer number of connections or by their position in a network.

Much literature is available on the uses and practices of social network analysis. While most of the published work is academic in nature, it can help shed light on the theories and methods of data collection. Highly recommend works include *Social Network Analysis: A Handbook* by John Scott and *Social Network Analysis: Methods and Application,* by Stanley Wasserman and Katherine Faust. Scott's book is a great place to learn the basics, but once you get going, you'll find the technical explanations from Wasserman and Faust to be helpful. Also, be sure to consult *Introduction to Social Network Methods*, a free, online handbook by Robert A. Hanneman (<faculty.ucr.edu/~hanneman/nettext/>).

Here are some ideas for just about any beat in all types of communities:

- **Local government power**   Which city council members are connected to others outside of government via business or organizations? How might these relationships affect important decisions being made in your community?
- **Campaign contributions**   Which candidates are drawing in the most money and who is donating? Are there special interests that the donors are trying to promote? Are there any political action committees in your community? How is everyone involved?
- **Crime**   Criminologists have used social network analysis to track the criminals at the heart of many problems within inner cities. Police can then take that information to target criminals who are committing the most crimes.
- **Public health**   Researchers have used this method to track the spread of HIV and SARS. Reporters could look at the spread of West Nile and other diseases throughout the nation.
- **Contracts and bids**   Who is getting public money for performing services in your community? Who are the winners and losers in the contract game? Are there any connections between local businesses and government officials that might influence which companies are awarded contracts? How is the public being served through this process?

Bringing It All Together

In this chapter you have learned about a number of advanced utility techniques. You may not need all of them, or ever use any of them, but don't forget to refresh your memory of them from time to time—they can help smooth the way when you hit roadblocks.

Notes

Chapter 1

1. Brant Houston, *Computer-Assisted Reporting: A Practical Guide*, 3rd edn (New York: Bedford/St Martin's Press, 2004).
2. Margaret H. DeFleur, *Computer-assisted Investigative Reporting: Development, and Methodology* (Mahwah, NJ: Lawrence Erlbaum Associates, 1997), 99.
3. Bill Doskoch, *Spreadsheet Manual* (self-published, 1994).
4. Interview with authors.
5. Ibid.
6. Ibid.
7. CBC Radio Manitoba, infrastructure investigation, May 1995.
8. CBC Radio Manitoba, second infrastructure investigation, 1996.
9. Adrian Humphreys, 'Wife-killers face hard prison time: Courts taking domestic murder very seriously', *Hamilton Spectator*, 24 Nov. 1997, A1.
10. Paul Schneidereit, 'Time passages', *Halifax Chronicle-Herald*, 17 Nov.–5 Dec. 1997.
11. Kevin Donovan, 'Housing millions down drain', *Toronto Star*, 20 May 1995, A1.
12. Interview with authors.
13. Interview with authors.
14. Interview with authors.
15. Interview with authors.
16. Interview with authors.
17. Robert Cribb, 'Dirty dining', series, *Toronto Star*, 19–22 Feb. 2000.
18. Interview with authors.
19. Fred Vallance-Jones, 'Reservations', *Hamilton Spectator*, 23–29 Nov. 2001.
20. Karen Kleiss et al., 'Behind the kitchen door', *Edmonton Journal*, 30 Sept.–2 Oct. 2006.
21. Interview with authors.
22. Jim Rankin et al., 'Race and crime', *Toronto Star*, 19–27 Oct. 2002.
23. Fred Vallance-Jones et al., 'Smokescreen', *Hamilton Spectator*, 18–23 Sept. 2004.
24. 'Faint warning', CBC Radio, Feb. 2004; 'Prescribed to death', CBC Radio, Apr. 2005.
25. 'Dying for a job', CBC Radio, Apr. 2006.
26. Interview with authors.

Chapter 2

1. Julian Sher's account of his documentary, which aired 12 Apr. 2007 on the CBC, can be found at: <www.cbc.ca/doczone/battleforbaghdad/sher.html>. He produced the documentary in collaboration with the *New York Times*. See <www.nytimes.com/ref/world/middleeast/2007_BAGHDADATTACKS.html>.
2. Interview with authors, 6 Apr. 2007.
3. Interview with authors, 5 Apr. 2007.
4. Julian Sher, 'A beginner's guide to the web', *Media* magazine (winter 1995): 7.
5. Nora Paul, 'Six steps to sensible searching of the World Wide Web', Poynter Institute, IRE tipsheet, June 1999, 2
6. Ibid.
7. Tu Thanh Ha, 'Worker didn't think the overpass would fall', *Globe and Mail*, 12 Apr. 2007, A1.

8. Peter Rakobowchuk, 'Police say five people dead after overpass collapse near Montreal', Canadian Press, 31 Sept. 2006, at: <www.cbc.ca/cp/national/061001/n100106.html>.

9. Quebec Auditor General report can be found at: <www.vgq.gouv.qc.ca/HTML/Welcome.html>.

10. <www.vgq.gouv.qc.ca/publications/Rapp_2003_2/Highlights/html/04.html>.

11. The cbc.ca version of Derek Stoffel's story can be found at: <www.cbc.ca/canada/story/2006/10/06/bridges-inspections.html>.

12. Interview with authors.

13. Erik Schatzker, 'Backgrounding U.S. businesses', IRE tipsheet presented at the CAJ/IRE 'Crossing the 49th' workshop, Montreal, 4 Oct. 2003, 2.

14. Ibid.

15. Robert Cribb, 'Dirty dining' series, *Toronto Star*, 19–22 Feb. 2000.

16. Robert Cribb, Dean Jobb, David McKie, and Fred Vallance-Jones, *Digging Deeper: A Canadian Reporter's Research Guide* (Toronto: Oxford University Presss, 2006), 138.

17. Drew Sullivan, 'Access—Hands-on CAR training', IRE tipsheet, 31 Mar. 2001.

18. <www.library.ubc.ca/home/evaluating/>.

19. Stephen C. Miller, 'M.I.D.S. (Miller Internet Data Integrity Scale)', *New York Times*, Oct. 1998, IRE tipsheet, 1–2.

20. Jim Carroll and Rick Broadhead, *1997 Canadian Internet Handbook* (Toronto: Prentice-Hall Canada, 1997), 287.

21. <search.ottawa.ca/help_en.asp>.

22. Ibid.

23. Carroll and Broadhead, *1997 Canadian Internet Handbook*, 287–8.

24. The CBC's series on biotech foods, which aired in 1999, was called 'Field of Genes', and can be found at: <www.cbc.ca/news/radionews/context/biotech.html>.

25. Drew Sullivan, 'Access—hands-on CAR training', IRE tipsheet, 31 Mar. 2001, 9.

26. <www.degreetutor.com/library/research-tools/librarian-searchguide%20>.

27. <www.google.com/help/basics.html>.

28. Carroll and Broadhead, *1997 Canadian Internet Handbook*, 289.

29. <www.degreetutor.com/library/research-tools/librarian-searchguide%20>.

30. Ibid.

31. Ibid.

32. Ibid.

33. Ibid.

34. Ibid.

35. Ibid.

36. Sullivan, 'Access—Hands-on CAR training'.

37. <clusty.com/about>.

38. Ibid., 6.

39. Unlike the US Food and Drug Administration, Health Canada does not have a complete list of all its advisory committees; and unlike the FDA, Health Canada doesn't provide verbatim transcripts of its closed-door meetings. However, a partial list can be found at: <www.hc-sc.gc.ca/dhp-mps/prodpharma/activit/sci-consult/index_e.html> and reading the summaries can provide clues for story ideas.

40. William Boei and Darah Hansen, 'Two million told: Don't drink the water', *Vancouver Sun*, 17 Nov. 2006.

41. Interview with author, 6 Apr. 2007.
42. Carolyn Edds, 'Finding databases on the web', *Investigative Reporters and Editors*, 2.
43. Ibid., 2–3.
44. Wes Williams, 'Backgrounding the individual by web and computer', *Investigative Reporters and Editors* (1999): 1.
45. Julian Sher, 'Steven Truscott: His word against history', *Media* magazine, at: <www.caj.ca/mediamag/summer2001/tv.html>.
46. Ibid.
47. Interview with authors, 6 Apr. 2007.
48. To learn how to spy on people, go to Julian Sher's home page at: <www.journalism net.com/spy/spychat.htm>.
49. <www.cbc.ca/news/background/seniorsdrugs/>.
50. For more detailed information on joining mailing lists, go to Julian Sher's home page at: <www.journalismnet.com/people/listserv.htm>. For information on how to join journalism-related mailing lists, go to: <web.syr.edu/%7Ebcfought/>.
51. <www.technorati.com/live/top100.html>.
52. Interview with authors, 5 Apr. 2007.
53. <davidakin.blogware.com/>.
54. Ibid.
55. Ibid.
56. Mary McGuire, Carlton University, Interview with authors, 5 Apr. 2007..
57. Alan Finder, 'For some, online persona undermines a resume', *New York Times*.
58. Interview with authors, 5 Apr. 2007.
59. Interview with authors, 6 Apr. 2007.
60. Natalie Johnson, 'Using Facebook to Find Sources', *Media* magazine 13, 3, 2008 (<www.caj.ca/mediamag/Winter%202008/(David%20McKie,%20Dec.%20 17,%202007)CAJ_rev4MediaMag1207.pdf>).
61. Ibid.
62. Joseph C. Ben-Ami, 'Institute for Canadian Values applauds end of Court Challenges Program, cuts to Status of Women funding', Institute for Canadian Values, 25 Nov. 2007.
63 Julian Sher, 'The credibility test: There are ways to identify the individuals running certain websites', *Media* magazine 10, 1 (2003): 5.
64. <direct.srv.gc.ca/cgi-bin/direct500/BE>.
65. Andrew Mayeda, 'RCMP lays income trust charge: Financial official has been suspended after 14-month probe', *Ottawa Citizen*, 16 Feb. 2007, A1.
66. Cribb et al., *Digging Deeper*, 61.
67. <www.elections.ca/scripts/webpep/fin/select_search_option.aspx>.
68. The campaign donation information for Quebec, Ontario, and BC can be found at: <www.electionsquebec.qc.ca/fr/recherche_donateurs_app.asp>; <www.elections ontario.on.ca/en/finances_returns_en.shtml>; <www.elections.bc.ca/fin/finance. htm>.
69. Cribb et al., *Digging Deeper*, 44.
70. <www2.parl.gc.ca/content/hoc/Committee/391/FINA/Evidence/EV2230165/ FINAEV07-E.PDF>.
71. The websites of SEDAR and the SEC can be found at: <www.sedar.com/search/ search_en.htm> and <www.sec.gov/cgi-bin/srch-edgar>.
72. Interview with authors, 6 Apr. 2007.

73. Julian Sher, RSS: Real Simple News feeds, 2005, at: <www.journalismnet.com/tips/rss.htm>.
74. Ibid.
75. <davidakin.blogware.com/blog/_archives/2007/2/27/2769133.html>.
76. Interview with authors, 14 Apr. 2007.
77. Ibid.
78. <forjournalists.com/cookbook/index.php?title=Wiki_Panel_H>.
79. Interview with authors 14 Apr. 2007.

Chapter 3

1. Jack Rupert, 'Overtime nightmare: Procedures abused, costs skyrocket: city auditor', *Ottawa Citizen*, 3 May 2006, C1.
2. April Lindgren, 'Probe of fat hydro salaries to cost $300,000: Ontario Liberals hiding panel instead of taking action, critics say', *Ottawa Citizen*, 30 Jan. 2007, A5.
3. Rich Gordon, 'Spreadsheets vs. Databases', Tipsheet at the Investigative Reporters, and Editors conference, Albuquerque, New Mexico, 12–13 Nov. 1993.
4. John Walkenbach, *Excel 2007 Bible* (Toronto: Wiley, 2007), 51.
5. Ibid., 51.
6. <www.electionsquebec.qc.ca/fr/recherche_donateurs_app.asp>.
7. <www.fin.gov.on.ca/english/publications/salarydisclosure/2007/electric07.html>.
8. <www.cbc.ca/news/background/workplace-safety/media.html>.

Chapter 4

1. Glen McGregor, 'Rapid fire' series, *Ottawa Citizen*, 10–14 Feb. 2007.
2. Email correspondence, 15 Mar. 2007.
3. David Akin, email correspondence, 13 Mar. 2007.
4. <www.tbs-sct.gc.ca/est-pre/20072008/me-bd/part1/ME-017_e.asp>.
5. John Walkenbach, *Excel 2007 Bible* (Toronto: Wiley, 2007), 175.
6. Sarah Cohen, 'Numbers in the newsroom: Using math and statistics in news', *Investigative Reporters and Editors* (2001): 2.
7. [re *Hamilton Spectator*]Ibid., 5.
8. [Phil Harbord]Interview with authors, 27 Mar. 2007.
9. Glen McGregor, 'Shooters in your neighbourhood: They live down the block from you. But don't fret, they say their weapons are a safe, and wholesome hobby, even a family activity', *Ottawa Citizen*, 11 Feb. 2007.
10. Ibid.
11. Cohen, 'Numbers in the newsroom', 66.
12. Ibid, 1.
13. Interview with authors, 27 Mar. 2007.
14. Ibid.
15. April Lindgren, 'Let the sun shine in: Thousands added to Ontario list of top PS earners', *Ottawa Citizen*, 31 Mar. 2007, A4.
16. Robert Cribb, Dean Jobb, David McKie, and Fred Vallance-Jones, *Digging Deeper: A Canadian Reporter's Research Guide* (Toronto: Oxford University Press, 2006), 222.
17. Walkenbach, *Excel 2007 Bible*, 223.
18. Ibid, 225.
19. John Walkenbach, *Excel 2007 Formulas* (Toronto, Wiley, 2007), 181.
20. Ibid, 275.

21. Ibid, 351.
22. Ibid, 370.
23. Cribb et al., *Digging Deeper*, 256.

Chapter 5

1. Robert Cribb, Tamsin McMahon, and Fred Vallance-Jones, 'Dangerous skies', part 1 of 'Collision course', *Hamilton Spectator*, *Record* of Waterloo Region, *Toronto Star*, 3 June 2006.
2. Interview with authors.
3. Ibid.
4. Brant Houston, *Computer-Assisted Reporting, A Practical Guide*, 3rd edn (New York: Bedford/St Martin's, 2004).
5. Robert Cribb, Tamsin McMahon, and Fred Vallance-Jones, part 2 of 'Collision course', *Hamilton Spectator*, *Record* (Waterloo Region), *Toronto Star*, 5 June 2006.
6. Fred Vallance-Jones, 'Power and the Tories: Cash sale', *Hamilton Spectator*, 22 Apr. 2002.

Chapter 6

1. Robert Cribb, Rita Daly, and Laurie Monsebraaten, 'How system helps shield bad doctors: College admits flaws in process', *Toronto Star*, 5 May 2001.
2. Fred Vallance-Jones, Laurie Monsebraaten, and Phinjo Gombu, 'How parties bend rule on donations', *Toronto Star*, 24 May 2003, A1.
3. Ibid.
4. Data supplied by Transportation Safety Board of Canada.

Chapter 7

1. 'The highs and lows of voter participation', *Hamilton Spectator*, 15 Nov. 2006.
2. Jim Rankin et al., 'Race and crime', *Toronto Star*, 19–27 Oct. 2002.
3. Interview with authors.
4. Interview with authors.
5. Ibid.
6. Ibid.
7. 'What Went Wrong', *Miami Herald*, Dec. 1992.
8. Tim Ormsby et al., *Getting to Know ArcGIS* (ESRI Press, 2004), 332.
9. Electronic map data, City of Hamilton, 2006.
10. Statistics Canada map data, used with permission.
11. Ibid.

Chapter 8

1. Ziva Branstetter, 'Five steps to finding and obtaining data', IRE conference, 2006, Fort Worth, Texas.
2. online at <www.cna-acj.ca/Client/CNA/cna.nsf/object/FOIAUDIT07/$file/FOI %20AUDIT%20REPORT-English.pdf>.
3. Bob Warner, 'Negotiating for data with reluctant local officials', National Institute for Computer-Assisted Reporting panel discussion in Boston, Mar. 1999.
4. Carla Heggie, Interview with author 2 May 2007.

5. Municipal Property Assessment Corporation v. Mitchinson, 2004 CanLII 17632.
6. Carla Heggie, Interview with authors 2 May 2007.
7. Branstetter, 'Five steps'.
8. Heggie, interview.
9. Ibid.
10. <blogs.ukings.ca/carincanada/2001/01/11/writing-queries-is-not-programming-under-ontario-foi-acts/>
11. Heggie, interview.
12. Jim Rankin et al., 'Singled out: Star analysis of police crime data shows justice is different for blacks and whites', *Toronto Star*, 19 Oct. 2001, A1.
13. Jim Rankin, Powerpoint presentation for Michener Award ceremony, Ottawa, 10 Apr. 2003.
14. Rankin, interview with authors 2 May 2007.
15. Ibid.
16. Ibid.
17. Glen McGregor, 'The hornet's sting, inside Ottawa's parking ticket system', *Ottawa Citizen*, 9–14 June 2007.
17. Ibid.
18. Ibid.
19. Ibid.
20. Ibid.

Chapter 9

1. Karen Kleiss, Interview with author.
2. <www.cbc.ca/news/background/seniorsdrugs/>.
3. <blogs.ukings.ca/carincanada/wp-content/uploads/2008/01/driveclean2.pdf>.
4. Jim Rankin, Powerpoint presentation for the Michener Award ceremony, Ottawa, 10 Apr. 2003, 11.
5. Carl Sessions Stepp, *Writing as Craft and Magic*, 2nd edn (New York: Oxford University Press, 2007), 112.
6. Joel Sappell, IRE tipsheet, 1.
7. Ibid.
8. Charles Duhigg, 'Bilking the elderly, with a corporate assist', *New York Times*, 20 May 2007, 20.
9. Interview with authors, 22 May 2007.
10. Shawn McIntosh, 'Storytelling with data', NICAR tipsheet, 2003, 1.
11. Interview with authors, 1 May 2007.
12. Glen McGregor, interview with authors, 10 May 2007.
13. Ibid.
14. Bob Carty, interview with authors, 16 May 2007.
15. Ibid.
16. Rob Washburn interview with authors, 16 May 2008.
17. Stepp, *Writing as Craft and Magic*, 125.
18. Ibid.
19. George Kennedy, Daryl Moen, and Don Ranly, *Beyond the Inverted Pyramid: Effective Writing for Newspapers, Magazines, and Specialized Publications* (New York: St Martin's Press, 1993), 165.
20. Bob Carty Interview with authors, 16 May 2007.
21. Rob Washburn interview with authors, 16 May 2008.

22. Ibid.
23. Jim Rankin et al., 'Singled out: Star analysis of police crime data shows justice is different for blacks and whites', *Toronto Star*, 19 Oct. 2001, A1.
23. Interview with authors, 2 May 2007.
24. David McKie, 'American public journalism: Could it work for the CBC?', Masters of Journalism thesis (Carleton University, 2002), 4.
25. Stepp, *Writing as Craft and Magic*, 61.
26. James Neff, 'Writing the story: Getting people in and numbers out while building the CAR narrative', IRE tipsheet, 1999, 1.
27. *Hamilton Spectator*, May 2007.
28. Neff, 'Writing the story', 1.
29. <www.cbc.ca/news/background/seniorsdrugs/>.
30. Kennedy et al., *Beyond the Inverted Pyramid*, 182.
31. Ibid.
32. Hanke Gratteau, 'Writing for impact', IRE conference.
33. <www.pulitzer.org/year/2002/investigative-reporting/>.
34. Shawn McIntosh, 'The *Clarion Ledger*, Special issues in CAR stories', IRE tipsheet.
35. Kennedy et al., *Beyond the Inverted Pyramid*, 183.
36. Don Bartlett and Jim Steele, 'The big story: How to conceive and carry out meaningful investigative projects', Globe Investigative Conference, 2003, 3.
37. Richard Galant, 'Writing the story', IRE tipsheet, 1997, 2.
38. David Boardman, 'Writing and editing the CAR story the right way: Making the data and numbers work for you', NICAR tipsheet, 2000, 1.

Chapter 10

1. Aaron Kessler, interview with author, 12 Dec. 2007.
2. Gordon Hickey, Michael Martz, and David Ress, 'Who runs Richmond?', *Richmond Times Dispatch*, 14 Aug. 2005.
3. David Ress, '4 power brokers help shape city's landscape', *Richmond Times Dispatch*, 14 Aug. 2005.
4. <media.gatewayva.com/rtd/multimedia/TheyRunRichmond/>.

Index